# TRANSFORMING
# QUALITATIVE DATA

RONALD JETTY

*Let it not be said that I have said nothing new.*
*The arrangement of the material is new.*

—Blaise Pascal,
French philosopher and mathematician,
1623-1662

# TRANSFORMING
# QUALITATIVE DATA

## Description, Analysis, and Interpretation

Harry F. Wolcott

**SAGE** Publications
*International Educational and Professional Publisher*
Thousand Oaks   London   New Delhi

*The author wishes to thank reviewers David Snow and Calvin Morrill from the Department of Sociology, University of Arizona.*

*For information address*:

SAGE Publications, Inc.
2455 Teller Road
Thousand Oaks, California 91320

SAGE Publications Ltd.
6 Bonhill Street
London EC2A 4PU
United Kingdom

SAGE Publications India Pvt. Ltd.
M-32 Market
Greater Kailash I
New Delhi 110 048 India

Printed in the United States of America

**Library of Congress Cataloging-in-Publication Data**

Wolcott, Harry F., 1929-
    Transforming qualitative data: description, analysis, and
interpretation / Harry F. Wolcott.
        p.    cm.
    Includes bibliographical references.
    ISBN 0-8039-5280-5 (cl).—ISBN 0-8039-5281-3 (pb)
    1. Ethnology—Methodology.  2. Ethnology—Authorship.
3. Educational anthropology—Methodology.  I. Title.
GN345.W64   1994
306'.01—dc20                                                    93-44425

94  95  96  97  98  10  9  8  7  6  5  4  3  2

Sage Production Editor:  Rebecca Holland

# Contents

# 1

# Something Old, Something New

*It is time now to worry about something that has been implicit through-
out the discussion of methodology . . . those mysterious procedures by
which you transform what you see and hear into intelligible accounts.*
—Michael H. Agar, *The Professional Stranger*, p. 189

- How do qualitatively oriented researchers "transform" what they see and hear into intelligible accounts?
- Is it always necessary to go "beyond" one's data in a descriptive study? May a researcher present data solely in a descriptive mode, leaving to the reader—or to a future time—the task of analysis/interpretation?
- If analysis and interpretation are ways to go beyond one's data, are the two processes virtually interchangeable, or can a useful distinction be made between them?
- If a useful distinction can be made, should researchers try to accomplish *both* analysis and interpretation in the same study, or should efforts be directed exclusively to one or the other?

These questions prompted the preparation and organization of everything that is new about this book. My thesis is that the real mystique
of qualitative inquiry lies in the processes of *using* data rather than in
the processes of *gathering* data. In Michael Agar's terms, what are "those
mysterious procedures" by which initial observations are transformed
into intelligible accounts?

1

A major new chapter proposing a working distinction among the terms *description, analysis,* and *interpretation* (Chapter 2) sets the tone by providing the rationale for three sets of illustrative chapters that follow. Each part has further explication, and each illustrative chapter is introduced with a new preface describing how it came to be written with its particular emphasis.

The final part of the book takes a different turn, attending to the mysterious procedures of transformation by addressing how they *may* be taught and must be learned. Recent years have seen a burst of interest in questions of what and how to teach "qualitative inquiry" or "qualitative methods" as a formal subject, particularly among faculty in professional schools suddenly given responsibility for teaching a subject in which they themselves have had neither training nor experience. I have addressed a chapter specifically to that audience, followed by a complementary one from the perspective of what qualitative researchers need to know, independent of what can be accomplished in formal coursework designed for them.

That's what is new. Ah yes, and the arrangement of the material is new.

The book is not entirely new and speculative, however. The questions I have posed afford an opportunity to pull together in one volume some of my substantively oriented work, writing that represents the efforts of a professional lifetime. I have included nine such pieces here. Editor Mitch Allen once referred lightheartedly to that part of the collection as "The Best of Harry."

As an author, the opportunity to pull together and reexamine a collection of previously published pieces engaged me in a task that occupied my thoughts and energy for months and months. (Indeed, everything about the volume took longer than I originally envisioned; writing always does.) To editor Mitch Allen, acting on behalf of a publishing house that has taken a lead in pioneering the development of a literature of qualitative research, "The Best of Harry" offered something of a mixed blessing. For marketing purposes, he cautioned, the emphasis would have to be on what was new and original. Those chapters that had passed the test of time (in most cases literally having been "pre-owned," to borrow a euphemism from used-car dealers) would have to be regarded as a bonus or unexpected dividend.

The book does contain nine pieces that have appeared earlier in some published form. Brought together here, those chapters constitute a "reader" of completed studies, illustrating a range of approaches and topics in qualitative inquiry. I present them consistent with my strongly held belief that if you want to engage in this kind of work you should invest more time looking at what others have done than in listening to what they say you should do. But in the five new chapters, as well as in new prefaces accompanying previously published pieces, I offer whatever advice and suggestions I can. The emphasis throughout is on using rather than gathering data.

Mitch also expressed some initial reservation when I proposed *Transforming Qualitative Data* for my title. He was not exactly transfixed with my choice of *transforming*, but that term seemed to me to give the emphasis on process that I wanted to convey. And I know he would not have minded had I slipped in *ethnographic* in addition to, or in place of, *qualitative*. As I note below, however, I have drawn from ethnographers rather than have written expressly for them. The more encompassing term *qualitative* is intended to communicate that.

*Transforming* was the critical term in the title. By the time I had convinced Mitch of its suitability, I was beginning to have doubts of my own about the other two words I had chosen. Just what are *qualitative data* and how are they distinguished from quantitative data? It had not occurred to me that through the years the phrase *qualitative data* has stolen its way into my vocabulary, one more instance of the powerful influence the physical sciences exert on contemporary ways of knowing. Thinking back, I realize that I was reared at the end of an academic era when ethnographers did not have to insist that they were "collecting data," something regarded at the time as better suited to laboratory conditions. They had their own term, one that aptly described their approach: *doing fieldwork*. I recall once parroting in a draft a declaration I had heard only a short time earlier, "Anthropologists do not gather data." A younger colleague returned my draft with a comment written in the margin, "Maybe you don't, but I do!"

These days there are a lot more data around, not only because of the information explosion but because a lot more people lay claim to be doing "research." If you do research, data are the first evidence of your efforts, something you gather or collect or generate or create, depending on the tradition in which you are working.

Everything has the potential to be data, but nothing *becomes* data without the intervention of a researcher who takes note—and often makes note—of some things to the exclusion of others. That process of taking note brings us back to the idea of "transforming" data. My attention here will be directed primarily to that part of the transformation when a researcher does something with whatever has already been identified, or is otherwise immediately retrievable, as data. Strictly speaking, that is the *second* stage in the process of data transformation, one that can occur only after data are already at hand. Having such data in the first place is a prior stage. What a reader subsequently makes of the researcher's transformations is another. And on it goes.

How then are qualitative data distinguished from quantitative data? My inclination is to sidestep this semantic trap by labeling data according to the self-ascribed role of the researcher who identifies them. Thus qualitative data are data that qualitative researchers generate, or, with a slight refinement, qualitative data are whatever data qualitatively oriented researchers collect that are not intentionally and recognizably quantitative. Resolving the issue this way takes cognizance of a critical point: The same data can have quite different meanings and uses for researchers of different persuasions.

The focus in the chapters that follow will be on the purposes to be achieved with data already at hand, not on distinguishing qualitative data from quantitative. Were we not so generally attuned to wanting to do "research" and anxious to be perceived as researchers, these matters might not draw attention. I have frequently used the term *qualitative inquiry* rather than *qualitative research* in these pages to suggest a broad range of scholarly activity that encompasses creative dimensions beyond a preoccupation with data per se. Yet our use of *inquiry* is taken by some as another indication of a concern with how we wish to be perceived rather than with what we are trying to accomplish. I do not intend it that way; I hope to illustrate how qualitative approaches allow far broader scope in what we recognize among the issues we address and what we draw upon as data in addressing them. "Data in use" rather than "research in action" is the central theme; not all the illustrative chapters here are research based. Qualitative inquiry, broadly defined, would never insist that they need to be.

Given under the guise of an authoritative reading of "the market," Mitch's advice and influence can also be traced in the organization (more accurately, the reorganization) of the material. My original plan, reflecting an enduring faith in inductive approaches to teaching, had been to write only the briefest of introductions to each illustrative chapter and to follow each set of chapters with an essay—one each on description, analysis, and interpretation—drawing the lessons from the readings. The three sets of illustrative-chapters-plus-summary-explication were then to be summarized and integrated into a Big Definitive Essay at the end. I began drafting new material and new introductions with that organization in mind.

Mitch suggested turning it all around. People want to know what they are supposed to be looking for when you ask them to read material that makes or illustrates your arguments, he insisted. As a result, the Big Definitive Essay appears first, the chapter immediately following this brief introductory one. Coming so early in the presentation, it now must anticipate in the abstract, rather than review through example, how qualitative data are transformed. It has not become quite the definitive statement I once hoped to write, but it is a beginning, and that is something. A focused discussion precedes each of the major parts. Following Mitch's advice, additional and highly specific comments pertaining to each illustrative chapter now precede rather than follow it.

The concluding part on teaching and learning qualitative inquiry allows me to summarize the whole process of qualitative research and to review the description-analysis-interpretation distinction. Readers totally unfamiliar with qualitative inquiry may want to read that part, particularly the chapter devoted to learning qualitative inquiry (Chapter 13) first, for orientation, and again later, for a summing up. Keep in mind, however, that this is not a fieldwork manual, although it might be considered a "deskwork" one.

I benefited greatly from Mitch's counsel in preparing an earlier publication for Sage, and I decided to follow it this time, in spite of the fact that it required a major change in organizing the material. At the time, I already had drafted the commentaries designed initially to follow the illustrative chapters. These were easily reworked into process-oriented introductions, each of which came quickly to the point, because they were written as though the reader were already familiar with the material. The proposed concluding essay that was now to become an introductory one had to be developed along lines more applicable to qualitative work in general rather than focused exclusively on my own. I could not even assume that readers familiar with some of my method-related writing were necessarily acquainted with the more substantively oriented selections included here.

Yet I admit to initial misgivings in not remaining true to my intuition to follow a more inductive approach. I was able to discuss the dilemma with George Spindler, my longtime colleague and former mentor at Stanford University, whose name appears frequently in these pages. Spindler offered a helpful perspective on how preparing a book on a topic and teaching a course on it present different pedagogical problems. I share his observation here, rather than postponing it for the chapter in which other matters of teaching will be discussed, because it relates as well to how we ourselves use, and might better use, qualitative studies with our many and varied audiences.

As I explained to "Spin," I never tell students how to read an assigned text or what they should find in it, and I did not expect to tell my readers what they should expect to find here. I found a sympathetic ear, for Spindler is every bit as much the gifted and effective teacher as he is the astute editor. I felt certain that he does not tell his students today what to read "for," any more than he did when I was his student years ago. And he agreed.

Spindler also reminded me, however, that an instructor is present *in person* to sequence and guide reading and discussion as an ongoing intellectual activity. The instructor can shape and direct dialogue, raise critical questions, pull threads of ideas together, make connections between early discussions and subsequent ones, and draw attention to important points. In short, an instructor can orchestrate a set of readings in terms of some larger curricular design. In preparing text material, by contrast, an author whose message is not made explicit in the text risks that his or her purposes may never be accomplished at all! That is not to say authors' purposes will necessarily be accomplished anyway, but at least authors have a fighting chance if they are explicit about what their texts have been designed to do.

Through subtle maneuvering and exquisite choices among these selected essays, I would like to have had you discover for yourself, quite independently, that qualitative study has three major dimensions: description, analysis, and interpretation. To trust that you would discover that intended message in the lifeless pages of a book did seem to leave a lot to chance, however, so I have had to "spill the beans," letting you in on my grand design from the outset. As you read, you can judge for yourself whether the description-analysis-interpretation distinction I propose is helpful. Know in advance that my efforts are designed to show that it is.

Whether or not the distinction proves helpful, you have before you an integrated set of new essays and time-tested old ones. And whether you are here as an old hand at this work, an interested student or newcomer to it, or an instructor who has chosen the book as a text, you are free to make of all this whatever you will. In realizing my dual opportunity—to address the basic problem in qualitative research of what to do with data and, at the same time, to bring a number of my own articles together in one place by way of illustration—I have accomplished my immediate and tangible purposes. If what follows proves to be of help to you in accomplishing yours, I will have achieved my hoped-for purposes as well.

My own academic biography unfolds in the chapters that follow. For readers new to qualitative inquiry, I should underscore that the chapters represent *a* point of view, not *the* point of view. That view reflects my anthropological training and orientation, my opportunities for extended fieldwork—especially on issues related to the field of education—and my efforts to bring the perspective of the former to the practice of the latter through efforts on behalf of "anthropology and education." My observations and suggestions are drawn most often from ethnographic research. They represent one particular field- and discipline-based research approach as understood by one particular fieldworker. The references that accompany each chapter or introduction are drawn most often from the writings of other ethnographers or ethnographically oriented qualitative researchers. And my examples are drawn most often from research into aspects of education, although here that means education "writ large" in its anthropological sense rather than restricted too singularly to what goes on in schools.

I will be flattered if colleagues or students in cultural anthropology find the discussions and illustrative chapters helpful, but I have not written particularly with them in mind. My intent has not been to help neophyte anthropologists in the conduct of ethnographic research as much as to draw upon the ethnographic experience as a resource for others whose research or practice may benefit from it.

# Reference

Agar, Michael H. (1980). *The professional stranger: An informal introduction to ethnography.* New York: Academic Press.

**2**

# Description, Analysis, and Interpretation in Qualitative Inquiry

*If ethnography produces cultural interpretations through intense research experiences, how is unruly experience transformed into an authoritative written account?*

— James Clifford, *On Ethnographic Authority*, p. 25

*Having notes—all neatly typed or bound, all stored safe and sound—is one thing: it validates our anthropological communications. But using notes is quite another: that activity shows fieldnotes to be not a fixed repository of data from the field but a reinterpretable and contradictory patchwork of perspectives.*

— Rena Lederman, "Pretexts for Ethnography: On Reading Fieldnotes," p. 90

"No one ever flunked fieldwork!" John Van Maanen once noted during a luncheon conversation on the subject. That may be overstatement, but it would seem unusual for anyone to initiate fieldwork yet gain nothing from the experience. On the other hand, it is not at all uncommon to complete fieldwork, accumulate a mountain of data, and have nothing to show by way of a completed study. So the greater problem for first-time qualitative researchers is not how to get data but how to figure out what to do with the data they get.

9

With experience, most researchers become less compulsive about collecting data and more proficient at using the data they collect, but the problem of transforming unruly experience into an "authoritative written account" never totally disappears. This question—what to do with data—provides the unifying concern in this volume, drawing heavily upon examples for illustration and exegesis. This chapter introduces and explores the issue at a general level. The parts that follow look at applications.

What I propose by way of an answer to the question is to take three ordinary terms—the trio revealed in my chapter title—and invest them with somewhat restricted definitions in discussing the transformation of qualitative data. The entire process is often glossed as *analysis*, but I am reluctant to use that word in its all-encompassing sense when I am about to suggest a more specialized meaning for its use among qualitative researchers.

I have identified and discussed elsewhere (in Wolcott, 1992) three major modes through which qualitative researchers gather their data: participant observation (experiencing), interviewing (enquiring), and studying materials prepared by others (examining). Here I propose that there are also three major ways to "do something" with descriptive data. No coincidence that I identify three ways to get data and three ways to present data, however; that simply reveals my penchant for sorting things in threes.

One way of doing something with data in rendering an account is to stay close to the data as originally recorded. The final account may draw long excerpts from one's fieldnotes, or repeat informants' words so that informants themselves seem to tell their stories. The strategy of this approach is to treat descriptive data as fact. The underlying assumption, or hope, is that the data "speak for themselves."

A second way of organizing and reporting data, one that typically builds upon the first, is to expand and extend beyond a purely descriptive account with an analysis that proceeds in some careful, systematic way to identify key factors and relationships among them.

A third way, calling for interpretation, may follow from the second or spring directly from the first. It does not claim to be as convincingly or compulsively "scientific" as the second, being neither as loyal to nor as restricted by observational data only. The goal is to make sense of what goes on, to reach out for understanding or explanation beyond the limits of what can be explained with the degree of certainty usually associated with analysis. It is not entirely unknown for interpretation to be both starting point and culmination for qualitative inquiry. At the interpretive extreme, a researcher-as-writer may seem merely to swoop down into the field for a descriptive morsel or two and then retreat once again to the lofty heights of theory or speculation, something like the touch-and-go maneuvers of novice pilots practicing landing and takeoff techniques.

By no means do I suggest that the three categories—description, analysis, and interpretation—are mutually exclusive. Nor are lines clearly drawn where description ends and analysis begins, or where analysis becomes interpretation. Nor is this particular set of terms, in this particular combination, something unique. As a matter of fact, in this instance, I would not even insist that the arrangement is new, for not only do the three terms appear frequently in discussions of qualitative research, they are usually listed in the same order. That is not necessarily the order followed in our accounts, however; note that this interpretive chapter sets the framework for everything that follows.

I do suggest that identifying and distinguishing among the three may serve a useful purpose, especially if the categories can be regarded as varying *emphases* that qualitative researchers employ to organize and present data. I propose that qualitative researchers keep this distinction in mind as they go about transforming their observational data—all that stuff collected on tape, film, and paper, plus all that other intangible stuff in one's head—into authoritative written accounts.

I will offer my own brief working definitions to help distinguish among the terms as I use them here. Researchers seem to follow no consistent pattern in employing them. The terms are often combined (e.g., *descriptive analysis, interpretive data*) or used interchangeably. I can illustrate the latter—*analysis* and *interpretation* appearing as virtual synonyms—with two sentences from one of my favorite ethnographers, Michael Agar, who writes,

> In ethnography . . . you learn something ("collect some data"), then you try to make sense out of it ("analysis"), then you go back and see if the interpretation makes sense in light of new experience ("collect more data"), then you refine your interpretation ("more analysis"), and so on. The process is dialectic, not linear. (Agar, 1980, p. 9)

If Mike Agar accepts the distinctions I propose here (he found the idea provocative when I first suggested it in informal conversation), he might someday rewrite sentences like these employing the phrase *analysis and interpretation* where heretofore he has taken either term to stand for both. Alternatively, being the systematic fieldworker that he is, he might be inclined to use only one term, *analysis,* leaving interpretation to ethnographers more oriented toward meanings and symbols, less concerned than he with systematic procedures in ethnographic research. More likely, as with most qualitative researchers, he will leave the way open to do a bit of both, after first providing readers with a richly layered descriptive account.

Each of the three terms—*description, analysis, interpretation*—is introduced here with a terse definition of its role in qualitative inquiry. The terms are developed more fully in the essay that follows.

> *Description* addresses the question, "What is going on here?" Data consist of observations made by the researcher and/or reported to the researcher by others.
>
> *Analysis* addresses the identification of essential features and the systematic description of interrelationships among them—in short, how things work. In terms of stated objectives, analysis also may be employed evaluatively to address questions of why a system is not working or how it might be made to work "better."
>
> *Interpretation* addresses processual questions of meanings and contexts: "How does it all mean?" "What is to be made of it all?"

## Description

Neophyte qualitative researchers, especially graduate students in professional fields such as education, nursing, or social work, who never dreamed they might someday have to do a study of their own, are easy to scare. Words like *objectivity, reliability, validity,* or *replicability* can send them rushing back to their word processors to rewrite thesis proposals that safeguard against, or effectively dispel, any suggestion that their intended studies can be faulted simply because they are dependent on a human observer.

One of the more obvious strategies for accomplishing this during the reporting phase of a study is for researchers to remove themselves from the picture, leaving the setting to communicate directly with the reader, as early ethnographic accounts often did. Another is to have informants present their accounts "entirely" in their own words or faithfully (alas, sometimes too faithfully) to preserve and report *every word* spoken by both interviewer and interviewee in formally taped sessions. This strategy, passing on "raw" rather than "cooked" data, presupposes a reader capable of overcoming all the problems that the researcher tried to avoid. Done in good faith—although built on a misunderstanding of how to keep an account "scientific" or "objective"— it falls of its own weight unless the neophyte realizes in time that there is no such thing as "pure" description.

In the very act of constructing *data* out of *experience*, the qualitative researcher singles out some things as worthy of note and relegates others to the background. Because it takes a human observer to accomplish that, there goes any possibility of providing "pure" description, sometimes referred to lightheartedly as "immaculate perception." (I first came across that phrase in a brilliant essay by ethnologist C. G. Beer, 1973, p. 49, although the concept can be traced back to Nietzsche.) Nevertheless, qualitative researchers typically introduce their studies with an *essentially* descriptive account. They may stop, or hope to stop, at a point where the data still speak for themselves. However reluctantly they acknowledge that such accounts are filtered through their own perceptions, they stoutly defend them as free from intentional bias—which may well be the case. Some researchers believe that such descriptively oriented accounts most closely approximate true science: lots of data heaped on readers thereby *empowered* (a 1990s verb of choice) to reach independent conclusions as to what is going on or how things come to have particular meanings in particular contexts.

"Heaped data" as a presentation format carries risks of its own. Readers are likely to get the idea that the researcher has been unable to sort out (or unwilling to throw away) data and has simply passed the task along. This is comparable to a "dump truck" approach college students sometimes employ in answering essay examinations if they cannot directly answer, or do not fully understand, the question asked. They respond with the-answer-must-be-in-there-somewhere approaches in which they relate everything they remember about a topic, throwing themselves on the mercy of the reader to pick out what is relevant. The problem? Data that do not "speak" to the person who gathered and

reported them are not likely to strike up a conversation with subsequent readers either. Occasionally, qualitative researchers do get
away with an excess of descriptive reportage. When they do, it may be
through exploring a fascinating topic or (less likely) developing so engaging a style that readers accustomed to being bored with research read
on—for a while, at least—out of appreciation and amazement.

Style alone cannot save a study, however. Readers always want to
know what the point is and need to be reassured that there is one. The
focus must narrow, the level of detail must be relevant and appropriate.
Every newly introduced detail of questionable relevance raises reader
suspicion: Is all this really adding up?

During early stages of writing, while data are still being sorted and
sifted, it may be helpful for the researcher to include too much detail:
somewhat similar examples or illustrations, protocols too lengthy,
details of questionable relevance. Everything can be edited later. With
the miracle of modern word processing, neither including nor eventually deleting excessive detail poses a problem. The advantage of moving data from fieldnotes to a working draft is that in so doing you flag
items of *possible* importance. That is easier to do the first time than having
to sift through everything again later for detail recalled but omitted.
Qualitative studies suffer for their length, however, and subsequent
efforts to pare overwritten drafts must be as vigilant as are initial efforts
to be inclusive.

Do qualitative researchers have some special way of describing things
and rendering those descriptions in final accounts? Not that I know of,
but the question has been asked of me, suggesting that would-be researchers sometimes have little idea of what should go into their fieldnotes and, of that, what should find its way into their working drafts.
Other than the implication that it must be preferable to "thin," there
is no consensus on what exactly constitutes the "thick description"
Clifford Geertz immortalized in a provocative essay by that title, an essay
quoted frequently in the pages that follow (Geertz, 1973; see also
Denzin, 1989, pp. 83-103, on this topic).

Every decision about the appropriate level of detail returns ultimately
to the immediate purposes being addressed and to overriding considerations that map a course between extremes of too-selective reporting
or hopeless obfuscation. Every detail considered for inclusion must be
subjected to a critical judgment: "Is this relevant to the account?" If I

could provide the magic formula for recognizing, remembering, recording, and subsequently transforming relevant data, here is where I would reveal it. But the only advice I offer is to make judgments in terms of sufficiency and to screen *all* description in those terms, the data to be excluded as well as the data to be included.

Be honest about identifying your purposes. Do not be too singular, or too academic, if your purposes also include curiously personal motives in addition to obvious and acceptable career ones. If, for example, you intend to indulge your latent talent for literary panache, you may as well admit it, at least to yourself. Whatever hallmark you intend to stamp on your work must nonetheless be appropriate to your purpose. There is no such thing as immaculate perception, and there is no immaculate description, either. One of the unheralded qualities of qualitative inquiry is purposiveness, and the more explicit we can be about our purposiveness as both fieldwork and deskwork progress, the better our position to judge what needs to be described, and at what level of detail.

The descriptive adequacy of an account is often difficult for the researcher-as-author to judge. That is one among several compelling reasons to invite readers unfamiliar with a setting to act as critical reviewers of early drafts. The images conjured up in their minds are limited to the account you provide. They are unable to hear nuances that you may hear; they were not present to hear them when originally spoken. Phrases that do not sound redundant, because of the way you heard them uttered, may nonetheless read redundantly to others who encounter them only in print. Be informed by what invited reviewers tell you they find in your working drafts. Never forget that in your reporting, regardless of how faithful you attempt to be in describing what you observed, you are creating something that has never existed before. At best it can only be similar, never exactly the same as what you observed. And at worst . . .

Just as some researchers prefer to build their cases essentially through the descriptive account, others appear obviously impatient to get beyond "mere description" (but see Erickson, 1977, p. 59, who cautions against rushing the journey, because description is never *mere* description) and on to analysis or interpretation. For researchers of either persuasion, a critical question is where and how to make the shift, whether reluctantly and in closing ("Can't I just raise a couple of questions at the

end?") or eagerly and early, perhaps introducing an analytical or theoretical framework as a means of introducing the reader to the problem
at hand.

There is no one best way to accomplish any of this. Doctoral students
worriedly anticipating when and how to introduce their analytical or
interpretive frameworks sometimes find the advice helpful to "stay
descriptive as long as possible." This advice is biased in favor of the
descriptive account while alerting students that there will come a point
at which they will find it necessary to introduce something more than
descriptive labels to keep the account moving forward in a purposeful
way. Should even that advice prove too "writerly," how about this:
"Tell the story. Then tell how that happened to be the way you told it."

In thinking about a point at which analysis enters the reporting process, beginning researchers who can maintain a critical stance toward
their own descriptive data—data they initially may have regarded as
objective—become aware that data are tainted with an analytical or
interpretive cast *in the very process of becoming data*. To go a step further,
as Mary Anne Pitman insists, "Data are already theory" (personal communication; see also Pitman & Maxwell, 1992, p. 761, with the more
cautious claim—reflective of dual authorship—that data are already
"theory laden"). The descriptive aspects of an account might better be
regarded as implicit analysis or implicit interpretation. Instead of anticipating some tangible point at which description abruptly stops and
analysis begins, we can be looking for the often subtle shift as implicit
analyses or interpretations gradually give way to explicit ones in even
the most descriptively oriented account.

One problem with descriptively oriented researchers striving too
hard to be objective is a tendency to treat everything at the same level
of detail. Observers get fixed (or perhaps transfixed) behind a wide-
angle lens that attends unselectively, recording everything from the
same distance rather than zooming in to particular details consonant with
the purposes of the study. For example, in a study of computer use in
the classroom that I was asked to review, the researcher had attended
dutifully to an entire class, especially the teacher-pupil dialogue, during a lengthy period of group instruction. When pupils finally were
released to their own keyboards and screens, however, my suggestion
was that both researcher and reader might learn more through attention directed to any *one* of those screens rather than remaining fixed at

the same vantage point from which the entire class had been observed earlier. Further, whatever appeared on the screens offered rapid feedback into what pupils had understood of their instructions. Like fieldworker observations themselves, descriptive narratives can move in and out like zoom lenses. The world is not flat; we should discourage any tendency of descriptive researchers to make it seem so.

## Ways to Organize and Present Description

Qualitative researchers need to be storytellers. That, rather than any disdain for number crunching, ought to be one of their distinguishing attributes. To be able to tell (which, in academia, essentially means to be able to write) a story well is crucial to the enterprise. When we cannot engage others to read our stories—our completed and complete accounts—then our efforts at descriptive research are for naught.

Regardless of the topic—presentation of a case study, discussion of method, examination of underlying philosophical issues—we ordinarily expect qualitative researchers to build their cases, or at least to draw their illustrative examples, from stories. Qualitative researchers of analytical or interpretive bent are nonetheless expected to ground their reflections in observed experience. So there must be something of the storyteller in each of us. Let me turn to this customary starting point of qualitative reporting—development of the narrative or presentational account—before proceeding to explore the analytical and interpretive dimensions that accompany it.

In the paragraphs that follow, I identify a number of ways to organize and present the descriptive portion of a qualitative study. I stop at 10; my purpose is to be suggestive rather than all inclusive. One can reduce such a list to the fewest basic plots (I would begin by looking for three all-consuming ones, as you must realize) or expand it ad infinitum. I have used variations and adaptations of these approaches in developing my own narratives, but always in combination, never in the pure forms described below.

*(1) Chronological order.* Events always can be related in the order that they occurred, with relevant context introduced as needed. Relating events in ordinal (first, second, . . . ) or chronological sequence (if that

does not violate confidences) offers an efficient alternative to the sometimes lengthy bridges written to give an account the appearance of flow when significant events do not seem all that continuous. Events can also be related in *reverse* chronological order, introducing the account by looking at how things are—or were—before turning to how they got that way. (Note my preference for the past tense here rather than for the often awkward "ethnographic present." See Sanjek, 1991, for a thoughtful examination of the phrase *ethnographic present*.)

*(2) Researcher or narrator order.* Chronological order is a fallback position for relating an account, as well as an obvious way to organize and code fieldnotes. Researchers should be attentive to other logics in addition to the logic of time so dominant in our own thinking. Thus an informant's way of unveiling his or her life story ought to be examined for its own internal logic before a researcher unwittingly reorganizes it into an orderly chronological sequence. The way the story has been revealed to the researcher may offer another way to organize. (This fits well with the idea of presenting an account as a mystery, to be discussed below.) Researchers endowed with a gift for storytelling—or self-consciously developing their own "theory" of it—may see many alternative ways to relate events through narrative strategies. The underlying issue, as Josselson (1993) defines it, is the question of what must be added to *story* to make it *scholarship*, how to "transform story material from the journalistic or literary to the academic and theoretically enriching" (p. xi; see also Spence, 1982).

*(3) Progressive focusing.* If a study is built around a carefully specified problem, the descriptive account may be revealed through a progressive focusing that goes in either direction, slowly zooming from broad context to the particulars of the case, or starting with a close-in view and gradually backing away to include more context. Most likely the zooming will move in both directions. Whether one zooms from outside in (ground to figure) or vice versa probably reflects disciplinary orientations, the psychologist or biographer predictably opening and closing with a focus on the individual, the anthropologist or sociologist more likely to open and close with a focus on the social setting. Relating an account through progressive focusing is not unlike the "funnel approach" Agar (1980, p. 136) suggests as a model to guide fieldwork.

*(4) Day-in-the-life.* This approach can take a reader immediately to the scene of the action. The day-in-the-life need not be interpreted too literally. Readers might be privy to a real or a fictionalized account, an entire day, or some customary sequence of events. A variation is to take readers along on a reconstruction of the first day of fieldwork, so that others are introduced to the setting in much the same way the researcher first met and reacted to it. This approach can accommodate an impressionistic introduction that allows the researcher to communicate a "feel" for the setting as well as to make use of first impressions that may be part of a stereotype the researcher intends to examine or to correct.

I advise fieldworkers to make extensive notes during the first days of research as well as to ensure that their data are sufficient for the reconstruction of an entire "day" or a complete sequence of events. I have heard arguments pro and con about note-taking during the early stages of fieldwork, critics insisting that early impressions are poorly informed and note-taking is not well focused. Personally, I attach great importance to "first impressions." Although I find such data invaluable in their own right, I think extensive early note-taking can be defended solely on the basis of keeping open the option to use this narrative technique.

To my surprise, when I decided to use a day-in-the-life approach for the opening descriptive chapter of my study of the principalship (Wolcott, 1973), I found that, in spite of conducting fieldwork for 2 years, I had sufficient data to portray a "real" day in the principal's life for only 2 days. Had I thought about it earlier, I would have made a conscious effort to record several full days' events to broaden my options for the write-up.

*(5) Critical or key event.* Just as no researcher as fieldworker can ever hope to *get* the whole story down to every last little detail, no researcher as author can ever expect to *tell* the whole story either. One way to circumvent the problem of never being able to tell the whole story is to focus on only one or two aspects, creating a story-within-a-story in which the essence (but not the detail) of the whole is revealed or reflected in microcosm. Anthropologists often report phase-denoting life cycle events this way. In numerous accounts, the activities surrounding birth, marriage, or death are presented and examined, not only for the events themselves but for the way an entire cultural ethos is reflected

in them. Focusing on a key event is one example of "doing less more thoroughly" in qualitative inquiry, a guideline I have discussed elsewhere (Wolcott, 1990, p. 62).

*(6) Plot and characters.*  Where individuals or sociological roles are central to a study, the researcher may proceed as though staging a play. First, the main characters are introduced. Then the story is put into motion. At that point, the researcher may either fade into the wings or assume the role of narrator, taking responsibility to ensure that the audience understands what is happening by guiding or "talking over" as the plot develops.

*(7) Groups in interaction.*  In the same way it is necessary in some tellings to keep individual characters clearly identified (and in others to assure anonymity), it often proves helpful to researcher and reader alike to create distinct group identities to emphasize differences important to a case.

Addressing himself specifically to efforts at planned change, for example, anthropologist George Foster advises researchers to attend first and separately to the target group and to the donor group, and only then to put the two groups in motion together in their interaction setting (Foster, 1969). I have found Foster's suggested sequence well suited to *any* study of interacting groups. The advice may prove as useful for organizing and presenting material as for orienting fieldwork. The format draws attention to change agents themselves, so that the target group is not perceived as the only "beneficiary" of change efforts. Nor should attention be directed too narrowly to identifying only two groups in the transaction; efforts at social engineering need to be examined in broad contexts.

*(8) Follow an analytical framework.*  The previous point suggests developing a narrative around one framework that has proved particularly helpful. Adopting *any* framework imposes structure on the descriptive account, if structure is what the research—or the researcher—needs. By having the framework in mind during fieldwork, the researcher, like a well-prepared chef, is assured that, when the various descriptive ingredients of the case are called for in an ensuing analysis, they will be at hand.

Making sure that the descriptive portion of an account will include the detail necessary for subsequent analysis or interpretation raises an important issue: how to ensure that one does not gather only data that support a preconceived framework. I think the antidote is to maintain a healthy skepticism toward everything one hears, sees, remembers, records, and writes in the course of developing a study. A guiding question: Am I attending as carefully to what *is* going on as I am attending to what I *think* is going on?

On the other hand, perhaps in anticipation of being overly selective or subjective, neophyte researchers sometimes seem to assume that, once drafted, their own descriptive accounts must be treated as gospel. They take that to mean that materials formed into sentences cannot later be changed, even by the author who constructed them, lest the truth-value of the account become suspect. This is not the case. Development of the descriptive material is every bit as much an interactive process as is any subsequent analysis or interpretation. Not until we try to make sense of data do we necessarily begin to understand what is central, what is peripheral.

Whether one is following a chronology, doing progressive focusing, or imposing an analytical model, what proves important in later stages for developing a manuscript should help guide subsequent revision of earlier sections, not only the descriptive account but sometimes the problem statement itself. That is why fieldwork and initial deskwork need to go hand in hand, preferably with writing begun while one still has access to the field. Howard Becker (1986, p. 12) has reminded budding social science authors that the only version that matters is the last— that is, the final—one. His advice prompted from me a writer's (and researcher's) guideline that I incorporated in *Writing Up Qualitative Research* but borrowed from the instruction sheet for assembling a wheelbarrow: "Make sure all parts are properly in place before tightening" (Wolcott, 1990, p. 47).

*(9) The "Rashōman Effect."* Japanese director Akira Kurosawa's 1950 film classic *Rashōman has lent its name to social science (e.g., Lewis,* 1959, p. 17; see also Heider, 1988). The film depicts a violent encounter as seen through the eyes of four witnesses, lending dramatic emphasis to the lesson that there is not one version of any event but as many versions as there are viewers. As a storytelling technique, any descriptive account

can be related through the eyes of different participants, seemingly freeing the researcher from having to disclose his or her own view—except for the presence of the authorial hand that has guided each viewer's recounting.

This Rashomon Effect can be adapted as a teaching device as well as a narrative strategy. An instructor might suggest that students conclude their fieldwork inquiries by examining data in terms of the way scholars in different disciplines (e.g., anthropologist, historian, sociologist) or qualitative researchers of different persuasions (e.g., microethnographer, biographer, ethnomethodologist, phenomenologist) typically present data and offer their interpretations. This is somewhat akin to the scientist's search for and systematic examination of rival hypotheses, except that in the science game a single hypothesis usually emerges as victor, while adherence to the Rashomon Effect may make alternative interpretations equally compelling. In *A Thrice-Told Tale*, for example, Margery Wolf provides a superb example of multiple interpretations of the same set of events as reported by the same fieldworker reporting in three distinct styles: fiction, fieldnotes, and reflexive account (Wolf, 1992).

*(10) Write a mystery.* My final suggestion, one that may appeal to compulsive problem-solvers as well as to fans of the genre, is to organize and present qualitative studies as though writing a mystery novel. (Marion Dobbert reminded me of this refreshing idea.) The problem focus becomes the mystery to be solved. With the researcher in the key role of detective, data are introduced in the manner of accumulating evidence, to be sifted, sorted, and evaluated according to their contribution to solving the mystery. The challenge (and reminder) is to write with a sense of excitement and discovery. How satisfying to have a reader say of a qualitative study, "I just couldn't put it down."

Whether or not they are particularly keen on portraying themselves as "solvers of mysteries," all researchers are advised to think about their problem and what it is they are trying to discover or solve. A researcher who cannot complete the following sentence (in the proverbial 25-words-or-less) is not likely to be effective as a fieldworker or ever be able to bring a study to fruition: "The purpose of this study is . . ."

I do not mean to suggest that everything must be specified in advance, for that would deny qualitative researchers the capacity to refine their studies as they proceed. Yet even the most fervent advocates of emergent approaches need to have, and to be able to communicate, a sense of what they seek. Comforted as we may be by the freedom of our inductive style, we must recognize that nothing emerges from qualitative inquiry without considerable assistance on the part of the researcher.

## Analysis

To underscore the distinction between analysis and interpretation, it may be helpful to distinguish between key terms and word pairs often heard as descriptors in qualitative inquiry. I have in mind a rather literal sorting, the same approach I use at a rudimentary level to sort data bits into broad categories. Into the pile or bin labeled "analysis" I would place such terms as *cautious, controlled, structured, formal, bounded, scientific, systematic, logico-deductive, grounded, methodical, objective, particularistic, carefully documented, reductionist, impassive.* Into the pile or bin labeled "interpretation" go a set of terms largely complementary to the first: *freewheeling, casual, unbounded, aesthetically satisfying, inductive, subjective, holistic, generative, systemic, impassioned.*

There are additional terms whose counterparts do not necessarily belong with "analysis." If interpretive results can sometimes be creative, speculative, conjectural, fresh, surprising, unpredictable, imaginative, inspirational, and insightful, that does not mean that analytical findings invariably are uncreative, unimaginative, uninspiring, unsurprising, or lacking in insight. Nevertheless, an inherent conservatism and caution is associated with the work of analysis, a mantle of restraint worn proudly, somewhat akin to the laboratory coats worn by technicians to proclaim, "Scientist at work." Even in the social sciences, where virtually nothing is known with certainty, an analytically based report may all but shout, "Based on careful analysis, this much we can say for sure . . ." or, in short, "We *found* . . ."

Because qualitative data gathering is conducted through such everyday techniques as participant observation and interviewing, it is comforting to employ a term like *analysis* to suggest that in what we do with data we are able to wrest them from their humble origins and transform them into something grand enough to pass for science. To avoid confusion, I have taken the phrase *transforming data* to refer to *analysis* in this broad, everyday sense. For our special purposes in qualitative inquiry, I want to infuse the term *analysis* with a more carefully specified definition. *Data analysis* as employed here may be regarded a special subset of *data analysis* in its broad everyday use.

I propose a working distinction between *analysis* in that broad "transforming data" sense—referring to virtually anything one does in the management and reporting of data—and a less expansive definition in which *analysis* refers quite specifically and narrowly to systematic procedures followed in order to identify essential features and relationships consonant with the descriptors noted above. That does not require us to drop the general meaning of the term as much as to recognize, for our own purposes, an additional, more restrictive meaning that distinguishes between analytical affirmability and interpretive plausibility.

I admit to some difficulty in my effort to avoid using the term *analysis* in its customary, broad sense in these pages. The word slips easily into any discussion as a gloss for everything we do in transforming data. I argue here on behalf of using it as well to refer quite specifically to one aspect of that transformation.

The day before I first penned this part (and I was writing in long-hand, as I continue to do when literally "thinking on paper"), a colleague recently returned from overseas stopped at my campus office to remark on the inordinate time the "analysis" of data recently collected during fieldwork was taking. In the more restricted use of the term I am proposing here, I would not describe what she was doing as *analyzing* data. As she recounted the tedious business of coding and entering data into a computer program, *processing* seemed an appropriate term. (Miles and Huberman, masters at qualititative data analysis and coauthors of a major treatise on the topic—1984/1994—suggest *data management* as another.) Contrasted with the weeks and weeks in which she will be engaged in mechanical processing, the truly analytical moments will occur during brief bursts of insight or pattern recognition, some of which must already have occurred for her to have identified even the most rudimentary categories and coding procedures. Other such moments seem destined yet to come in exploring relationships among the categories or discerning critical elements from casual ones.

In this technical sense, the analysis of our nontangible social data is similar to the analysis of tangible substances like soil, water, blood, or investment portfolios. From anyone who advertises as an "analyst," we expect a straightforward identification of elements present, most likely reported in comparison with a previous analysis or with some generally accepted standard. Analysis rests, ultimately, on agreed-upon knowledge, the recognition of mutually recognized properties or standards.

For example, in some areas in my community, arsenic can be a problem in drinking water supplies. Those of us with our own domestic water systems watch for a "maximum contaminant level" of 0.05 mg/l in periodic test reports. I have no idea who decided on my behalf that a little arsenic wouldn't hurt me, nor have I actually checked on whether laboratory technicians who conduct such analyses can test to that level of accuracy. I am satisfied to hear what I want to hear: that an agreed-upon standard exists, and that my water supply meets it— that is, compares favorably. (This issue of comparison is integral to analytical work and raises intriguing questions for qualitative researchers. I take it up separately in the introduction to Part II in order to proceed with this overview.)

Analysis always suggests something of the scientific mind at work: inherently conservative, careful, systematic. Analysis does more than merely hint at fact, however: it presumes to *be* fact. If, as researcher, I choose and follow procedures correctly, you as reader can—and, if we are to maintain a dialogue, you must—accept my findings. Analysis does not preclude interpretation, but in the very act of shifting from strict quantification (so many milligrams per liter of arsenic) to meanings ("So, you see, you have nothing to worry about"), the analyst is likely to signal a dramatic shift of role or manner intended to mark a boundary between fact and interpretation.

The analytically minded consumer or client may expect such shifts to be marked, although in our daily lives we experience ambivalence toward how strictly we want to see them observed. Our visits to the family physician, for example, are confounded by the blurring of lines between certainty and speculation: We find ourselves wishing doctors knew more than they do while suspecting that their pronouncements already far exceed what they know with comforting certainty. I was impressed when my own doctor once admitted to a "diagnosis of exclusion" in attempting to identify a fleeting problem of dizziness for which I seemed to show no sign of related telltale symptoms. George Homans (1950) observed that scientific analysts (would he have included medical doctors?) always need "the most brutal reminders" of all that they leave out because they are "so charmed with their pictures they mistake them for the real thing" (p. 15).

Results couched in analytical terms are often accepted as what is known "with certainty." Our field data themselves, contradictory, subjective, unruly, partial as they invariably are, provide little basis for knowing with certainty. Subjecting them to rigorous analysis offers a way to achieve credibility. As J. Clyde Mitchell (1983) pointed out in an article on case and situation analysis, the essential point in making inferences from case material is in realizing "that the extrapolation is in fact based on the validity of the analysis rather than the representativeness of the events" (p. 190). For some problems, for some researcher personalities, and for some circumstances, the need to be right is so crucial that what is passed off as analysis may consist of little more than a reorganization of the basic descriptive data, a retreat to coding and labeling, observational data upgraded to be rewritten as fact.

Researchers weaned on quantitative methods may succumb to overwhelming urges to reduce their qualitative data to numerical categories or neat variables, seeking to achieve respectability for their results at the cost of more penetrating analyses (or interpretations) that might raise questions rather than put them forever to rest. In this sense, analysis might be considered the quantitative side of qualitative research. (Better to regard them as two sides of the same coin than argue for the divisive quantitative/qualitative split, I think.) Analysis is the more orderly, less speculative side of data transformation. Whatever I present under the rubric of "analysis" you may accept with assurance. The deal has already been cut. I wouldn't employ that label unless I was certain, and you must reciprocate with equal evidence of your own good faith. Any differences must be traced to other sources, such as questions of *what* should be analyzed or what to analyze *for*. And there is plenty of room for argument there, plenty of room for closer attention not only to our procedures but to our purposes for analyzing! But as for the analysis itself—it stands as given. As a colleague working on socially sensitive issues in AIDS research pointed out, the risk of being sued is greatly diminished when one sticks to analysis. Computers are good allies under such constraints; they do not propose interpretations.

Most often the term *analysis* is preceded by a qualifying adjective. Some designated analyses are hopelessly broad, pointing as they do with an elbow instead of a finger: comparative analysis, computer analysis, cultural analysis, illuminative analysis, logical analysis, meta-analysis, policy analysis, statistical analysis. Given their imprecision, such phrases as these might stand accused of giving analysis a reputation for being loose. More commonly, the qualifying term identifies not only a particular subset of technical procedures to be followed but also a particular subset of researchers who customarily employ them: analytical induction, analytical mapping, analysis of variance, clique analysis, cluster analysis, componential analysis, compositional analysis, configurational analysis, consensus analysis, constructive analysis, content analysis, conversational analysis, conversion analysis, correspondence analysis, crime analysis, discourse analysis, discriminant analysis, document analysis, domain analysis, exploratory and confirmatory factor analysis, extended case study analysis, generative analysis, graphic analysis, impact analysis, interaction analysis, latent variable analysis, market analysis, miscue analysis, mode of production analysis, multivariate analysis, panel analysis, path analysis, power analysis, reconstructive analysis, processual analysis, psychoanalysis, qualitative analysis (in chemistry, of an unknown sample), reconstructive analysis, (simple and multiple) regression analysis, repeated measures analysis, retrograde analysis, semantic analysis, situational analysis, social drama analysis, social network analysis, soil analysis, spectral analysis, statistical power analysis, stepdown analysis, structural analysis, structural equation an-alysis, textual analysis, thematic analysis, thematic field analysis, time allocation analysis, transactional analysis, visual analysis, wave analysis.

As long as one collects the kind of data required by these procedures and rigorously follows the (typically rigorous) rules for applying them, rightness—at least of a procedural kind—should be in the offing. In effect, the procedures impose order on the management of data, no matter how unruly the data themselves. As an essentially deductive activity, the certainty associated with analysis derives from those procedures.

Analysis has political dimensions as well as scientific ones. Every researcher faces choices leading as readily to the charge that one has underanalyzed as has overanalyzed one's data, or has totally submerged the fieldwork in the subsequent management of data. The potential of qualitatively oriented inquiry can be lost more easily in the temptation to overpower, rather than surrender to, one's data. And the lure of certainty, coupled with ever-expanding computer capabilities, poses a new threat to qualitative inquiry. John Seidel expresses concern for what he terms "analytic madness," prompted by programs such as his own ETHNOGRAPH, that tempt researchers to gather great volumes of data and thus invite analyses in breadth rather than in depth (Seidel, 1992).

One way to maintain the analytical aura, although it can become an academic cop-out, is to raise rather than attempt to resolve questions posed or implicated by the data. If questions are to bear the brunt of the analysis, they need to provide coherence and a sense of direction, with a few penetrating questions rather than a multitude of minor ones of little consequence. No one expects a researcher to know everything, of course, but even humility needs to be approached with moderation. An old saying reminds us, "Any fool can ask questions." Questions posed need to be real, not rhetorical, and a researcher must give evidence of having taken the analysis as far as possible before insisting that the reader share the responsibility.

Whether the analysis is to serve as a diagnosis on which a prescription for action should be made, a launchpad for further study, or a case examined and closed, is yet another strategy decision that may be linked to the way the problem was originally set or to the intended outcomes of the research. Researchers need always to have before them the question of whether they have set and approached their problem in an appropriate way. The possibility of better stating or further refining a problem, or of altering the course of future inquiry, should always remain open.

On the other hand, there is a threat of infinite regression in all inquiry. A realistic cost-benefit appraisal needs to be part of any decision to pursue or drop a given line of research. Throughout my professional life, well-meaning friends and associates have continued to point to things they think might be "interesting" for me to study. I have learned to smile and bite my lip rather than raise the issue of exactly how interesting each suggested study might prove to be. Each of us has the potential to pursue only a limited number of studies; we should not squander them. Indeed, we are reminded that far too little attention is given to how we go about making choices as to which problems to study. As Charles Lindblom (1990) observes, "What is most worth inquiry" might well be "among the questions most worth probing" (p. 44).

## Ways to Approach Analysis

To summarize this brief description and analysis of analysis, I have identified several strategies one might employ for pursuing it. I stopped with a list of 10, enough to suggest a range of alternatives. Once again, I repeat that although discrete when presented in the abstract, the approaches overlap considerably in practice.

If some of these approaches appear a bit diversionary, keep in mind the importance for the analytically oriented researcher to draw attention to aspects of a study that are (or appear to be) incontrovertible. When a study seems not to have turned out too well, the researcher must discern what—or what else—remains that one can be "sure" about and thus address with confidence. That is what this list of strategies explores. They are not strictly parallel to the previous list of descriptive approaches, in which procedures also pointed to outcomes. As suggested in a previous paragraph with a seemingly endless list of its own, the outcomes of analysis are often quite specific. Here I treat analysis more as a general mind-set, as, for example, a researcher who wants to present conversation analytically without necessarily subjecting it to the rigors of conversation analysis.

*(1) Highlight your findings.* In the very act of observing, a qualitative researcher makes myriad choices in looking at some things rather than others, in taking note of some things rather than others, and in subsequently reporting some things rather than others. In the analytical mode, that process becomes increasingly selective as some of the data now receive most of the attention. Depending on how the researcher has chosen to build the descriptive base, the researcher may double back to highlight certain information already presented or may use the sharper focus to present new material or a finer level of detail.

The traditional ethnographic concern for context, with attention to how things are and how they got that way, must bow here to a focus on only certain facets and certain relationships among them. The specificity associated with analysis also suggests how to get the process started if it seems too overwhelming: keep breaking down the elements until there are small enough units to invite rudimentary analysis, then begin to build the analysis up from there. My colleague Dianne Ferguson summarizes this procedure as "chunking it out" until you have a segment of data small enough that you finally see a way to begin.

Here is where one reports or summarizes whatever was counted, measured, inquired about, and so on. No more story, just the facts, now organized in such a way as to reveal those underlying properties and structures and relationships that are the stuff of analysis.

Ordinarily, we do accumulate some nice, neat data to draw upon, but there is a certain irony in realizing that what we have along those lines is often more tangential than central to our efforts at qualitative inquiry, the likely consequence of uncharacteristically systematic efforts such as census-taking, questionnaires, or archival research. Nonetheless, at write-up time, such tangible data are comforting not only to have but to report. Thus the data at hand may exert an unanticipated, perhaps not even welcome, influence on how analysis proceeds. And the more of this kind of data you are able to present, the more you may have to ask yourself why you took a qualitative approach at all. You may be about to discover that qualitative approaches are an inefficient way to conduct surveys!

This is not to suggest for a moment that qualitative researchers do not or should not collect relevant systematic data. To the contrary, there are systematic approaches to fieldwork (as in item 3 below) based almost exclusively on collecting so-called hard data, yet somehow able to slip in under the big tent of qualitative research. At the least, anyone doing qualitative work needs to be alert to counting those things that need to be counted.

Early in the fieldwork that led eventually to publication of *The Man in the Principal's Office: An Ethnography* (1973), one of my major studies, I had the good fortune of a conversation with sociologist Robert Dubin. He expressed interest in my ethnographic approach in a field he defined as the sociology of work. But he also expressed concern that I had no plans for collecting any systematic data. He counseled me to include some systematic observation, particularly in terms of time distributions, even going so far as to suggest that I do some "time and motion" study. "You wouldn't have to do a great deal of it in order to have some interesting material to report," he promised, "and I think someday you will be glad you did." Totally oblivious to a precedent well established by the applied anthropologists of the 1940s and 1950s, I nonetheless followed his suggestion to do something that seemed to me the very antithesis of anthropological fieldwork. Yet Dubin proved to be quite right. Not only did I appreciate having such data to report, it is my impression that the time and motion data I collected briefly and intermittently during a 2-week period, and however far afield from the basic thrust of my study, remain the most frequently cited "findings" from the entire 2 years of fieldwork.

*(2) Display your findings.* One of the most important lessons in Miles and Huberman's *Qualitative Data Analysis* (1984 and in a 1994 expanded second edition) is to "think display." For the findings-oriented researcher, graphic presentation offers an alternative to prose not only for conveying information but for dramatizing or emphasizing particular aspects of a study. Tables, charts, diagrams, and figures are one way to do it.

I assume that how (or whether) each of us uses graphics reflects the way we conceptualize our studies. The walls of my study are never lined with blank sheets of newsprint, with felt pens nearby at the ready; the chalkboard in my office is always clean. With me, it's all words, all linear. My impression is that, like me, most researchers make too little use of graphics and visualization. Conversely, researchers who use them are inclined to excess. Miles and Huberman's wonderfully helpful and widely acclaimed text (14 printings of the original edition) serves as something of a case in point, with its 31 figures, 67 charts, 20 boxes, and 26 informal tables and diagrams.

"Thinking display" also brings to mind other visual approaches, particularly photographs, film, and videotaping. Photography offers the analysis-minded researcher a way of incorporating ambiguity without getting caught up in it, by including photographs as "visual facts" that can be presented with or without interpretation. (For further references and a case study using photographs as data for a "layered" sociological analysis, see Dowdall & Golden, 1989; see also Ball & Smith,

1992; Wagner, 1979; and, of course, the anthropological classic, Bateson & Mead, 1942.)

The advent of the "poster session" format for presentations at national meetings lends further impetus for "thinking display" and offers an edge for younger colleagues while seniors remain wedded to traditional talk formats. Meanwhile, computer graphics software has put opportunities for visual display virtually at our fingertips—to the extent that presentation-minded students purporting to learn fieldwork techniques already show signs of acting like survey researchers and pollsters gathering data especially amenable to graphic display. Anything that weans us from our dependency on prose is a blessing, however. That includes quantitative researchers as well, and there are sources addressed to both audiences (see, for example, Tufte, 1983; Wainer, 1992; or a brief comment and list of citations by Roper, 1989).

*(3) Follow and report "systematic" fieldwork procedures.* The terms *fieldwork* and *systematic* are not antithetical. There is an inevitable tension among qualitative researchers themselves between those insisting on making fieldwork more scientific and those dedicated to its interpretive and humanistic side. Although they were the "fads" of decades now past, the systematic approaches of the ethnoscientists and ethnosemanticists are not entirely out of vogue. These approaches seem especially to appeal to researchers who want more structure than they find under the broad rubric "doing fieldwork." Because these approaches lay out in recipelike fashion the data one should collect, they pretty much dictate the course of the ensuing presentation and analysis as well.

Spradley and McCurdy's *The Cultural Experience,* originally published in 1972 and reissued in 1988, offers an excellent introduction followed by examples of 12 student ethnographies. Beginning researchers seeking a recipelike approach to either informant interviewing or participant observation continue to find Spradley's two field guides (1979, 1980) instructive, his Developmental Research Sequence a godsend, and his several completed studies invaluable models. More recently, the two-volume set *Systematic Fieldwork,* by Werner and Schoepfle (1987a, 1987b), and an overview by Dobbert and Kurth-Schai (1992) offer procedural guidelines.

*(4) Flesh out whatever analytical framework guided the data collection.* This strategy has already been noted as a narrative technique. As with the systematic fieldwork procedures, data are collected according to the requirements of the framework being followed; one collects and reports what the framework calls for. The following are a few examples used frequently in qualitative work: componential analysis, consensus analysis, content analysis, discourse analysis, analysis of social settings.

*(5) Identify patterned regularities in the data.* Although we are all constantly admonished for the human tendency to stereotype and to overgeneralize, we would suffer long days indeed if our every new encounter required us to start fresh rather than rely on previous experience in discerning an essentially predictable world. Our work as social scientists is largely dependent on that same capability, and we often walk a fine line between the few repetitions we actually observe and the behavior patterns into which we quickly transform them in our accounts. Nevertheless, this is where we look for and discuss the relationships, the what-goes-with-what that realizes in the study of a single case the potential for understanding something beyond it. Our small samples and always too-brief opportunities to observe preclude us from reporting authoritative correlations, but careful reporting of what we actually observe—even in single instances—is an important contribution from our work. As well, our observations can serve as a powerful restraint on overgeneralizations made by others, a phenomenon Alan Beals has described for anthropologists as their spoiler role: "It's not so in my village" (Beals, 1973, p. 359).

*(6) Compare with another case.* With the emphasis on similarity (rather than the kind of metaphorical language befitting interpretation), controlled comparison between a known case and the unknown case being analyzed offers a way for the analyst to exercise control—assuming, of course, that the comparative basis itself is appropriate. (As noted, this topic will be further developed in Part II.)

*(7) Evaluate (i.e., compare with a standard).* Evaluation is a form of comparison in which some explicit or implicit standard supplies the comparability by which judgments can be made. The critical element is to have a recognized or agreed-upon standard. When evaluation

constitutes the major underlying purpose for conducting research, necessary agreements about what is to be looked at and how it is to be judged can (and presumably should) be worked out in early negotiation. When the researcher prefers not to assume the role of evaluator, an alternative approach is to include within the purview of the research how those immediately involved or affected evaluate what is going on, the researcher acting as information processor.

*(8) Contextualize in a broader analytical framework.* Another way for the analyst to maintain control is to draw connections with external authority. Most often this is accomplished through informed references to some recognized body of theory in one's special field, or to its recognized classics, in the tradition of the literature review. More recently, the researcher has been allowed, even encouraged, to make the connections personal or part of everyday experience—such as to one's own expectations, to experience, to conventional wisdom, to social norms. There is no way for the reader to controvert a researcher's declaration, for example, that something is—or is not—what the researcher as person had anticipated all along.

*(9) Critique the research processes.* I have cast analysis here as a strategy of reporting in which it is critical for the researcher to maintain authority and control. Although we seldom expect to know anything with complete certainty, we expect the analyst to offer at least the equivalent of a double-your-money-back guarantee. But what happens to a need to report with assurance when the analysis itself provides no comforting level of certainty?

Well, for one thing, you might simply try to break loose and be more speculative. This can be accompanied by "full disclosure," advising your readers that, although what you are able to convey from your observations does not conform to your own customary standard of reporting, the possible significance or implications of those observations seem too great to ignore.

In that regard, not even the great observer naturalist Charles Darwin serves as a good model. Darwin sat uncertainly on his observation-based theory of natural selection for 20 years, reluctantly driven to publish only because Alfred Russell Wallace was about to announce essentially the same theory, arrived at independently. But neither was

Darwin rushed by June deadlines or a forthcoming meeting of the Promotion and Tenure Committee; nor was he anxious to introduce a Grand Theory so contradictory to prevailing doctrine. Your work is probably of more modest scope and consequence. What you cannot report with a comforting level of certainty may nonetheless warrant being reported with a becoming level of uncertainty.

Along with that—or, alternatively to it, if you simply cannot cross over to the interpretive side—focus your analytical attention on the research process itself, becoming your own critic but drawing attention to your methods rather than to your results. This may not be as diversionary as it first seems if you take as a guiding question to all your research, "What can be learned from this experience?" Whether or not the research provides results, something can usually be learned about research approaches. A first place to look in this self-appraisal is for patterned regularities (or systematic neglect) in your own ways of observing and managing data that may have precluded the possibility of identifying important elements.

In professional fields, where research is more often treated as an add-on, introduced after one's initial training rather than as an integral part of it, there appears to be far more concern with qualitative research processes than with qualitative research results. It remains our own paradox that a report drawing lessons on method is likely to have more impact than anything offered by way of substance. On the other hand, that is also a reminder that method is a way—perhaps *the* way—to reach qualitative audiences, this volume a case in point! Never turn away from a careful examination of process. Should research processes seem to be taking too much attention away from the content of the research, consider treating that topic separately.

*(10) Propose a redesign for the study.*  Following from the previous point, if the problem with the research was more serious than one of inadequate techniques or inadequate data, you may still have something important to contribute—and may still maintain control—if you turn your analytical efforts to issues of conceptualization or design. "Design" is itself something of a convenience in qualitative work, for it can be faulted in retrospect even in the absence of any prior attention given to it. Thus a so-called emergent or itinerant design in a proposed study can later be analyzed for its inadequacies. The researcher goes free

("The design did it"), maintains control ("I'll now show you exactly what went wrong"), and, in spite of thinly disguised academic posturing, we all stand to learn something.

## Interpretation

Associated as it is with meaning, the term *interpretation* is well suited to mark a threshold in thinking and writing at which the researcher transcends factual data and cautious analyses and begins to probe into what is to be made of them. My intent in assigning *analysis* its more restricted definition is to set *interpretation* apart, recognizably distinct from *analysis* rather than either a synonym for or logical extension of it. The imagery that springs to mind here is that of a teeter-totter or seesaw, balanced at a midpoint but responsive to whichever end is more heavily weighted. Description is the fulcrum, the pivotal base on which all else hinges, but it is the researcher who decides how the description is to be played out—whether to bear down more heavily on the side of analysis or interpretation or, risking the dull equilibrium of a static state, to try for "perfect balance" between them.

Interpretation is also subject to excesses: One can be faulted for offering too much or too little as well as for committing both sins simultaneously (e.g., too much unwarranted personal opinion, too little truly insightful commentary). Interpretation is more subtle than analysis. Like gift giving or joke making in an unfamiliar cultural setting, one may see others doing it without being able to ascertain exactly how to go about it, while those able to perform with aplomb seem unable to provide helpful guidelines.

I hope I offer useful advice in suggesting that novice researchers who feel uncertain about how far to go, how much interpretation to offer, should err on the side of too much description, too little interpretation. The prudent course is to bank on the contribution to be made through careful descriptive efforts and cautious analysis. My experience has been that if critical readers (dissertation adviser or committee members, invited colleagues, reviewers or editors considering an article for publication) judge an account to be underanalyzed and/or in need of more interpretation, they not only will request it but are likely to suggest what direction further development might take. Needless to say, the cogency of their recommendations will reflect upon the adequacy of the descriptive account.

A pervasive problem with interpretation is the temptation to reach too far beyond the case itself in speculating about its meanings or implications. Interpretation is not bound to the descriptive account as tightly as analysis (as defined here), but that does not free the researcher to float away with no discernible link to the case at all. Qualitative researchers are welcome to their opinions, but focused inquiry is not a soapbox from which researchers may make any pronouncement they wish. Plainly put, studies purported to be research-based must be just that. When the claim is made that an interpretation derives from qualitative/descriptive inquiry, the link should be relevant and clear.

It is hardly unknown for author-researchers to go off on a tangent, of course, and interpretation is where that is most likely to happen. Although we may be inclined to regard interpretation as the culprit, research often enough serves as a ruse for presenting "interpretation" as little more than a point of view in disguise. Recoil as we may in righteous indignation at flagrant violations of the research claim, my guess is that we are all guilty at times of coasting far beyond our data, if for no other reason than not to seem excessively picayune or apologetic about what is sometimes a thin basis in observed fact.

Nevertheless, we do ourselves and our work no harm by exercising caution with our research claims. Casual observations are not diminished when reported as just that, and even systematic observations should be reported with full disclosure as to the basis they provide for subsequent interpretation. As Sanjek (1991) states, "The relationship between fieldnote evidence and ethnographic conclusions should be made specific" (p. 621; see also 1990, p. 403). Too seldom does one find such straightforward reporting as this remarkable example drawn from the writing of anthropologist A. I. Hallowell: "I regret that my field notes contain no information about the uses of direct verbal address in the other cases mentioned. But it may well have taken place" (Hallowell, 1960/1976, p. 364). Yet how much more commendable is reporting with his disarming honesty than the all-too-frequent and pseudoauthoritative, "My research shows . . ."

Let me hasten to add that this caution extends only for rendering unto research what properly belongs to research. Research is a means of organizing our thoughts to reach understanding, not an end in itself.

The sheer accumulation of data carries no accompanying guarantee that anything of importance will be learned. Painstakingly thorough researchers of any ilk may scoff at such activities as armchair theorizing, idle speculation, quick and dirty studies, secondary analyses—but anything that provides inspiration for good ideas deserves its place. Where or how we derive our interpretive insights matters not; the ultimate judgment must be based on their worth, not their source. Ideas are judged by their explanatory power or their capacity to inspire the work of others.

Thorough, focused observation provides the basis for our claims-making as field-based researchers, however. We need to be clear to ourselves, and make clear to our audiences, which of our claims are based on field research. Find whatever insights you can, where you can, whenever you can, but be highly circumspect about insights you attribute directly to research. If you can maintain a healthy skepticism toward description, analysis, and interpretation as facets of research, extend it to the whole research ethos as well. Watch for the tendency to employ research as a basis for self-validation. You may discover that it is more important to free yourself from the yoke of research than to harness yourself to it. If your best ideas come while lecturing, fishing, cooking, or reading the words of others, then pursue those activities with a vengeance. As a courtesy to those whose insights do come from original fieldwork, avoid laying claim to research when it is not your true source.

Given the difficulty of assessing the adequacy of an interpretation—which by definition not only invites but insists that the researcher say what he or she makes of it all—the basis for judging that adequacy tends to shift subtly from interpretations themselves to the status and persona of the interpreter. Careers are oriented accordingly. Beginning researchers are expected to offer detailed accounts and may be discouraged from offering much in the way of interpretation. Established scholars whose writing continues to be based on substantial new fieldwork are relatively rare, for along with seniority comes license to construct interpretive essays on more modest data, perhaps providing no more than a vignette or two in the touch-and-go manner discussed earlier.

Freeing oneself from the limitations of one's own primary data is not only a matter of moving up in academic rank. Time itself fosters the seasoning both of the data and of the individual who gathered them. In about the same number of years that it takes for the award of promotion and tenure, for example, an academic researcher might be ready to offer a provocative interpretation for a dissertation study completed several years earlier.

Data and scholar alike mature within social contexts that exert a sometimes subtle influence on interpretation that we fail to recognize. In that sense, the interpretative dimensions of qualitative studies contain the true germ of life. Descriptive details are not likely to change through time; descriptive statements stand pretty much as written. What may for a time become an all-consuming effort at analysis—for the most part meaning the tedious business of data processing—comes eventually to an end. I do not recall hearing the statement "I'm reanalyzing my data" spoken with great enthusiasm; the implication is that somebody goofed the first time. On the other hand, the idea of finally finding a way to interpret one's data, or suddenly realizing how to go about reinterpreting it, denotes the possibility of fresh insight or a long-awaited breakthrough.

Interpretation does have its day. I don't believe you can rush it, and I don't recommend you try. Keep on mulling the questions you are asking, as well as mulling whether the questions you are asking are the important questions to ask. Consider, too, that you may have more to say at some time in the future about what they may mean.

### Ways to Approach Interpretation

This third list stretched to 11 possibilities, enough to suggest a variety of ways to address the issue of interpretation, ranging from simply "jumping in" to avoiding altogether any temptation to go beyond the data. I realized as I explored these possibilities that, like analysis, interpretation also can be approached cautiously and conservatively. Strategy decisions are never as clean-cut as we make them out to be when we reflect on them in public; in addition to complex professional reasons, our choices are influenced by complex personal ones as well. Several of the alternatives below offer a safe harbor for the researcher willing to go beyond analysis without becoming imprudent in reaching too far beyond.

*(1) Extend the analysis.* A cautious researcher can speculate on speculation itself, noting the implications or influences that one might draw, without actually drawing them. This is a strategy for pointing the way rather than leading the way.

One can safely point the way by offering a (comparative) perspective sufficiently outrageous that, although not intended literally, raises doubts or questions not lightly dismissed. Given current concern about domestic violence and intrafamily abuse, for example, a researcher investigating these topics might leave a reader with unsettling questions as to why, in the face of so much stress and uncertainty, there isn't more rather than less violence and abuse? How does it happen that the majority refrain from such conduct, given that they are subject to the same social malaise as their neighbors? What is the nature of resilience in the face of so much adversity? Such questions are neither born of analysis nor pointedly interpretive. They put a researcher at little risk, yet manage to convey a caution against accepting overly simplistic explanations of complex social phenomena or always looking at issues from the same perspective.

*(2) Mark and then make the leap.* If you are not saddled with a personal need to present your every written statement with certainty, there is vast interpretive possibility in the world of uncertainty. The bridge from the known to the unknown goes by many names. I have always been partial to the term *inference,* probably because John Platt's influential article "Strong Inference" appeared in 1964, just as I was starting my career as a professional (i.e., post-Ph.D.) researcher. Another phrase, *inductive reasoning,* may be more familiar; I borrow a definition from Rudolph Carnap, "I mean . . . by inductive reasoning all forms of reasoning or inference where the conclusion goes beyond the content of the premises and therefore cannot be stated with certainty" (Carnap, 1953, quoted in Sarana, 1975, p. 3). The idea of inductive inference goes back to Baconian times, and researchers through the years have employed similar phrases to assure both themselves and others that they were "doing science." (Some humanistically or interpretively inclined researchers today may be equally adamant about insisting that they are not.)

Whether sticking to the facts dooms one to be forever stuck with the facts remains the Grand Debate. Those who emphasize interpretation cast their lot with a creative human imagination capable of being informed rather than bound by an ever-expanding universe of facts. If you would join them, I suggest that you give clear indication wherever in your account your efforts at description or analysis yield to interpretation. Be sensitive as well in recognizing those arenas where interpretive efforts are appreciated and applauded. They are not universally welcome or invariably appropriate.

*(3) When you come to the end, stop!* Nobody insists that a weak interpretation is better than no interpretation at all. If you cannot put an otherwise adequate account into some suitable interpretive framework, don't detract from what you have accomplished by tacking on a wimpy interpretation. Take the account as far as you can with confidence, then stop while ahead. If possible, try to point to what seems to be needed next and what will be necessary in order to take that step. And do consider some of the possibilities explored below that might help you move toward interpretation without pushing you farther than you feel ready to move.

*(4) Do as directed.* I have grown used to hearing the gatekeepers of qualitative research (faculty members, editors, reviewers) rail about how beginning researchers—doctoral students in particular—tend either to overinterpret or, more often, to underinterpret their studies. There is no absolute rule as to the proper ratio of description to analysis to interpretation, an issue I explore in concluding this chapter. But one can easily draw a pragmatic rule: As long as it does not violate your integrity (and not just offend your feelings), try to comply with the demands put upon you. Whether you are directed to provide more or less by way of interpretation, work toward your immediate objective: to get the dissertation passed, the article published, the research project completed.

The solitary nature of most qualitative inquiry makes most of us overly sensitive to criticism, but it is well to keep in mind that those whom we perceive as holding power or being supercritical may nonetheless be trying genuinely to help us achieve more powerful contributions through our work. Even when someone's efforts strike you as self-serving or misguided (e.g., a pet theory rather than an appropriate one is suggested to you), keep in mind that most of the seeming power holders are also stakeholders in the qualitative enterprise. Inadequately developed accounts reflect on us all. When plain old disagreement is at issue, through careful attribution you may be able to signal to your reader when ideas expressed are not your own: "I am indebted to Professor Snark for suggesting that in his view . . ."

*(5) Do as suggested.* This strategy is similar to the previous point except that now your critics are your own invited colleagues or perhaps editors and anonymous referees invited implicitly through material submitted for review.

If you are struggling with and seemingly stumped by the challenge of interpretation, I know of no better way to overcome that hurdle than to place your case, literally and figuratively, before interested associates and to invite their comments. The crucial element in soliciting feedback seems to be to engage in dialogue about interpretive possibilities. As with writing, engaging in a dialogue requires that you first give voice to your thought processes. In the process of giving voice to your thoughts, you give others access to them as well.

There is some subtle reciprocity involved here; you are never totally free to ignore the suggestions of invited critics. Colleagues quickly learn not to offer suggestions or critique if you dismiss their comments or react too personally. Suggestions forwarded from editors' offices are usually prerequisites for getting a manuscript accepted. You aren't obligated to follow them, but if you don't intend to, start looking around for a different journal or publisher. Every invited reviewer is, nonetheless, a potential source of insight into the adequacy of your descriptive account, the incisiveness of your analysis, the depth of your interpretation. Every opinion offered is also a reminder that for every additional viewer there is an additional view.

A related consideration that has grown with interest in collaborative research is to turn to those in the setting you have been studying for joint authorship, for critique of manuscript drafts, or for contributed written statements of their own. Don't be disappointed if nothing is forthcoming; not everyone takes this business as seriously as we do, and those who do may feel overwhelmed by the invitation. But keep open the possibilities. Your conscience also may rest more easily if the invitation for collaboration or review was offered, even if declined. Minor disagreements as to fact are easily adjusted. Disagreement on matters of interpretation may raise questions deserving to be revealed rather than resolved. Issues of confidentiality and the ethics of reporting, on the other hand, do need to be resolved. I think they are best addressed at about the final draft, not as an abstraction but after the researcher's own proposed resolution of every reporting dilemma is well beyond the "What if . . . ?" stage.

*(6) Turn to theory.* Theory can serve both analytically and interpretively. It is probably employed more often analytically, for the purpose of providing structure. For interpretation, theory provides a way to link our case studies, invariably of modest scope, with larger issues. I suspect it is this linking power, rather than explanatory power, that makes theory so popular with individual researchers. This seems especially true in the field of education, where little theories are a dime a dozen, big theories are borrowed from the social sciences, and no overarching rival theories ever arose to replace the preoccupation with learning theory dominant at midcentury.

One interpretive tack is to examine a case in terms of competing theories and then proclaim the winner or, more often, attempt some eclectic resolution. Theory can be pitched at so many levels that the same theory may provide a safe harbor for some (I've always found it difficult to think of anything that can't be linked with communication theory) and a radical one for others (e.g., today's feminist theory or critical theory). At any moment, there is always some prevailing theory-of-the-day (Freudian theory, Marxist theory, general systems theory, chaos theory) for those determined to stay current or who find theory itself sufficiently engaging that they continue to reinterpret the same data set in terms of each new theory to come along.

*(7) Refocus on interpretation itself.* Sometimes intentionally, sometimes not, interpretation works its way to center stage, the descriptive account serving only as introduction or example for a major effort at interpretation. More than simply linking up with theory or leaning on it for an interpretive framework, the objective here is to develop that framework. Descriptive research previously reported may be reviewed briefly for illustration or inspiration, or some newly proposed conceptual apparatus may be turned back on original data as a test of its explanatory power or completeness. Any urgency as to the "theoreticalness"

of a particular interpretation is most likely to be determined by traditions existing within individual disciplines. Some fields, and some individual practitioners, are more theory-compulsive than others. One researcher's hunch may be another's middle-range theory, and even that, you must realize, is a matter of interpretation.

*(8) Connect with personal experience.* In the self-reflexive mood dominant in the 1980s, the distance an observer was expected to maintain to assure objectivity disappeared altogether in some camps. Clifford Geertz described the prevailing theme as "I-witnessing" (Geertz, 1988, pp. 73-101). Personal reflection once begrudgingly tolerated became not only accepted but expected.

"I-witnessing" offers two interpretive options. The first is to personalize the interpretation: "This is what I make of it all." The second is to make the interpretation personal: "This is how the research experience affected me," a style to which John Van Maanen affixed the label Impressionist Tale (Van Maanen, 1988, pp. 101-124). What differs between the two is the extent of personal revelation called for. The latter option turns attention back on the fieldworker, reflecting the stance that consciousness is private, and thus the only true understanding a human observer can hope to achieve is of oneself. Excesses of the approach are reflected in a quip in which a "postmodern" ethnographer, concluding an informant interview, says to the interviewee, "Well, that's the story of my life. Do you have anything to add?"

*(9) Analyze the interpretive process.* In lieu of the solid interpretation you may have hoped to provide, you might instead analyze the interpretive process. Explain what seems to be holding you back or what pieces of the puzzle are still missing. You can always plead for more time; in that regard, Darwin's 20-year procrastination established a useful precedent after all. Try to identify other factors as well, considerations that may leave your readers with a clearer sense of the problem in spite of the fact that you yourself feel no closer to an answer.

*(10) Interpret the analytical process.* Although you may not be up to offering an interpretation, you may be able to examine the analytical process you employed with your data, leaving your reader with war

ranted doubt about an analysis that may have been as irrelevant as it was satisfying. Or you might consider how your analysis may reflect fashionable points of view rather than important underlying issues. A shorthand label suggested by Schlechty and Noblit (1982, p. 290) to describe this interpretive strategy is "making the obvious dubious." (For a powerful but disquieting example reinterpreting an ostensible research effort in the mental health field as an essentially promotional one instead, see Kirk & Kutchins, 1992.)

From his vantage point as an acquisitions editor, Mitch Allen also notes variations related to the cyclical nature of the social sciences themselves, pointing to the success of some scholars (and, presumably, the delight of their publishers) at debunking one's academic ancestors and/or being, in Mitch's phrase, "counterintuitive," sensing and seizing a propitious moment for challenging conventional wisdom and setting a new course.

My personal assessment is that the most deeply committed field researchers are neither likely fountainheads of major theoretical shifts nor likely to find fieldwork itself much affected by them. There is always the possibility for putting a new spin on ideas generated elsewhere, however, and close inspection of the interpretative process seems a good place to do it. To the extent that a novice must choose between keeping an eye either on his or her fieldwork or on his or her pontificating colleagues, I would recommend the former, taking the risk of being too cautious rather than trying to catch the biggest wave of the day.

*(11) Explore alternative formats.* The more imaginative you may want to be in your interpretation, including the exploration of personal feelings and beliefs, the more you may feel hampered rather than empowered by your academic heritage. Never give up on trying to get an article published until it has been submitted to a number of journals (and even to the same journal after a change of editors, if you are convinced that your choice of journals is appropriate). But consider alternative literary forms: poetry and poetics (e.g., Brady, 1991; Richardson, 1992), historically or ethnographically accurate fiction (e.g., Richardson, 1990; Wilson, 1966). Of late, there has also been interest in the performance of text (for discussion, Paget, 1990; for ideas, Delue, in press; Shaftel & Shaftel, 1982). Although such alternatives are out of the mainstream of

research reporting, they are also a reminder that others, including film-makers as well as writers, share your frustration and continue to seek other formats and reach out to other audiences.

## Description, Analysis, and Interpretation: Achieving a Balance

If you find the proposed distinction among the three categories useful for thinking about the relative emphasis in organizing and presenting a qualitative study, a next question is this: How does one apportion energy, effort, and allotted space among them?

My answer, the same one I give for almost every direct question about qualitative research: It depends. ("It depends" may be the all-purpose answer among qualitative researchers: see Glesne & Peshkin, 1992, p. xii; Miles & Huberman, 1984, p. 43.) That is not to say it is entirely arbitrary, however. There are multiple factors to be considered.

The purposes of the research are always paramount. As discussed earlier, if they are to provide genuinely helpful guidelines, one must be scrupulously honest—at least with oneself—in assessing what those purposes are, in addition to recognizing what can be admitted in public (i.e., what they are supposed to be). The stated purpose of dissertation research, for example, is to shed light on some original and significant problem, but I know of few doctoral students who, when the end was almost in sight, did not mutter in exasperation, "Just tell me what I have to do to get the damn thing approved."

At the postdissertation stage, either in revising the dissertation for publication or when initiating original new research, younger colleagues find themselves again having to capitulate, this time to unseen and probably unknown editors or funding agencies that indirectly guard access to tenure in a publish-or-perish world. This is the real world of research, and those who survive it learn to live with its politics, just as we learn to live with the machinations of institutional administrations. (How little attention we give to trying to understand our own research contexts. Are such concerns too close to home? Do we believe that we alone have been able to elude the social forces we examine so pains-takingly in the lives of everyone else?)

There are also personal and career dimensions in decisions regarding how analytical or interpretive to be. Those impatient with the plodding nature of fieldwork may be content to pursue a lifetime of professional writing based on a modicum of early experience and a relentless effort at reinterpretation, riding in on new waves such as the feminist and postmodernist preoccupations of the 1980s. Devotees of fieldwork who find their métier in providing painstakingly careful descriptive accounts must steel themselves against likely criticism that their work is underanalyzed or undertheorized. Although professors often decry the lack of interpretation or the low level of analysis evident in dissertations submitted by their students, those students may have realized that they are better off to be faulted for interpretive shortcomings than to be accused of interpretive excess.

Most assuredly, it is preferable to overdo the descriptive detail, especially in early drafts, than to go overboard with analytical or interpretive efforts obviously too heavy for the descriptive account to bear. But there are always questions of balance: how best to achieve a project's potential—or one's own—in apportioning one's efforts among description, analysis, and interpretation. And how might, or should, those ratios shift during the course of a career? Is careful descriptive fieldwork the stuff of energetic young scholars, interpretation the sole prerogative of older ones? Can research vigor be demonstrated only through proposing new studies, or can it also be demonstrated by advancing new interpretations for fieldwork completed earlier?

By way of analogy, and apart from the idiosyncrasies of individual careers, let me offer a way to think about balance. I will cast the discussion in terms of the ratio of description to analysis to interpretation as revealed through the relative space devoted to each in final text.

I hasten to repeat that where one facet ends and another begins may seem like tangible points when examined like this, but they do not occur that way in our thought processes. As anthropologist Jules Henry suggested years ago (by way of interpretation), humans are not only capable of learning, and, by extension, of thinking, about more than one thing at a time, they are incapable of learning, and thus of thinking, about only one thing at a time. He termed this phenomenon "polyphasic learning" (Henry, 1955, pp. 196-199). In like manner, the three processes discussed here occur simultaneously in thought. I cannot imagine that a human observer ever does or ever could attend solely to descriptive concerns in one sitting, analytical ones in the next. Thoughts related to data analysis and interpretation may linger for years, just as details of events long forgotten may pop into one's head, or experiences in a new field setting may suddenly prompt a fresh perspective for rethinking the meaning of events in an earlier one. Barbara Frankel (1987) has noted in this regard:

> While it has been trendy for some years to take sides "for" or "against" interpretive social science, no one has yet paused in the game long enough to explain how one would go about doing *non*interpretive science of any sort. (p. 170)

## A Proposal: The D-A-I Formula

I draw my analogy for discussing balance in qualitative inquiry from a comparable problem faced by the manufacturers of plant food. For each separate product marketed, of any kind or quality, manufacturers of commercial fertilizer must decide upon a ratio among three primary macronutrients required for plant growth. Their decisions are reported to consumers in terms of an "N-P-K" formula familiar to household green-thumber and professional agriculturalist alike. The formula accounts for the three linked numbers that appear on even the tiniest bottle of plant food, as well as on every bag of commercial fertilizer, in combinations such as 8-8-4, 10-15-10, or 8-32-16.

How is this ratio determined, and what is the proper balance among the three ingredients? The more scientifically oriented grower recognizes (and the McGraw-Hill *Encyclopedia of Science and Technology*, sixth edition, 1987, confirms) that the first number in the N-P-K formula represents elemental nitrogen, the second number represents anhydride of phosphoric acid, the third number represents oxide of potassium (chemical symbol K from *kalium*) or "soluble potash." The figures state, in terms of percentage composition, how much of each key ingredient is present. If one of the three is absent, that, too, must be noted, which accounts for the "0" in a 0-10-10 product, advertised to stimulate blossoming without stimulating further growth, that I apply to hanging baskets of flowering plants after midsummer.

The lore of precisely the effect of each ingredient varies among gardeners and nursery workers, but, in general, nitrogen is said to encourage lush, fast growth; phosphoric acid, to stimulate flower and seed production; potash (potassium), to build overall strength, especially roots and branches. Secondary nutrients and trace elements, when present, are listed separately, also as a percentage of the total. For example, the "guaranteed analysis" on a 7-15-10 product designed especially for application on rhododendrons, camellias, and azaleas that grow well in the Pacific Northwest also includes sulfur 4.0%, calcium 2.0%, magnesium 1.0%, iron 0.6%, zinc 0.5%, manganese 0.225%, copper 0.1%, boron 0.09%, and even a guaranteed trace of molybdenum, 0.0009%.

In like fashion, I suggest that *description, analysis, and interpretation are the three primary ingredients of qualitative research.* And they too are variously combined to achieve particular purposes. No single combination can be regarded as best, nor is a researcher required to include all three, although in our work it is as hard to imagine a pure analysis or interpretation as it is a pure description. Like the commercial preparations, our studies also contain other "elements" as well. These may include the customarily appearing ones (comparable to secondary elements like sulfur, calcium, and magnesium) such as acknowledgments, literature review, significance of the study, implications for practice and/ or further research. They may also contain trace elements such as compassion, humor, insight, and personal revelation in which, as with plants, boundaries between deficiency and toxicity are sometimes difficult to define.

I do not suggest that this idea be taken too literally. Most assuredly, I do not propose that every qualitative study now be accompanied by its D-A-I rating. Nevertheless, pressing the analogy does offer perspective, which is what analogy should do. Establishing such a rating scale in itself would precipitate an interesting dialogue as researchers attempt to reach agreement as to what qualitative research's basic ingredients are. I have proposed three (of course!). Yet I doubt that proponents of evaluation—particularly in professional fields where evaluation tends to be a critical application for qualitative work—would be satisfied to see it subsumed under analysis, as I have suggested here. (A bit more on issues related to evaluation in the introduction to Part II.)

Another issue is whether all three ingredients ought to be present for a qualitative study to be judged acceptable. I note here that the 0-10-10 fertilizer I buy to encourage blossoming is neither less expensive nor an inferior product. It is designed for a particular purpose. A comparable hypothetically rated 0-10-10 qualitative study might suggest that the prerequisite descriptive component has already been provided elsewhere. Such a 0-10-10 ratio would also announce that the author's efforts have been divided equally between analysis and interpretation.

The critical function my hypothetical formula would serve is to make explicit the ratio of the three primary ingredients to each other and to the whole. The combined percentage of the three elements in the N-P-K formula never totals 100%. The formula indicates only the nutrient portion of the three compounds and does not account for other materials present. Similarly, the hypothetical D-A-I formula cannot total 100%, for it does not account for other "materials" that contribute to the total, the secondary and trace elements, plus all the "inert" material that finds its way into academic writing.

Plant requirements for the three macronutrients can be satisfied by the separate application of individual elements. Reportedly, however, "pure" forms rarely are applied, in part because they are not easily assimilated. In like vein, although technical monographs and appendixes sometimes contain description or analysis in the almost pure form of charts, tables, or interview protocols, we find them difficult to assimilate as well. For plant or reader growth alike, it seems, the elements are most effective when applied in purposive combination.

Given my bias in favor of the descriptive element in qualitative work, I would advise beginning researchers to organize and present their accounts in such a way as to ensure, were we actually to employ this hypothetical rating scale, that the first number (percentage composition devoted to description) be large, the ratio between the two remaining numbers (percentages devoted to analysis and interpretation, respectively) revealing of the researcher's purposes and capabilities. Thus a 40-15-5 combination might indicate a detailed description accompanied by a computer-generated analysis; 40-5-15, a well documented, highly interpretive study of the sort one might expect from a meanings and symbols anthropologist or a phenomenologically oriented or interpretive interactionist sociologist.

Playing with figures suggests that a combination that on first inspection may appear optimum, such as 20-20-20, might instead raise questions as to why the researcher couldn't make up his or her mind as to what needed to be emphasized, what purpose was to be met, and why description was actually slighted through such a seemingly "equal" distribution of effort. A hypothetical 50-3-2 study might describe a novice researcher's early draft, with an overreliance on descriptive detail and too much faith in the self-evidence of data. With encouragement and carefully focused assistance to further the analysis and/or interpretation, the final draft might shift in the direction of slightly less detail (sharper focus, less extraneous material), coupled with a more extensive analysis or more than just a hint of interpretative possibility.

The purpose of my analogy to the N-P-K formula is not to set us arguing over the optimum combination and minimum requirements for all qualitative inquiry but to recognize, for the intents and purposes of any particular study, how to direct one's efforts. Determining the desired results brings me back again to the teeter-totter analogy, analysis and interpretation variously weighted but the whole enterprise hinging on descriptive adequacy. Whenever qualitative research is the basis for subsequent claims-making, description must provide an adequate base for whatever follows from it.

Some readers may be disappointed (and others relieved!) that I have not assigned D-A-I ratings to my own illustrative chapters that follow. I have arranged the chapters in that sequence, the more descriptively oriented chapters appearing first, the more interpretively oriented ones last, but that takes the idea far enough. Assigning percent ratings could lend rigidity to an idea intended to help researchers in transforming qualitative data of their own, not entice them into rendering numerical comparisons in the work of others. Discussing and defending different assessments of these (or any other) accounts might foster lively dialogue, but the ultimate intent should be to probe the usefulness of the distinctions rather than to strive for rater reliability. Finally, there remains a question of whether researchers are in the best position to assay their own studies. What a researcher intends is not necessarily what the reader actually finds. Nor do my plants necessarily respond as they are supposed to, consistent with purposes I have clearly in mind for them.

# References

Note: References appear immediately following each chapter or separate new introduction. In that way, the references for chapters published earlier could be left intact. A final select bibliography identifies frequently cited materials and additional sources that may be especially helpful for qualitative researchers.

Agar, Michael H. (1980). *The professional stranger: An informal introduction to ethnography.* New York: Academic Press.

Ball, Michael S., & Smith, Gregory W. H. (1992). *Analyzing visual data.* Newbury Park, CA: Sage.

Bateson, Gregory, & Mead, Margaret. (1942). *Balinese character: A photographic analysis.* New York: Academy of Sciences.

Beals, Alan. (1973). *Culture in process* (2nd ed.). New York: Holt, Rinehart & Winston.

Becker, Howard S. (1986). *Writing for social scient..._s.* Chicago: University of Chicago Press.

Beer, C. G. (1973). A view of birds. In Anne D. Pick (Ed.), *Minnesota Symposia on Child Psychology* (Vol. 7, pp. 47-86). Minneapolis: University of Minnesota Press.

Brady, Ivan (Ed.). (1991). *An anthropological poetics.* Savage, MD: Rowan and Littlefield.

Carnap, Rudolph. (1953). Inductive logic and science. *Proceedings of the American Academy of Arts and Sciences, 80,* 189-197.

Clifford, James. (1986). On ethnographic authority. In James Clifford (Ed.), *The predicament of culture* (pp. 21-54). Cambridge, MA: Harvard University Press.

Delue, Norman. (1994). *A class act: A creative drama guide for teachers.* Carthage, IL: Good Apple.

Denzin, Norman K. (1989). *Interpretive interactionism.* Newbury Park, CA: Sage.

Dobbert, Marion L., & Kurth-Schai, R. (1992). Systematic ethnography: Toward an evolutionary science of education and culture. In Margaret D. LeCompte, Wendy L. Millroy, & Judith Preissle (Eds.), *Handbook of qualitative research in education* (pp. 93-159). San Diego, CA: Academic Press.

Dowdall, George W., & Golden, Janet. (1989). Photographs as data: An analysis of images from a mental health hospital. *Qualitative Sociology, 12*(2), 183-213.

Erickson, Frederick. (1977). Some approaches to inquiry in school-community ethnography. *Anthropology and Education Quarterly, 8*(2), 58-69. (Revised and reprinted in *Anthropology and Education Quarterly, 15*[1], 51-66, 1984)

Foster, George. (1969). *Applied anthropology.* Boston: Little, Brown.

Frankel, Barbara. (1987). Comment on *Anthropology as interpretive quest,* by Roger M. Keesing. *Current Anthropology, 28*(2), 169-170.

Geertz, Clifford. (1973). Thick description. In C. Geertz (Ed.), *The interpretation of cultures* (pp. 3-30). New York: Basic Books.

Geertz, Clifford. (1988). *Works and lives.* Stanford, CA: Stanford University Press.

Glesne, Corrine, & Peshkin, Alan. (1992). *Becoming qualitative researchers: An introduction.* White Plains, NY: Longman.

Hallowell, A. Irving. (1976). Ojibwa ontology, behavior, and world view. In *Contributions to anthropology: Selected Papers of A. Irving Hallowell.* Chicago: University of Chicago Press. (Original work published 1960)

Heider, Karl G. (1988). The Rashomon Effect: When ethnographers disagree. *American Anthropologist, 90*(1), 73-81. [See also Heider's reply to Freeman and Rhoades, *American Anthropologist, 91*[2], 450, extending the discussion.]

Henry, Jules. (1955). Culture, education, and communications theory. In George D. Spindler (Ed.), *Education and anthropology* (pp. 188-215). Stanford, CA: Stanford University Press.

Homans, George C. (1950). *The human group*. New York: Harcourt, Brace and World.

Josselson, Ruthellen. (1993). A narrative introduction. In Ruthellen Josselson & Amia Lieblich (Eds.), *The narrative study of lives* (Vol. 1, pp. ix-xv). Newbury Park, CA: Sage.

Kirk, Stuart A., & Kutchins, Herb. (1992). *The selling of DSM: The rhetoric of science in psychiatry*. New York: Aldine de Gruyter.

Lederman, Rena. (1990). Pretexts for ethnography: On reading fieldnotes. In Roger Sanjek (Ed.), *Fieldnotes: The makings of anthropology* (pp. 71-91). Ithaca, NY: Cornell University Press.

Lewis, Oscar. (1959). *Five families*. New York: Basic Books.

Lindblom, Charles. (1990). *Inquiry and change: The troubled attempt to understand and shape society*. New Haven, CT: Yale University Press.

Miles, Matthew B., & Huberman, A. Michael. (1984). *Qualitative data analysis*. Beverly Hills, CA: Sage.

Miles, Matthew B., & Huberman, A. Michael. (1994). *Qualitative data analysis: An expanded sourcebook* (2nd ed.). Newbury Park, CA: Sage.

Mitchell, J. Clyde. (1983). Case and situation analysis. *Sociological Review, 31*, 187-211.

Paget, Marianne A. (1990). Performing the text. *Journal of Contemporary Ethnography, 19*(1), 136-155.

Pitman, Mary Anne, & Maxwell, Joseph A. (1992). Applications of qualitative and ethnographic research. In Margaret D. LeCompte, Wendy L. Millroy, & Judith Preissle (Eds.), *The handbook of qualitative research in education* (pp. 729-770). San Diego, CA: Academic Press.

Platt, John R. (1964). Strong inference. *Science, 146*, 347-353.

Richardson, Laurel. (1992). The consequences of poetic representation: Writing the other, rewriting the self. In C. Ellis & M. G. Flaherty (Eds.), *Investigating subjectivity: Research on lived experience* (pp. 125-137). Newbury Park, CA: Sage.

Richardson, Miles. (1990). *Cry lonesome and other accounts of the anthropologist's project*. Albany: SUNY Press.

Roper, Donna C. (1989). The role of graphic analysis of quantitative data. *American Anthropologist, 91*, 450-452.

Sanjek, Roger (Ed.). (1990). *Fieldnotes: The makings of anthropology*. Ithaca, NY: Cornell University Press.

Sanjek, Roger. (1991). The ethnographic present. *Man: The Journal of the Royal Anthropological Institute, 26*(4), 609-628.

Sarana, Gopala. (1975). *The methodology of anthropological comparisons: An analysis of comparative methods in social and cultural anthropology* (Viking Fund Publications in Anthropology No. 53). Tucson: University of Arizona Press.

Schlechty, Phillip, & Noblit, George W. (1982). Some uses of sociological theory in educational evaluation. In Ronald G. Corwin (Guest Ed.), *Research in sociology of education and socialization* (Vol. 3, pp. 283-306). Greenwich, CT: JAI.

Seidel, John. (1992). Method and madness in the application of computer technology to qualitative data analysis. In Nigel G. Fielding & Raymond M. Lee (Eds.), *Using computers in qualitative research* (pp. 107-116). Newbury Park, CA: Sage.

Shaftel, Fannie R., & Shaftel, George. (1982). *Role playing in the curriculum* (2nd ed.). Englewood Cliffs, NJ: Prentice-Hall.

Spence, D. P. (1982). *Narrative truth and historical truth.* New York: Norton.

Spradley, James P. (1979). *The ethnographic interview.* New York: Holt, Rinehart & Winston.

Spradley, James P. (1980). *Participant observation.* New York: Holt, Rinehart & Winston.

Spradley, James P., & McCurdy, David W. (1988). *The cultural experience: Ethnography in complex society.* Prospect Heights, IL: Waveland. (Original work published 1972)

Tufte, Edward R. (1983). *The visual display of quantitative information.* Cheshire, CT: Graphics Press.

Van Maanen, John. (1988). *Tales of the field: On writing ethnography.* Chicago: University of Chicago Press.

Wagner, Jon (Ed.). (1979). *Images of information: Still photography in the social sciences.* Beverly Hills, CA: Sage.

Wainer, Howard. (1992). Understanding graphs and tables. *Educational Researcher, 21*(1), 12-23.

Werner, Oswald, & Schoepfle, G. Mark. (1987a). *Systematic fieldwork: Vol. 1. Foundations of ethnography and interviewing.* Newbury Park, CA: Sage.

Werner, Oswald, & Schoepfle, G. Mark. (1987b). *Systematic fieldwork: Vol. 2. Ethnographic analysis and data management.* Newbury Park, CA: Sage.

Wilson, Carter. (1966). *Crazy February.* Philadelphia, PA: Lippincott.

Wolcott, Harry F. (1973). *The man in the principal's office: An ethnography.* New York: Holt, Rinehart & Winston.

Wolcott, Harry F. (1990). *Writing up qualitative research.* Newbury Park, CA: Sage.

Wolcott, Harry F. (1992). Posturing in qualitative inquiry. In Margaret D. LeCompte, Wendy L. Millroy, & Judith Preissle (Eds.), *Handbook of qualitative research in education* (pp. 3-52). San Diego, CA: Academic Press.

Wolf, Margery. (1992). *A thrice-told tale: Feminism, postmodernism, and ethnographic responsibility.* Stanford, CA: Stanford University Press.

# Emphasis on Description

*Beginning at a point which is the Northwest corner of the Northeast ¼ of the Southwest ¼ of Section 19, Township 18 South, Range 3 West Willamette Meridian, Lane County Oregon, said point being 1313.15 feet North 2°08' East of the Southwest corner of the Northeast ¼ of the Southwest ¼ of said section, said point also being the Northwest corner of the above described property, thence South 89°49' East 660.0 feet along the North line of said property, thence South 2°08' West 660.0 feet to a point; thence North 89°49' West 660.0 feet to the West line of said property; thence North 2°08' East 660.0 feet to the place of beginning, in Lane County, Oregon.*

—Legal description for a tract of land purchased by the author

*In the strict sense . . . description is a specific, rather uncommon, form of writing.*

—James Clifford, "Notes on (Field)notes," p. 67

Description—in its everyday sense, not the *strict* sense illustrated above—is at the heart of qualitative inquiry. If we could just get the description right—which we never quite do—ours would be the noblest of scientific achievements. When we do not get much of it right, then what "follows" does not really follow at all, and we render our efforts at field-based research nothing more than self-validating and very time-consuming exercises. Firsthand description is not the only basis on which provocative analysis and interpretation may be founded, but whenever it is the basis we claim, it is worthy of our painstakingly thorough and adequately comprehensive efforts to try to get things right, in spite of the impossibility of ever fully succeeding.

Description entails both art and science and seems to suffer more in the absence of the former, for it is an intuitive as well as an objectifying act. It requires not only a sense of what to observe and report but exquisite judgment about what not to report, a keen sense of what is focus, what is periphery, and how to maintain a perspective and balance between them. As methodological issues, those aspects of fieldwork will not be addressed in this volume except as they are introduced in Chapter 5. That chapter, "Confessions of a 'Trained' Observer," is included in this part to suggest how description can be turned on itself to examine the very process through which we derive our accounts.

Although Chapter 5 is the only chapter dealing explicitly with observation, each of the illustrative chapters represents an implicit statement of what one observer observed and how he subsequently transformed those observations into a formal written account. No doubt there will still seem to be a little black box wherein mysterious procedures magically transform initial sensory observations into a final printed version. Through discussion and, especially, illustration, I have tried to unmask the process as much as I am able, for that is my overriding purpose here.

Because the emphasis in this part is on descriptive dimensions of qualitative work, the analytical and/or interpretive aspects of this first set of chapters will go largely unremarked. Yet even in that seeming omission, there is an important lesson: Emphasis itself is a critical aspect of descriptive work. One draws attention to some things while slighting others. Similarly, one can give precedence to description without diminishing the influence of analytical or interpretive concerns. A bit more on this question of relevance in descriptive work.

## There's Always a "Dark and Stormy Night" Somewhere

On the day I first drafted this introductory part (June 30, 1992), I also happened upon two "dark and stormy nights" in my reading. The first encounter occurred during perusal of the morning newspaper. I read how torrential rain the previous evening had forced the opening performance of a new production in Ashland's Oregon Shakespeare Festival, 175 miles to the south, to be cut short after less than half an hour. Although the performance was being presented in the new and semicovered Allen Pavilion officially opened only 2 nights earlier, the festival's general manager explained that "the sound of the downpour drumming on people's rain gear made it impossible to hear the actors, and the slippery stage made it dangerous to perform a wrestling scene."

Later in the day's reading, I encountered my second dark and stormy night, this one reported in a descriptively oriented doctoral dissertation. The chapter described a collective bargaining meeting between a local school district's management team and its classified (i.e., non-teaching) employees.

What struck me in reflecting on the two accounts was how central the stormy night was to the telling of the first story, when it became impossible to hear actors on stage, and how incidental to the telling of the second, in which the real storm center *for purposes of the research* was at the negotiation table, not outdoors. My impression is that there are many phrases of the "dark and stormy night" sort in reported research these days, especially in doctoral dissertations, a consequence of a certain literary license felt by contemporary researchers. Purportedly intended to give readers a "feel" for context, they also give their author-researchers an opportunity, however circumscribed, to dabble with style.

But the news isn't all good. However harmlessly interjected into qualitative accounts, dark and stormy nights signal a practice that at its extreme approaches the "haphazard descriptiveness" of which even widely acclaimed ethnographers such as Bronislaw Malinowski and Margaret Mead have been accused: describing things simply because they are there, without regard to their immediacy for the account at hand. I have the impression that writing one or two paragraphs of enchanting introductory description has now become as much a part of the ritual of writing qualitative dissertations as has the inevitable (and usually tedious) chapter reviewing the literature. Once completed, neither of these two exercises is likely to be referred to again!

Whatever is to be included in a descriptive account needs to be assessed for its relevance and contribution to the story being developed.

Everything comes back to the purposes for initiating the research and preparing the account in the first place. Along with the current welcome embrace for qualitative approaches, we must recognize that considerable misunderstanding has been generated about its strictures. A colleague in a Third World country recently asked, for example, how one goes about describing a building "qualitatively." I hope I was helpful in responding that there is no set way to go about it. The prior question for a qualitative researcher might be not how but whether to describe a building in which something important is happening. Why not take us directly to that part of the building where something of significance to the account has occurred?

Observers in schools, for example, continue dutifully to record what is posted on the walls or written on chalkboards as well as to note or map the location of desks, tables, chairs, windows, exits—and then typically make no further reference to anything in the physical setting. I was dismayed to realize that the researcher studying collective bargaining duly reported the dark and stormy weather outside but did not detail seating arrangements at the negotiation table that might have revealed a great deal. I cannot recount the number of times I have looked at classroom observation protocols that are rich with detail up to the moment the formal lesson begins, at which time the account stops abruptly, as though the official lesson—what is supposed to be happening—can simply be assumed or is of no consequence for understanding schools. (See an insightful discussion in this regard in Erickson, 1982.)

As discussed in Chapter 2, if a descriptive account is to be rendered as some kind of story, the researcher needs to think like a storyteller. What is to be presented, in what sequence? More than just any story, some qualitative researchers suggest that our accounts ought to read like mystery stories, with a problem to be solved, clues dropped along the way, and a mounting file of evidence to be weighed and considered, including facts that do not fit, evidence that may contradict other evidence. The reader ought to have sufficient information to be able to arrive independently at the same conclusions as the researcher or to arrive at alternative and equally plausible explanations. Literary panache can be welcome relief, but it cannot substitute for critical detail or divert either author or reader from the focal story. If there must be diversions, we have conventions for marking them so readers can make their own way among options (e.g., parenthetical sentences or paragraphs, footnotes, materials presented separately or in accompanying appendixes).

So, now, a set of three chapters selected to illustrate an emphasis on description, to be followed by parts devoted, respectively, to analysis and to interpretation. Although the organization of the book follows the description-analysis-interpretation sequence discussed in Chapter 2, I note again that I have not assigned D-A-I "ratings" for the illustrative chapters. Nor do I single out any chapter as an example of one of the approaches outlined for each category. The approaches are highly interactive; I may have gone too far in suggesting that the three chapters in this part are more descriptive, the two selected for the next part essentially analytical. The operative term is *emphasis*, not exclusiveness. What is more, not only the various approaches, but the very idea of distinguishing among description, analysis, and interpretation, or of thinking about the relationship among them in terms of a ratio, occurred after the fact. The idea provided a framework for organizing and presenting these chapters, and I propose it as a way both to examine studies conducted by others and to guide the transformation of data in studies not yet written. But things were not so orderly the first time around, and even now I propose the idea as guide, not a magic formula.

## References

Clifford, James. (1990). Notes on (field)notes. In Roger Sanjek (Ed.), *Fieldnotes: The makings of anthropology* (pp. 47-70). Ithaca, NY: Cornell University Press.

Erickson, Frederick. (1982). Taught cognitive learning in its immediate environments: A neglected topic in the anthropology of education. *Anthropology and Education Quarterly, 13*(2), 149-180.

# 3

# Adequate Schools and Inadequate Education

## The Life History of a Sneaky Kid

---
### PREFACE
---

The first of the three illustrative chapters in this part is titled "Adequate Schools and Inadequate Education: The Life History of a Sneaky Kid." From here on, the account will be referred to by its obvious short title, "Sneaky Kid."

This chapter was originally prepared as a commissioned paper for the School Finance Project. It was submitted as a report to the U.S. Department of Education in 1982 with the title "Adequate Schools and Inadequate Education: An Anthropological Perspective." Subsequently it was rewritten for publication in the *Anthropology and Education Quarterly* in 1983.

The federal project officer who prompted the original writing was not particularly interested either in promoting anthropological life history or in a case study of a high school dropout. Her task at the time was to commission a set of papers presenting the views of social scientists from different disciplines on the topic "educational adequacy." By the time she contacted me, she already had lined up numerous contributors who promised to address that issue from traditional and predictable perspectives. She was searching for other ways to view the problem of defining educational adequacy to suggest what, if any, role or action the federal government might take if funding were to become available. It was all rather hypothetical, but Congress had allocated money for a set of position papers on the topic, and that part of the mandate had to be met, even if nothing more was to come of it.

My proposal to present a case study of one youth, rather than to provide another equalization formula for the distribution of school funds, was not only acceptable but, if for the sake of variety alone, greeted with enthusiasm. I had only to agree to address the formally assigned topic and to meet project limits regarding due dates (soon) and length (short). There was no objection to conducting new research, although neither project expectations nor the modest honorarium warranted more than a position paper. The interviews were something I had been contemplating, however, and the project's unusual focus (educational "adequacy"?) provided the direction and impetus I needed to get started.

Some of this is spelled out in two additional chapters dealing with Brad, the self-styled "sneaky kid" of this story, that appear in subsequent parts. Together, the three chapters constitute what I now regard as the Brad Trilogy.

When colleagues or students ask which of my articles might prove helpful as models for writing of their own, there are two that I mention. Sneaky Kid is one of them. I commend it first for its length, to show that a life history can be presented even within customary length limits for a journal article. David Mandelbaum's 1973 article on the life of Gandhi, which includes both an extended discussion of the anthropological life history method as well as the Gandhi material as illustrative content, serves as both an excellent model and a helpful resource. I am pleased to see life history gaining a more prominent role in research, particularly in the fields of education and mental health. I hope life history studies in these fields will extend beyond professional domains to include individuals like Brad who are either peripheral or absent altogether from formal institutional settings.

Brad's life history is not complete here. The aspects of his life emphasized in this telling were selected to achieve the dual objectives of providing a broad look at his present circumstances and then, in sharper relief, to make a telling contrast between schooling and education. That contrast, it must be remembered, was imposed upon the data as a way to organize and present the case. Brad himself would never have made as much of his schooling as I do here, a point he neatly summarized with his pithy observation, "I've always liked learning. I just didn't like school."

Brad's words are excerpted from interviews tape-recorded over a period of several relatively brief interview sessions. I transcribed his statements in sentences or brief paragraphs, writing them by hand directly onto 5" × 8" note papers for easy labeling and sorting into broad categories suggested by the account itself, such as "early schooling," "family," "growing up." Brad talked easily but not a lot; I usually had to prompt to keep him going. Initially I was concerned whether his brief statements were sufficient to allow me to convey his story in his words, but that concern melted as I came to appreciate his terse and to-the-point prose.

The idea persists that categories should (will?) emerge from the data. My experience is that they cannot do it on their own. As author-researcher, you must go to their rescue or they will perish. In that process, you have no choice other than to transcend any commitment you may have felt toward pure description. Although you may try to stay "close to the data," in even the most rudimentary sorting some structure must be imposed. Doing so creates the task and tension confronting the qualitative researcher, a constant reminder that description, analysis, and interpretation are a matter of emphasis. They are neither independent of one another nor mutually exclusive. As already noted, the chapters in this part were chosen because they emphasize description, not because they are only descriptive. Even this chapter, which I consider one of the most descriptive accounts I have written, concludes with four pages explicitly subtitled "An Interpretation." That label may be presumptuous for the modest reflections I offer, but it is a good reminder of Frederick Erickson's point noted in Chapter 2 that description is never "mere" description.

That our categories reveal implicit theory does not necessarily say as much about our capability as theory-builders as it does about theory-building as an everyday activity in which all humans engage constantly. Nevertheless, in this account, I was trying to stay close to the data, particularly to words recorded on tape. My tentative categories bore descriptive titles, some of which gave way to phrases in Brad's words (e.g., "I'm Not Going to Get Caught," "Hiding Out From Life," "I've Been More Places and Done More Things"), some drawn from other texts (e.g., *A New Life, The Bicycle Thief, Home Is the Hunter*).

Sequencing and editing were my two other tasks in managing the protocol data, along with the obvious responsibility of providing the framework into which the whole story fit. There are accounts in which informants do, or at least appear to, present life stories entirely in their own words—the works of Oscar Lewis and Leo Simmons are cited as examples in the chapter—but the likelihood of finding such giftedness in informants, together with concern about the unseen hand of the researcher as editor, raise unresolved methodological issues. I think researchers are well advised to play a visible role, even when their goal is to have an informant's own story related *essentially* in the informant's own words.

Given the educational focus of my assignment—knowing where the account had to end up—I decided to arrange the story sequence so that the reader meets Brad on his own ground, first through a recounting of major events and everyday aspects of his life, next through important dimensions of his worldview. Only then do I present a discussion of Brad vis-à-vis my major thesis and paradoxical title, "Adequate Schools and Inadequate Education." By the time readers arrive at the point where I offer *my* thoughts as to what might be done, I want to be sure they have a sufficient background to form their own assessment of Brad and his circumstances.

Brad read only one draft of the original report. Once was enough for a project he saw as bound more closely with my future than his own. I was reminded again that informants and researchers can have quite different views as to what constitute sensitive issues and whether or not anonymity is one of them. I did not give Brad veto power, but I honored my promise not to include anything he had declared "off the record" during our interviews, and I was ready to hear any objection he might raise. He requested that I delete only one phrase he had used that, I believe, he felt might make him appear "out of it" in the eyes of other youth. Even as each of us read, we had entirely different audiences in mind, my peers looking over my shoulder, Brad's peers looking over his. In his words, each of us had his own way to "think about things."

It is always a relief to get through the stage when one shares what has been written with those written about, but my reaction to Brad's reaction to the draft is probably a common one. I was relieved that he could "live with it" but doubted that he felt I had captured the essence of the real Brad. Nor did the reading prompt any new revelation or insight, other than confirm that, as far as Brad himself was concerned, his actions seemed justified.

There were two Brads now, a real-life one and a story one I was creating on paper. As a check on the fidelity of the latter, I listened to Brad's current accounts of his exploits and problems, always keeping the developing draft in mind. I also listened repeatedly to the full set of taped interviews. I needed to discern how well Brad's story—as portrayed by me—was both accurate and adequate as a depiction of Brad himself. Having such a "reality check" is testimony to the value both to begin one's writing while still having access to field site or informants and to audio- or videotaped materials that allow one to return again and again to an original source rather than having to depend on what has been filtered through "headnotes" and fieldnotes. In whatever form one's field data exist, they should always be reviewed again after an account has been drafted.

In reading the initial drafts of interpretive statements written by other researchers, especially the early drafts of studies prepared by students with no prior experience at fieldwork, I sometimes wonder whether they have attended carefully to the descriptive portions of their own accounts, to what their informants were trying to tell them. Descriptive data need to be studied, not merely skimmed. Even now, more than a dozen years after the interviewing, I discover ideas that might have been explored. For example, eventually I realized that Brad marked life by "experiences," while I busied myself supplying neat but largely irrelevant categories like "early years," "elementary school years," "middle and high school years," and "dropping out of school." Dropping out of school was not an "experience" in Brad's terms; it was more like a habit, one he began to develop as early as the fifth grade. On the other hand, being in reform school was an experience. In building a case on his behalf, I may have gone a bit overboard in marking Brad's sense of moderation. You may judge for yourself after reading further in the trilogy.

I assembled my collection of telling quotes and supplementary journal entries into my tentative categories. I was not familiar with word processing when I started this project (1981). Especially on a project of larger scope, I might be inclined today to manage the protocol data on one of the software programs developed for qualitative work that allows a researcher to identify, code, and manipulate segments of data (see, for example, Fielding & Lee, 1992). However, in spite of the miracle of word processing, especially for revising and editing, I must admit that even now I would feel a strong urge to do this processing manually, on tangible cards or slips of paper that could be spread out before me, sorted and resorted, written upon, filed neatly in boxes. I need to see in concrete form what I am doing. That is what those sheets of paper help me to do. For much the same reasons, I continue to write first drafts in longhand, and I usually do heavy editing on printed copy, where all the text is displayed at one time, rather than on the screen. Those are personal preferences and styles. I continue to follow them because they continue to work.

A comment here about editing the words spoken by an interviewee. The underlying issue of editing original text, like every other decision in doing and writing up research, goes back to the purposes of the study. Nevertheless, my working guideline is to strive for readability. I edit spoken words as necessary to help readers read and to put informants in the best light possible. I have no qualms about editing out extraneous material that may technically be part of the record but is of no consequence to the purpose at hand. I am reluctant even to report phrases spoken in nonstandard English without first "correct-ing" them, unless I feel that the usage communicates something of an individual's idiolect (e.g., Brad's "Maybe school could of did better") or a regional dialect (e.g., "So I booked" for "So I left/departed/split"). In the case of Brad's protocols, it is of little importance for my purposes here to include his "uh huhs" or "you knows," or my questions ("Do you want to say any more about that?") or procedural points ("Shall I turn the tape recorder off for a while?"). Note one exception in which my question ("Can I trust you?") is included in the narrative because it provides the only context for his truncated but, I think, revealing reply: "Yeah. Pretty much. I dunno . . ."

In some contexts, it may be critical to report one's questioning strategies or reactions, but here they would only have been in the way, so I edited them out. A linguistic analysis of informant pauses and interjections can be revealing, but that was not a concern in this study. (For some second thoughts about editing interview data, however, see Blauner, 1987, or DeVault, 1990.) My transcription was adequate for my purposes; a linguist would have to go to the original tapes before proceeding with a technical analysis. Each level of detail implicates others requiring still more detail; there is no logical stopping place without a clear idea of purposes.

I have read studies in which interviewers have tried so hard to be faithful to "science" that the set of interviews forming the basis for the accounts are reproduced intact in the body of the study, leaving readers with comments now recorded for posterity such as the interviewer's own, "Well, suppose we turn now to a different topic." I do not quarrel with the idea of making full transcripts available *somewhere*, but I do not feel that the place for them is in the body of the text, unless there is a compelling reason to capture *and report* every phrase spoken. Overburdening readers with data seems an academic cop-out on the part of a researcher holding too tightly to the belief that data speak for themselves. If the data were telling the researcher something, the message certainly was not getting through to me. The help I needed was not forthcoming; instead, researchers apparently unable to decide what was important, or who mistakenly thought that it was all important, passed the entire burden of sifting through data on to me.

## References

Blauner, Bob. (1987). Problems of editing "first-person" sociology. *Qualitative Sociology, 10*, 46-64.

DeVault, Marjorie L. (1990). Talking and listening from women's standpoint: Feminist strategies for interviewing and analysis. *Social Problems, 37*(1), 96-116.

Fielding, N. G., & Lee, R. M. (Eds.). (1992). *Using computers in qualitative research.* Newbury Park, CA: Sage.

Mandelbaum, David. (1973). The study of life history: Gandhi. *Current Anthropology, 14*, 177-206.

Wolcott, Harry F. (1982). Adequate schools and inadequate education: An anthropological perspective. Commissioned paper prepared for the School Finance Project, U.S. Department of Education.

Wolcott, Harry F. (1983). Adequate schools and inadequate eduaction: The life history of a sneaky kid. *Anthropology and Education Quarterly, 14*, 3-32.

# ADEQUATE SCHOOLS
# AND INADEQUATE EDUCATION

## The Life History of a Sneaky Kid

"I guess if you're going to be here, I need to know something about you, where you're from, and what kind of trouble you are in," I said to the lad, trying not to reveal my uncertainty, surprise, and dismay at his uninvited presence until I could learn more about his circumstances. It wasn't much of an introduction, but it marked the beginning of a dialogue that lasted almost two years from that moment. Brad (a pseudonym, although as he noted, using his real name wouldn't really matter, since "no one knows who I am anyway") tersely stated his full name, the fact that his parents had "split up" and his mother was remarried and living in southern California, the local address of his

The chapter is reprinted by permission from the *Anthropology and Education Quarterly*, Volume 14, Number 1, pages 3-32. Copyright by the Council on Anthropology and Education, 1983. The version that appears here was revised slightly to accompany my chapter "Ethnographic Research in Education," which appeared in 1988 in a publication of the American Educational Research Association, *Complementary Methods for Research in Education*, edited by Richard M. Jaeger.

father, and that he was not at present in any trouble because he wasn't "that stupid." He also volunteered that he had spent time in the state's correctional facility for boys, but quickly added, "It wasn't really my fault."

It was not our meeting itself that was a surprise; it was that Brad already had been living at this remote corner of my steep and heavily wooded 20-acre home-site on the outskirts of town for almost five weeks. In that time he had managed to build a 10-foot × 12-foot cabin made of newly cut sapling logs and roofed with plywood paneling. A couple of weeks earlier, I had stumbled across his original campsite, but I assumed it had been made by some youngster enjoying a bivouac en route to hiking a nearby ridge that afforded a fine view, a popular day hike for townspeople and occasional overnight adventure for kids. I also found a saw, but thought it had been left by a recent surveying party. Brad had been watching me at the time and later admitted cursing to himself for being careless in leaving tools about.

I did not realize I now had both a new cabin and an unofficial tenant until a neighbor reported that his 8-year-old son claimed not only to have seen but to have spoken to a "hobo" while wandering through my woods. The "hobo" turned out to be the then 19-year-old youth, of medium build and slightly stoop-shouldered, standing opposite me. And it is his story that I am about to relate.

As intrigued and involved as I eventually became with Brad and his story, my purpose in providing this account transcends the individual case even though I will tie my remarks closely to it. That purpose is related to my professional interest in anthropology and education and, particularly, in cultural acquisition, drawing upon anthropology both for approach and for perspective on looking at educational issues (see Wolcott, 1982). There is no shortage of case study materials about alienated youth.[1] Attention here will be drawn particularly to educationally relevant aspects of this case. Brad's story underscores and dramatizes the critical distinction that anthropologists make between *schooling* and *education* and raises questions about our efforts at education for young people beyond the purview of the schools.[2] Adequate schools may be necessary but they are not sufficient to ensure an adequate education.

At first impression, Brad's strategy for coping with his life seemed as bold, resourceful, and even romantic, as was his building of a cabin. Faced with jobs he did not want to do (he abhors dishwashing, yet that seemed to be the only work he felt he could get, because "those jobs are always open") and expenses he could not afford (renting an apartment, buying and operating a motorcycle), he had chosen to change his lifestyle radically by reducing his cash needs to a minimum. What he could not afford, he would try to do without.

Never before had he done the things he now set out to do. He had never lived in the woods (though he had gone camping), never built a log house (though he had occasionally helped his father in light construction), never thought about a personal inventory of essential items. He had identified the cabin site, hidden from view but with a commanding view of its own, during one of his endless and solitary explorations of streets, roads, and paths in and around the city. The location was near a section of the city where he once lived as a child. He went deep into a densely wooded area, entering from the east and failing to realize how close he had come to my house on the country road around the west side of the ridge. But he knew he had to be near town. He needed to be where, one way or another, he could pick up the things essential to his anticipated lifestyle. He did not need much, but what he did need—hammer, saw, nails, sleeping bag, stove, cooking utensils, flashlight and lantern, pants and shoes, containers for carrying and storing water—he scrounged, stole, or, occasionally and reluctantly, purchased.

Brad displayed few qualities that would earn him the title of outdoorsman. His tools and equipment often were mislaid or neglected. He proved terrible at tying knots. He cut trees unnecessarily and turned his own trails into slippery troughs of mud. In spite of occasional references to himself as "Jungle Boy," he was basically a city boy making whatever accommodation was necessary to survive inexpensively. His fuel and food came from town; he was totally dependent on the city even though he could not afford to live in it. If his menu gradually became more like that of the woodsman (potatoes, onions, pancakes, melted cheese sandwiches, eggs, soup, canned tuna, powdered milk, and powdered orange juice) it was because he realized that these items could almost stretch $70-worth of food stamps into a month's ration of food. He washed and dried his clothes in coin-operated machines at night at a nearby apartment house complex. His battery-operated radio played almost constantly, and he became even more cabin-bound watching a small battery-operated TV set purchased for him by his mother during a brief visit, their first in over two years.

It was not Brad's wont to take leisurely walks in the woods, spend time enjoying sunsets, or listen to bird calls. He brought what he could find (and carry up steep, narrow trails) of his urban environment with him. Though not very sociable, he calculatingly mismanaged his purchases so that on many days he "had to" bicycle two miles each way to his favorite store to get a pack of cigarettes and perhaps buy a can of beer or "smoke a joint" in a nearby park. Town was the only direction he traveled. Yet almost without exception he returned to his cabin each evening, usually before darkness made the trip hazardous on an unlit bike. The security of having literally created a place all his own lent a critical element of stability to his life. He was proud of what he had built, even though he acknowledged that, were he starting over, his cabin would be "bigger and better in every way." His dreams for improving it never ceased.

For a while he envisioned building a tree house high in a giant Douglas fir nearby. A fearless tree-climber, he attached a high pulley and cable swing so he could trim branches and hoist construction materials. The tree house idea occupied his thoughts for weeks. During that time, few improvements were made on the cabin. The idea of being virtually inaccessible high in a tree proved more appealing than practical, however, and eventually he gave it up, brought his tools back to the cabin, and began work in earnest on improvements that included cutting out a section of wall and adding a lean-to bunk bed. The cable was removed from the tree house site and found its permanent place as a hillside swing with a breathtaking arc amongst the treetops on the slope below. Swinging was a literal as well as figurative high for him; pausing to rest between turns at the strenuous exercise, he volunteered the only positive comment I ever heard him make regarding the future: "I'll swing like this when I'm 60."

In brief glimpses, others people's lives often appear idyllic. Brad's "Robinson Crusoe" life had many appealing qualities. He seemed to have freed himself of the trappings of the Establishment, what he saw as a curiously roundabout and unappealing system that required him to take a job he hated in order to earn enough to provide transportation to and from work and money for the rent of some cheap place where he would rather not live. He had seen his father work hard, dream even harder, and yet, in Brad's opinion, "get nowhere." Brad was trying to figure out for himself what he wanted in life and whether it was really worth the effort.

I found it hard to argue on behalf of what some menial job would get him. I heard quite well his argument that, lacking in skill or experience, he would probably have to do work at once physically harder and lower paying than most jobs today. He could be an indefatigable worker, but I think he felt some anxiety about being able to "keep up" on jobs requiring hours of continuous hard physical labor. An earlier and short-lived job as tree planter had convinced him that hard work does not ensure success.

A glimpse into Brad's daily life does not dispel the romantic view of his existence. He arose when he wanted and retired when he wanted (although, with the cold, dark, and perennial dampness of the Northwest's winters, and with little to do, he spent so much time "in the sack" that getting to sleep became a constantly compounding problem). He could eat when he chose and cook or not as mood—and a rather sparse cupboard—dictated. Food and cigarette needs dominated his schedule of trips to town. A trip to the store, or to see about food stamps (in effect he had no address, so he went to the Welfare Office in person) or to secure other supplies (a tire for the bicycle, fuel for lanterns or the stove, hardware items for the cabin) occurred once or twice a week. Dirty clothes were washed regularly. And if there was no needed trip, he was free to decide—quite consciously, though rather impulsively, I think—how to spend the day.

Although the cabin was sometimes untidy and utensils were seldom washed before they were to be used again, Brad kept his person and his clothes clean. He brushed his teeth regularly. He never went to town without "showering" or at least washing his face and hair. In warm weather he underscored the nymph-like nature of his existence by remaining almost, or totally, unclad in the seclusion of his immediate cabin area, though he was excruciatingly self-conscious in public settings. His preference for privacy was highlighted by recollections of his distress at regimented public showering "on procedures" at reform school, and such experiences had made options like joining the armed services something he insisted he would only do if he had to. Brad was, at first glance, a free spirit. He regarded himself that way, too: "I do what I want."

## The Cultural Context of a Free Spirit

There is no absolute set of things to be wanted or ways to fill one's days and dreams, just as there is no absolute set of things to be learned (see Wallace, 1961b, p. 38). What people learn or want or do or dream about is embedded in particular macro- and micro-cultural systems.

Brad was aware of many things in his "culture" that he felt he could do without, including—up to a point—seeking much involvement within his society, seeming to heed its expectations, or depending on its resources. But he was accustomed to technological innovations and had been reared in a society where everyone appeared, at least to him, to have everything they needed. Although he saw himself as living figuratively, as well as literally, at the edge of society, he was still society's child. He was free to insist, "I do what I want," but he was not free to do what he wanted. What he had learned to want was a function of his culture, and he drew narrowly and rather predictably from the cultural repertoire of the very society from which he believed he was extricating himself.

Brad needed to cook. An open fire is slow and quite impractical on a rainy day. One needs a camp stove in order to cook inside a cabin. And fuel. And then a better stove. Cold water is all right for washing hands but it can be a bit too bracing for washing one's hair or torso, especially when outside with the wind blowing. One needs a bigger pan to heat water for bathing. Soap and shampoo. A towel. A new razor. A mirror. A bigger mirror. Foam rubber mattress. A chair. A chaise lounge.

One needs something to look at and listen to. Magazines are a brief diversion, but rock music is essential. One needs a radio. Flashlight batteries are expensive for continual radio listening; a radio operated by an automobile battery would be a better source—and could power a better radio. An automobile battery needs to be recharged. Carrying a battery to town is awkward, and constantly having to pay for battery charges is expensive. As well as access to a power supply (in my carport), one needs a battery charger. No, this one is rated too low; a bigger one is needed. Luckily not a harsh winter, but a wet one. The dirt floor gets muddy; a wood floor would be better. The roof leaks; a heavier grade of plywood and stronger tarpaulin to place over it are required. The sleeping bag rips where it got wet; a replacement is necessary. Shoes wear out from constant use on the trails; clothes get worn or torn. Flashlights and batteries wear out. Cigarettes (or tobacco), matches, eggs, bread, Tang, Crisco, pancake flour, syrup—supplies get low. An occasional steak helps vary the austere diet.

One needs transportation. A bicycle is essential, as are spare parts to keep it in repair. Now a minor accident: the bicycle is wrecked. No money to buy a new one. Brad "hypes" himself up and sets out to find a replacement. Buy one? "When they're so easy to get? No way!"

## The Life History of a Sneaky Kid

Here is the place to let Brad relate something of his life and how he had tried to make sense of, and come to grips with, the world about him.

Ideally, in relating a life history through an ethnographic autobiography, informants tell their stories almost entirely in their own words (e.g., classics such as Leo Simmons's *Sun Chief*, 1942, or Oscar Lewis's *Children of Sanchez*, 1961; see also Brandes, 1982). There should be a high ratio of information to explanation in a life story; sometimes there is no explanation or explicit interpretation at all. Time, space, and purpose require me to proceed more directly. I have worked with a heavy hand in reorganizing material and selecting the most cogent excerpts from months of informal conversations and many hours of formal interviews that Brad volunteered for this purpose.[3]

I have given particular attention to aspects of Brad's story that illustrate the two major points of this paper: that education consists of more than schooling, and that we give little systematic attention to the course of a young person's education once out of school. For these purposes I have dwelt more on social concerns than on personal or psychological ones. Brad had some personal "hang-ups," focused largely on his acceptance of his body and a preoccupation with sexual fantasy as yet unfulfilled, *Portnoy's Complaint* personified. In time (or, more candidly, not quite in time, before he sank unexpectedly into a mood of utter despair and abruptly announced he was "hitting the road" because he saw no future where he was), I realized he had some deep-seated emotional hang-ups as well, but my concern in this paper is with Brad as a social rather than a psychological being, and thus with personality-in-culture rather than with personality per se.

### "In the Chute"

A speaker at the American Correctional Association meetings in 1981 was reported in the national press to have used the phrase "in the chute" to describe individuals whose lives seem headed for prison even though they have not yet arrived there: "People who are in the chute, so to speak, and heading toward us, are beginning that movement down in infancy."

Brad was not yet "in the chute." It is not inevitable that he end up in trouble, but he could. Excerpts from his life story suggest how things point that way. Here he recalls a chain of events that started at age 10 with what proved a traumatic event in his life, his parents' divorce:

*On the loose.* "After my parents got divorced, I was living with my dad. I had quite a bit of freedom. My dad wasn't around. If I didn't want to go to school, I just didn't go. Everybody who knows me now says,

'That guy had the world's record for ditching school.' My dad was at work all day and there was no one to watch me. I was pretty wild. My dad took me to a counseling center at the university; they told me I was 'winning the battles but losing the war.'

"After my dad got remarried, I had no freedom any more. I had a new mother to watch me. I got mad at her a couple of times, so I moved in with her parents. I went to seventh grade for a while and got pretty good grades. Then I went to southern California to visit my mother. When my dad said he'd have to 'make some arrangements' before I could return, I just stayed there. But I got into a hassle with my stepdad, and I ditched some classes, and suddenly I was on a bus back to Oregon.

"My father had separated again and I moved into some little apartment with him. He wanted me to go to another school, but I said, 'Forget it, man, I'm not going to another school. I'm tired of school.' So I'd just lay around the house, stay up all night, sleep all day.

"Finally I told my mom I'd be a 'good boy,' and she let me move back to southern California. But I got in another hassle with my stepdad. I ran out of the house and stayed with some friends for a few months, but then the police got in a hassle with me and they said I'd have to go back with my dad or they were going to send me to a correctional institution. The next thing you know, I was back on the bus."

*Getting busted.* "By then my dad had remarried again. I wasn't ready for another family. I stayed about two days, then I left. I figured any place was better than living there. But they got pissed at me because I kept coming back [breaking into the house] for food, so they called the cops on me. Running away from them, I broke my foot and had to go to the hospital. Then I got sent to reform school. They had a charge against me [contraband], but I think the real reason was that I didn't have any place to go. I was in reform school for eight months."

*Second-rate jobs and second-rate apartments.* "I finally played their 'baby game' and got out of reform school. They sent me to a halfway house in Portland. I got a job, made some money, got a motorcycle, moved to another place, then that job ended. I got another job with a church-going plumber for a while, but I got fired. Then I came back and worked for my dad, but there wasn't nothing to do, and I got in some family hassles, so I got a few jobs and lived in some cheap apartments.

"For a while I was a bum down at the Mission. I'd get something to eat, then I'd go sleep under a truck. My sleeping bag was all I had. I knew winter was coming and I'd have to do something. I saw a guy I knew and he said 'Hey, I've got a place if you'd like to crash out until you get something going.' So I went there and got a job for about four months washing dishes. Then my mom came up from California to visit and found me an apartment. God, how I hated that place, with people right on the other side of those thin walls who know you're all alone and never have any visitors or anything. I quit washing dishes; they cut me down to such low hours I wasn't making any money anyway. So I just hibernated for the winter."

*A new life.* "When the rent ran out, I picked up my sleeping bag and the stuff I had and headed for the hills at the edge of town. I found a place that looked like no one had been there for a while, and I set up a tarp for shelter. I decided to take my time and build a place for myself, because I wasn't doing anything anyway. I just kept working on it. I've been here a year and a half now. I've done some odd jobs, but mostly I live on food stamps.

"I used to think about doing something like this when I lived in Portland. I read a book called *How to Live in the Woods on Pennies a Day*. I even tried staying out in the woods a couple of times, but I didn't know exactly what to do. I wasn't thinking about a cabin then. All I knew was that I needed some place to get out of the wind and some place to keep dry. I saw this piece of level ground and knew that if I had tools and nails I could probably put up some walls. As I went along I just figured out what I would need.

"I put up four posts and started dragging logs around till the walls were built. There were plenty of trees around. It took about a week to get the walls. I slept in a wet sleeping bag for a couple of nights, cause I didn't have a roof. The first roof was some pieces of paneling that I carried up from some kids' tree fort. I had a dirt floor but I knew I'd have to have a wood floor someday. I knew about plaster because I had worked with it before, so I smeared some on the walls. All that I really needed at first was nails. I got the other stuff I needed from new houses being built nearby."

*"Picking up" what was needed.* "I got around town quite a bit. Any place where there might be something, I'd take a look. If I found anything that I needed, I'd pick it up and take it home. I just started a collection: sleeping bag, radio, plywood for the roof, windows, a stove, lanterns, tools, clothes, water containers, boots. If you took away everything that's stolen, there wouldn't be much left here. Like the saw. I just walked

into a store, grabbed it, put a piece of cloth around it to hide it, and walked out.

"Before I got food stamps, I'd go to the store with my backpack, fill it with steaks and expensive canned food, and just walk out. If anybody saw me, I'd wave at them and keep walking. I didn't have much to lose, I figured. The closest I ever got to being stopped, I had two six-packs of beer and some cooked chicken. The guy in the store had seen me there before. I just waved, but he said, 'Stop right there.' I ran out and grabbed my bike, but he was right behind me. I knew the only thing I could do was drop the merchandise and get out of there with my skin and my bike, and that's what I did. He didn't chase me; he just picked up the bag and shook his head at me."

*The bicycle thief.* "We lived in the country for about three years while I was growing up. Moving back into town was kinda different. I went pretty wild after moving to town. Me and another kid did a lot of crazy stuff, getting into places and taking things. I'd stay out all night just looking in people's garages. I'd get lots of stuff. My room had all kinds of junk in it. That's when I was living with my dad, and he didn't really notice. He still has an electric pencil sharpener I stole out of a church. He never knew where I got it.

"Instead of going to school, I'd stay home and work on bikes. We used to steal bikes all the time. We'd get cool frames and put all the hot parts on them. I've stolen lots of bikes—maybe around 50. But I probably shouldn't have never stolen about half of them, they were such junk. I just needed them for transportation."

*Being sneaky.* "I've always been kind of sneaky, I guess. That's just the way I am. I can't say why. My mom says that when I was a small kid I was always doing something sneaky. Not always—but I *could* be that way. I guess I'm still that way, but it's not exactly the same. It's just the way you think about things.

"I don't like to be sneaky about something I could get in trouble for. But I like to walk quietly so no one will see me. I could get in trouble for something like sneaking in somebody's backyard and taking a roto-tiller. I did that once. I sold the engine.

"I guess being sneaky means I always try to get away with something. There doesn't have to be any big reason. I used to tell the kid I was hanging around with, 'I don't steal stuff because I need it. I just like to do it for some excitement.'

"Last year I went 'jockey-boxing' with some guys who hang around at the park. That's when you get into people's glove compartments. It was a pretty dead night. One guy wanted a car stereo. He had his tools and everything. So we all took off on bicycles, five of us. I was sort of tagging along and watching them—I didn't really do it. They got into a couple of cars. They got a battery vacuum cleaner and a couple of little things. You go to apartment houses where there's lots of cars and you find the unlocked ones and everybody grabs a car and jumps in and starts scrounging through.

"I've gone through glove compartments before and I probably will again someday if I see a car sitting somewhere just abandoned. But I'm not into it for fun anymore, and it doesn't pay unless you do a lot. Mostly young guys do it.

"I'm still mostly the same, though. I'll take a roll of tape or something from the supermarket. Just stick it in my pants. Or if I saw a knife that was easy to take. That's about it. Oh, I sneak into some nearby apartments to wash my clothes. I pay for the machines, but they are really for the tenants, not for me. And I'll sneak through the woods with a piece of plywood for the cabin."

*I don't have to steal, but . . .* "I'm not what you'd call a super thief, but I will steal. A super thief makes his living at it; I just get by. I don't have to steal, but it sure makes life a hell of a lot easier. I've always known people who steal stuff. It's no big deal. If you really want something, you have to go around looking for it. I guess I could teach you how to break into your neighbor's house, if you want to. There's lots of ways— just look for a way to get in. It's not that hard to do. I don't know what you'd call it. Risky? Crazy?

"I can be honest. Being honest means that you don't do anything to people that you don't know. I don't like to totally screw somebody. But I'll screw 'em a little bit. You could walk into somebody's garage and take everything they have—maybe $5,000 worth of stuff. Or you could just walk in and grab a chain saw. It's not my main hobby to go around looking for stuff to steal. I might see something, but I wouldn't go out of my way for it."

*Breaking and entering.* "I remember busting into my second-grade class-room. I went back to the schoolground on the weekend with another kid. We were just looking around outside and I said, 'Hey, look at that fire escape door—you could pull it open with a knife.' We pulled it open and I went in and I took some money and three or four little cars and a couple of pens. There wasn't anything of value, but the guy with me stocked up on all the pens he could find. We got in trouble for it. That was the first time I broke in anywhere. I don't know why I did it. Maybe too many television shows. I just did it because I could see that you could do it.

"And I've gotten into churches and stores. I've broken into apartment house recreation rooms a lot, crawling through the windows. And I've broken into a house before.

"I went in one house through the garage door, got inside, and scrounged around the whole house. God, there was so much stuff in that house. I munched a cake, took some liquor, took some cameras. Another time I thought there was nobody home at one house, and I went around to the bathroom window, punched in the screen and made a really good jump to the inside. I walked in the house real quietly. Then I heard somebody walk out the front door, so I split. I didn't have nothin' then; I was looking for anything I could find. I just wanted to go scrounging through drawers to find some money.

"If I ever needed something that bad again and it was total chaos [i.e., desperation], I could do it, and I would. It's not my way of life, but I'd steal before I'd ever beg."

*Inching closer to the chute.* "Just before I started living at the cabin, I kept having it on my mind that I needed some money and could rob a store. It seemed like a pretty easy way to get some cash, but I guess it wasn't a very good idea. I had a B-B gun. I could have walked in there like a little Mafia, shot the gun a few times, and said, 'If you don't want those in your face, better give me the money.' There were a couple of stores I was thinking of doing it to.

"I was standing outside one store for about two hours. I just kept thinking about going in there. All of a sudden this cop pulls into the parking lot and kinda checks me out. I thought, 'Oh fuck, if that cop came over here and searched me and found this gun, I'd be shit.' So as soon as he split, I left. And after thinking about it for so long.

"But another time, I really did it. I went into one of those little fast food stores. I had this hood over my head with a little mouth hole. I said to the clerk, 'Open the register.' And she said, 'What! Are you serious?' I knew she wasn't going to open it, and she knew I wasn't about to shoot her. So then I started pushing all the buttons on the cash register, but I didn't know which ones to push. And she came up and pulled the key. Then someone pulled up in front of the store and the signal bell went 'ding, ding.' So I booked.

"Another time I thought about going into a store and telling this cashier to grab the cash tray and pull it out and hand it to me. Or else I was going to wait till near closing time when they go by with a full tray of 20-dollar bills and grab it. Or go into a restaurant right after closing time, like on a Saturday night or something, and just take the whole till. I was going to buy a motorcycle with that. All I needed was $400 to get one.

"If I was ever that hurting, I could probably do it if I had to. It's still a possibility, and it would sure be nice to have some cash. But you wouldn't get much from a little store anyway. I'd be more likely just to walk in and grab a case of beer."

*I'm not going to get caught.* "I can't straighten out my old bike after that little accident I had the other day, and that means I need another bike. I'll try to find one to steal—that's the easiest way to get one. I should be able to find one for free, and very soon, instead of having to work and spend all that money, money that would be better off spent other places, like reinstating my driver's license.

"The way I do it, I go out in nice neighborhoods and walk around on people's streets and look for open garages, like maybe they just went to the store or to work and didn't close the door. I walk on streets that aren't main streets. Someone might spot me looking around at all these bikes, but even if somebody says something, they can't do anything to you. The cops might come up and question me, but nothing could happen.

"Now, if I was caught on a hot bike . . . but that's almost impossible. If I was caught, they'd probably take me downtown and I'd sit there a while until I went to court, and who knows what they'd do. Maybe give me six months. They'd keep me right there at the jail. But it's worth the risk, because I'm not going to get caught. I did it too many times. I know it's easy.

"Even if I worked, the only thing I'd be able to buy is an old Schwinn 10-speed. The bike I'm going to get will be brand new. Maybe a Peugeot or a Raleigh. A $400 bike at least. It might not be brand new, but if I could find a way, I'd get a $600 bike, the best one I could find. And I'll do whatever I have to, so no one will recognize it."

*Home is the hunter.* "I think this will be the last 'bike hunting' trip I'll ever go on . . . probably. I said it *might* be the last one. I could probably do one more. When I get to be 24 or 25, I doubt that I'll be walking around looking for bikes. But, if I was 25 and I saw a nice bike and I was in bad shape and really needed it, I'd get it. I'm not going to steal anything I don't need. Unless it's just sitting there and I can't help it, it's so easy. I'm not really corrupt, but I'm not 'innocent' anymore. I can be trusted, to some people." ["Can I trust you?" I asked.] "Yeah. Pretty much. I dunno. When it comes to small stuff . . ."

*Growing up.* "When I was growing up, I was always doing something, but it wasn't that bad. My parents never did take any privileges away or give me another chance. Anytime I did something in California, my mother and stepdad just said, 'Back to Oregon.' They didn't threaten, they just did it. My mom could have figured out something better than sending me back to Oregon all the time. She could have taken away privileges, or made me work around the house. And in Oregon, my dad could have figured a better way than throwing me out of the house. Bad times for me were getting in a hassle with my parents. Then I wouldn't have no place to go, no money or nothin'. That happened with all of them at different times."

[By my count, including a time when Brad lived with his mother at her sister's home, and when he lived with one stepmother's parents for a while, he was reared in six families. That fact seemed not particularly disconcerting to him, but the abruptness of being dispatched among them was.]

"The last time I got kicked out in California, I moved back to Oregon, but I only stayed in the house a couple of days. My stepmom and my dad started telling me I wasn't going to smoke pot anymore, I would have to go to school, I was going to have to stop smoking cigarettes, and other shit like that. And I didn't like anything about that fucking house. Another reason is that my dad said I couldn't have a motorcycle. So I split. I just hung around town, sleeping anywhere I could find. I ripped off a quilt and slept out on a baseball field for awhile. I stayed in different places for a couple of weeks. Then I got busted, got sent to reform school, then I got some work and the first thing I did was buy a motorcycle. I was riding without a license or insurance for a while. Even after I got a license, I kept getting tickets, so finally my license got suspended, and my dad took the motorcycle and sold it to pay for the tickets.

"If I had kids, I would just be a closer family. I would be with them more and show that you love them. You could talk to your kids more. And if they do something wrong, you don't go crazy and lose your temper or something."

*Getting paid for dropping out.* "I've earned some money at odd jobs since I came here, but mostly I live on food stamps. I knew that if I wasn't working and was out of money, food stamps were there. I've been doing it for quite a while. When I was at the Mission I had food stamps. A guy I worked with once told me, all I had to do was go down there and tell 'em you're broke, that's what it's there for. I haven't really tried looking for a job. Food stamps are a lot easier. And I'd just be taking a job away from someone who needs it more. Now that I've figured out the kinds of things to buy, I can just about get by each month on $70 for food. If I couldn't get food stamps, I'd get a job. I guess food stamps are society's way of paying me to drop out."

*Hiding out from life.* "So now I've got this cabin fixed up and it really works good for me. This is better than any apartment I've ever had.

"I guess by living up here I'm sorta hiding out from life. At least I'm hiding from the life I had before I came up here. That's for sure. The life of a dumpy apartment and a cut-rate job. This is a different way of life.

"This place works a lot for me. What would I have been doing for the year and a half in town compared to a year and a half up here? Like, all the work I've done here, none of it has gone for some landlord's pocketbook. I should be able to stay here until I get a good job.

"I like living like this. I think I'd like to be able to know how to live, away from electricity and all that."

The romantic Robinson Crusoe aspects of a young man carving out a life in the wilderness, what his mother referred to as "living on a mountaintop in Oregon," is diminished by this fuller account of Brad's lifestyle. Brad would work if he "had to," but he had found that for a while—measured perhaps in years rather than weeks—he did not have to. If he was not hiding out from life, he had at least broken out of what he saw as the futility of holding a cut-rate job in order to live a cut-rate existence.

Brad kept a low profile that served double duty. He had a strong aversion to being "looked at" in settings where he felt he did not "blend in," and his somewhat remote cabin protected him from the eyes of all strangers—including the law. His cabin became his fortress; he expressed concern that he himself might be "ripped off." On sunny weekends, with the likelihood of hikers passing through the woods, he tended to stay near the cabin with an eye to protecting his motley, but nonetheless precious, collection of tools and utensils, bicycles and parts, and personal belongings. He sometimes padlocked the cabin (though it easily could have been broken into) and always locked his bike when in town if he was going to be any distance from it. Had he been ripped off, he would hardly have called the police to help recover his stolen items; few were his in the first place.

Technically he was not in trouble with the law. To some extent the law exerted a constraining influence on him. In his view, to get caught was the worst thing that could happen to him and would have been "stupid" on his part. That tended to circumscribe both the frequency and extent of the illicit activities in which he engaged. But the law also menaced him as a down-and-outer and as a relatively powerless kid, a kid without resources. The law works on a cash basis. Working for me, Brad earned and saved enough money to purchase an engine for his bicycle in order to circumvent his earlier problems with the motorcycle, only to discover via a traffic violation of over $300 (reduced to $90 with the conventional plea, "Guilty, with explanation") that a bicycle with an engine on it is deemed a motorized vehicle, and that he was required by law to have a valid operator's license (his was still suspended), a license for the vehicle, and insurance. To make himself "legal," he needed about $175 and would continue to face high semi-annual insurance premiums. In his way of thinking, that expense got him "nothing"; he preferred to take his chances. Traffic fines were actually a major budget item for him, but his argument remained the same, "I won't get caught again."

Margaret Mead once commented that most Americans would agree the "worst" thing a child can do is to steal (in MacNeil & Glover, 1959). As a "sneaky kid," Brad had already been stealing stuff—little stuff, mostly—for more than half his lifetime. He seemed to me to be approaching the moment when he would have to decide whether to dismiss his stealing as a phase of growing up and doing "crazy things" (jockey-boxing, breaking into the classroom on weekends, petty shoplifting, stealing bicycles) or to step into the "chute" by joining the big leagues. With mask and gun, he had already faced the chute head-on. That event might have ended otherwise, had not someone called his bluff. With the occurrence of repeated traffic fines, the courts themselves could conceivably precipitate for him a desperate need for quick and easy money.

## Worldview: "Getting My Life Together"

The material presented thus far lends ample support for Brad's depiction of himself as a "sneaky kid" with a number of antisocial and unsociable traits. In the last 10 of his 20 years, Brad's antics often had resulted in trouble ("hassles") and had paved the way for more trouble than actually had befallen him. (In that regard, it is ironic that being sent to reform school, though on the technically serious charge of "Supplying contraband" coupled with "Harassment," was, in his opinion, more a consequence of having "nowhere else to go" than of the offenses themselves.)

From mainstream society's point of view, Brad's story would seem to reflect the enculturation process going awry, a young person growing apart from, rather than a part of, the appropriate social system. Brad did not behave "properly" on certain critical dimensions (e.g., respect for other people's property, earning his way), and therefore his almost exemplary behavior on other dimensions (his lack of pretense, his cleanliness, and, particularly, his resourcefulness and self-reliance) was apt to be overlooked. He was not a social asset, and he seemed destined for trouble.

Yet in both word and deed (and here is the advantage of knowing him for two years, rather than depending solely on formal interviews), Brad repeatedly demonstrated how he was more "insider" than "outsider" to the society he felt was paying him to drop out. In numerous ways he revealed a personal worldview not so far out of step with society after all. Adrift though he may have been, he was not without social bearings. The odds may have been against him, but they were not stacked. This was not a "minority" kid fighting the immediate peril of the ghetto, nor a weak kid, nor a dumb kid, nor an unattractive kid, nor a kid who had not, at some prior time in his life, felt the security of family. Indeed, somewhere along the way he learned to value security so highly that his pursuit of it provided him an overriding sense of purpose.

Both Brad's parents had worked all their adult lives and, judging from statements I personally heard them make, took pride in their efforts. If, as Brad sized it up, they were "not really rich," they were at least comfortable. Perhaps from Brad's point of view they had paid too high a price for what they had or had given up too much to attain it, but they are the embodiment of the American working class. As Brad expressed it, "My dad's worked all his life so he can sit at a desk and not hold a screwdriver any more. But he just works! He never seems to have any fun."

Absolutely no one, including anthropologists who devote careers to the task, ever learns the totality of a culture; conversely, no one, including the most marginal or socially isolated of humans, ever escapes the deep imprint of macro- and micro-cultural systems in which he or she is reared as a member of a family, a community, and a nation. Evidence of that cultural imprinting abounds in Brad's words and actions. I have combed his words and found evidence that in examining his world-view one can find glimmers of hope, if only he does not "get caught doing something stupid" or in some unexpected way get revisited by his past. Though he occasionally makes some deliberate, unsanctioned responses, Brad appears well aware of the "cultural meanings" of his behavior (see Wallace, 1961a, p. 135).

If Brad does "make it," it will be largely because of the cultural imprinting of values instilled at some time in that same past. Let me here make the point to which I will return in conclusion: There was no constructive force working effectively on Brad's behalf to guide, direct, encourage, or assist him. He had no sponsor, no support system, virtually no social network. The agencies poised to respond to him will act when and if he makes a mistake and gets caught. He cannot get help without first getting into trouble. The only social agency that exerted a positive educative influence on him was an indirect consequence of the mixed blessing of food stamps that kept him from having to steal groceries but made it unnecessary for him to work. He had learned to spend his allotment wisely in order to make it last the month.

The following excerpts, selected topically, suggest the extent to which Brad already had acquired a sense of middle-class morality and an ethos of working to achieve material success. They point, as well, to loose strands that remain someday to be woven together if he is to be bound more securely to the Establishment.

*A job—that's all that makes you middle class.* "A job is all that makes you middle class. If I'm going to have a job, I've got to have a bike that works. I've got to have a roof, I've got to have my clothes washed. And I'd probably need rain gear, too. You can't go into any job in clothes that look like you just came out of a mud hut.

"Even though I've worked for a while at lots of different things, I guess you could say that I've never really held a job. I've worked for my dad a while—altogether about a year, off and on. I helped him wire houses and do other things in light construction. I scraped paint for a while for one company. I worked for a graveyard for about eight months, for a plumber a while, and I planted trees for a while.

"I wouldn't want to have to put up with a lot of people on a job that didn't make me much money. Like at a check-out counter—that's too many people. I don't want to be in front of that many people. I don't want to be a known part of the community. I don't mind having a job, but I don't like a job where everyone sees you do it. Working with a small crew would be best—the same gang every day. I'd like a job where I'm out and moving. Anything that's not cleaning up after somebody else, where you're not locked up and doing the same thing over and over, and where you can use your head a little, as well as your back.

"My mother said, 'If you had a little job right now, you'd be in heaven.' Yeah, some cash wouldn't hurt, but then I'd have to subtract the $70 I wouldn't get in food stamps, and there might not be a whole hell of a lot left. So I'm living in the hills and I'm not workin'. No car, either. So no girl friend right now. No big deal.

"If I did have a job, the hardest thing about it would be showing up on time and getting home. Living out here makes a long way to go for any job I might get.

"If you get your life together, it means you don't have to worry so much. You have a little more security. That's what everybody wants. Money: a regular job. A car. You can't have your life together without those two things.

"My life is far better than it was. I've got a place to live and no big problems or worries. I don't worry about where I'm going to sleep or about food. I've got a bike. Got some pot—my home-grown plants are enough now, so I don't have to worry about it, even though it's not very high class. But you've got to have a car to get to work in the morning and to get home. I can go on living this way, but I can't have a car if I'm going to do it.

"Sometimes my mom sends me clothes, or shampoo, or stuff like that. But if I had a job, I wouldn't need that. She'll help me with a car someday, if she ever thinks I'm financially responsible."

*Building my own life.* "I'm not in a big hurry with my life. If I can't do super-good, I'll do good enough. I don't think I'll have any big career.

"Maybe in a way I'll always be kind of a survivalist. But I would like to be prepared for when I get to be 50 or 60—if I make it that far—so that I wouldn't need Social Security. I get my food stamps, so I guess I'd have to say I'm part of the Establishment. A job would get me more into it.

"Over a period of time I've learned what food to buy and what food not to buy, how to live inexpensively. I get powdered milk, eggs, dry foods in bulk, and stuff like that. Food costs me about $80 per month. I could live on $100 a month for food, cigarettes, fuel, and a few little extras, but not very many, like buying nails, or a window, or parts for a bike. But I don't really need anything. I've got just about everything I need. Except there is a few things more.

"I might stay here a couple of years, unless something drastically comes up. Like, if a beautiful woman says she has a house in town, that would do it, but if not for that, it isn't very likely. I'll have to build my own life.

"I wouldn't mind working. I wouldn't mind driving a street-sweeper or something like that, or to buy a $30,000 or $60,000 piece of equipment, and just make money doing stuff for people. You see people all over who have cool jobs. Maybe they just do something around the house like take out washing machines, or they own something or know how to do something that's not really hard labor but it's skilled labor.

"But living this way is a good start for me. I don't have to work my life away just to survive. I can work a little bit, and survive, and do something else."

*Being by myself.* "At this time of my life it's not really too good to team up with somebody. I've got to get my life together before I can worry about just going out and having a beer or a good time.

"Being by myself doesn't make all that much difference. I guess that I'm sorta a loner. Maybe people say I'm a hermit, but it's not like I live 20 miles out in nowhere.

"I don't want to be alone all my life. I'd like to go camping with somebody on the weekend. Have a car and a cooler of beer and a raft or something. It's nice to have friends to do that with. If I had a car and stuff, I'm sure I could get a few people to go. Without a car, man, shit. . . ."

*Friends.* "A friend is someone you could trust, I suppose. I've had close friends, but I don't have any now. But I have some 'medium' friends. I guess that's anybody who'd smoke a joint with me. And you see some people walking down the street or going to a store or to a pay phone. You just say, 'Hi, what's going on?'

"I know lots of people. Especially from reform school. I've already seen some. They're not friends, though; they're just people you might see to say hello and ask them what they've been up to and ask them how long they did in jail.

"The first time I met one guy I know now, I was pushing my bike and I had my backpack and some beer and I was drinking a beer. I'd never seen him before. He said, 'Hey, wanna smoke a joint?' I said, 'Sure.' So I gave him a couple of beers and we smoked some pot and started talking. I told him I lived up in the hills. I see him around every now and then. He's known me for a year and I talk to him sometimes and joke around. He's sort of a friend.

"I had a few friends in southern California, but by the time I left there I wasn't too happy with them. I guess my best friend was Tom. I used to ride skateboard with him all day. His older brother used to get pot for us. That's when I think I learned to ride the very best. We always used to try to beat each other out in whatever we did. I was better than him in some things and after a while he got better than me in a couple of things. But I think I was always a little bit more crazier than he was—a little bit wilder on the board."

*I've been more places and done more things.* "I've lived in a lot of different places. Like going to California. Living out in the country. Living different places in town. Dealing with people. Living at the reform school. Living in Portland. Living here.

"I've definitely had more experiences than some of the people I went to school with, and I've had my ears opened more than they have. In *some* things, I'm wiser than other kids my age.

"I saw a guy a few weeks ago who is the same age as me. He lived in a house behind us when I was in fifth grade. He still lives with his parents in the same place. I think about what he's been doing the last nine years and what I've been doing the last nine years and it's a big difference. He went to high school. Now he works in a gas station, has a motorcycle, and works on his truck. I guess that's all right for him, so long as he's mellow with his parents. That way he can afford a motorcycle.

"But you've got what you've got. It doesn't make any difference what anybody else has. You can't wish you're somebody else. There's no point in it."

*Some personal standards.* "In the summer I clean up every day. When it starts cooling down, I dunno; sometimes if it's cold, I just wash my head and under my arms. Last winter I'd get a really good shower at least every three days and get by otherwise. But I always wash up before going to town if I'm dirty. I don't want to look like I live in a cabin.

"I don't really care what people on the street think of me. But somebody who knows me, I wouldn't want them to dislike me for any reason.

"And I wouldn't steal from anybody that knew me, if they knew that I took something or had any idea that I might have took it. Whether I liked them or not. I wouldn't steal from anybody I liked, or I thought they were pretty cool. I only steal from people I don't know.

"I don't like stealing from somebody you would really hurt. But anybody that owns a house and three cars and a boat—they're not hurtin'. It's the Law of the Jungle—occasionally people get burned. A lot of people don't, though. As long as they've got fences and they keep all their stuff locked up and don't leave anything laying around, they're all right. The way I see it, 'If you snooze, you lose.'

"If you say you'll do something, you should do it. That's the way people should operate. It pisses me off when somebody doesn't do it. Like, you tell somebody you're going to meet them somewhere, and they don't show up. But giving my word depends on how big of a deal it is; if it's pretty small, it would be no big deal.

"Sure, stealing is immoral. I don't like to screw somebody up for no good reason. But my morals can drop whenever I want.

"I went to Sunday School for a while and to a church kindergarten. I guess I heard all the big lessons—you get the felt board and they pin all the stuff on 'em and cut out all the paper figures: Jesus, Moses. But our family doesn't really think about religion a whole lot. They're moral to a point but they're not fanatics. It's too much to ask. I'd rather go to hell. But any little kid knows what's right and wrong."

*Moderation: Getting close enough, going "medium" fast.* "One of my friend's older brothers in southern California was a crazy fucker. He'd get these really potent peyote buttons and grind them up and put them in chocolate milkshakes. One time they decided to go out to the runways where the jets were coming in, 'cause they knew somebody who did it before. Planes were coming in continually on that runway. They'd go out there laying right underneath the skids marks, just right under the planes. I never would get that close. Just being out there, after jumping the fence and walking clear out to the runway, is close enough. I never did lie on the runway. . . .

"On the skateboard, I just go medium fast. . . .

"The fun part of skiing is knowing when to slow down. . . .

"When those guys went jockey-boxing, I didn't actually do it with them. I was just tagging along. . . .

"Robbing a store seemed like a pretty easy way to get some cash, but I guess it wasn't a very good idea. . . .

"I don't know why I didn't get into drugs more. I smoke pot, but I've never really cared to take downers and uppers or to shoot up. I don't really need that much. . . .

"I like to smoke pot, but I don't think of myself as a pothead. A pothead is somebody who is totally stoned all day long on really good pot, really burned out all the time. I smoke a joint, then smoke a cigarette, and I get high. I just like to catch a buzz. . . .

"If you really get burnt out your brain's dead. You can get burned out on anything if you do it too much. I don't do it enough to make it a problem. If you take acid you never know who's made it or exactly what's in it. I've taken it before and gotten pretty fried. I don't know if it was bad acid but it wasn't a very good experience. . . .

"Sometimes when I want to be mellow, I just don't say anything. I just shut up. Or somebody can mellow out after a day at work—you come home, smoke a joint, drink a beer—you just sort of melt. . . . "

*Putting it all together.* "Anything you've ever heard, you just remember and put it all together the best you can. That's good enough for me."

## Formal Schooling

I knew little of Brad's schooling when I began systematically to collect life history data from him. By his account he had often been "slow" or "behind the rest of the class." He could read, but he faltered on "big words." He could write, but his spelling and punctuation were not very good. He had trouble recalling number sequences and basic arithmetic facts. ("Lack of practice," he insisted.) In one junior high school he had been placed in "an EH [educationally handicapped] class with the other stonies." As he recalled, "I don't know if I felt I was special or not, but I didn't like those big classes."

Measures of IQ or scholastic achievement did not really matter anymore. Brad was well aware of his capacities and limitations. How far he was once "below average" or "behind" in his schoolwork had become, as it always had been, purely academic. Schooling for him was over; he was out.

Formal schooling aside, for practical purposes Brad could read, he could write, he could do simple arithmetic. The only book he "requisitioned" for his cabin was a dictionary. That alone was incredible; even more incredibly, he occasionally labored through it to find a word —no easy task when the alphabet had to be recited aloud in order to locate an entry.

Schooling had played a part in Brad's life, but not the vital part educators like it to play. In 10 years he enrolled in eight schools in two states, ranging from early years at a small country school to a final eight months at a state reformatory, and including attendance at urban elementary, junior high, and senior high schools. I traced his attendance record where he boasted having "the world's record for ditching school." Perhaps it was not the world's record, but following his midyear enrollment in grade 5 he maintained 77 percent attendance for that year and 46 percent attendance in grade 6 the year following. He changed schools during the academic year at least once in grades 4, 5, and 6, as well as beginning the term in a new school four different years: "I guess I was in school a lot, but I was always in a different school."

In Brad's assessment, school "did what it's supposed to do. . . . You gotta learn to read." He laid no blame, noting only that "Maybe school could of did better." He acknowledged that *he* might have done better, too.

"I was just never that interested in school. If I knew I had to do something, I'd try a little bit. I could probably have tried harder."

The earliest school experience he could recall was in a church-sponsored kindergarten. Hearing Brad use objectionable language, the teacher threatened to wash his mouth with soap. At the next occasion when the children were washing their hands, he stuck a bar of soap in his mouth: "I showed the kids around me, 'Hey, no big deal, having soap in your mouth.' "

He recalled first grade as a time when "I learned my ABCs and everything. It was kind of neat." Apparently his enthusiasm for schooling stopped there. He could think of no particular class or teacher that he especially liked. His recollection of events associated with subsequent grades involved changes of schools, getting into trouble for his classroom behavior, or skipping school altogether. As early as fourth grade he remembered difficulty "keeping up" with classmates.

By his own assessment Brad did "OK" in school, but he recalled excelling only once, an art project in clay that was put on display and that his mother still kept. During grade 7 his attendance improved and, for one brief term, so did his grades, but he was not really engaged with what was going on and he felt lost in the large classes.

"In those big classes, like, you sit around in a big horseshoe, and you've got a seat four rows back, with just one teacher. Like English class, I'd get there at 9:00 in the morning and put my head down and I'd sleep through the whole class. It was boring, man.

"Another class they tried to get me in was typing. I tried for a little while, but I wasn't even getting close to passing, so I just gave up."

Brad's public schooling ended in southern California. When he got shunted back to Oregon, he did not enroll in school again, although after being "busted" schooling was his principal activity during his eight months in reform school. He felt that he had attended "a couple of pretty good schools" in southern California during grades 8, 9, and, briefly, 10, but, as usual, the times he remembered were times spent out of class, not in it.

"By the end of school, I was cutting out a lot. Like, I didn't need PE. Look at this kid—he's been riding bicycles and skateboards all day all his life. I didn't need no PE. I don't need to go out in the sun and play games. I wasn't interested in sports. So I'd go get stoned. I'd take a walk during that class, go kick back in an orange grove, maybe eat an orange, get high, smoke a cigarette, and by the time I'd walk back, it was time for another class. I did it for a long time and never got caught. Anyhow, then I switched schools."

Brad felt that his lack of academic progress cost him extra time in reform school, "So I started to speed up and do the stuff and then I got out." In his assessment, "I was doing 9th-grade work. I probably did some 10th- and 11th-grade stuff, but not a lot."

Although young people seldom return to public schools after serving "time," I asked Brad to identify the grade levels to which he might have been assigned had he gone back to school.

"For math, if I went back, I'd just be getting into 10th grade. In reading, I'd be a senior or better. Spelling would be about 8th grade. I can spell good enough. Handwriting, well, you just write the way you write. My writing isn't that bad if I work on it. I don't worry about that much."

On the other hand, he did recognize limitations in his command of basic school skills. He had "kind of forgotten" the multiplication facts, and he was pretty rusty on subtracting and recalling the alphabet. To be a good speller, he once mused, you've got to "do it a lot," but at reform school he did only "a little bit." His awareness of these limitations is revealed in a letter intended for his mother but later abandoned in favor of a cheerier style:

> Hi
> if I sit hear and stair
> at this pieac of paper
> eny longer ill go crazy
> I dont think im scaird

of witing just dont like
to remind myself I
need improvment. its
raining alot past
few days but its warm
'n dry inside. . . .

Reading was the school skill at which Brad felt most proficient, and his confidence was not shaken by the fact that some words were difficult for him. He said he did not enjoy reading, but he spent hours poring over instruction manuals. My impression was that although his oral reading was halting, he had good reading comprehension. That was also his assessment. When, at his father's insistence, he briefly entertained the idea of joining the Army, Brad had first to take the G.E.D. exam (for his high school General Equivalency Diploma) and then take a test for the Army. He felt he passed "pretty high" on the Army test and on some parts of the G.E.D., "like reading and a couple of other ones" he felt he did "super, super good."

Brad once observed philosophically, "The people in college today are probably the ones who didn't sleep when I was in English class." At the same time, school was a closed chapter in his life. Other than to acknowledge that he "might have tried harder," however, he expressed no regrets over school as an opportunity missed. Anticipating that his lack of school skills would prove a barrier to enrollment in any technical training program, he could not imagine ever returning to the classroom. And, like most school leavers, he could not think of anything that might have been done that would have kept him in school.[4]

## Adequate Schools and Inadequate Education:
## An Interpretation

It might be socially "desirable" if Brad could read better, write better, do arithmetic better, spell better. With better spelling skills, he would "stare" rather than "stair" at a blank page and perhaps feel less self-conscious about needing "improvment." Considering that he devoted some (although certainly not exclusive) attention to schooling for 10 of his 20 years, he does not do these things very well.

On the other hand, that he can do them as well as he does might also be regarded as a tribute to the public schools. Brad's level of school achievement may be disappointing, but it is not inadequate. He is literate. He did get "something" out of school. True, his performance at the 3 Rs could be more polished, but the importance of his proficiency with such amenities pales before problems of greater social consequence. Brad's schooling has stopped, but his learning continues apace. Exerting some positive, constructive influence on that learning as it pertains to Brad's enculturation into society presents society's current challenge. That challenge has not been taken up.

Schools can affect the rate and level of academic achievement, but they do not set the course of students' lives. Schools are expediters for many, but they do not and cannot "reach" everyone, even though they may ever so briefly touch them. Schooling is not everyone's cup of tea. As Brad put it, "I've always liked learning. I just didn't like school."

Learning—in the broad enculturative sense of coming to understand what one needs to know to be competent in the roles one may expect to fulfill in society, rather than in the narrow sense of learning-done-at-school—is an ongoing process in which each human engages throughout a lifetime. In Brad's case, the direction that process was taking seemed to reflect all too well what he felt society expected of him: Nothing. He was left largely to his own resources to make sense of his world and create his own life (see Mann, 1982, p. 343). He endeavored quite self-consciously ro "figure things out," but his resolutions often put him at odds with society; what appeared as inevitable conclusions to him were neither inevitable nor necessarily appropriate in terms of community norms.

Maybe we cannot reach him; surely we cannot reach everyone like him. But I was astounded to realize that no systematic, constructive effort was being exerted to influence the present course of Brad's life. No agency offered help, or direction, or concern, and neither did any of the "institutions" that ordinarily touch our lives: family, school, work, peer group. If it is naive to regard these influences as invariably positive and constructive, our interactions with them do, nonetheless, contribute to our sense of social "self." Brad was, for the most part, out of touch with them all.

If Brad is able to "get his life together," it will have to be almost entirely through his own effort. Perhaps his personal style as a loner helped buffer him from peer influences that seemed to me, as a wary adult, as likely to get him into trouble as to guide him on the straight and narrow; that he could find time and space "on a mountaintop in Oregon" rather than on a beach or under a freeway in southern California seemed to me to give him an advantage over his fellow "street people." His lifestyle was not overly complicated by urban trappings or the quickened pace of city life. He was not crowded or pushed. At the same time, he could neither escape the influence of material wants and creature comforts so prevalent in the society in which he lives nor deny a deeply felt need to connect with someone, somewhere. Seeming loner that he often appeared, even Brad could acknowledge, "There must be a group that I would fit in, somewhere in this town."

He had learned to "hunt and gather" for his necessities in the aisles of supermarkets, in neighborhood garages, and at residential building sites. He conceded that stealing was wrong, but, among his priorities, necessity (broadly defined to allow for some luxuries as well) took precedence over conformity. He saw "no alternative" for getting the things he felt he needed but could not afford. Still, he took only what he considered necessary, not everything he could get his hands on. He was not, nor did he see himself ever becoming, a "super thief."

I do not see how society can "teach" Brad not to be sneaky or to shoplift or to steal. Most families try to do that. His family wasn't entirely successful, though more of the message seems to have gotten through than one might at first assume.[5] In that regard I find useful the distinction between deviant *acts* and deviant *persons* as suggested by anthropologist Robert Edgerton (1978). In spite of occasional deviant acts, Brad's statements reveal his underlying enculturation into the prevailing ethos of mainstream American society. He was well aware of the meanings of his acts to others; as he noted, "Any little kid knows what's right and wrong." Although he prided himself on the cunning necessary to survive his "hard life" by whatever means necessary, he staunchly defended his behavior—"I couldn't get by without stealing stuff"—as well as himself: "I am not that rotten of a kid!"

There was a foundation on which to build, but there was neither external help, nor support, nor a modicum of encouragement shaping that process. Was schooling "an" opportunity in Brad's life, or is it the only directed opportunity he gets? It seems to me there might, and should, be a more concerted effort to exert a positive influence to provide him with reasonable and realistic routes of access back into the cultural mainstream. To have any effect, however, such efforts would have to be in the form of increasing the options available to him, rather than trying to "shove" him in some particular direction; he has already heard the lectures about good citizenship.

The community's best strategy would seem to be to assure that *opportunities* exist for a person like Brad to satisfy more of his wants in socially acceptable ways. Fear of getting caught isn't much of a deterrent to someone who thinks he's "too smart" to get caught. Armed robbery is already within the realm of things Brad could, and might, do. With an attitude toward behaviors like shoplifting, "ripping things off," burglary, operating a vehicle with a suspended license, or even his preoccupation with obtaining an adequate supply of "pot," that "just about everybody—or at least everybody my age—does it," he can too easily find himself "in the chute" without realizing that everybody isn't there after all. Having gotten out of mainstream society, he does not see a way back in. Nor is he convinced it is worth the effort to try.

It is convenient—and an old American pastime—to place blame on the schools. Questions concerning educational adequacy, when directed toward the schools, invite that kind of blame-setting by relating the present inadequacies of youth to prior inadequacies of the schools (see Levin, 1983). Employing the anthropologist's distinction between schooling and education encourages us to review the full range of efforts the community makes to exert a positive educative influence on our lives, not only during the school years but in the postschool years as well.[6] The problems Brad now poses for society are not a consequence of inadequate schooling. They dramatize the risk we take by restricting our vision of collective educational responsibility to what can be done in school.

One hears arguments that today's youth vacillate between extremes of taking what they want or expecting everything to be handed to them on a silver platter. One finds a bit of both in Brad's dreams of pulling off a robbery or suddenly finding himself owning and operating a $60,000 piece of machinery, as well as his reluctance to do work like dishwashing that entails cleaning up after others and where everyone can watch you perform a menial job.

But I wonder if young people like Brad really believe that society "owes" them something? Perhaps that is an expression of frustration at failing to see how to *begin* to accumulate resources of their own comparable to what they perceive "everyone else" already has. A willingness to defer gratification must come more easily to those who not only have agonized during deferment but have eventually realized some long-awaited reward. Nothing Brad had ever done had worked out that well—at least prior to his effort to build both a new cabin and a new lifestyle. He had virtually no sense of deferred gratification. With him, everything was "now or never."

In a society so materialistic as ours, opportunity is realized essentially with money rather than "school" or "work." To Brad, money represented security and he had limited access to it. That is why food stamps, in an annual amount less than $900, figured so importantly to him. His use of the stamps has left me wondering whether it might be possible to design some governmental agency that would calculatedly confront individuals like Brad in an educative way.

But the educative value of a welfare dole is limited, and, as Brad discovered, the power of the dole-givers and their labyrinth of regulations is ultimate. The stamps made a better consumer of him (buying generic brands, buying large quantities, buying staples), but he realized that the first $70 of any month's take-home pay would be money he would otherwise have received free from the food stamp program. To "earn" his stamps, he had to remain poor.[7] Had he found the second-rate job he so dreaded, part of his earnings would simply have replaced the dole, his other expenses (transportation, clothes, maybe a second-rate apartment) would have increased dramatically, and he would have again been trapped in a second-rate life. Until his food stamps were summarily canceled for two months, after he failed to participate in a ritual midwinter job search during a period of staggering recession and regional unemployment, he did not aggressively seek work. When he finally realized he was destitute and began in earnest to look for work, 38 days passed before he even got turned down for a job! He put in many hours at painting and yard clean-up for me (although he refused to equate working for me with "real work") and reverted to "ripping off" items he felt he needed but could not afford.

I invited Brad's thoughts on what might be done to help people like him. His idea, other than a dream of finding "just the right job" (never fully specified) without ever going to look for it, was of a "day work" program wherein anyone who needed money could appear at a given time, do a day's work, and promptly receive a day's pay. I'm sure Brad's thoughts turned to the end of the day when each worker would receive a pay envelope, while I wondered what one would do with a motley pick-up crew that wouldn't inadvertently make mockery of work itself. Yet implicit in his notion are at least two critical points.

First is a notion of a right to work: If (when) one is willing, one should be able to work and, if in dire need, be paid immediately in cash. Brad found no such right in his life. Although he had been able to find—but not hold—a number of jobs in the past, now he heard only "No Help Wanted" and read only "Not Presently Taking Applications." He was not entirely without social conscience when he observed that if he found a job he would only be taking it away from someone who needed it more. Brad did not really need a job. And, as he had begun to "figure out," no one really needed him. Maybe he was right; maybe $70 in food stamps was society's way of paying him to drop out.

Second is a notion of an overly structured wage and hour system that effectively prices most unskilled and inexperienced workers like Brad out of the job market and requires a full-time commitment from the few it accepts. Brad's material needs were slight. He could have pre- served the best elements in his carefree lifestyle by working part time. However, the labor market does not ordinarily offer such options ex- cept for its own convenience. Either you want a job or you do not want a job. But work for its own sake cast no spell over Brad; he did not look to employment for satisfaction, for meaningful involvement, or for achieving self-respect. Money was the only reason one worked.[8]

School provides opportunity and access for some youth; employment provides it for others. Neither school nor work presently exerted an influence on Brad. He was beyond school, and steady employment was beyond him. Without the effective support of family or friends, and without the involvement of school or work, he was left to his own devices. In his own words, he could not see a way to win and he did not have anything to lose. From mainstream society's point of view, we would be better off if he did.

After so carefully making provision for Brad's schooling, society now leaves his continuing education to chance, and we are indeed taking our chances. But educative adequacy in the lives of young people like Brad is not an issue of schooling. Schools provided him one institutional opportunity; they no longer reached him, and no other agency was trying. His next institutional "opportunity," like his last one, may be custodial. If it is, we all lose; Brad will not be the only one who will have to pay.[9]

## Summary

"The important thing about the anthropologist's findings," writes Clifford Geertz (1973), one of anthropology's more articulate spokesmen, "is their complex specificness, their circumstantiality" (p. 23). Whatever issue anthropologists address, they characteristically begin an account and look for illustration through real events or cases bounded in time and circumstance. The effective story should be "specific and circumstantial," but its relevance in a broader context should be apparent. The story should make a point that transcends its modest origins. The case must be particular, but the implications broad.

Following that tradition, I have related a specific and circumstantial life story to illustrate the necessity of regarding education as more than just schooling and of pointing out how little we attend to that broader concern. That may seem a roundabout way to address so complex an issue, but it is a way to bring an anthropological perspective to the problem.

Brad's story is unique, but his is not an isolated case. He is one among thousands of young people who simply "drift away." His uninvited presence on my 20-acre sanctuary, in search of sanctuary himself, brought me into contact with a type of youth I do not meet as a college professor. He piqued my anthropological interest with a worldview in many ways strikingly similar to mine but a set of coping strategies strikingly different. It is easy for people like me to think of people like Brad as someone else's problem, but, for a moment that lingered out to two years, he quite literally brought the problem home to me. I do not find ready answers even in his particular case; I am certainly not ready to say what might, can, or must be done in some broader context.

Little is to be gained from laying blame at the feet of Brad's parents or his teachers, and to do so is to ignore indications of repeated, if not necessarily effective, efforts to help and guide him. Though our extended conversations may have been enlightening to Brad, as they surely were to me, my more direct efforts to help seemed to go awry. At the end, he departed almost as unexpectedly as he had arrived. I am not sure what I think "society" can accomplish for an amorphous "them" when my own well-intended efforts with just one youth seemed only to demonstrate to him that I had my life "together" (his term) in a manner virtually unattainable for himself. The easiest course is to blame Brad, but to do so is to abandon hope and a sense of collective responsibility.

The only certainty I feel is that it is in our common interest to seek ways to provide opportunities intended to exert a continuing and constructive educational influence on the lives of young people like Brad. I do not know whether Brad can or will allow himself to be reached effectively or in time. I do know that from his perspective he saw neither attractive opportunities nor sources of potential help; by his own assessment, he simply did not matter. He was not free of his society but he had become disconnected from it. Once adrift, nothing seemed to beckon or guide him back.

Because we tend to equate education with schooling, we are inclined to look to the past and ask where the schools went wrong. Brad's story, in which school played only a minor role, serves as a reminder of the importance of other educative influences in our lives. It also points out how little systematic attention we give to discerning what those influences are or how we might better use them to augment, complement, and otherwise underwrite the massive efforts we direct at youth during their in-school years. In that broad perspective, our efforts at *education* appear woefully inadequate in spite of the remarkable accomplishments of our schools. Until I found Brad living in my backyard, however, the problem remained essentially abstract. Now it has confronted me with the "complex specificness" of one young human life.

## Notes

*Acknowledgments.* A portion of the work on which this article is based was performed pursuant to Contract No. NIE-P-81-0271 of the National Institute of Education dealing with issues of educational adequacy under the School Finance Project. Data collection and interpretation are, however, the responsibility of the author. Appreciation is expressed to W. W. Charters, Jr., Stanley Elam, Barbara Harrison, Bryce Johnson, Malcolm McFee, and Esther O. Tron, as well as to "Brad," for critical reading and helpful suggestions with early drafts of this paper.

1. If I found any surprise in reviewing the literature, it was in discovering some remarkable similarities between Brad's story and the ground-breaking classic first published half a century ago, Clifford Shaw's *The Jack-Roller: A Delinquent Boy's Own Story* (1930).

2. Meyer Fortes, writing in 1938, noted the firmly established axiom that "education in the widest sense is the process by which the cultural heritage is transmitted from generation to generation, and that schooling is therefore only part of it" (p. 5). Melville Herskovits (1948) subsequently introduced the encompassing term *enculturation* for referring to education in Fortes's "widest sense," but he retained the term *education*, suggesting that it be restricted to "its ethnological sense of directed learning," in turn distinct from and more encompassing than *schooling*, defined as "that aspect of education carried out by specialists" (p. 311; see also Wallace, 1961b).

3. I have been careful to observe the few conditions Brad imposed on my use of the information; he, in turn, was paid for time spent interviewing and for later checking the written account, and early drafts were informed by his comments. That is not to imply that he was entirely satisfied with my portrayal or my interpretation, but he was satisfied that what I reported was accurate. If only to please me, he even commented that he hoped his story might "help people understand."

4. See, for example, the *Oregon Early School Leavers Study* (Oregon Department of Education, 1980), in which only one third of the young people interviewed responded that "something might have been done to affect their decision to quit public secondary school" (p. 16).

5. Brad expressed only resentment toward his father, but his mother's efforts to provide a positive influence on him were often mentioned. When Brad introduced us, after proudly showing her the cabin during her brief but long-anticipated visit, I asked whether she felt she could exert a guiding influence over him living 1,000 miles away. "We've always been a thousand miles apart," she replied, "even when we were under the same roof."

On a different occasion, responding to Brad's announcement that he needed to "find" another bicycle, I asked, "What would your mother think about you stealing a bike? That it's dumb; that it's smart?"

"Neither," he replied. "She'd just think that I must have needed it. She wouldn't say anything. She doesn't lecture me about things like that. But she used to cut out everything they printed in the paper about 'pot' and put it on my walls and she'd talk about brain damage."

6. Although the distinction between education and schooling is sometimes acknowledged, it is not necessarily regarded as having much significance, at least for understanding contemporary society. To illustrate, note in the following excerpt how educator/economist Henry Levin, addressing the topic *Education and Work* (1982), at once recognizes the distinction between education and schooling but bows to what he describes as the "convention" of equating them:

> Although the term education is sometimes used interchangeably with schooling, it is important to note that schooling is not the only form of education. However, schooling represents such a dominant aspect of education in modern societies that the convention of equating education and schooling in the advanced industrialized societies will also be adopted here (p. 1).

7. The irony of the implications and consequences when *not* working is prerequisite to maintaining a steady income is nicely spelled out in Estroff, 1981. See especially Chapter 6, "Subsistence Strategies: Employment, Unemployment, and Professional Disability."

8. Paul Willis (1980) notes in his study of working-class youth that it is this "reign of cash" that precipitates their contact with the world of work (p. 39). As one of his informants explained, "Money is life." Brad's mother expressed a similar view: "Money, not love, makes the world go round."

9. For a grim scenario, including some discomforting parallels and similarities, see Mailer, 1979. The protagonist of Mailer's "true life novel" makes special note of the impact of reform school on his life (Chapter 22). Brad did not reveal the extent of the impact on his own life of the same reform school, but he did include it specifically in his brief inventory of significant "experiences." Similarities noted earlier between Brad's account and Shaw's *The Jack-Roller* (1930) seem less pronounced in a subsequently published follow-up, *The Jack-Roller at Seventy* (Snodgrass, 1982).

# References

Brandes, S. (1982). Ethnographic autobiographies in American anthropology. In E. A. Hoebel, R. Currier, & S. Kaiser (Eds.), *Crisis in anthropology: View from Spring Hill, 1980*. New York: Garland Publishing Company.

Edgerton, R. (1978). The study of deviance—Marginal man or everyman? In G. D. Spindler (Ed.), *The making of psychological anthropology*. Berkeley: University of California Press.

Estroff, S. E. (1981). *Making it crazy: An ethnography of psychiatric clients in an American community*. Berkeley: University of California Press.

Fortes, M. (1938). *Social and psychological aspects of education in Taleland*. Supplement to *Africa*, 11(4).

Geertz, C. (1973). *The interpretation of cultures.* New York: Basic Books.

Herskovits, M. J. (1948). *Man and his works: The science of cultural anthropology.* New York: Alfred A. Knopf.

Levin, H. M. (1982). *Education and work.* Program Report No. 82-B8. Palo Alto, CA: Institute for Research on Educational Finance and Governance, Stanford University.

Levin, H. M. (1983). Youth unemployment and its educational consequences. *Educational Evaluation and Policy Analysis, 5*(2), 231-247.

Lewis, O. (1961). *Children of Sanchez: Autobiography of a Mexican family.* New York: Random House.

MacNeil, I., & Glover, G. (Producers). (1959). *Four families* (Film narrated by Ian MacNeil and Margaret Mead). National Film Board of Canada.

Mailer, N. (1979). *The executioner's song.* New York: Warner Books.

Mann, D. (1982). Chasing the American dream: Jobs, schools, and employment training programs in New York State. *Teachers College Record, 83*(3), 341-376.

Oregon Department of Education. (1980). *Oregon early school leavers study.* Salem: Oregon Department of Education.

Shaw, C. R. (1930). *The jack-roller: A delinquent boy's own story.* Chicago: University of Chicago Press.

Simmons, L. (Ed.). (1942). *Sun Chief: The autobiography of a Hopi Indian.* New Haven: Yale University Press.

Snodgrass, J. (Ed.). (1982). *The jack-roller at seventy: A fifty-year follow-up.* Lexington, MA: D. C. Heath & Company.

Wallace, A. F. C. (1961a). The psychic unity of human groups. In B. Kaplan (Ed.), *Studying personality cross-culturally.* Evanston, IL: Row Peterson and Company.

Wallace, A. F. C. (1961b). Schools in revolutionary and conservative societies. In F. C. Gruber (Ed.), *Anthropology and education.* Philadelphia: University of Pennsylvania Press.

Willis, P. E. (1980). *Learning to labour: How working class kids get working class jobs.* Hampshire, England: Gower Publishing Co. (Originally published 1977).

Wolcott, H. F. (1982). The anthropology of learning. *Anthropology and Education Quarterly, 13*(2), 83-108.

# 4

# The Elementary School Principal

## Notes From a Field Study

---

### PREFACE

---

This second illustrative chapter is also the second of the two articles that I commend as possible models for other qualitatively oriented researchers. The "Sneaky Kid" of Chapter 3 offers a prototype for a brief life history. This chapter offers a prototype for an event-focused account in which a subset of activities is examined as a representation of the whole. The evolution of the chapter proved something of a major turning point in my career as ethnographer.

It is hardly surprising that my two models both appear in this part, "Emphasis on Description." I take description to be the cornerstone of qualitative inquiry, the foundation on which all else rests. My own work is heavily descriptive, and I recommend the same emphasis to anyone wondering how to guide an uncertain entry into qualitative work. Whatever more we achieve through rigorous analysis or brilliant interpretation rests or collapses on the strength of a descriptive base. The question is always a matter of emphasis, however, not of exclusiveness. The idea of pure description was laid to rest (once again) in the discussion of Chapter 2. Neither analysis nor interpretation, most often in combination but sometimes singularly, is ever a mere add-on. Cornerstones are necessary to a solid construction built upon them, but a cornerstone is not the entire edifice. On the other hand, good description does have remarkable survival qualities, often outlasting conceptual frameworks too hastily placed upon them.

The balance among description, analysis, and interpretation "feels right" to me in pointing to "Sneaky Kid" and to this chapter as models. In the present chapter, the descriptive account provides the basis for an analysis that ranges from a close inspection of demographic data to a wide-ranging identification of cultural themes. The chapter concludes with a broad interpretive speculation that invites reexamination of the seemingly straightforward question, "What is going on here?"

The most ambitious of my own studies in terms of time, scope, and resources was the research and writing that led to publication of this chapter and to my monograph, *The Man in the Principal's Office: An Ethnography* (Wolcott, 1973). Both the chapter and the monograph remain in print today in reissues by Waveland Press. The 1984 reissue of the monograph includes a new preface and bibliographic update.

I initiated the fieldwork for this study in 1966. I planned to devote 1 year to research, a second to writing. That is what I had done with dissertation research initiated 4 years earlier: 1 year of fieldwork in 1962-1963, followed by a year devoted exclusively to writing. I was part of the academic establishment now, however, and never again would there be such luxury (or tyranny, depending on how one looks at it) as an uninterrupted year—or even an uninterrupted week—to devote *exclusively* to anything! Furthermore, year two found me spending most of my available research time still following the principal around, the balance of it organizing an extensive collection of observer notes, tape-recorded interviews, and archival records.

In agreeing to write the chapter, I inadvertently allowed myself to get sidetracked writing a brief piece about the study for someone else's book rather than devoting myself single-mindedly to my own, as I should have done. At the time, George Spindler, Professor of Anthropology and Education at Stanford University, was contemplating his next iteration in the series of edited volumes (one each in 1955, 1963, 1974, and 1982, and two in 1987) through which he largely created and subsequently guided the emerging field of "anthropology and education" for 4 decades. Anticipating (correctly, as it turned out) that my new monograph about the principal might eventually join my previously reported research on the Kwakiutl as another volume in his edited series of cases, Spindler suggested that I might like to (i.e., "ought to") prepare a chapter from *each* of my two studies for inclusion in his projected book.

Spindler argued that such writing would not only give my studies greater visibility but also offered an opportunity to draw upon my fieldwork experience in new and different ways. But that was the catch—he wanted original material that would complement the cases rather than segments simply lifted from the cases themselves. By accepting his invitation, I had created unforeseen dilemmas for myself.

The Kwakiutl material had been revised from the dissertation and was already published in the original set of four monographs that launched the series Case Studies in Education and Culture in 1967. Returning to the Kwakiutl data presented my first dilemma, for it meant stealing time I should have devoted to the new study. Having a monograph in print was heady stuff, however, and I was eager to help in any possible way to publicize it. I also wanted to add whatever insight I could about the education of native American groups as well as to demonstrate how "anthropology and education" might inform educational practice. Furthermore, I had an idea in mind, and Spindler had a publisher in hand. Who could ask for anything more? (The selection from the Kwakiutl study is included as Chapter 8 in this volume.)

That same logic—writing with publication virtually guaranteed—led me to agree as well to contribute something from the principal study. The catch was that this piece also had to be new. That posed another dilemma, because the principal study was yet to be written. It was *all* new, meaning, in this case, nonexistent. Nonetheless, I felt I should bank on the sure thing—that is, set aside work on the big study, which had only the interest of a publisher, while I developed a shorter article that might easily appear 2 or 3 years in advance of any monograph. By then I had been in academia long enough to have succumbed to its publish or perish ethos. The federally funded Research and Development Center supporting my work was experiencing that same pressure to provide sufficient evidence of past accomplishments to support requests for continued funding. A preview of my study would be a welcome addition to its arsenal.

I did not realize that materials invited for edited collections go through such a slow process of production; my monograph reached the shelves more than a year ahead of the chapter prepared for Spindler's book.

There is a lesson here about staging one's work as well as about publishing. My bigger mistake was not my decision to prepare a chapter for someone else's book when I should have been working on my own but to accept a writing assignment that drew upon a larger study not yet written.

As I began writing, the material I was drafting for Spindler began to look more and more like a condensed version of the yet-to-be-written monograph. At this first opportunity to report *something* from my study, I seemed unable to resist the temptation to tell all. To try to accomplish that in a few pages, I found case study detail getting in the way of all that I now wanted to say about the elementary school principalship in general.

Some 38 pages into a draft of the chapter for Spindler, and with no end in sight, I realized that I needed to refashion my introduction to give me license to proceed as I was, writing a broad ethnography of the principalship, rather than the ethnography of a principal. I wrote what I felt was a convincing rationale for the tack I had taken. Sensing a need for feedback ("Is this sorta what you have in mind?" we ask, hoping the reply will be "It's perfect!"), I sent the draft off to Spindler. Here was my rationale:

> A brief account such as this provides the opportunity for making a general overview of a study but it precludes the possibility of presenting the descriptive data from which any insights or tentative generalizations are drawn. I have chosen to make some rather broad statements, and I have chosen to speak about the elementary school principalship in general, rather than restrict my comments only to the specifics of one man over a given period of time. (Draft of August 1968)

Spindler returned the draft with a powerful one-word question written in the margin opposite my beautiful rationale: "Why?" On page after page, in a firm but gentle way, his brief editorial comments took me to task for ignoring the carefully detailed observations of the case study in my rush to generalize about the role. At about this same time, Clifford Geertz may have been framing the statement I quoted in the previous chapter: "The important thing about the anthropologist's findings is their complex specificness, their circumstantiality" (Geertz, 1973, p. 23). Spindler cautioned more succinctly; the heart of ethnography, he admonished, is "singularity." Again and again throughout the manuscript he had written in the margin, "Don't generalize." To make his point, at every instance where I had written "they," a reference to all principals, he had rewritten "he" in an effort to pull me back to my case study.

The generalizations themselves were not the problem. They revealed my own efforts to identify patterns, extract themes, and begin to distinguish beliefs and behaviors unique to the case study principal from beliefs and behaviors that could be attributed to some or all other principals. By August 1968, I had been a "principal investigator," both literally and figuratively, for almost 2½ years. I had been in education a dozen years, and in schools another 16 years prior to that. With all that experience to provide both general context and specific observations, I felt quite adequate to the task of organizing an account, both in my head and now on paper. But that neither was what Spindler wanted in a chapter for his book nor, as he was trying to help me realize, was that the contribution ethnography has to offer. Lucky for me things happened as they did, because this time the idea of "complex specificness"—the essence of careful descriptive work—finally took.

From that lengthy first draft I salvaged only the section on method. I began casting about for some part of the whole study that could be related with case study specificity yet revealing of principal "subculture." I realized that I could never encapsulate the entire story of my case study principal in one chapter. I decided to focus on one particular set of events. Five principals had been appointed as an ad hoc screening and advisory committee to interview and rank the contenders from a panel of candidates eager to fill newly announced vacancies. The case study principal was a member of the committee, and its story was the story I chose to tell.

The episode selected was not one I planned to include in the monograph. The retelling might have added another entire chapter to a proposed table of contents already beginning to look too long. On the other hand, this story-within-a-story seemed laden with insight too rich to be sloughed by relating only a few high points. Excerpts from the candidate interviews and the ensuing deliberations warranted reporting with a level of detail adequate to communicate the essence of what was going on.

A problem with presenting the story in isolation was the absence of context in which to place it. Nor was there a point of reference so that

I could tell the reader where to find information on topics neglected in this telling. This was especially so in regard to method. I felt compelled to provide a description of how I had conducted the study; never before had I made that explanation. Later, when I turned full attention to writing the monograph, the same problem reappeared in reverse: I felt I had already paid sufficient attention to method. In the late 1960s, however, an educator audience unfamiliar with ethnographic approaches wanted that information spelled out in detail.

Still, Spindler suggested paring my discussion of method, to keep the focus on the descriptive account. Were I writing the article today, I would devote even less space to method than you will find here. I do not believe that every time we sit down to draft a qualitative study we must reinvent qualitative research all over again. Whenever I make that statement to an audience of students or faculty, however, there is always someone to remind me that in his or her department one is expected to defend the entire approach at each calling forth. If there is room for compromise, my recommendation is to report in adequate detail how one obtained those data *actually used in preparing the account*, not the "methodology" (as it is so often referred to) of the entire study.

The article was written to stand alone, independent from the monograph, and that it does. It illustrates how a subset of data from a larger study can be used to suggest aspects of the whole, the synecdoche about which we have been hearing in recent preoccupation with ethnography as text. I also call attention to the way chronological events have been rearranged to allow the story to unfold in a sequence different from the way the events occurred. The sequence for this retelling derives from the (important) way candidates were ranked in a final assessment rather than from the (unimportant) order in which they were interviewed.

Following an overview and discussion of method, the descriptive account details the proceedings of the Principal Selection Committee. Under the subtitle "Discussion and Comments," three themes are identified to pull the account together and connect it to the full study. Keep in mind, however, that it is I who put the themes there: I did not find them, discover them, or uncover them; I *imposed* them. I offer them as a perspective, a way to view these events (as well as others observed and not reported) in some encompassing way that points to underlying behavior patterns rather than to discrete events. In the chapter's final pages, in what I then subtitled "Conclusion" but today would call "An Interpretation," I suggest a broad perspective that invites another way of viewing continuity and change in schools. That topic has been a focal point of educational research for decades.

A further and rather lighthearted reason for my claim that this writing can serve as an exemplary model is that not only does it have the requisite elements for a proper account—clearly stated purpose, literature review (in this case, pointing instead to the absence of literature), method, description, analysis, interpretation—it also has a lengthy two-part title. I must admit that such titles are an academic affectation to which I have become somewhat addicted. Although the title of this chapter is hardly an example, even academic titles can be fun. The traditional colon provides opportunity to be playful with part of a title yet studiously descriptive as well, as illustrated by the titles of both chapters in the next part. Our works are not overburdened by playfulness.

With further revision, the rewritten draft accomplished what Spindler and I hoped it would. It complemented the intended monograph, drawing on that fieldwork in a different way. My problem as storyteller was to get as quickly as possible to the proceedings of the Principal Selection Committee without burdening the reader with the level of detail planned for the full account. I realized, for example, that it did not matter which member of the committee was the case study principal. Nor was the order in which candidates actually appeared for interviews of any consequence. Introducing only some candidates, rather than all 14, and presenting them in the order in which they ultimately were ranked, seemed a way to help readers focus on the subtle winnowing process taking place.

All the successful candidates were known by name or reputation to the members of the selection committee. That familiarity, coupled with the casual manner of the proceedings, precluded anyone on the committee from discerning the pattern evident in their choices. Nor did I recognize it myself until I stopped thinking in terms of individual personalities and started thinking in terms of demographic data: age, sex, background, recent experience, type and amount of formal education, marital status. Never have I been more surprised by the analysis of my own data, and simple demographic data at that! Perhaps this once, the data really did speak for themselves, if only softly, only to me.

But they didn't, of course. And in the late 1960s, it was hardly earth-shattering that an all-male group of principals would find a subset of slightly younger replicas of themselves best qualified to fill vacancies in their ranks. That did not seem any more remarkable at the time to me than it did to them, except that they prided themselves for serving and contributing to a school system recognized for being both fair and progressive.

I pondered themes I could discern in the data that were consistent with my observations throughout the fieldwork. I came up with a complementary set of two. First was the lack of either esoteric knowledge or esoteric language evident in their efforts to assess the candidates or to match candidates' talents with the requirements of the position. Second was the high regard that committee members demonstrated for the feelings and sensitivities of each other and for the candidates as people. One of the worst things going—or not going—for any candidate was to have no member of the committee who could speak positively and personally on his or her behalf. That circumstance conveniently excluded any outsider from serious consideration, whether external to the school system or working at another level within it.

I have acknowledged my tendency to cut things up or put them together in sets of three. Nevertheless, two themes were all I had identified when I was ready to circulate an early draft of my revised article among other colleagues.

I was particularly anxious to strengthen any anthropological insight that could be added, and my circle of reviewers included anthropologist Alfred G. Smith, then a colleague at the University of Oregon. Smith's broad-ranging interests at the time included his course "Cybernetics and Anthropology." In place of providing me with some insight from the anthropological study of social organization, Smith drew upon cybernetics to suggest how the principals in my account seemed to be engaging in what he called "variety-reducing" rather than "variety-generating" behavior.

My initial reaction was one of disappointment. I was trying self-consciously to make the paper "more anthropological," and my second anthropologist-critic was proposing a term that I have never heard uttered by another anthropologist, before or since. Variety-reducing behavior indeed! Nevertheless, Smith not only lauded my draft for its "little whitecaps of insight" but anticipated my preoccupation with demonstrating its strong disciplinary roots. "What do you care whether or not the paper is 'anthropological'?" he noted. "What you really want is a good paper, right?"

Wrong! Well, no, I did want a good paper. But I also wanted it clearly to demonstrate an anthropological perspective. That was the reason I chose cultural themes as my vehicle of analysis, following the "technical sense" of the concept—the tacitly approved postulates of a society—suggested earlier by Morris Opler (1945, 1959; see also Agar, 1979, 1980). Although I failed to recognize it initially, Smith had shown me the way, viewing my data through a perspective from general systems theory.

I realized that how Smith perceived this small group of principals to be acting, in their temporary assignment as members of the Principal Selection Committee, might also provide a perspective for organizing the entire account. Their efforts served to help keep things manageable in the face of a constant buffeting from the forces of change whirling about them. That "coming into clearer focus" is presaged in the first paragraph of my Conclusion. It not only added a closing comment to the chapter I was preparing for Spindler but heralded a major shift in my conceptualization of the principal's role in writing once again under way for the monograph. "Variety-reducing behavior" helped me identify an overriding ethos that seemed to account not only for role behavior but for the paradoxes that principals themselves observed between their ideal role and their real one (as discussed in "Patience and Prudence," one of the final chapters of the monograph).

## On Reflection

"And what if Peter *hadn't* caught the wolf? What then?" muses grandfather in the tale of Peter and the Wolf. And what if the Principal Selection Committee had selected different finalists—the 61-year-old female candidate, for example? Or I had chosen a different event to portray? Or different reviewers had been invited to critique the draft? What role did serendipity play here?

That the selected candidates were so strikingly similar had indeed escaped me initially. Although that observation lends drama to the anecdote, the similarity may not be as crucial as one might think. Had the committee selected their only female candidate, for example, the concept of variety-reducing behavior might nonetheless have remained suitable. With such a selection, they would have appeased mild pressure to admit more women into administrative ranks (there were three female principals in the school district at the time), while the few years of service remaining to her would not have threatened prevailing male domination of the role.

As far as the choice of episodes, this one had particular appeal as a brief, self-contained story with a natural beginning and ending. But it was not atypical of the way principals interacted in the conduct of other collective business transacted during school hours and almost exclusively among themselves (who else is free then?), away from their individual schools. As noted in the text, their mandate to screen applicants who would become their successors was not unlike Pettitt's observation of the challenge to elder tribesmen among North American Indians to "review, analyze, dramatize, and defend their cultural heritage" before each new group of initiates (Pettitt, 1946, p. 182). In deliberations as members of a selection committee, that is exactly what an anthropologically oriented observer saw them doing.

Had I missed those sessions (I was there because the case study principal happened to be assigned to the committee, and, at that, it was only my good fortune that my schedule allowed me to attend all three sessions for their full duration), some other set of observations would have served as well. The test is whether the broad interpretation beginning to emerge would have been appropriate and adequate in those other settings. I can only offer a hope—no, I'll state that more strongly: a firm conviction—that it would have.

What seems most fortuitous was my choice of reviewers. Most certainly I would not have come upon the variety-reducing concept on my own. I trust that I would have realized that principals' spoken-of roles as change agents, another dominant theme in the educational administration literature at the time (and still bandied about today), contrasted sharply with the maintenance role they played from day to day in their effort at containment. (That is a good example of the kind of paradox discussed in the next chapter, "Confessions of a 'Trained' Observer.")

Most important was the lesson Spindler finally got across to me—after only 8 years!—of the ethnographic commitment to detail and how best to use ethnographic data by staying case specific. In what may have been the biggest generalization he ever made, he cautioned in his concluding suggestions about my first draft, "An ethnography never generalizes to other cases. One might, in interpretation, compare with *specific* other cases, or hypothesize about a broader scope of phenomena."

Of course, there must be a *capacity* for generalization; otherwise there would be no point to giving such careful attention to the single case. The art of descriptive research, I believe, is in portraying the case at hand so well that readers themselves make the generalizations for us. They fill in or complete the pattern work that we outline only faintly.

Whether this was ethnography at all is quite another matter, a topic I have addressed elsewhere (Wolcott, 1982). That is why the monograph has a two-part title. My important declaration "An Ethnography" follows the colon to reassure the reader of my intent. Anthropological life history was well established at the time, but there was less precedent for so role oriented a study. As Richard Fox (1991) has subsequently paraphrased it (p. 12), I think Spindler was anxious to have me "writing about the everyday life of persons, not the cultural life of a people. This has been described as the ethnography of the particular (see Abu-Lughod, 1991, pp. 149-160). Attending to the "everyday life of persons" seems good advice for all qualitative researchers, not just the more anthropologically oriented ones.

## References

Abu-Lughod, Lila. (1991). Writing against culture. In Richard G. Fox (Ed.), *Recapturing anthropology: Working in the present* (pp. 137-162). Santa Fe, NM: School of American Research Press.

Agar, Michael M. (1979). Themes revisited: Some problems in cognitive anthropology. *Discourse Processes, 2*(1), 11-31.

Agar, Michael M. (1980). Stories, background knowledge and themes: Problems in the analysis of life history narrative. *American Ethnologist, 7*, 223-239.

Barnhardt, Ray, Chilcott, John, & Wolcott, Harry F. (Eds.). (1979). *Anthropology and educational administration*. Tucson, AZ: Impresora Sahuaro.

Erickson, Donald A. (Ed.). (1977). *Educational organization and administration*. Berkeley, CA: McCutchan.

Fox, Richard G. (Ed.). (1991). *Recapturing anthropology: Working in the present*. Santa Fe, NM: School of American Research Press.

Geertz, Clifford. (1973). Thick description. In C. Geertz (Ed.), *The interpretation of cultures* (pp. 3-30). New York: Basic Books.

Opler, Morris E. (1945). Themes as dynamic forces in culture. *American Journal of Sociology,* *51,* 198-206.

Opler, Morris E. (1959). Component, assemblage, and theme in cultural integration and differentiation. *American Anthropologist, 61,* 955-964.

Pettitt, George A. (1946). *Primitive education in North America* (Publications in American Archaeology and Ethnology 43). Berkeley: University of California.

Spindler, George D. (Ed.). (1955). *Education and anthropology.* Stanford, CA: Stanford University Press.

Spindler, George D. (1963). *Education and culture: Anthropological approaches.* New York: Holt, Rinehart & Winston.

Spindler, George D. (1974). *Education and cultural process: Toward an anthropology of education.* New York: Holt, Rinehart & Winston.

Spindler, George D. (1982). *Doing the ethnography of schooling: Educational anthropology in action.* New York: Holt, Rinehart & Winston. (Reissued 1988 by Waveland Press, Prospect Heights, IL)

Spindler, George D. (1987a). *Education and cultural process: Anthropological approaches* (2nd ed.). Prospect Heights, IL: Waveland.

Spindler, George D. (Ed. with Louise Spindler). (1987b). *Interpretive ethnography of education: At home and abroad.* Hillsdale, NJ: Lawrence Erlbaum.

Wolcott, Harry F. (1967). *A Kwakiutl village and school.* New York: Holt, Rinehart & Winston. (Reissued 1984, 2nd printing 1989, by Waveland Press, Prospect Heights, IL)

Wolcott, Harry F. (1973). *The man in the principal's office: An ethnography.* New York: Holt, Rinehart & Winston. (Reissued with a new preface in 1984 by Waveland Press, Prospect Heights, IL)

Wolcott, Harry F. (1982). Mirrors, models, and monitors: Educator adaptations of the ethnographic innovation. In George Spindler (Ed.), *Doing the ethnography of schooling: Educational ethnography in action* (pp. 68-95). New York: Holt, Rinehart and Winston. (Reissued 1988 by Waveland Press, Prospect Heights, IL)

# THE ELEMENTARY SCHOOL PRINCIPAL

## Notes From a Field Study

"Harry, you ought to watch the company you keep," quipped a colleague from the university when he encountered me at lunch one day with a group of five elementary school principals. "He does!" came the immediate retort from the principal sitting next to me.

The principals had just completed an all-morning meeting at the school district central office, where they had been appointed to serve as a Principal Selection Committee for the school district. As such, they were to interview and recommend candidates to fill new positions as

"The Elementary School Principal: Notes from a Field Study" first appeared in Spindler's edited volume *Education and Cultural Process: Toward an Anthropology of Education*, pp. 176-204, published by Holt, Rinehart and Winston in 1974. Subsequently it was reprinted in two edited collections focusing on educational administration: Donald Erickson's *Educational Organization and Administration* (McCutchan, 1977) and Ray Barnhardt, John Chilcott, and Harry Wolcott, *Anthropology and Educational Administration* (Impresora Sahuaro, 1979). In 1987 Spindler brought out a second edition of *Education and Cultural Process*, this one subtitled *Anthropological Approaches* and published by Waveland Press. The chapter was retained in the second edition and appears on pages 245-273. It is reprinted here with permission of Waveland Press.

elementary school principals for the following school year. I had been
present at their morning session in the role of an ethnographer inquiring into the life and work of the elementary school principal from an
anthropological perspective.

This chapter draws upon a larger study designed to provide an
ethnographic-type account of the elementary school principalship by
means of an extensive case study of one principal (Wolcott 1973). In
the present chapter, I have selected from the field notes an episode in
which attention is drawn to the behavior of a small group of principals
rather than to the behavior of an individual. The context of this episode
is the proceedings of the Principal Selection Committee. A major portion
of the chapter is devoted to a descriptive account of the proceedings
of this committee and a discussion and comment based on the data
presented. The chapter begins with an overview of the perspective and
methods basic to the entire field study.[1]

## The Ethnographic Approach

The apparent neglect of attention to the *actual* behavior of school
administrators in the literature on educational administration led to
the proposal for conducting this research. That literature could well be
augmented by a series of detailed ethnographic-type accounts of the
actual behavior of people occupying roles in professional education,
contextualized not only in terms of the formally organized institution
in which they work but also in terms of their lives as human beings
interacting within the context of a broader cultural milieu. This study
was designed specifically to provide such data about the elementary
school principalship.

The ethnographer's task is the recording of human behavior in cultural
terms. The standard ethnography provides an account of some cultural
process, such as law or divorce, or the way of life of some particular
group of people, such as the Tikopia or the Children of Sanchez. This
study is ethnographic to the extent that the principal who provides
the focus for it is seen as an interacting member of a cultural system.
Because the study is social and cultural rather than psychological in
orientation, its scope includes not only the behavior of the principal
himself but also the behavior of those with whom a principal interacts
in the course of his professional life. This includes to some degree his
spouse, his family, and his friends, and to a greater degree teachers,
other administrators, parents, and pupils. These roles, and the inter-

action of the people filling them, are the human elements of a cultural system, the school system of one community. To the extent that the cultural system involved in this study is similar to other cultural systems serving the same purpose, this ethnography of a single principal should produce knowledge relevant to the understanding of such roles and cultural systems in general.

There are other ways one might proceed in studying a school administrator, one of which would be for the ethnographer to obtain such a position. In prior fieldwork, however, I had become acutely aware of the limitations on one's ability to objectively observe processes in which he is deeply involved as a participant (Wolcott 1967).

The literature dealing with school administration might have been expected to serve as a source of information about administrative behavior, but that body of writings is susceptible to several of the limitations which characterize the literature of professional education more generally. One such limitation is that much of the literature is hortatory or normative in content. It tells principals (or teachers, or superintendents) how they *ought* to act. It is prescriptive rather than descriptive. Literature of this type can provide a source for inquiring into the *ideal* world of formal education (Lee 1963), but it fails to provide an account of what actually goes on or how the ideals are translated into real behavior. The literature that *is* empirically based, on the other hand, provides factual data which tend to tell too little about too much. Such data prove valuable as a source of census information; for example, we can readily obtain a description of the "average" American elementary school principal (DESP 1968):

a male
married
between the ages of 35 and 49
has had 10 to 19 years total experience in schools
was an elementary classroom teacher just prior to assuming
  his administrative post.

This description fits the case-study principal perfectly. Yet the data provide little insight into how one becomes a principal, how a principal acts, or what he finds satisfying and perplexing about his role.

The barrage of questionnaires that confront public school personnel to inventory their training, habits, and preferences might also be expected to provide data about the principalship. However, the people who compose these questionnaires have frequently failed to do careful preliminary fieldwork. The information obtained in answer to questions like "Should a principal attend church regularly?" may reveal little more than the tendency of school administrators to give "expected" responses. Such studies seem to ignore the consequence that if the questions one asks are not crucial, differences in responses are not crucial either.

The nearest approximation we usually get to the actual behavior of administrators is from data based on self-reporting techniques. These techniques have frequently been employed in studies of school principals. Although self-reporting is somewhat comparable to one of the standard methods by which ethnographic accounts have been obtained— intensive interviews with a single or a few selected informants—it is far more subject to problems of informant reliability than is the method of intensive interviewing employed as one of a number of data-gathering techniques in the ethnographer's multi-instrument approach.

The ethnographic approach taken in this study has not been widely employed in conducting research in school settings. To my amazement I have occasionally been asked, "Did the principal know you were making the study?" I spent weeks searching for a suitable and willing subject, and I did not request formal permission from the school district to conduct the study until I had the personal permission and commitment of the selected individual. His family, his faculty and staff, his fellow principals, and many visitors to the school knew something about the research project. The faculty assigned me the nickname "The Shadow" as a way to jokingly acknowledge my presence and purpose at their school, and the name was learned by some of the pupils, too.

In order to learn how it is to be a principal, every aspect of the principal's life had some potential relevance for the study. I was once asked (somewhat facetiously, I suppose) whether I planned to take the principal's temperature each day. I replied, not at all facetiously, that were it readily available I would have recorded that information, just as it might be interesting to know what the principal and his family ate at each Sunday dinner, but I would obviously need priorities in my data gathering. My attention has been drawn primarily to such aspects of the principal's life as the who, what, where, and when of his personal encounters, the cultural themes manifested in his behavior and in his attempts to influence the behavior of those about him, and the problems and paradoxes inherent in the role of the principal. Although the behavior of one principal served as the focus of the study, the fieldwork provided extensive opportunities for observing many principals, ranging from the rather frequent and often informal contacts of the case study principal with administrators at nearby schools to his participation in the official sessions and formal meetings of his school district and his memberships in county, regional, and state organizations of elementary school principals.

## Methods in Fieldwork

An "ethnographic approach" implies commitment to a perspective in both the methods of field research and the handling of data in subsequent writing, but it does not explicate the methods for doing either. Whenever it has been expedient to describe my research methodology by a brief label I have leaned to the term "field study." Zelditch (1962) has stated a case for the merits of the participant observer approach in the field study without going to the extreme of insisting that participant observation entails only participating and observing. He argues, "a field study is not a single method gathering a single kind of information" (1962, p. 567); rather, the participant observer employs three different modes in his research: "enumeration to document frequency data; participant observation to describe incidents; and informant interviewing to learn institutionalized norms and statuses" (566). I shall use these three categories—enumeration, participant observation, and interviewing—to describe the specific techniques employed during my fieldwork.

### Enumeration and Census Data

1. Collecting copies of official notices sent to and from school to pupils, parents, or faculty (greatly facilitated by having a faculty mailbox in the office and by a school secretary who did not mind making an extra carbon of routine reports and correspondence).
2. Collecting copies of records (or, at the end of the year, the records themselves) of enrollments, reports, the principal's personal log of events, and daily notices written in a faculty notebook.
3. Collecting "time and motion" data by noting, at 60-second intervals over a carefully sampled period of two weeks at school, what the principal was doing, where he was, with whom he was interacting, and who was talking.
4. Mapping and photographing the school and neighborhood.[2]

## Participant Observation

The primary methodology used at the beginning of the study was that of participant observation. Customarily the principal introduced me by saying, "This is Harry Wolcott. He is from the university and doing some research in which I'm involved." This brief introduction seemed to serve as a sufficient explanation of my presence to all but the most curious, but anyone who asked was welcome to a fuller description. The principal and staff were remarkable in their capacity for allowing me to observe and record without insisting that I become an active participant in their conversations and activities. Although simply "keeping up" with a busy principal precluded the possibility of my ever being a totally passive observer, my active participation at school was limited primarily to engaging in the social banter of the faculty room during lunch or at coffee breaks.

I made it a practice to carry my notebook with me and to make entries in it almost continuously. My intent was to create a precedent for constant note-taking so that the people would feel it was natural for me to be writing regardless of the topics or events at hand. Notes were taken in longhand in complete and readable form whenever possible. When I could not make complete notes and still remain present as observer, I jotted brief notes in the margins of my notebook and completed the full account later, often before leaving the school building. I never returned to the school until a complete account from a previous period of observation was finished. Nothing was gained by my mere presence as an observer; until the notes from one visit were a matter of record, there was no point in returning to school and reducing the impact of one set of observations by imposing a more recent one. Ultimately the longhand entries were transcribed onto 5 by 8 papers, each entry describing a single event, whether a lengthy transcription such as that containing my notes of the three meetings of the Principal Selection Committee or brief entries such as

The principal said that when he called his wife to tell her he would be home by 5:30 this evening she replied, "So early! Why—what's wrong?"

As the principal is trying various keys in the lock [he had just received some duplicates from the central office but did not know which doors they fit] a little girl from grade two comes up quietly behind him, pokes him gently in the ribs, and says, "Boo." "Oh, my," he says. The little girl continues happily down the hall.

One of the objectives of this research was to see the principal in as many different settings appropriate to an ethnographic study as possible. It was easier, of course, to intrude on his professional life in connection with his work as a school administrator than to intrude into his personal life. At the school I was excluded, by prior arrangement, only from a few "touchy" parent conferences. Although more symbolic than functional, a table and chair were moved into the principal's office for my use. My observation extended to such settings as any school or school district activity or meeting, meetings of local, regional, and state educational organizations; formal and informal staff gatherings; in-service programs; and traveling to meetings with groups of principals.

In reviewing plans for the fieldwork with colleagues, I had been cautioned against becoming "overidentified" with the principal, particularly since he was the formally appointed status leader of the school. I visited often with teachers and staff members, including visits at school on days when I knew the principal was away. "Oh, checking up on us, eh?" someone would inevitably joke, leading me to feel that the caution against being overidentified with "the boss" had been well given.

My apprehension about being overidentified with the principal did not extend to those settings where he was away from his school. However, there are few guidelines for a researcher in accompanying a subject to see about a new battery for his automobile or to attend a service club luncheon. I was able to include within the scope of my observations such settings as the principal's home and family, business meetings at his church and the Sunday School class he teaches, trips to local businesses for school and personal reasons, Kiwanis luncheons, a family wedding and reception, and brief meetings with friends and neighbors.

## Informant Interviewing

These interviews were of several types. First were taped interviews of approximately one hour duration, structured but open-ended, which provided excellent data concerning the principal's family life (interviews with his wife and mother) and the perceptions of him as a school administrator (interviews with thirteen faculty and two staff members). The interviews took time to arrange and conduct, and they seemed to take an eternity to transcribe, but they proved extremely valuable for uncovering the range of perceptions and the extent of the affective content expressed by the teachers regarding their work and the people with whom they associated professionally. The fact that I requested each interview as a personal favor and that no interviewing was done until I had spent over half a year at the school undoubtedly contributed to the extensive and useful data gathered via this method.

Another approach was to ask all the pupils in each fifth- and sixth-grade classroom to write briefly (and anonymously) what they thought they would remember about the principal. The phrases which I suggested to them to start their writing were, "What kind of a principal is he?" "Pleasant memories are . . ."; and "One time I won't forget . . ." The comments I received ran the gamut of opinion, from the succinct response from a boy who wrote that his principal is "a Dam stopit one" to the reflection by a sixth-grade girl that "He is the kind of a principal who helps you figure it out." One boy wrote: "I won't fore get the time when my freind and I were blamed fore bilding a fire in the bath room."

The principal himself served as a primary informant, as he was not only the focus of the research but was to some extent a co-worker as well. I was never too explicit about what data I was gathering, nor did I often share my hunches or tentative analyses with him, but he correctly assumed that a brief recounting of what had occurred at school since my last visit would be helpful to the study. He enjoyed talking and visiting (I found that he did the talking one-third of the total school day during the "time and motion" study), so this self-appointed task came easily to him. At times he reflected on his personal feelings and philosophy and these statements provided valuable insights into his "ideal world." The juxtaposition of actual behavior and ideal behavior provides an excellent means for describing and analyzing a cultural system, and I was fortunate in having an informant who talked easily about aspects of his ideal world.

On a few occasions I emphasized the informant role and asked the principal to relate specific accounts. Plans were always discussed in advance when these sessions were to be taped. Important tapes included a session in which the principal summarized the opening of school and gave a forecast of the coming year, a session in which I asked him to review the wedding list and chat about the people who had been invited to his daughter's marriage and reception, and a session recorded in my automobile as we drove through the school-attendance area while the principal described the neighborhood to three new teachers who accompanied us.

A ten-page questionnaire designed for the study was distributed to all the faculty and staff at the end of the fieldwork. The questionnaire was particularly valuable in enabling me to obtain systematic data about the staff, as I could see no point in holding a long taped interview with each of the twenty-nine members of the regular and part-time staff. This questionnaire provided standard census data and information concerning each teacher's perceptions of the school, community, and classroom. It also provided an opportunity for all staff members to state their feelings about an "ideal" principal.

The use of the questionnaire provided me with a chance to thank the staff for their patience and help during the study. I felt that the questionnaire might also give me an opportunity to elicit staff reaction to the research project, and the last statement of the questionnaire was, "Some things the researcher may never have understood about this school are . . ." The question did not evoke much response, but it was flattering to read "I think you probably understand more than we may think." I delighted in the humor of one teacher who assumed (correctly) that I did not know "There is no Kotex dispenser in the [women's] restroom."

My presence in the school district throughout the study was, I suppose, viewed as a mixed blessing. The mild but constant surveillance produced little overt strain that could not be alleviated by joking, but I provided so little feedback that there was no "payoff" for the many people who shared their perceptions and feelings with me. Still, a sympathetic and nonevaluative listener can provide an unusual opportunity for emotional catharsis, and I was amazed at how often teachers and principals seemed to appreciate an opportunity to "speak their minds." In this regard I feel that my position as observer and information-getter was considerably enhanced by the fact that, like the teachers and administrators who were the subjects of the study, I spoke the "language" of educators and had been "on the firing line" as a classroom teacher. I believe the case-study principal also found some com- fort in having a part-time cohort with whom he could share something of the nature, complexity, and extent of problems which confronted him in the course of his daily work.

## From the Field Notes:
## Proceedings of the Principal Selection Committee

Any number of episodes recorded during the course of the fieldwork could have been drawn upon here to illustrate aspects of a principal's professional life. Many would call attention to the routine of a typical day and to the incessant questions, problems, and meetings that seem to make constant demands on a principal's time and resources. I have chosen instead to draw upon a rather unique set of events, the proceedings of the Principal Selection Committee. This committee met three times during one month in the spring of 1967. These meetings provided a special setting in which the principals appointed to an ad hoc screening committee found themselves compelled to review and define—for the purpose of evaluating candidates—the critical attributes and qualifications of their role. This charge to interview and endorse certain candidates to join their ranks, though directed only to the principals appointed to the committee, served as an annual renewal ceremony for all the elementary school principals of the district. The fact of their appointment and task, and the results of their interviews and deliberations, served to reaffirm publicly the standards and responsibilities of their office. The necessity for adding new members to their ranks occasioned a time when, like the elders among North American Indian tribes, the principals were obliged to "review, analyze, dramatize, and defend their cultural heritage" (Pettitt 1946).

The circumstances underlying the committee's existence—who appointed it, the task it was given, how binding its recommendations would be—provide clues about the formal context in which it worked. As the committee convened, for example, no one explained nor questioned why it had five principals (among the twenty-seven elementary school principals in the district), how or why the four new members had been selected by the director of elementary education and why one member had been retained from the prior year (especially after the director commented, "I tried to eliminate people who had ideas from the past"), how many vacancies or at which schools they would occur ("We will need two people, maybe three. We should pick our best people, not for [specific] positions but for ability, because we don't know where they will go"), or how binding the committee's actions would be on the ultimate recommendation which the superintendent would make to the school board. It was customary in this school district for the director of elementary education to appoint committees of varying sizes and varying purposes, and it was part of her job to "know" when she had sufficient authority to make appointments on her own or when she, in turn, needed the approval of the assistant superintendent or superintendent. The principals seemed to assume that she would be present during their meetings, and she slipped easily into the role of informal chairperson of the group.

For the principals appointed to the committee, to select "two, maybe three" candidates apparently provided sufficient parameters for their task, since in their ultimate decision they ranked the most "controversial" of the acceptable candidates as number four. No one pressed to learn why the number of vacancies was ambiguous. Two new schools were to be opened in the fall. If "maybe three" vacancies were to occur, there was more than mere conjecture about which principals might be in disfavor among the powers in the central office. (The third vacancy proved later to be due to an as yet unannounced plan for administrative reorganization which required the full-time services of one elementary school principal in the central office.)

Although the recommendation of the committee could be ignored by the superintendent, it did not necessarily mean it would be. The new members checked with the principal who had already served on the committee to reassure themselves that recommendations made the previous year had been honored. The confidence expressed in the superintendent was formal and reciprocal. The committee showed no inclination to test the extent of its power or to threaten the power of the superintendent by making radical or unexpected recommendations. Attention was addressed specifically to assessing each candidate's standing "in the eyes of the superintendent" during discussions prior and subsequent to the interviews. In turn, official recognition was accorded to the committee through brief appearances before and during its sessions by the director of personnel, the assistant superintendent, and the superintendent.

During the total twelve hours of interview and discussion through which members of the Principal Selection Committee sat, fourteen possible candidates were reviewed. A brief profile of the candidates as a group showed them to include male and female applicants from within and outside the district, all holding a master's degree and all experienced elementary school teachers. In age they ranged from thirty-one to sixty-one. Their total experience in professional education varied from eight to thirty-nine years.

The extent of significant variation among the candidates is less than this description implies. One applicant who was not seriously considered and who was not invited for an interview accounted for most of the variation. She was the only female applicant and had served in an administrative capacity for only one year some fourteen years previously. In age and teaching experience she had thirteen more years than the next most senior applicant. The committee shared the feelings of one principal who summarized, "I think she's a wonderful gal and a fine teacher, but I question anyone going into this at 61." While age provided the immediate basis for a decision not to consider her further, it is likely that sex would have been the critical issue had she been younger. Three of the district's twenty-seven elementary schools were administered by women. As one male principal had candidly remarked on a prior occasion, "It's going to be a long time before we put in another woman." Some candidates were dropped after only a brief comment as the committee sought ways to reduce the number of people who were to be accorded interviews and serious consideration. Regarding a relatively young newcomer in the district who had asked to be considered, for example, no one added any further comment after one principal expressed the opinion, "I see too many people ahead of him." Someone added, "The same with so-and-so." A third principal immediately suggested dropping both their names. Consideration of another applicant, an administrator from outside the district, was summarily ended when the personnel director, during a brief preview of the slate of candidates, recalled that this applicant had "already been hired [i.e., offered a contract] once in this district" and certainly should not have the opportunity to turn them down again. The committee agreed that there was no point in retaining names of people who were not going to be considered among the top eligible candidates, and they expressed concern over the problem of "getting the hopes up" among candidates called in for interviews. Yet any time a candidate's name was about to be dropped permanently, there was some hedging about giving everyone a chance. The frequent statement, "Let's just leave his name on for now" revealed a reluctance to take decisive and final action (eliminating a candidate) when less decisive action (ranking eight "top" candidates for three positions) accomplished the same purpose without requiring the ultimatum.

As the preliminary discussion of the candidates continued, based on the perusal of each candidate's folder of letters and recommendations, two procedural questions were discussed. The first was whether candidates would be selected only from within the district. The assistant superintendent observed that no outsider had been appointed to an elementary school principalship for many years. "We shouldn't overlook good people from outside, but in the past when things have been equal we have given preference for 'in-district.' " The tradition of selecting applicants from within the district was reaffirmed in the final recommendation made by the committee, although two out-of-district candidates were called for interviews. The rationale for interviewing "outsiders" was that the district did not wish to foster the impression that promotions to administrative positions were made only from within the ranks. To reaffirm among themselves that good candidates were always being sought, one principal recounted how an outstanding principal from California had "almost" been hired in a previous year. Another principal reminded the committee that any candidate "might come teach with us first" and work up into a principalship through promotion within the system.

The other procedural question dealt with the manner of conducting the interviews. The alternatives considered were to hold informal interviews, to ask candidates a set of prearranged questions (e.g., "What do you see as the role of the principal?" "How can the principal make the best use of teacher competencies?") or to guide the interview by using either an "in-basket"[3] or a problem approach. The pros and cons of each approach were discussed briefly. When the director of elementary education recalled that in a prior year one of the present applicants had been interviewed by using a structured interview technique, interest in that approach quickly subsided. Though never formally resolved, the actual procedure followed in the interviews was unstructured and was oriented primarily to getting a candidate to talk freely about his experiences, his beliefs about teaching, and his thoughts about the role of the school and the role of the principal.

Excerpts from the interviews and discussions are presented below. I have rearranged the actual order of interviews and have presented the candidates here according to the final rank order decided upon by the committee. The name of each candidate's ordinal position in the final ranking is used as a pseudonym.

## Mr. Seventh

Mr. Seventh, age forty-eight, was an out-of-district candidate. Off and on he had been working toward a doctorate in education at the local university. He had served in administrative capacities, first as a principal and more recently as an assistant superintendent, for twenty-two of his twenty-five years in education. At the beginning of his brief interview he was asked whether he would plan to stay in the district if he completed his doctorate. He said that even with a doctorate he felt he might be able to advance sufficiently in a district of this size (over 20,000 students) to keep him there. He added that he might not finish his doctorate anyway. One principal joked with him about wanting to "go beyond" the principalship: "Isn't the principal about the best thing you can be?"

One of the interviewing principals had served years before as a teacher in a school where the candidate was principal, and he later said of him, "I think he'd be a pretty good candidate—he's pretty strong." At age forty-eight, however, the committee seemed reluctant to endorse him. Their reservations were reinforced by their suspicion that he wanted to get into their school district only because of its proximity to the university so he could complete his graduate work. When it finally came time to draw the line on candidates, Mr. Seventh's presumed lack of commitment to the principal role and his potential mobility, especially were he to complete his graduate studies, served as the basis for a low ranking. As one principal summarized, "I would have ranked Seventh higher, but I think of the elementary principalship as a career. He's a stronger candidate than some of the others, but I just don't think he's going to stay—he'll stay about four or five years and use us as a stepping stone."

## Mr. Fifth

Mr. Fifth, 39, also from outside the district, had been principal of a large elementary school in a growing but still rural community for the previous five of his twelve years in public school work. In spite of his long tenure, his experience, which was confined primarily to rural schools, was regarded as a serious handicap. "Coming from those rural communities, he will be facing a real change if he comes here to be an elementary school principal," noted one committee member. "Would he be willing to come here as a *teacher*?" asked another. At the time they decided to invite him for an interview, members of the committee also tacitly assumed that his age and experience had probably narrowed the range of positions he would accept to that of a principalship. They found themselves in agreement that his rural-conservative school experience had probably failed to provide him with a sufficiently "exciting" background from which he might make a contribution to their own schools (thus rather subtly reinforcing the explicit preference for candidates who have worked in their own district, one they perceive as a school system in which the program *is* exciting).

Committee members were cordial in their greetings and introductions when Mr. Fifth appeared for his interview. He was directed to choose one of the (few) comfortable chairs in the meeting room, prompting the personnel director to joke, "It won't be this comfortable again." After a folksy prelude, the director of elementary education asked, "What things have you been doing and how have you been involved?"

**Mr. Fifth:** Ma'am?

**Director Of Elementary Education:** Well, if you were a principal, what kinds of changes would you want to make?

**Mr. Fifth:** It would depend on what I found. If I found some needs, I would move in and meet those needs.

**Interviewing Principal:** How do you see the role of the counselor in relation to the principal?

**Mr. Fifth:** I see the principal as a sort of mediator—right in the middle—if there is a middle.

He described a two-stage role for the principal, first in getting the cooperation of the staff, then in a "selling" role to convince the parents. To illustrate, he elaborated upon an experimental "group counseling situation" recently set up at his school, a topic of immediate interest to the interviewing principals because of districtwide efforts to develop a counseling program at each elementary school.

**Interviewing Principal:** How were the children selected for your group counseling?

**Mr. Fifth:** Well, being in the school for four years, I pretty well knew which children needed help. Our goals were to help Bill Jones get some subjects so he could do his doctorate. But of course if I was setting up a [real] program, I would identify which kids needed certain things.

**Interviewing Principal:** How have you gotten teacher involvement in curriculum development in your district?

**Mr. Fifth:** We gave them their choice: "Do you want math or do you want social studies?" You see, they had a choice of what they would do. [There was some laughter at this. One interviewer asked, "No third choice?" Another joked, "Oh, there's a third choice, all right."]

**Interviewing Principal:** Is everyone on one of the two committees?

**Mr. Fifth:** Yes.

**Interviewing Principal:** Why do you say you like autonomy?

**Mr. Fifth:** I like to be an individual, just like you do.

**Interviewing Principal:** Do you like your teachers to be individuals, too?

**Mr. Fifth:** Yes. As a matter of fact, I encourage it.

**Interviewing Principal:** What do you feel is the role of the departmentalized program in the elementary school?

**Mr. Fifth:** We have "self-contained,"[4] yet I guess there are more exceptions than the rule. [He described his reading program, a one-hour uninterrupted period during which the children are regrouped.] It's a sort of modified Joplin plan. . . . We have Bible class but we don't let it interfere with reading.

His discussion of the reading program prompted him to comment about the extensive "help" received at his school from a nearby teacher's college:

**Mr. Fifth:** So much help can be a problem. For example, in our building we have fourteen teachers, two aides, nine high school cadet helpers, twenty-eight teacher trainees (ranging from part-time observers to student teachers), plus our own music and special education people, plus five more coming in doing research from the college. After describing how many people are in and out of the building, you could see why I would want to leave.

**Interviewing Principal:** It's not so rare here, either. This morning I had thirteen visitors, four teacher trainees, seven students observing from the university, and three policemen, plus the regular faculty.

The question of salary was introduced as a point of information by one of the interviewing principals, who explained that in the district an administrator's salary is not dependent upon school size but on tenure. The personnel director explained the administrative salary schedule in some detail: "Roughly, a principal gets one-fifth above the teaching schedule. So in your case, the teaching salary of $8,000 for a teacher with a master's degree and ten years of experience [the maximum years of nondistrict experience acceptable in the school district for purposes of salary evaluation] plus one-fifth is about $11,000 for ten months. A total of 205 days; $11,000." Mr. Fifth said that at present he was on an eleven-month contract. "You gain a month there," was the reply. He was informed that many school personnel work for the school district in the summer, writing curriculum or teaching summer school, "but not on the administrative [salary] schedule, of course."

Following the interview, committee members chatted as they watched Mr. Fifth walk out onto the parking lot, get into his pick-up truck, and drive away. "My wife once applied for a teaching position in that district," commented one principal. "It was *very* conservative!!"

In the review of the candidates at the conclusion of all the interviews the following comment of one interviewing principal seemed to summarize the reaction to Mr. Fifth: "We're doing *so much* here for boys and girls. We've gone about as far as we can. These fellows from outside have a real disadvantage, because they're still talking about getting kids in and out of rooms, holding ball games, and so on. I think he'd come along pretty well in a couple of years. He'd know our lingo and he'd be doing a good job. It might just take him a little longer."

A second principal concluded the discussion: "The more he talked, the farther I got from him."

Mr. Fifth, Mr. Seventh, and, in all, the names of ten applicants were excluded from the list of candidates recommended to the superintendent. Slight as the variation was among the original panel of fourteen candidates, the variation among the final four candidates chosen was even less. The four were married males between the ages of thirty-one and thirty-four. They had been in professional education from eight to twelve years, had all taught in the upper elementary grades, and all held degrees received five to ten years earlier at the master's level. Each candidate had been with the district from five to ten years. Although they held somewhat different positions at the moment (administrative intern, teacher on leave to pursue a doctoral program, resource teacher, junior high vice principal), each candidate had managed to alter his status from that of the full-time elementary classroom teacher he had once been; none now had direct teaching responsibilities. With the exception of the resource teacher (an extra teacher assigned full-time to a school to provide instructional assistance to the staff), all had held positions specifically entailing administrative duties. All four were considered eminently qualified to assume a principalship. Each candidate had achieved his present visibility *within* the district. With the exception of Mr. Fourth, each had achieved this visibility without stepping on the wrong toes.

Mr. Fourth's problem, at least in part, was that he had run head-on into a not-unknown obstacle in the path of a young man heading for the elementary principalship—the female administrator. A brief comment here concerning the different roles played by men and by women in the hierarchy of the elementary school, particularly in the professional relationship of the administration-bound male vis-à-vis the authority-holding female, may help put Mr. Fourth's problems as a candidate into perspective.

At the teaching level, the world of the elementary school is a world of women. At the administrative level the ratio of men to women is almost exactly reversed: 85 percent of the elementary school teachers are females (NEA Research Report 1967: 14); 78 percent of the elementary school principals are males (DESP 1968:11). The administration-bound male must obviously be able to survive in a predominantly female setting among his teacher colleagues. In addition, he must be able to survive in such relationships as that of student teacher-master teacher, or teacher-supervisor, where his immediate superior is most frequently a woman. And finally, there is a considerable likelihood that among the principals under whom he serves as a teacher he will be assigned to a "woman principal"[5] at least once—an assignment which probably exceeds random chance because female administrators seem particularly sensitive about securing teachers with whom their male pupils can "identify." Thus while women administrators do not exert a majority influence in the formal organization of their peers (indeed, in that era just prior to Women's Lib, I believe I detected a tendency among male principals to keep their few female colleagues "in their place" in their professional organizations by relegating to them such assignments as taking charge of table decorations, sending out invitations and thank-you letters, and performing minor bookkeeping tasks), the women exert a powerful influence as gatekeepers to the principalship.

Among the fourteen candidates reviewed by the Principal Selection Committee the only two whose current dossiers contained overtly negative statements were two candidates working with female principals. Both had already achieved nonteaching assignments at their schools as resource teachers, and both maintained high involvement in the activities of the local teacher association. It was their active participation in the teacher association that provided the basis for some of the criticism which each candidate received in his evaluation. One principal noted two complaints in her written evaluation: one, that the candidate was "traditional" in his approach to teaching (an implied criticism and a somewhat irrelevant one since he was neither serving as a classroom teacher nor being considered for a teaching position); and two, that he conducted too much of the business of the teacher association at school, thus detracting from his responsibility as a resource teacher to assist the teaching faculty. "First things should be first," the principal had admonished in summary.

"In other words," the personnel director commented after the evaluation was read aloud to the committee, "the teachers aren't getting the help they need."

"That's the only man left on her staff," observed one principal. "As I recall, she wasn't satisfied with the only other guy on her staff last year, either."

## Mr. Fourth

Mr. Fourth had been highly regarded as a candidate the previous year. His candidacy was critically reviewed because members of the committee expressed some hesitation about his present status, particularly concerning a prevalent rumor that Mr. Fourth and his principal were not getting along very well. Differences between Mr. Fourth and his woman principal were more than hinted at, they were openly aired by committee members. The candidate himself commented on their relationship during his interview, "She's not too good for a man's ego—especially if you're a little inefficient like I am."

Unlike the procedure followed with any other candidate, Mr. Fourth's principal was invited to meet with the committee to share her views about his candidacy. Her discussion began with these comments:

> I think his one big problem is relating to people, because he tends to want to move too fast. . . . One thing he feels inadequate about is making small talk that makes people feel comfortable when they come to school. . . . I think he is better with men than women. I've talked to him about how as an administrator he will be working mostly with women, and he'll have to observe certain amenities.

To the direct question, "Do you think he should be an administrator—say, for example, in a smaller school or some special setting?" she replied, "If I had my druthers, I'd like to have him in a situation where he could get some help—especially in human relations. I think we need to realize he's been in a very difficult position this year, working with a woman. . . . He has told me, 'It hasn't been any morale boost to work *with you.*' "

Immediately after the conference with Mr. Fourth's principal, one principal said, "Well, she hasn't changed my ideas any. We talked last year about his impulsiveness and these other problems." Another principal said, "There's no question of his ability. But I do feel some reservations about him." Another added, "A member of my staff said he walked right by her the other day without speaking. She felt badly about it. Of course, that doesn't pertain here."

Mr. Fourth's position as a former favorite was altered only slightly, but it was sufficient to put him out of the running. One committee member noted that no doubt the outcome would have been different had Mr. Fourth still been assigned to his former school, working with a male principal who had helped both to groom and to sponsor him for the step into administration.

## Mr. Third

Mr. Third was less well known among committee members than any other in-district candidate. He had the briefest tenure in the district (five years), and this was his second consecutive year on leave in order to pursue graduate study toward a doctoral degree at the university. He helped reestablish his longevity by remarking to the committee as he entered for his interview, "I sat *here* last year," but the committee had already been reminded by the holdover member that Mr. Third had been "high on our list" the year before.

The search for topics to discuss was more difficult with a candidate who had not been active in the district for the past year and a half. As Mr. Third noted, "I've sort of lost track of some of these different programs." The discussion soon turned to the candidate's observations on the doctoral program at the university. The committee was receptive to his criticism that the "whole question of curriculum and administration at the university is all geared to secondary school." He told them that the set of qualifying examinations he had just written were all of the order, "Imagine yourself the principal of a *secondary school*. What would you do if . . ."

One interviewing principal asked how Mr. Third's previous school district compared with this one.

**Mr. Third:** The principals in this school district have a little more autonomy in the selection of staff.

**Interviewing Principal:** Is this autonomy a good thing?

**Mr. Third:** I think this situation is good.

**Interviewing Principal:** Why do you?

**Mr. Third:** So a staff can develop its abilities to the maximum. For example, maybe one staff can do more with "flexibility" than another.

Several times during the interview Mr. Third reaffirmed his belief in the importance of the elementary school principalship. In his concluding remarks he summarized, "I think the elementary principalship is a great challenge and quite different from other areas. You are working closely with individuals and different programs. . . . I've been an assistant principal, and now I'd like to try another notch up the ladder."

Mr. Third seemed to have made a good impression among the members of the committee. Their favorable reaction created some dilemmas which they discussed following his interview. One problem was his brief tenure: "He's the least experienced." Although his experience prior to coming to the district included two years as a teaching vice-principal, it was noted that he had held no position other than classroom teacher in his three active years in the district. An earlier bias expressed in the case of Mr. Seventh, who had been suspected of planning to come to the district in order to pursue a doctoral program at the university and then "moving on," was reinterpreted to differentiate between in-district candidates and out-of-district ones. "It's different in using the district if you've come up through the ranks or from outside it," suggested one principal. Mr. Third "might just be willing to stick around," posited another.

Mr. Third's recent efforts as a conscientious and effective supervisor of student teachers, fulfilling a part-time position on the university staff along with his program of studies, were duly noted by principals who had seen him in action: "Often these guys on a degree program don't have time to spend in supervising, but that's not the case here." Another principal added, "We've had some supervisors from the university who have missed a whole term."

Someone questioned, "We don't have anything on the salary schedule for a Ph.D. Couldn't he do better somewhere else?"

"He's told us he likes this district and wants to stay here," assured the assistant superintendent. "He doesn't want to be a professor."

I am quite sure I was the only person at the meeting who did not realize that the candidate was the superintendent's son-in-law.

## Mr. Second

Enthusiastic support of Mr. Second's candidacy was expressed before, during, and after his formal interview. His excellent performance as a teacher and resource teacher, that he "dealt with difficult situations very well" as an active member of the local teacher organization, his "energy and interest," his active role in church work, even that his father had been a principal—all were duly reviewed before the interview began. If there was any reservation expressed at all, it was only to suggest that a promotion to the principalship might be a bit premature at present. While comments like "he was highly considered last year" and "I think he has matured greatly" tended to dispel such reservations among committee members, one principal reminded the committee, "He'll be around another year."

Mr. Second's interview began with the suggestion that he describe his "present situation," his experience, and the new programs he was working on. He launched easily into a fifteen-minute description of

the educational program in the school where he was presently assigned. The following discussion was precipitated by his account of
that program.

**Interviewing Principal:** I think we've heard a lot about the program at your
school, and it's been a real good education. Now let's hear about how you
think of *yourself* in a program—what do *you* want in a program?

**Another Interviewing Principal:** Yes, what do you think is the unique role of
the elementary school?

**Mr. Second:** I think it is to take each child where he is and take him as far as
he can go. But that isn't unique to the elementary school. It's also junior
high, isn't it? Yet I'm not qualified for the junior high.

**Another Interviewing Principal:** Who has the responsibility for making
improvements in a school's program?

**Mr. Second:** That's the principal's job—along with the whole faculty, of course.
As an administrator, you should be the last one to take the glory.

To signal the start of the closing ritual during the interviews each
candidate was asked if he had questions to address to the members of
the committee. No candidate seemed to have a crucial question he
wanted to ask, but none forfeited the implicit challenge to be able to
ask *something*. The out-of-district candidates wondered which position
they were being interviewed for. The in-district candidates already
knew that this information was not yet available and that the decision
about the annual "administrator shuffle" had not been announced and
probably had not been made. Their questions concerned the dates
when appointments were to be announced or the types of appointments
to be made. The top two candidates expressed their concern about
appointments to smaller schools, since the word was out that one of
the new appointments might be for a "two-role" person (e.g., principal
of two smaller schools, or principal plus some other assignment in one
school). Mr. Second's query set off the following series of remarks in
this regard.

**Mr. Second:** I've been curious as to just how the joint principalships between
two schools work out?

**Interviewing Principal One:** I've worked with it and it leaves a lot to be desired.

**Interviewing Principal Two:** I think we took a step backward when we went
to it.

**Interviewing Principal One:** I think it is better to combine a half-time principal and a half-time resource teacher in *one* school.

**Interviewing Principal Three:** That looks good on paper but it never seems to work out.

**Interviewing Principal Two:** Of course, you know which one will give—just like when we principals have a conflict between supervision and administration.

**Interviewing Principal One:** There are no half-time jobs.

**Interviewing Principal Four:** How about combining the role of principal and the role of counselor?

**Interviewing Principal One:** With the role we're trying to create for the counselor, those two roles are not always compatible. When the axe has to fall, I'm the one who has to do it.

## Mr. First

Presently serving in his second year as a full-time junior high school vice-principal, Mr. First had already established himself in an administrative niche. His request to get "back" into the elementary schools was met with a pose of suspicion by members of the committee which masked (but just barely) the significance they attributed to his application as a reaffirmation of the importance of the role of the elementary school.

The discussion prior to Mr. First's interview included the following comments:

**Assistant Superintendent (reviewing his record):** He's been a junior high vice-principal two years, but it only took one year to make him want to come back.

**Interviewing Principal One:** He's been so nice to work with over there that for selfish reasons I'd like to see him stay at the junior high level. How did he happen to get put into junior high?

**Director Of Elementary Education:** They talked him into it one summer when I was away. They desperately needed a junior high vice-principal. He didn't know what his chances were for an elementary school position, so he took it.

**Interviewing Principal One:** Should he stay at junior high? Can he do any good there? Can he move up?

**Interviewing Principal Two:** I think we should interview him and find out his feelings about junior high, whether he wants to get back into elementary, and if so, why.

**Interviewing Principal Three:** How often do we ask people to do things in the district because it will be good for the district rather than for them? I'm not sure we're even doing these guys a favor.

**Assistant Superintendent:** Do you think that First's role on the Teacher-School Board Salary Committee has made a difference in how the Board might regard him? When we bring names to the Board, they react.

**Interviewing Principal One:** It might, but it shouldn't.

Mr. First's interview got off to a late but jovial beginning—he had thought his appointment was 11:40 a.m. instead of 10:40 a.m. and had to be telephoned at his school. His arrival precipitated the exchange of a few moments of raillery among those present. He knew everyone on the committee.

**Interviewing Principal:** What makes you think you want to be in a gang like this?

**Mr. First:** Are you serious? Do you want me to answer?

**Interviewing Principal:** Yes. That's really why we are all here.

**Mr. First:** Well, this is where I belong. This is where my training and my interest is.

Mr. First described programs and problems at his junior high school. He explained how he had tried to break down the resistance of those parents who "have the attitude that the school only calls once a year and that's when the kid is in trouble." He cited several aspects of secondary school administration which he disliked: "I don't like the sports emphasis in high school, the problems with buses and scheduling, the court cases. Last year I spent one day out of every two weeks in court. I'd rather be working with kids earlier in their lives, not in the kind of conference I sat in recently with a parent when a doctor told the mother her alternatives are either to give the daughter 'The Pill' or lock her up in a cage."

Another question gave him an opportunity to remind the committee of both his prior experience as a school administrator ("When I was an elementary principal in the Midwest," he began, "we had this problem . . .") and of an early encounter he had had with administrative rigidity. He described the attendance area of that school, a predominantly black slum area in a large city, as a "third-generation ADC neighborhood."[6] He discussed the program he had tried to initiate at the school: "It was a very peculiar nongraded program for a very peculiar neighborhood, a program for which the teachers and I were ready but the administration was not. I felt like I'd been kicked real hard when they turned down the program. That was about the time the director of elementary education came through recruiting teachers for this district. That's how I happened to come here."

**Interviewing Principal:** When you went back to the classroom after being an administrator, what were some of the problems?

**Mr. First:** Unwinding!! Not worrying so much about 50-minute programs.

**Mr. First:** One of my goals once was to go into teacher education. I used to think you could do the most good there, but I think now that's too far removed. You can do more good in the public schools—you're closer there. But it has some distasteful parts, too, like worrying over school budget elections or hassling with the school board over a $100 raise.

## Final Deliberation

Members of the Principal Selection Committee deliberated for almost an hour after interviewing the last of the candidates before reaching a decision on their recommendation to the superintendent. One principal suggested a straw vote to rank all candidates and "see how near we are to one mind." The director of elementary education proposed that they identify and rank the top five candidates. Selecting a panel of five candidates for a maximum of three positions followed the earlier recommendation of the personnel director who had suggested they rank more candidates than needed because "someone might not take it." When the straw ballot was taken, four "favorite" in-district candidates topped the list. That number was informally adopted as the number of candidates the committee would recommend. Another straw vote was taken which reaffirmed the original ranking of the top candidates but revealed that one committee member was disrupting what was an otherwise highly agreed upon rank order.

**Interviewing Principal One:** There's someone who is ranking a top candidate low. I wonder if there is something we should have talked about?

**Interviewing Principal Two:** I'm the one voting him low. Not because I have anything against him, but I still feel we have an obligation to another candidate. So I'm voting higher for him than I really feel about him. Yet I don't know if that's right, either.

Discussion, without further voting, revealed that all the members were satisfied with the composite results of the ranking and with the specific recommendation of the top candidates, as agreed upon from Mr. First to Mr. Fourth. The director of elementary education summarized: "I'll give these results, and our first vote, to the assistant superintendent. I'll tell him that before we would recommend anyone besides these top four we would want to discuss it."

The meeting, and the Principal Selection Committee itself, disbanded. "I'd much rather interview teachers," commented the case study principal. "So would I," added the director of elementary education.

## Discussion and Comments

The proceedings of the Principal Selection Committee were presented here because that event, though well removed from the daily routine of any principal, brought into bold relief several aspects central to the professional life of the case study principal and to the principals with whom he worked. The present discussion is limited to three interrelated dimensions of the principalship which seem to pervade the life and work of a principal and which are substantially reflected in the data presented. These dimensions are (1) the lack of professional knowledge associated with the role, (2) an esteem for personal feelings, and (3) a proclivity toward variety-reducing behavior.

### Lack of Professional Knowledge Associated With the Role

Throughout my fieldwork I was struck with the number of occasions in which principals communicated to each other uncertainties about what they "should" be doing and what is their "real" role. To any outsider, whether teacher, pupil, parent, or even researcher, the principals I met were always ready to describe and defend the importance of the elementary school and their contribution to its mission. In their own gatherings, however, free from their usual audiences and oblivious to the observer, they probed constantly for guidelines to answer one common and basic question, "What is the role of the principal?"

The role uncertainty of the principalship seems due in part to the problem of the lack of any professional (i.e., private and/or technical) knowledge or skill which clearly distinguishes the administrator from those administered. This problem is referred to broadly in the field of educational administration as that of working from a "limited knowledge base." Evidence of the limited knowledge base is illustrated in two ways in the proceedings of the Principal Selection Committee. First, in examining dialogue recorded during the committee's proceedings, one becomes aware of the absence of an esoteric technical vocabulary which might have been expected in other settings in the deliberations of such a "board of examiners." Except for Mr. Fifth's use of the terms "self-contained" and "a sort of modified Joplin plan" the vocabulary evident throughout the proceedings reflects the ambiguous and general terms that characterized the professional language of administrators observed throughout the study: "real challenge," "meeting needs," "good situation," "involvement . . . more autonomy," "unique program," "doing so much for boys and girls," and so forth. Indeed, to the extent that there is an esoteric language shared among professional educators (a language sometimes referred to jokingly within their circles as "pedagese"), principals express concern with their own ability to keep up with the latest changes in techniques or terminology. One principal observed, "You hire one or two new teachers and listen to them and you don't even know what they're talking about."

A second example of the problem of a limited knowledge base is suggested by the lack of systematic procedures by which the principals made evaluations necessary for ranking candidates. Having to make judgments which result in identifying one person as superior to another or which distinguish qualified from unqualified personnel can be a difficult and for some people a distasteful business. Nonetheless, the work of the schools is inexorably bound up with evaluating the performance of both staff and pupils. One of the crucial aspects of the principal's job in this school district, as it is elsewhere, is the annual process of preparing evaluative recommendations regarding personnel, particularly for those on probationary status. The lack of special skill or knowledge available to principals in performing this evaluative function was reflected collectively by the Selection Committee in the haphazard approach they took in interviewing and assessing candidates for the principalship. Whatever specific criteria each member of the committee used as a basis for judgment seemed to be assiduously avoided as a topic for mutual discussion and concern. One senses that each principal felt that regardless of the criteria he or his cohorts used, ultimately the group would reach substantially the same decisions regarding the selection and ranking of the candidates at hand. It should be pointed out in this regard that the final decision of the Committee did reflect just such a consensus.

### An Esteem for Personal Feelings

The case-study principal and his colleagues seemed to share a distaste for formal evaluative tasks. Their reluctance was particularly
apparent in the comments and jokes they made throughout the year
about preparing their formal "teacher evaluations" and by the collective anxiety they exhibited as the deadline neared for submitting those
reports to the central office. The same distaste was apparent throughout the meetings of the Principal Selection Committee as they spoke
of "getting this over with." But their lack of regard for the formality of
evaluation *procedures* should not be confused with their regard for the
personal feelings of those whom they were evaluating. Their esteem
for the feelings of the candidates, for the feelings of each other, and for
their own feelings and intuitions as part of the assessment task, are
repeatedly revealed in the dialogue. If the role of the principal can be
characterized by a lack of professional knowledge, as suggested above,
a compensating behavior of those who serve in it may be to give the
affective domain considerably more importance than one generally
associates with the processes of administration.

All candidates were interviewed graciously under circumstances in
which the formalities inherent in the setting, such as meeting by a tight
schedule of appointments at the central office, or holding most interviews seated around a large conference table in the formally designated
Board Room, were consciously underplayed. The interviewers attempted to engage candidates in light social banter as they arrived for
interviews. They asked open-ended questions, starting always with
a question intended to put each candidate at ease and let him "tell
something about himself." No question addressed to or response of a
candidate was treated with the air of a grueling interrogation. Concern
was expressed about interviewing any candidate for whom an invitation to appear for an interview might serve inappropriately to arouse
his hopes. At the same time, the names of persons whom the committee
never intended to consider as serious candidates were gently retained
rather than summarily dropped. The only candidate really "rejected,"
and this primarily at the suggestion of the personnel director, was an
out-of-district candidate who had once accepted and then rejected a
contract offered him by the school district.

The personal feelings of the interviewing principals also made their
way into the discussion of literally every candidate. Some of the
statements regarding personal feelings were quite explicit: "I think I
know him less well than some of the others, but I have a better feeling

about him"; or, "I feel some reservations about how he relates to kids, but there's no question of his ability."

Not only were feelings of the interviewers introduced into the discussions, so also were feelings imputed to the candidates themselves. Most often such descriptions put the candidate in a favorable light or showed concern for his own feelings: "He has as good a feeling about children as anyone I know." "I think it would be a terrible blow to him if he didn't get a principalship."

Under conditions in which most comments are favorable, however, even the least hint of negativism served as a signal of caution: "He may be a bit bitter about education. He's talked to me about changing jobs and about being an administrator." [This comment brought a retort from another principal: "If he's somewhat bitter now, this would be the worst possible thing for him."]

### A Proclivity Toward "Variety-Reducing" Behavior

The proceedings of the Principal Selection Committee reveal a tendency among the principals to engage in what might be described as "variety-reducing" behavior.[7] This terminology comes from the field of general cybernetic systems. In the present case it draws attention to the fact that when the principals had to express preferences or to exercise choices which might be expected either to generate or to reduce the variation in certain aspects of the schools, their behavior reveals an inclination to reduce and to constrain. Their attention was directed toward keeping things "manageable" by drawing upon and reinforcing the existing system rather than by nurturing or even permitting the introduction of variation. This behavior is exemplified most clearly in the results of the major task confronting them, identifying candidates to receive official sanction. In that gentle but effective culling a panel of fourteen applicants was reduced to a final trio in which the successful members appeared so similar as to be virtually interchangeable. Whatever potential for variation extant among that original panel in terms of age, sex, background, recent experience, type and amount of formal education, marital status—in this instance even height, weight, and manner of speech and dress—was successfully narrowed in the final selection. And while this process was going on, the principals also lent whatever support they could to reducing the potency of other variety-generating agents with whom their work brings them into continual contact, such as local colleges and universities, or central office administrators ready to saddle the principalship with a double role.

That the behavior of the principals in the episode gives such overt evidence of variety-reducing behavior is, in one sense, hardly surprising. The task to which they were assigned was by definition a variety-reducing task: there were almost five times as many aspirants as positions to be filled. Further, the very terms which the concept of "variety-reducing" calls to mind are terms which are descriptive of management processes: organize, systematize, categorize, constrain, control. What may be unusual is the extent to which variation was so thoroughly and systematically reduced, albeit this seemed to be neither an immediate nor a conscious concern of any of the principals on the committee.

## Conclusion

I would like to conclude with a note of reflection relating the role of the principal to the emphasis placed on "change" in the public schools. This observation relates particularly to the preceding discussion on the phenomenon of variety-reducing behavior observed during the proceedings of the Principal Selection Committee.

The public schools have a seeming penchant for change. School people write, read, and talk constantly of new programs, new "hardware," new approaches. One can gather the impression from educators that anything "old" is suspect and that "changed" is automatically assumed to be "improved." In the last decade a whole vocabulary of change, including terms particularly familiar to students of cultural dynamics like "change agent," "acculturation," "innovation," and "diffusion," became the vogue in educational circles.

The school principal, charged directly with the role of being the instructional leader of his school, is often described as both instrumental and essential in the continuing process of introducing change into the school. The case-study principal and his colleagues recognized this charge and responsibility. They acknowledged not only their formal obligation but their personal commitment to fostering change in the interests of a better education for children.

In looking at the totality of a typical "live" elementary school as the person charged with administering it might do, rather than at what is going on in any particular setting within it, one can appreciate that a school is a very dynamic institution. An elementary school is in a constant state of change without anyone having to do anything to induce or encourage the process. More than 500 people moved constantly into, out of, and within the school in this case study each day. New pupils, parents, teachers, substitutes, specialists, solicitors, sales- and service-men, and visitors arrived constantly to replace former ones or to swell the ranks of those already present. New problems, programs, and personnel are introduced constantly in schools as pupils graduate or move away, teachers "turn over," or interest groups demand and govern-mental agencies offer to subsidize new curricula and services.

Regardless of what he *says* about the desirability of creating a climate for change, the principal already lives with incessant change as a way of life. If an occasional principal demonstrates such a tolerance of or personal need for change that he actually becomes an innovator who induces significant change into his own school, really creating some-thing new or introducing new degrees of freedom into the setting (rather than simply manipulating or restructuring what was already present), I would think he would be a rare principal indeed. I do not believe I encountered such people among the career administrators with whom I came in contact during my fieldwork. The life of innovative programs or schools, and the tenure of innovative administrators, is frequently short-lived (see Fleming 1967; Miles 1964; Redefer 1950; Rogers 1962; Smith and Keith 1971).

Faced as he is with the inevitability of change as an inherent and major aspect of his task, even though he may not recognize it as such, the school principal is successful in his work as he is able to contain and to constrain the ever-changing group which he is assigned to administer. If his survival in that role necessitates his constant effort at variety reduction, we may have an important clue in helping to explain why certain dimensions of public school education remain so relatively unchanged in spite of the constant attempts to change them both from within and from without. For it may be that the only way one can hope to maintain any control in a system which is inherently so volatile and constantly changing in some dimensions—in this case, its personnel—is to exert all the influence one can in reducing the potential variety which might enter the system via routes more ame-nable to restraint. Although it presents a curious paradox between their ideal and actual roles as "agents of change" if principals actually serve to constrain rather than to facilitate the dynamic aspects of formal education, that is exactly the paradox which I am suggesting here.

The paradox may be explained by reanalyzing the extent to which managing change is already an inherent and significant part of the principal's role. Change comes in the form of a constantly changing population, both in the local community of parents and children and, perhaps even more, in the day-to-day composition of the adult cadre present at school. How long does it take to orient a new substitute teacher so that her day at school will not be a fiasco? What amenities are required for meeting a parent new to the community or orienting a relief custodian or secretary new to the school? How much more variation might a principal be expected to seek out per day after spending a not-so-unusual two hours orienting "thirteen visitors, four teacher trainees, seven students observing from the university, and three policemen" plus handling the new problems generated by over 500 pupils and staff members already part of the daily complement?

Programmatically the public schools may still warrant the assertion made by Willard Waller years ago that they are "museums of virtue" (Waller 1932:34), but while the air of virtue about them may have remained, the characteristic of "museum-ness" has not. Most urban elementary schools today are large, bustling institutions. The people who manage them live their professional lives among a constantly changing and volatile group of children and adults in which everyone, including themselves, has only relatively temporary status. The irony for the elementary school principal is that the extent of change with which he lives is neither acknowledged by those about him nor even necessarily recognized by himself. Indeed, he listens to the cries for change and often joins ritually with those who attempt to bring it about. Yet ultimately his own actions, in a constant press to keep the institution manageable at all, may tend to reduce the variation with all the ploys and powers characteristic of administrators in general and an elementary school principal in specific: "We'll have to see about that." "Mrs. X has some good qualities as a teacher, but she and I just aren't seeing eye to eye. I'm going to have to suggest that she either transfer or resign." "It's a grand idea, but there's no money in the budget for it." "These fellows from outside have a real disadvantage. . . . I think he'd come along pretty well in a couple of years. He'd know our lingo and be doing a good job."

Could it be that those people who seek to become and are able to survive as principals, through a perhaps inadvertent but apparently critical and essential proclivity toward variety-reducing behavior, have their greatest impact on education not as agents of change but rather as advocates of constraint? If so, we may be better able to account for the remarkable stability and uniformity that has characterized American elementary schools in spite of the forces for change swirling constantly about them.

# Notes

Grateful acknowledgment is expressed to Max Abbott, Norman Delue, Joanne M. Kitchel, and George D. Spindler for critical comment and editorial assistance in the preparation of this material. At the time of this writing, the author was professor of education and anthropology and a research associate at the Center for the Advanced Study of Educational Administration (CASEA) at the University of Oregon. The author wishes to acknowledge the support of CASEA during a portion of his time devoted to the preparation of this chapter.

1. A discussion of the methodology employed here has also appeared in *Human Organization* (Wolcott, 1970). A more thorough discussion appears as Chapter 1, "A Principal Investigator in Search of a Principal" in the completed monograph (Wolcott 1973).

2. This part of the research was conducted by my research assistant, an experienced geographer, who developed a socioeconomic map of the school-attendance area (Olson 1969). Although I carried out the balance of the field research, it was invaluable to have assistance in the analysis of enumeration and interview data by someone less closely connected with the school setting and thus presumably more able to restrict his analysis to the data at hand.

3. The in-basket approach (see Hemphill et al. 1962) presents a series of hypothetical problems typical of those which require the attention of an administrator, presented in the form in which they might come across his desk in notes, memoranda, notices, letters. A whole set of simulated materials has been developed for use in graduate courses in elementary school administration (UCEA 1967, 1971).

4. "Self-contained" refers to the organizational program of a school in which one teacher remains with the same group of pupils throughout the day.

5. In this regard note how the term "principal" is often qualified with the adjective "woman" if the role occupant is female, just as the term "teacher" is usually qualified with the term "man" when the role occupant is male, particularly in referring to teachers at the elementary school level.

6. An ADC, or Aid to Dependent Children, neighborhood, i.e., a neighborhood with many families on welfare.

7. I am indebted to anthropologist Alfred G. Smith for suggesting to me the concept of variety-reducing versus variety-generating behavior as a means of analyzing administrative strategies.

# References and Further Reading

Department of Elementary School Principals, NEA, 1968, *The Elementary School Principalship in 1968*. Washington, D.C.; Department of Elementary School Principals, National Education Association.

Fleming, Emett E., 1967, "Innovation Related to the Tenure, Succession and Orientation of the Elementary Principal," Northwestern University, unpublished doctoral dissertation.

Fuchs, Estelle, 1966, *Pickets at the Gates*. New York: The Free Press.

———, 1969, *Teachers Talk: Views from Inside City Schools*. New York: Anchor Books, Doubleday & Company.

Griffiths, Daniel E., Samuel Goldman, and Wayne J. McFarland, 1965, "Teacher Mobility in New York City," *Educational Administration Quarterly* 1:15-31.

Hemphill, John K., Daniel E. Griffiths, and Norman Frederiksen, 1962, *Administrative Performance and Personality.* New York: Bureau of Publications, Teachers College, Columbia University.

Lee, Dorothy, 1963, "Discrepancies in the Teaching of American Culture." In George D. Spindler, ed., *Education and Culture: Anthropological Approaches.* New York: Holt, Rinehart and Winston, Inc.

Miles, Matthew B., ed., 1964, *Innovation in Education.* New York: Bureau of Publications, Teachers College, Columbia University.

National Education Association Research Report, 1967, "Estimates of School Statistics 1967-1968." *Research Report 1967 R-19.* Washington, D.C.: National Education Association.

Olson, John A., 1969, "Mapping: A Method for Organizing Data about Your School Attendance Area," *Oregon School Study Council Bulletin,* vol. 12, no. 7.

Pettitt, George A., 1946, *Primitive Education in North America.* Berkeley: University of California Publications in Archaeology and Ethnology 48 (Excerpted in Walter Goldschmidt, ed., *Exploring the Ways of Mankind.* New York: Holt, Rinehart and Winston, Inc., 1960).

Redefer, Frederick L., 1950, "The Eight Year Study . . . After Eight Years," *Progressive Education* 18:33-36.

Rogers, Everett M., 1962, *Diffusion of Innovations.* New York: The Free Press.

Sarason, Seymour B., 1971, *The Culture of the School and the Problem of Change.* Boston: Allyn and Bacon.

Smith, Louis M., and Pat M. Keith, 1971, *Anatomy of Educational Innovation: An Organizational Analysis of an Elementary School.* New York: John Wiley & Sons, Inc.

Spindler, George D., 1963, "The Role of the School Administrator," in George D. Spindler, ed., *Education and Culture: Anthropological Approaches.* New York: Holt, Rinehart and Winston, Inc.

University Council for Educational Administration, 1967, *The Madison Simulation Materials: Edison Elementary Principalship.* Columbus, O.H.: University Council for Educational Administration.

———, 1971, *The Monroe City Simulations: Abraham Lincoln Elementary School.* Columbus, O.H.: University Council for Educational Administration.

Waller, Willard W., 1932, *The Sociology of Teaching.* New York: John Wiley & Sons, Inc. (Science Edition, 1965.)

Wolcott, Harry F., 1967, *A Kwakiutl Village and School.* New York: Holt, Rinehart and Winston, Inc.

———, 1970, "An Ethnographic Approach to the Study of School Administrators," *Human Organization* 29:115-122.

———, 1973, *The Man in the Principal's Office: An Ethnography.* New York: Holt, Rinehart and Winston, Inc.

Zelditch, Morris, Jr., 1962, "Some Methodological Problems of Field Studies," *American Journal of Sociology* 67:566-576.

# 5

# Confessions of a "Trained" Observer

The focus throughout this book is on what to do with data rather than on how data are collected. Although explicit attention is given to fieldwork techniques in some chapters (see especially Chapters 4 and 11), every chapter has implications for data gathering as well as data use, particularly in suggesting and illustrating a broad conception of the potential "data base" in qualitative inquiry. This chapter is the only one devoted exclusively to data collection, specifically to the question of what it is that we do when we say we are observing. I hope readers will find the discussion itself provocative. My rationale for including it, and for placing it in this part, is to show how even methodological issues can be addressed descriptively.

The chapter was originally prepared in response to an invitation to participate in a seminar, "Field-Based Methodologies in Educational Research." The seminar, sponsored by the University of Wisconsin Research and Development Center for Individualized Schooling, in cooperation with the National Institute of Education and the Johnson Foundation, was convened at Wingspread, the foundation's meeting facility in Racine, Wisconsin, in November 1978. Invited participants were asked to prepare a paper addressing one of several "problem areas" related to growing interest in field-based educational research. My self-selected topic fit with other papers related to the training of students as field researchers. Papers were to be circulated in advance so that the sessions could be devoted to discussion rather than to hearing formal presentations. A book was in the offing.

I saw an opportunity in this writing to explore two questions: what we actually do when we go about observing, and what anyone might do to try to make a better observer of someone else. Anticipating the original seminar discussion, I rather expected to have my thoughts and questions dismissed as hopelessly naive. Instead, as I recall, they were mostly evaded, which left me wondering whether perhaps these were the right questions after all. If so, it was the questions that were significant; my answers were only a start.

This is the only chapter to undergo major revision; the other chapters either are totally new or, except for minor corrections, have been preserved in their original form. Unlike the other published papers, however, this one deals with research *processes*, issues that cannot be closed like completed studies. My alternatives were to leave the paper alone and treat it as historical artifact or burrow deep inside it, leaving the structure intact but reexamining every point and taking note of contributions to the topic since I first grappled with it in the late 1970s.

Discussions of method offer a common denominator for dialogue among qualitative researchers whose subject matter foci vary widely. It has surprised me to realize how often in my own career I have lectured or written about method, especially as I do not regard myself a methodologist. I have delighted in cultural anthropology's eclectic approaches and emphasis on content. For years I have sought to entice colleagues in educational research to relax their preoccupation with method in favor of substantive issues. At one time I believed the new interest in qualitative approaches would move us farther in that direction, but somehow method retains its central position, serving as the lingua franca of educational researchers. Alas, even the substantive essays that constitute the core of this collection are bound together under a common cover by two key issues in qualitative method: What do we take for data? What do we do with the data we take? This chapter addresses the first, and seemingly prior, question. In the book's final part, I will suggest how the transformation of data can also inform the collection of data if we think through our studies in reverse order to the way we actually conduct them.

The chapter is built around the issues I saw—and continue to see—in explaining to others what we do, or what we think we do, when conducting the observations so critical to qualitative inquiry. The questions are genuine, not rhetorical, and I have dealt with them descriptively. My purpose was to pose the questions as well as I could and thus to engage the reader in assessing with me whether these are the right questions to ask.

I developed the narrative through the story of the evolution of a course on ethnographic research that I taught for more than two decades. Within that story was embedded still another, going back to an account published at the turn of the century. To my surprise as I began drafting the original paper, I realized that the point of my "story within a story" was not all that clear when transformed from a brief anecdote to the studied prose of a written document. So I described that dilemma as well.

I have attempted to deal directly, honestly, and descriptively in this paper with questions about the process of observation, questions that remain genuinely intriguing to me. Even today I can take these issues just so far. The description extends beyond what I have understood, to probe into questions still to be formed. Our own questions as researchers offer opportunities to turn attention on ourselves and to inquire, "What is going on here?" My point is that description literally can be turned on itself to help us maintain a perspective on what we are up to, or think we are up to, as the self-appointed observers of others.

# CONFESSIONS OF A "TRAINED" OBSERVER

*What a splendid pursuit Natural History would be if it was all observing and no writing!*
  —Charles Darwin, Letter to J. D. Hooker, February 1868

A number of years ago I proposed and first offered a graduate class that I continued to teach for many years under some variant of the title "Ethnographic Research in Education." The only feedback I received

---

This chapter is a substantially revised version of the chapter that originally appeared in 1981 in *The Study of Schooling: Field-Based Methodologies in Educational Research and Evaluation*, Thomas S. Popkewitz and B. Robert Tabachnick, eds. (Praeger Publishers, an imprint of Greenwood Publishing Group, Inc., Westport, CT, 1981), pp. 247-263, used with permission. Copyright to this revised version has been retained by the author.

to the idea of offering the course was from my longtime colleague, W. W. (Sandy) Charters, Jr., who remarked, "What a great idea. The course will make a substantial contribution just by helping students to become better observers."

The title "Ethnographic Research" should suggest that my ambitions for the seminar were far greater than merely teaching students to become "better observers." I wonder if I really believed at the time that one three-unit course was adequate formal preparation for doing genuinely *ethnographic* fieldwork, especially for students lacking prior study in cultural anthropology. More recently my primary objectives in teaching *any* qualitatively oriented method course or workshop have been for participants both to gain some experience in participant observation and interviewing and to wrestle with the concept of "participant observation" itself.

But because Sandy Charters was interested enough both to offer encouragement and to point to the importance of a specific skill that seemed within the purview of a fieldwork seminar, I have often thought about what I do—or might do—to help students become better observers. For me, that has meant helping them become oriented to observing and reporting in the manner of *ethnographic research* in the field and as *ethnography* in the final product. If one course is not sufficient for accomplishing such lofty purposes, at least it is a beginning.

Prior to thinking about how to present the course, however, I had not really grappled with the nexus between "how to look" and "what to look for." Granted that these processes are inextricably woven together, can we isolate and discuss observer skills just as we sometimes do for note-taking, writing, or storytelling skills? Can we talk about how to observe, apart from addressing why? Is observation necessarily an esoteric process best left to experts, or is it an everyday activity at which we can all improve our performance? Let me turn first to my experience in the seminar and my professional concern for, and problems with, ethnographic observation. Later I will return to questions about observing as a basic skill.

## Ethnographic Observation

To the end of alerting students to the critical need for observer skills, I sometimes began the class by reading an excerpt from the autobiography of Nathaniel Shaler, published in 1909. The excerpt, titled "I Become Agassiz's Pupil," was reprinted in Houston Peterson's edited volume, *Great Teachers*, which first appeared in 1946 and subsequently was reprinted in Gilbert Highet's popular *The Art of Teaching* (1950).

In this sketch, Shaler recalls his initial encounter with the eminent biologist-naturalist Louis Agassiz midway through the last century. Shaler was 18; Agassiz was 52. Agassiz, who was then at Harvard, had agreed to take Shaler as a student under a tutorial arrangement common at the time by which professors subsidized meager salaries through tuition payments from private students.

On the appointed day, Shaler arrived at Agassiz's laboratory in the Lawrence Scientific School to begin his apprenticeship and training. He was directed to sit at a table on which Agassiz then placed a small fish in a rusty pan, directing Shaler to "study it." Agassiz cautioned his new student about damaging the specimen and instructed him to confine attention to the specimen itself rather than to consult printed sources or converse with others in the laboratory. Agassiz concluded his brief instructions by adding that, when he thought the youth was ready, he would return to question him.

Shaler reports that after about an hour he had completed his examination of the fish and was ready to proceed to a more challenging task (and be done with what he termed the "loathsome" stench of old alcohol in which the specimen had been preserved). To his dismay, however, he realized that Agassiz, although present in the laboratory and covertly watching his pupil, had no immediate intention of returning to question him. Not that day, not the next, not for a week. And so Shaler committed himself anew to the task of observation—and in due course felt he had learned a hundred times more than during his cursory initial inspection. Still he received nothing more than a cheery "good morning" from his new mentor. At last, on the seventh day of his sustained observations, Agassiz approached and inquired, "Well?" The question prompted an hour-long explication on Shaler's part, while Agassiz sat on the edge of the table and puffed a cigar. Suddenly, Agassiz interrupted to exclaim, "That is not right," and abruptly walked away.

Fortunately, Shaler interpreted Agassiz's behavior as a test of whether he was capable of sustained independent work. He reports that he returned to his observer task afresh, discarding his original set of notes and working on detailed new ones for 10 hours each day for the next week. At the end of that time, he writes, he had results that astonished himself and apparently satisfied Agassiz, for although there were no words of praise, Agassiz subsequently placed before him a new and more complicated task and told him to see what he could make of it. That task took two months, broken only occasionally by Agassiz's invariable correction, "That is not right." But Shaler's overall reaction, at least as recalled years later, was an increasing sense of excitement and power as he honed skills of observation and comparison. Once past the period of trial, Shaler was free to converse, to consult published accounts, and to follow his own pursuits and interests. In time the relationship between the two men became more collegial, but Shaler reports that he never forgot his stern initiation into disciplined observation.

That account has always fascinated me. It seemed an appropriate story with which to introduce my students to a research approach in which the skills of the observer—the "self as instrument"—are so crucial. Unfortunately, however, that beguiling introduction marked the extent of our dialogue regarding the skills of observing. Although we examined the accounts provided by ethnographers whose fieldwork was conducted in traditional settings, as well as accounts of ethnographers and other participant observers who have conducted studies in educational settings, we never attended specifically and directly to observer skills. We touched upon all sorts of related topics but never seemed to address observation per se. I can identify at least six general issues in which observation skills are implied, although something else was emphasized instead. To illustrate:

1. We talked frequently about participant observation as a critical field technique, but instead of discussing the observer dimension, we digressed to discuss how much one should participate or how participation might unduly influence a field setting. Following the distinction proposed by Raymond Gold (1958), we became glib with nuances that differentiate participants-as-observers from observers-as-participants, typically forgetting that in formal educational settings investigators seldom are unable to overcome prevailing institutional norms that turn virtually every visitor into a passive observer. We also agonized over ethical issues, such as whether, and how "fully," our subjects should be informed of our research purposes. In exploring myriad related social aspects of the observer *role*, we eventually lost sight of basic questions about what and how one actually observes.

2. We talked about note-taking but were forever getting sidetracked onto such mechanical aspects as where and when to record, how to overcome the tediousness of the process, and of the importance of making full notes early in the fieldwork (i.e., hour one, day one, week one) when images are fresh and nothing is yet "taken for granted." We discussed how to break notes into manageable units and how to sort

them, and about who, if anyone, should have access to them. But we never seemed directly to address *what to put in them* and thus what and how one actually "documents" an observation. We appreciated efforts of experienced observers to help us understand that field notes are only mnemonic devices to prompt our memories for fuller details, thus assuaging anxieties that notes are never quite complete, but we did not then turn attention to why our notes for any one observation could not consist of a few well-chosen words rather than detailed and lengthy journals worthy of posterity. (How those discussions would have been enhanced by access to Roger Sanjek's wonderful edited volume, *Fieldnotes*, published in 1990.)

3. We talked about focus and periphery and about the concern for context that finds an observer's gaze shifting constantly between figure and ground. In sharp contrast to those committed to tight research designs, we talked about not narrowing a research focus too much or too soon, and about the need to attend to alternative explanations or concomitant events that might help us understand a setting. Yet we did not talk specifically about how to observe, and, almost perversely, the implicit lesson that seemed to emerge was that when observations are highly focused, one had better get back to examining the "big picture," but if the big picture is well accounted for, one had better get back to detailed observation.

4. We discussed observer lenses, observer perspectives, and—probably most constructively—observer bias. We talked about how biases, whether personal, theoretical, or undetected, influence what is observed. We always found easy agreement that "bias" needs to be explicated, although to the best of my recollection we never pressed that issue to examine our prejudices about biases, discuss how one could ever initiate research in the absence of bias, or distinguish between what we might term "good" bias and bad. Today, for example, gender bias has come to rank as high as theoretical bias as a pervasive threat to careful observation, while the American tendency to favor an "underdog" is largely applauded and religious views, party affiliation, or income tax brackets are deemed irrelevant. We are forever issuing warnings about what to look out for, but we never seem to turn the question around to state unequivocally what to look for. Routinely we comment on the quantity of observation (too little, too thin), but how do we measure quality? At what point does "thick" description become too thick, "rich" description too rich? And what distinguishes thick description from slick? Or dense?

5. We discussed objectivity and invariably decided in its favor—that is, to strive for it, at the same time acknowledging that we cannot actually attain it. But we confined the issue to objective *reporting*, seeming to accept without adequate reflection that there is such a thing as objective or "pure" *observing*. We examined anthropologist Hortense Powdermaker's notion that the observer may be "involved" or "detached," a theme that pervades her personal account of fieldwork in *Stranger and Friend* (Powdermaker 1966). Yet we never came to grips with the implications of how involvement or detachment might affect the quality of the observations, except perhaps for an implicit agreement that it seems more "scientific" (but, alas, less "humanistic") to be too detached rather than too involved, if one must choose between them.

6. We examined what other ethnographers have written—probably the best way to get a sense of what ethnography is about—but found it devilishly hard to know precisely what they were observing that prompted one thing and not another to come to their attention. In the long run, we always seem to find ourselves using the most intuitive of judgments—the kind we ordinarily reserve for real lives rather than professional ones—to judge whether a given account has "internal consistency" or "face validity." Two individuals who have made major contributions to the ethnography of education once flattered me during a seminar presentation by noting how they would "trust" my reporting of an event. Yet when questioned further by members of the seminar, they seemed at a loss to explain why they trust one observer and not another, or trust one observer more than another.

At the end of the workshop or term, I customarily announce that I regret having run out of time to say more on the topic of observing, and I remind students how the skills of observing have been integral—albeit implicit—to many of our discussions. The truth is, however, that were the class to continue for a year or more, I doubt that I would ever find time to say more about observer skills. Let me review some problems I encounter when thinking about how to teach those skills to anyone else.

1. In practice, I know that only a few of these students will actually do observational studies, and even for those few, I am loathe to create an impression that they have been formally "trained" as a consequence of one or two lectures or class exercises. Further, although many

students have sought my advice or blessing when proposing a descriptively oriented study, no student has ever requested "training" prior to conducting one. When I have been asked for written sources dealing with observational skills, I have felt hard pressed to suggest truly helpful sources. Even *Fieldnotes* (Sanjek 1990) deals essentially with the product rather than the process of observation, if the two can be separated. Prior to its publication, I discharged my professorial responsibility by citing a reference or two (e.g., Brandt 1972; Gearing et al. 1975; Sackett 1978; Spradley and McCurdy 1972; Stallings 1977, among earlier efforts; Adler and Adler, 1994; Agar 1980; Bernard 1988; Evertson and Green 1986; Fassnacht 1982; Hammersley and Atkinson 1983; Patton 1990; Werner and Schoepfle 1987, among later ones), though Shaler's brief account of his early days with Agassiz probably conveys as much about the *process* of observing as do these informative longer works.

2. Neither my program of studies for becoming an educational researcher, nor a Ph.D. minor in cultural anthropology, provided training as an observer. When I set out for a year of fieldwork to study formal and informal education among the Kwakiutl Indians of British Columbia, my adviser George Spindler, Professor of Anthropology and Education at Stanford University, gave me the same figurative pat on the rump that all neophyte fieldworkers of the day received and admonished me to "keep in touch."

What I learned about fieldwork—and anthropology in general—during my year of "initiation" was due far more to the influence of a fellow graduate student, Ronald Rohner, and to his wife Evelyn. Ron, who was also one of Spindler's students, was completing a degree in cultural anthropology (rather than in "education and anthropology" as I was) and was concurrently conducting fieldwork in a neighboring village. (For a published account, see Rohner and Rohner, 1970.) Even in that "natural laboratory," however, the three of us talked about what we were observing, not how. Our attention was on results, not process. We agonized over how much to participate in the social life of our respective villages and sought our mentor's counsel on that complex issue. But we never discussed what we felt we were doing, or thinking, or recording, that made "observations" or "data" of some of our experience but not all of it.

I am no longer hesitant to say that I have become a trained observer, but I am not sure how and when I got that way. Perhaps it is more appropriate to say that I am an "experienced" observer who has proven himself by successfully accomplishing still other tasks (e.g., producing published accounts) that presuppose some capability at observation.

3. I have always had difficulty responding to the question, "What do you look at?" In its abstract form, I avoid the question as a topic for fruitful dialogue, for the best answer I can offer is that ambiguous, all-purpose one: "It depends."

I do not experience that same uncertainty in actual field settings. When engaged in fieldwork, I find a strong, if largely intuitive, sense of purpose. What I have not found is an adequate way to explicate or to convey that sense of purpose to others. That is why I accepted the invitation years ago to confront the issue by drafting a paper describing my dilemma.

4. I think I am generally regarded by others as a thorough, capable, and sensitive observer (although neither my reviewers nor my students necessarily allow me the luxury of my personal biases, no matter how forthrightly I state them). Yet I can cite telling lapses in my own attention to detail. For example, not until several years after publication did a (Canadian) student point out that I had failed to note that the school where I carried out my study of an elementary principal was a *public* school (Wolcott 1973), a condition not as taken for granted on his side of the border as on my own. I was quite surprised to learn that the school principal, the central figure in that study, was not a teetotaler, as I portrayed him, but was willing (on rare occasions) to join in a social "drink," something I did not realize until I had known him *six years.*

I sometimes amaze friends and colleagues by my inattentiveness to details, conversations, events, social cues. I had grown rather skeptical of my own powers of observation or recall even before age started providing a plausible excuse. Now it takes myriad notes to myself just to get through the day, and it has become increasingly difficult to remember where I put the notes.

5. I have heard about classes, and occasionally participated in seminars or sessions, designed to "train" observers—or at least to sensitize people to cues that observers use. Unless "trainees" are given specific instruction about what to look for—especially with videotaped or filmed sequences that can be viewed again and again—the only inevitable lesson one can draw is that different people attend to different things. If you direct me to observe eye movements, gait, proximity, and so on, then we can talk about reliability, but, when you so direct me, I become *your* observer, an extension of *your* senses or *your* system. With Flanders, I floundered, wondering how a whole generation of "trained" classroom observers could abide with so few categories for sorting everything that goes on in classrooms.

Nevertheless, it took an anthropologist colleague (Robert Tonkinson) to jolt me into realizing years ago how the kinds of data American teachers were gathering "on" and "for" each other reflect the ethos of mainstream society and its educator subculture. "At Task" measures then in vogue particularly intrigued my colleague. "How incredible," he observed, "that educators would presume to measure classroom effectiveness by whether pupils appear to be busy. How like school people to confuse 'busy-ness' and learning? Might not classes of the slowest students or least creative teachers appear outstanding by such a measure?"

## Strategies for Ethnographic Observers

Although I seem to have avoided teaching specific observer skills to my students, I have not been reticent about the topic of how to approach a new research setting, at least for research that stems from ethnographic interests (see, for example, Wolcott 1987). For me, the ethnographic commitment provides a guide to the purposes that observations are intended to serve. When observations are linked to a particular discipline or professional interest (psychologist-observer, economist-observer, medical-observer), one immediately gains a sense of direction and purpose. Thus part of the answer to the question, "What do you look at?" is embedded in a counterquestion, "What do your professional colleagues look at?" Each occupational or professional group has both customary ways of looking and customary foci of concern. Commitments to ways of looking, or to what is looked at, are also implied and instructed by other terms: Marxist, behaviorist, revisionist, poststructuralist, even "educationist." Cultural anthropologists have revealed similar patterns through the years by contrasting historicists with diffusionists, emicists with eticists, traditionalists with postmodernists.

On the other hand, one of the special (but sometimes baffling) things about ethnography is its wide scope, especially called for in a commitment to "context" and a "holistic" approach. Problem-centered fieldwork provides a way out of the dilemma, but it also threatens the professed concern for context. The problem of "what to look at," although not necessarily dispelled for any observer in a professional role, is particularly vexing (as well as totally intriguing) for ethnographers of traditional bent. In my view, if a researcher knows in advance exactly what information is wanted (i.e., knows exactly what to look for), then ethnography is one of the least efficient ways to gather data.

The strategies described below suggest ways to approach a setting when the questions, as well as the answers, are problematic. The idea of identifying and contrasting these broad strategies was first suggested in conversation with anthropologist Alfred G. Smith many years ago.

### Strategy One: Observe and Record Everything

I have always insisted that one can conduct ethnographic inquiry anywhere. There is ethnographically relevant information in looking at anything: walls, games, tablecloths, advertisements, rubbish piles, footpaths, picnics, jokes, the *Congressional Record*—you name it. This first strategy is a logical extension of this idea: When you begin observing in a new setting, you can start by trying to observe and to record "everything." Attempting to record everything precipitates at least two helpful realizations.

First, because you cannot possibly record everything, you are immediately struck with the evidence of what you do actually record. Second, what you select provides important clues about your own observing. You need to uncover your observing and recording habits, and you may need to expand your gaze. You also need to bring into conscious awareness those events, things, and people that seem especially to attract your attention by promising the best payoff for your effort. Beginning with a broad sweep, you can proceed in a rather unstructured manner until you become better acquainted with the new setting, meanwhile establishing some precedents for your own role: how you intend to take notes, how you intend to take photographs, how and how much you intend to participate, whether you "write all the time," and so forth. While observing "everything," you can accumulate useful material for portraying the scenes you observe in a subsequent write-up. Remember that your readers may also appreciate the opportunity of a broad look around, to have for themselves an introductory overview similar to what you originally needed as a newcomer to the setting.

### Strategy Two: Observe and Look for Nothing— That Is, Nothing in Particular

The opposite strategy to looking at everything is to look at the observational setting as if it were "flat," with nothing in particular commending itself as more deserving of attention than anything else. What one actually looks for under this strategy are those elements that stand out from an otherwise flat landscape. In short, one watches for "bumps."

This strategy can be helpful both in too-familiar settings and in too-complex ones. Classrooms, for example, are too familiar to most educational researchers, and they experience an overwhelming urge to evaluate rather than to observe in them. Aware of being familiar with classroom routines, an experienced observer might initiate a new set of observations with the strategy that in yet another classroom one simply assumes "business as usual" until some event proves otherwise. The observer sets a sort of radar, scanning constantly for whatever it is that those in the setting are doing to keep the system operating smoothly.

Years ago, one of my doctoral students found himself looking at what pupils did to ensure "correct" answers, when correct answers became critical to progress in a so-called independent reading program (McGeever 1977). Similarly, a classroom observer might find his or her attention drawn to the handling of interruptions, because interruptions threaten what teachers conceive to be the optimal instructional environment. (See Lortie 1975 for insightful comments on classroom interruption as "the enemy.") What constitutes an interruption, and how interruptions are dealt with, offers a perspective for conducting classroom observations in this too-familiar setting. That is not because interruptions are part of the routine, but because they underscore the importance of routine and the limits to which those in charge will go to minimize disruption. One might also observe how students exert a counterforce within the system through the interruptions they devise.

Looking at "nothing in particular" is also a useful strategy in a setting so totally unfamiliar that the observer feels overwhelmed by the complexity of all that is going on. Backstage during the first dress rehearsal, the moments just prior to a news telecast, the kitchen of a busy restaurant, Saturday afternoon at an African beer garden, or a Hindu religious festival are examples of events where looking at "nothing in particular" might offer an observer like myself a way of coping when too much is occurring too quickly to allow anyone to take it all in.

### Strategy Three: Look for Paradoxes

Another strategy, implicating a more sophisticated level of observation, is to look for contradictions or paradoxes. I can provide an example from my fieldwork on the Northwest Coast, where I found myself among an indigenous people for whom the annual salmon run represented the most important economic activity of the year (Wolcott 1967). The fishing season, June to September, was a time of high earning and high living, and "weekends" often proved a high time, literally as well as figuratively. For conservation purposes, the Canadian government has always restricted commercial fishing to a few days per week. During many weeks, no boats were allowed to fish for more than two days. Thus a workweek of two days was followed by a weekend of five days. The topsy-turvy schedule coupled a weekend partying tradition with a week that consisted mostly of weekend. There was tension in the villages during the very season when one might have expected things to be going well, given the otherwise prevailing shortage of jobs and available cash income. Villagers spoke of better days ahead when everyone would be broke and have to remain at home.

Closer to the classroom scene, there is a paradox between the frequently heard opinion that it is hard to get teachers to try new things and the teacher-expressed belief that teachers have insufficient opportunity to show what they already are capable of doing (see, for example, Lortie 1975; Wolcott 1977). The lives of teachers and learners alike seem filled with paradoxes that warrant attention and provide a way to focus observer efforts.

Anthropologist Smith subsequently expanded his list of orienting categories to include looking for nothing, for differences, for distinctions, for contexts, for freedom, and for order (see Smith 1977 for a related discussion about developing taxonomies). For teaching purposes, I found the three strategies described above to be sufficient. Eventually I added one more.

## Strategy Four: Identify the Key Problem Confronting a Group

This fourth strategy was suggested by sociologist Howard Becker and is reflected in classic studies conducted with his coworkers (e.g., Becker et al. 1961, 1968). Becker suggests looking for *the* problem (or *a* problem) that confronts the group under study. For example, in *Boys in White*, a study of students in medical school, Becker and his colleagues identified the overriding concern facing medical students: to figure out what they absolutely had to learn *first*, once they realized that during their formal training they could not possibly learn everything they needed to know to practice medicine. Their resolution was to figure out what they needed to do and to know in order to remain in school. The immediate and critical objective along the route to their long-term goal was to become successful medical *students*; if they failed at that, they would never have the opportunity to become doctors.

In the medical school example, the solution was something of a paradox, but it need not necessarily be so. In my study of the principalship, for example, a major problem for school building administrators was to conduct effective evaluations of teacher effectiveness. That was not something administrators seemed especially adroit at doing. One can point an accusing finger and say that administrators *ought to do better*, but such a conclusion is not warranted simply from the observation that they seem not to conduct their evaluations with much confidence, or that they themselves expressed the wish that they could be more effective. Evaluation is a major problem, perhaps *the* major problem, for school principals. How they deal with that problem provides an effective way to observe them at work by focusing on *something* rather than *everything*.

## Context as an Observer Guide

Ethnographers hold "context" in high regard, and I would not want to miss the opportunity to point out that purposeful observation has contexts of its own. Context plays a key role in observation: Context always gives us a push (and usually a shove) in terms of what an observer should do. What is out there waiting to be observed is limitless: We never set out to observe it all. Let me review how past, present, and even the future exert their influence on us as observers.

*Past influences* include talking to and reading about others who have looked at settings similar to those we are observing. Their voices reflect both immediate experience and long tradition. For the ethnographer, this includes familiarity with the work of earlier ethnographers and with work in related fields. Each of the various social science disciplines has its distinct style, its patterns of reporting, its quoting circles.  Observing the strictures of the various intellectual traditions has its cost, but that need not cramp personal style. Those traditions make an essential contribution by making it unnecessary for each of us to reinvent a whole scholarly tradition in order to validate our methodological approaches or our conceptual orientations.

Because I work with a conceptual framework of the cultural anthropologist, I am duty-bound to identify "culture" in whatever I observe. If you are more at ease at conceptualizing in terms of institutions, power and status, the allocation of scarce resources, personality, or

Freudian interpretations, there are disciplines and traditions to guide you. Perhaps the social science disciplines, and the subtraditions or "schools" within them, can be likened to buying ready-made glasses: No pair suits everybody, and a pair that helps you see the fine print may not be the best pair to wear for driving on the freeway. (People sometimes choose glasses intended to make them look better without helping them to see better. Similarly, it can be distracting to read reports of capable observers who can't resist sprinkling their accounts with academic or literary references intended to make the research or researcher look better without helping the reader to see better.)

*Present influences* on one's observations often derive from the assignment itself. Such influences may seem incidental to the observational setting and are likely to be regarded as negative influences that hamper one from doing a more thorough job. I refer to limitations such as the funding or time available for fieldwork, the (obvious) inability of the observer to be in more than one place at a time, the duration of an effective observation period, the time that must be set aside for writing the final report (thus reducing fieldwork time by as much as fifty percent), the difficulty in gaining access to what you most want to see, or ethical fads that temporarily shut down certain avenues of inquiry. On the intellectual side, such restraints are matters of annoyance and concern. On the practical side, they often serve as blessings in disguise, for they impose limits that explicitly force the observer to recognize what can actually be accomplished in a given time, with given resources, under specific conditions.

Case in point: Describing research then in progress, one of my doctoral students explained during a guest lecture that, although she had been given formal permission to conduct an ethnography of an adult "mystery school," one condition imposed upon her reporting was that she not reveal any of the actual "secrets" passed on to neophytes. Sympathetic listeners in her audience of would-be ethnographers perceived this as a terrible obstacle to the research and were surprised to hear her add, "And thank goodness for that—otherwise my dissertation would have been twice as long as it was." (For the complete account, see Lincoln 1989.)

*Future influences* pose another set of limitations that help guide decisions about what to look at: the purposes that the observation is to serve. Whether the field observer, or a research coordinator, or a contracting agency makes the decisions, somebody someday has to decide the kind of statement that will result from the research, the intended audience, the format. Videotapes, films, monographs, or articles all impose limitations, and these limitations inform decisions about where and how to look. In my own work—and as advice I share freely with others—one of the most helpful activities for structuring both fieldwork and deskwork is to decide as early as possible the form in which I intend to report my research and to develop a tentative *outline* or *table of contents* (see Wolcott 1990).

These external influences—past, present, and future—although they may seem totally irrelevant to the setting being observed (no classroom or village ever cries out, "Monograph, monograph"), all impose limitations and structure upon a study. But one has to start somewhere. A realistic statement of the limitations and constraints under which one's observations will be conducted provides a starting point by helping to tease out what *can* be done in the face of so much that cannot. In that dilemma, Clifford Geertz consoles us with a reminder that "it is not necessary to know everything in order to understand something" (1973: 20).

## On Observing Better

It was unintentional but perhaps inevitable that my effort to examine the process of observing resulted in an ethnographic excursion. Originally I thought I could examine observation as though it were context-free. It is in the context of ethnographic description that my own concern for observation has evolved, and for the ethnographer, the question concerning "what to look at" is central and critical. But the question takes shape because it is given a focus in the critical preface, "*As an ethnographer,* what do you look at?" This becomes one of the compelling questions of the discipline: "What makes a study ethnographic?"

Recounting the story of Agassiz's new student has served to inform listeners that I take observation to be a critical research skill, yet I must note that I am not altogether certain what the message of the story is. Lucky indeed that Shaler was enough of a social observer to recognize a challenge and rise to it. (Or was he instead a hopeless sycophant, willing to cater to a new master? Or so ambitious as to endure any regimen in order to achieve his goals? Or . . . ?) Whatever the case, Agassiz instructed him exactly as to what to look at, and then imposed not only certain ground rules but even some conditions about the protection of specimens. Clues other than those Shaler subsequently reveals informed him that 10 hours a day for several successive days was long enough for the task, that the final report was to be oral, and that Agassiz would not in the end fault him for being subservient or slow rather than appreciate his capacity for being painstakingly thorough.

When we set out to conduct our fieldwork, we seldom receive as much guidance or instruction as Shaler did. To what would you have attended, had you been assigned to do an ethnographic study of the Lawrence Scientific School and chanced to arrive in Agassiz's laboratory the same day as Shaler? Would you have observed only Shaler, or would you have observed his fellow students as well? Would you have interfered with the natural course of events by asking Shaler and Agassiz to explain what was going on? Or, given your own experiences as a student, would you have supplied those meanings for yourself? Would you have felt you were observing cultural transmission, culture acquisition, socialization into laboratory life, an interaction ritual, or a historical moment in Agassiz's pioneering of American zoology? Would you have attempted to observe and record *everything*? If so, does that also include describing the specimen, or would Shaler's description of the fish have been adequate? Whose problem intrigues you more, Shaler's or Agassiz's? How easy to have someone narrow your gaze to a fish in a pan! Disconcerting, perhaps, but also comforting to have an authoritative figure standing nearby to announce, "That is not right," when later on you will have to rely on yourself to raise doubts that you are "not quite getting it right" (Geertz 1973: 29).

The meaning of the story is not precisely clear because meanings themselves are not all that apparent or clear, and when ethnographers talk about observing human social behavior they are talking about actions *and* their meanings. It is those meanings that confound our capacity to observe human behavior. The problem is rooted not in the fact that we do not know what other people mean but that as humans we are accustomed to supplying meanings of our own. We have a factual clue to the meaning (or part of the meaning) of Shaler's encounter with Agassiz only because Shaler narrated the story. Perhaps Agassiz was just absent-minded, or sadistic. Nevertheless, Shaler reports that he *believed* he was learning to be a better observer. Shaler has graciously supplied a meaning to guide both Shaler and the reader to an interpretation of the recorded events.

My experience has been similar to Shaler's. To whatever extent I have become a better observer—in the sense of actually seeing more detail, seeing *in* more detail, or recognizing what most warrants seeing— it is largely because other keen observers have lauded my ability to observe or, perhaps more often, announced expectations I subsequently endeavored to meet.

My fieldwork initiation among the Kwakiutl helped me become a better observer in at least two ways. The more dramatic aspect was the contrast in cultural settings that made so much behavior stand out in bold relief. It is this experience (sometimes fondly recollected afterward as culture shock) that prior generations of anthropologists have found crucial and that perpetuates the strongly held preference for having graduate students conduct their initial fieldwork in a setting culturally different than their own.

Too bad that we have not encouraged students in educational research to try looking at something else for a change. Instead, we continue sending them back to schools. The only doctoral student I sent off to a hospital to do fieldwork was a nurse-educator who subsequently returned to her faculty position in a school of nursing (Myers 1979). Only in the nick of time did my Korean-born doctoral student, Heewon Chang, and I realize that the place for her to conduct an ethnographic inquiry into high school adolescent life and ethos was in an American community rather than to return to her native Korea (see Chang 1992). The latter study can come at a later time. The opportunity for a genuine cross-cultural perspective was at our doorstep; we almost missed it.

A second way the Kwakiutl experience made a better observer of me was due to my Indian friends themselves. After I discharged my duties as village teacher, I had an opportunity to join the crew aboard the village chief's seine boat for several weeks. I returned briefly to the village and crew for the summer salmon run for many years. As a crew, we spent a lot of time "traveling," plying the waters from one fishing spot to another or going to and from the village. Whether by day or by night, "traveling" was a time for careful watching: for obstacles such as floating logs, for other boats (especially other seine boats on fishing days), for signs of fish, and for water and land animals, particularly deer. I wasn't much help in these activities, but I appreciated their importance. I endeavored to be vigilant. My efforts were sometimes chided, sometimes rewarded, but always with the same phrase, "Good eyes, Harry. You've got to have good eyes."

Like Shaler, I kept returning to the task and improved at it somewhat. I also learned that I am not a particularly astute observer. Time and again, I have been reminded that other people see things to which I do not ordinarily attend unless I make observing a self-conscious and intense activity, an effort I can sustain only for short periods of time. Under more urbane circumstances, a companion who uses totally different cues than I do (and is, of course, "untrained") can spot expensive jewelry or a bad wig at 25 paces; I have never been able to recognize either. What I *have* developed is an awareness that there is more going on than I am ordinarily aware of, and that I can increase my awareness by thinking about how the setting may appear to others in it. Anyone can observe better by asking that same question: What might another observer notice in this setting?

My academic training provides the basis for the only additional suggestion I have that might help other observers, and this brings us back to the problem of meanings and interpretations. It is a human tendency to assign meanings to what we see going on around us. For our own purposes, we "make sense" out of what reaches our senses, particularly sight and sound. I think the better observers are those who do not reflexively make sense out of what they see and hear when they are engaging in formal observation. They raise their sense-making abilities to the level of conscious awareness. In short, they distinguish between observed and inferred behavior, between what they sense and the sense they make of it.

Our capacity for inference is a wonderfully human quality. It enables us to figure things out, to make sense in a world of partial and incomplete transactions. But it plays havoc with our need at times or in certain roles (e.g., as researchers conducting field observations) to recognize the difference between what we actually observe and what we think things mean, how we wish things might be, or what we believe things ought to become. As a place devoid of meaning, the mechanically observed world is at once too stark and too cluttered to invite permanent occupancy, but it is essential for us to recognize that it is there, with or without our own meanings imposed on it. We do not have to withhold personal judgments, but we must be capable both of recognizing and of deferring them.

Had Shaler thought to describe in slightly more detail how he himself proceeded with his assignment, we would have a bit more data (albeit of a special and somewhat suspect type: self-reporting) of one individual's effort to become a scientific observer. In the harsh reality of carefully observed and recorded information, however, we are not only denied insight into his procedures, we lack even the assurance that Shaler sat there all day with his eyes open! Yet had I been seated nearby to observe what was going on, I think I would have been less preoccupied with details such as Shaler's eye movements, or how often he glanced up to see if Agassiz was watching, and more preoccupied with other ways of understanding what was going on in addition to what I saw and recorded.

"Sooner or later," I would have been thinking, "I've got to ask this chap what *he* makes of all this." For that is the breakthrough: *His* inferences become part of *my* arsenal of facts. If ever so slowly, a picture of observed behavior, plus its attendant meanings, begins to emerge. My description, my analysis, my interpretation, serve to flesh out that picture to help others not only to see but also to understand.

The vital processes of this first transformation and all that follows from it are dependent upon observers who recognize both how much and how little they observe. To the extent that we can help students to broaden their gaze and to recognize the distinction between what they see and what they make of it, perhaps we can help them become better observers after all.

# References

Adler, Patricia A., and Peter Adler
    1994 Observational Techniques. *In* Handbook of Qualitative Research. Norman K.
        Denzin and Yvonna S. Lincoln, eds. Newbury Park, CA: Sage.
Agar, Michael H.
    1980 The Professional Stranger: An Informal Introduction to Ethnography. New
        York: Academic Press.
Becker, Howard S., Blanche Geer, and Everett C. Hughes
    1961 Boys in White: Student Culture in Medical School. Chicago: University of Chicago
        Press.
Becker, Howard S., Blanche Geer, Everett C. Hughes, and Anselm L. Strauss
    1968 Making the Grade: The Academic Side of College Life. New York: John Wiley
        and Sons.
Bernard, H. Russell
    1988 Research Methods in Cultural Anthropology. Newbury Park, CA: Sage.
Brandt, Richard
    1972 Studying Behavior in Natural Settings. New York: Holt, Rinehart and Winston.
Chang, Heewon
    1992 *An Ethnography of high school.* Bristol, PA: Falmer Press.
Evertson, Carolyn M., and Judith L. Green
    1986 Observation as Inquiry and Method. *In* Handbook of Research in Teaching, 3rd
        Edition. Merlin C. Wittrock, ed. Pp. 162-213. New York: Macmillan Publishing
        Company.
Fassnacht, Gary
    1982 Theory and Practice of Observing Behavior. London: Academic Press.
Gearing, Frederick, Wayne Hughes, Thomas Carroll, Walter Precourt, and Allen Smith
    1975 On Observing Well: Self Instruction in Ethnographic Observation for Teachers,
        Principals, and Supervisors. State University of New York at Buffalo: Center for
        Studies of Cultural Transmission. (Final Report on the Project in Ethnography in
        Education. 128 pages. Mimeographed).

Geertz, Clifford
    1973 Thick Description. *In* The Interpretation of Cultures. Clifford Geertz, ed. Pp. 3-30. New York: Basic Books.
Gold, Raymond L.
    1958 Roles in Sociological Field Observations. Social Forces 36: 217-223.
Hammersley, Martyn, and Paul Atkinson
    1983NEthnography: Principals in Practice. London: Tavistock.
Highet, Gilbert
    1950 The Art of Teaching. New York: Vintage Books, Random House.
Lincoln, Letty C.
    1989 Reality, Meaning, and Transcendence: An Ethnography of an Adult Mystery School in the 1980s. Unpublished doctoral dissertation, University of Oregon.
Lortie, Dan C.
    1975 Schoolteacher. Chicago: University of Chicago Press.
McGeever, James M.
    1977 Student Activities in Traditional and Individualized Instruction in Selected Elementary Classrooms: A Descriptive Study. Unpublished doctoral dissertation, University of Oregon.
Myers, Loretta Ching
    1979 Socialization of Neophyte Nurses Within a Hospital Cultural System. Unpublished doctoral dissertation, University of Oregon.
Patton, Michael Q.
    1990 Fieldwork Strategies and Observation Methods. *In* Qualitative Evaluation and Research Methods. 2nd Edition. Pp. 199-276. Newbury Park, CA: Sage.
Peterson, Houston, ed.
    1964 Great Teachers, Portrayed by Those Who Studied Under Them. New Brunswick, NJ: Rutgers University Press.
Powdermaker, Hortense
    1966 Stranger and Friend: The Way of an Anthropologist. New York: W. W. Norton and Company.
Rohner, Ronald P. and Evelyn C. Rohner
    1970 The Kwakiutl Indians of British Columbia. New York: Holt, Rinehart and Winston. (Reissued 1986 by Waveland Press, Prospect Heights, IL)
Sackett, Gene P., ed.
    1978 Observing Behavior. Baltimore: University Park Press.
Sanjek, Roger, ed.
    1990 Fieldnotes: The Makings of Anthropology. Ithaca, New York: Cornell University Press.
Smith, Alfred G.
    1977 Taxonomy of Communication: Review and Commentary. *In* Communication Yearbook I. Brent Ruben, ed. New Brunswick, NJ: Transaction Books.
Spradley, James P. and David W. McCurdy
    1972 The Cultural Experience: Ethnography in Complex Society. Chicago: Science Research Associates. (Reissued 1988 by Waveland Press, Prospect Heights, IL)
Stallings, Jane
    1977 Learning to Look: A Handbook on Classroom Observation and Teaching Models. Belmont, CA: Wadsworth.

Werner, Oswald, and G. Mark Schoepfle
    1987 Systematic Fieldwork, Volume 1: Foundations of Ethnography and Interviewing. Newbury Park, CA: Sage.
Wolcott, Harry F.
    1967 A Kwakiutl Village and School. New York: Holt, Rinehart and Winston. (Reissued 1989 by Waveland Press, Prospect Heights, IL, with a new Afterword)
    1973 The Man in the Principal's Office: An Ethnography. New York: Holt, Rinehart and Winston. (Reissued 1984 by Waveland Press, Prospect Heights, IL)
    1977 Teachers Versus Technocrats: An Educational Innovation in Anthropological Perspective. Eugene, Oregon, Center for Educational Policy and Management, University of Oregon.
    1987 On Ethnographic Intent. In Interpretive Ethnography of Education: At Home and Abroad. George and Louise Spindler, eds. Pp. 37-57. Hillsdale, NJ: Lawrence Erlbaum Associates.
    1990 Writing Up Qualitative Research. Newbury Park, CA: Sage.

# Emphasis on Analysis

*An analytical science . . . picks outs a few of the factors at work in a particular situation and describes systematically the relations between these factors. Only by cutting down the number of factors considered can it achieve this systematic description.*
    —George C. Homans, *The Human Group*, p. 15

*In the five hundred double-spaced pages of transcripts that underlie this book, there are a total of 403 segments. Counting up the segments, 58 percent of them were accounted for by the analysis in this book. (By accounted for, I mean they were either directly quoted or referred to in the text, although the quote or reference may not cover everything in the segment.) . . . Looking at the amount of the transcript rather than number of segments . . . the material included in the analysis rises to 66 percent. When you find a pattern that draws from that much material—not to mention notes and other data—you know that the pattern is significant.*
    —Michael H. Agar, *Independents Declared*, Appendix I

In the description-analysis-interpretation distinction I have proposed, qualitative research reveals an analytical emphasis when confirmability is a primary objective: a determination to "get right" whatever you can. Realizing that we are never going to get it *all* right, analytical efforts are necessarily focused on parts or constituent elements and how they interact.

Underlying reasons for putting the emphasis on analysis may derive from different sources that lead to different results and depths. For example, researchers may be pressed for analyses they might have preferred not to make at all, as in situations where a granting agency, editor, or dissertation committee returns a manuscript insisting on more but not more of the same. "You can't just leave it at that," is the message; description per se is necessary but not sufficient.

As one among several analytical procedures reviewed in Chapter 2, analysis reflecting a conceptual or theoretical commitment may drive a research project from the beginning, data-gathering serving only as adjunct to a primary concern with analysis. On the other hand, analysis sometimes seems to be rather perfunctory, conducted out of a need to do "something" with one's data without a clear idea of just what that something should be. For anyone trying to play it safe by presenting an essentially descriptive account, cautious analysis may seem far more preferable to making the bold leap to interpretation.

Regardless of how it is motivated, analysis pulls data transformation toward the more scientific and quantitative side of our work. The analytically oriented researcher presents as "findings" selected results that have an air of undeniability about them. We engage in analysis to whatever extent it is important to be "correct," in the sense of being dependable, accurate, reliable—in short, of being right.

I have not meant to suggest that only the more cautious researchers turn to analysis; rather, analysis is what we all do in the process of cautiously constructing studies out of data. A conservative researcher might like to offer something more penetrating or profound by way of summary but cannot see a clear way to accomplish it or does not want to risk undermining the "facts" or the significance of a study by tacking on a speculative interpretation. So the researcher lays the case out before the reader with the message, "I've presented what I have observed. I have attempted to identify what I see as critical components. To this point I assume you concur with the analysis I have offered. I ask you to share responsibility in taking it from here."

Although it may not be readily apparent from the two chapters that follow, this last alternative was my strategy with them both. In neither case did I feel I had, or was likely ever to have, enough of the whole story. Nevertheless, there was something to be learned from what I could report. I wanted that "something" to be right; the possibility of more penetrating analysis or bold interpretation could be left for another time. I have always felt encouraged by Geertz's (1973b) assertion (noted in the previous chapter) that it is "not necessary to know everything to understand something" (p. 20). The business of analysis is to show— and show off—whatever it is we *know* we are getting right. Analysis exerts a kind of conservative centripetal force on the transformation of data, in contrast to interpretation's expansive, centrifugal one.

I recognize the attraction and power of presenting "undeniable" findings. My personal inclination, however, is toward the interpretive rather than the analytical. But I do not jump to broad or aesthetically satisfying interpretations unless I feel I have a handle on my topic. My interpretations are never offered as mere conjecture. To my own satisfaction, I personally must believe that I am almost getting it right, but it is not the same kind of rightness that is associated with analytical claims-making.

In the case of the two chapters here, I felt that neither did I have sufficient descriptive data, *nor* did I have sufficient insight into the data I had, to offer a more insightful interpretation or a more adequate analysis. I organized the presentations conservatively along analytical lines, picking out, as Homans (1950) observes, "a few of the factors at work in a particular situation" and describing systematically the relations among them (p. 15).

Analysis, as inherently conservative, is more concerned with being right as far as it goes than going as far as it can. That made it an appropriate strategy for me in these two chapters, just as it offers a good stopping place for beginning researchers, particularly doctoral students. I do not push students working at the dissertation stage to be broadly interpretive unless they show some intuitive sense about how to go about it. An analytical stance is usually far enough at that point: not all students are comfortable trying to achieve even that. If describing, sorting, and labeling are all a student feels competent to do, I too can live within those limits, settling for labels in lieu of insights, the traditional "implications for practice" and "implications for research" somehow managing to skirt underlying "So what?" issues altogether. In other academic roles—editor or reviewer, for example—I may call for more, but that does not assure that it will be forthcoming.

In electing to emphasize either analysis or interpretation (one can do both, but not emphasize both), qualitative researchers make their single most important strategy decision in the course of transforming data. Here is where the "closet quantifiers"—still a majority (and a respected one) among our colleagues in social research, and thus a majority among our students as well—bare their true colors and opt for careful number crunching and other systematic procedures that validate claims that they are "doing science." An equally committed minority—the more "daring" qualitative types—remain on the lookout for ways to be intellectually rigorous without succumbing to the rigor mortis of oversystemization.

Analysis offers the safer alternative, but that makes it neither better nor necessarily more inviting. I assume that many researchers think of themselves as simultaneously doing both analysis and interpretation, visualizing the process as a series of continuous and progressively more refined feedback loops. If, instead, analysis and interpretation are "opposites," as suggested by my teeter-totter analogy, they nevertheless are antithetical only in a contrastive way. Rather than attempt to see the two blended or balanced, however, I suggest that researchers regard them as sufficiently distinct to be able to recognize which process they are engaging in at any one time. The idea of a continuous feedback loop accommodates that relationship; the teeter-totter analogy dramatizes it.

Analysis underscores a particular mind-set, a resolve to get some part of our work right. When the analytical work is done well, we should not have to convince a reader of our rightness. As Agar (1986) asserts, there are times in working with your data when you "know" that the pattern is significant (p. 179). If you would venture beyond that point, better to recruit your readers as coinvestigators, even if they must remain passive partners. The analytical dimension in the three previous chapters (Chapters 3, 4, 5) was of the former type, "right as far as it went," ample description accompanied by modest analysis. In the two chapters selected for this part, the analysis takes each case as far as I felt I could go. That was the alternative to offering an interpretation I was not prepared to make. In both cases the descriptive base itself was limited, prompting me to offer a correspondingly conservative analysis derived largely through comparison.

Because comparison provides a ready-made and frequently employed vehicle for pursuing and presenting analysis, let me diverge briefly to examine its role in qualitative data analysis. Qualitative researchers may not realize how often their analytical procedures depend on comparison, especially when that comparative base derives from unexamined—and perhaps unrecognized—assumptions about what is right, or proper, or standard. The topic warrants a bit of analysis of its own.[1]

## The Role of Comparison in Data Analysis

All disciplines make use of comparison in their own way, although they are not equally bold in disclosing the extent of that dependency. I think cultural anthropologists are quite upfront among social scientists in acknowledging both their dependence on and their reservations about comparison, for their work is inherently comparative. As a panelist responding to the issue of comparison within the discipline, Ward Goodenough stated emphatically during the 1992 meetings of the American Anthropological Association, "We must compare, in order to know anything." But almost 100 years earlier, in a paper titled, "The Limitations of the Comparative Method of Anthropology," Franz Boas (1896) posed an early caution on a topic that has been widely debated ever since.

With just three terms, many cultural anthropologists sum up their entire disciplinary stance: *comparative, cross-cultural,* and *holistic.* To  ensure that these dimensions are operative, tradition suggests that fieldwork, particularly one's introductory experience to it, should be conducted among a people whose culture is decidedly different from one's own. Comparison remains the distinguishing feature of culture study. What counts as "different enough," however, is always at issue, particularly as access to unstudied peoples has seemed to each new generation of potential fieldworkers to become more restricted.

Today *ethnography* is something of a household word among nonanthropological researchers for fields in which culture itself is assumed rather than investigated. Clyde Kluckhohn noted years ago that it would hardly be fish who discovered the existence of water (Kluckhohn, 1949, p. 11), an observation intended as a reminder that things taken for granted are likely to escape an ethnographer's attention in familiar surroundings. As a consequence, contemporary fieldworkers often look quite self-consciously for ways to "make the familiar strange" (Erickson, 1973, p. 16; Spindler, 1982, p. 15) in otherwise too-familiar everyday settings.

This has generated new problems for anthropologists conducting fieldwork "at home" (see, for example, the 1981 volume edited by Messerschmidt dealing with aspects of this topic) and a particular problem in professional fields such as education that have so enthusiastically embraced qualitative research conducted by insiders. Try as we may, I remind colleagues doing educational ethnography that it is almost impossible to "make strange" such everyday circumstances of schools as the fact that chair and table heights change with the size of pupils, but doorknob heights do not, or to question just why it is that schools have and need front offices.

Historians, who work within extended time frames, and other researchers who conduct longitudinal studies in considerably briefer ones, make comparisons between how things were and how they have become. Researchers whose problems focus on change often fall into a ready trap of mistaking the rhetoric of change for change itself, believing themselves to be observing change-in-action before having established how things were in the first place. Nevertheless, a before-and-after comparison invites easy analysis—almost too easy, too uncritically accepted.

I have occasionally succeeded in encouraging doctoral students originally intending to study "change"—on what invariably proves too short a timetable ever to hope to see it—to direct their attention instead to what can be learned about any social system from its *efforts* to change itself. Alternatively, efforts to study change can be directed to examining how institutions intent on change adapt rather than adopt innovations (see Charters & Pellegrin, 1972), the adaptation of ethnography by educational researchers affording an excellent example. In that way, a "disappointing" effort to study change may become instead a provocative analysis of the maintenance functions of a social system—and perhaps even invite speculation (i.e., interpretation) as to why systems so seemingly dedicated to change usually manage to entrench the status quo.

## Evaluation as a Form of Comparison

The essence of comparison lies in calling attention to like features, typically showing how something to be understood is similar to something already familiar. A common form of comparative analysis—not always readily apparent—is a comparison between the phenomenon under investigation and some standard, whether explicit and widely accepted, as in the analysis of a soil or water sample, or implicit and perhaps ambiguous, as in the assessment of an educational or mental health program.

Program evaluations are, of course, explicitly evaluative, but all action-oriented research relies on comparative analysis to assess how things are against some set of standards, real or implied, that either describes how they should be or suggests what they could be. A useful practitioner-oriented resource of qualitative approaches to evaluation or "action research" is Patton's *Qualitative Evaluation and Research Methods* (1990). In a slightly differing conception of the same three terms I employ here, Patton sets *description* apart, to be balanced by *analysis* and *interpretation* (p. 430). For him, the researcher must assume a pivotal role of "evaluator-analyst" to ensure that analysis leads into interpretation.

I am reminded that as Elliot Eisner was developing his ideas and carving a niche for *connoisseurship/criticism* as a new qualitative approach in educational research, he made evaluation central to it at the very time that others of us were emphasizing the nonevaluative ("deferred judgment") dimensions of ethnography. "Educational criticism has three major aspects," Eisner (1977) stated in an early paper, "description, interpretation, and evaluation" (p. 72). Eisner defined description as "vivid rendering," and interpretation as the attempt to understand what has been rendered. Evaluation, his third aspect, runs an intriguing parallel to "analysis" in my D-A-I triumvirate, because it incorporates comparison. In Eisner's model, however, comparison is explicitly evaluative. More recently, Alan Peshkin has proposed another typology for qualitative researchers; to description, interpretation, and evaluation he has added a fourth category, verification (Peshkin, 1993).

There will always be argument as to whether research is inherently evaluative by the very act of singling out for attention certain things as worth having attention called to them. Perhaps a more immediate and useful distinction lies in a careful explication of purposes. Here the *role* assigned to comparison can signal another critical juncture. The less evaluatively oriented qualitative researcher compares in order to see, to bring things into awareness, without attempting to judge "worth." The more evaluatively oriented researcher takes responsibility for rendering judgment against some set of criteria, explicit or implicit. Eisner's model for the educational connoisseur/critic—the researcher who takes responsibility for making discerning judgments about the good teacher, good school, good curriculum—derives from the connoisseur of aesthetic achievement who renders an informed judgment about fine art, fine wine, or fine food.

Any of the approaches employed by qualitative researchers may be used evaluatively. None is completely "neutral," although that never excuses researchers from striving for objectivity. Perhaps because so much of my own work and teaching have been education related, in a field in which evaluations and evaluators wield great power and influence, I have argued on behalf of the contribution to be made by ethnography's nonevaluative side. I hoped ethnography would be recognized as an alternative to educational evaluation, in addition to its inevitable co-optation into becoming an alternative form of it.

I trust that my leaning in the direction of less judgmental, and thus less evaluative, approaches is apparent throughout these chapters. That is not to deny that one can find evaluative overtones in everything I have ever written, and I have conducted research that falls clearly within the parameters of ethnographic evaluation (see, for example, Wolcott, 1984). Nevertheless, I take analysis, rather than evaluation, to be the overarching concept. Analysis offers an umbrella broad enough to include comparison. Comparison, in turn, has both its evaluative and its nonevaluative sides.

## Making the Case for the Single Case

As frequent and useful as is comparison as a form of analysis, I am not much given to it other than in its literary form as analogy. I recall years ago reading a terse dismissal lamenting the disastrous consequences that comparative studies exerted on the development of the biological sciences. I presume the problem was in calling undue attention to cataloging likenesses between parts of different living systems rather than studying whole systems intact. All I recalled afterward was the strong message. If there is such a thing, I became "anticomparativist," resolved never to engage in the potentially mindless activity of simply cataloging similarities and differences. That may explain my lingering bias against comparative approaches in the social sciences such as the much touted "constant comparative method" suggested by Glaser and Strauss in their arguments both on behalf of (1967; Strauss & Corbin, 1990) and, more recently, about grounded theory (Glaser, 1993).

It may seem strange for an anthropologically oriented researcher to be stating a case against comparative study. Perhaps I can explain by turning the argument around to make anthropological fieldwork itself the basis of my argument. Like most (all?) cultural anthropologists, I work from a comparative basis, but my preference is for comparison only to the count of one. That is, I do not compare two or more things if I can learn what I want to know by studying only one of them, drawing upon my own experience—or the lack of it—to supply the necessary baseline. In my research, I have never studied more than one of anything. Only the unit of study changes: one village and school, one school principal, one major aspect of urban African life in one community in one southern African nation, one sweeping effort at educational change, one sneaky kid. My counsel to beginning researchers is to go and do likewise.

I note a tendency to increase the scale, rather than the depth, whenever the question of sample size is raised among qualitative researchers. Seasoned researchers are as vulnerable as newcomers to such temptation, sometimes proposing huge multisite, multiobserver studies based on seemingly blind adherence to the maxim that more is better. What drives this inclination toward multiple sites or cases is a desire to assure a strong basis for comparative analysis. The preference for larger N's is a legacy from quantitative research, where a small number of cases can seriously undermine the press for generalization. How fortunate some researchers are to be able to establish sample size by means of formula!

Doctoral students are especially likely to feel caught if problem and intuition alike suggest that a study of a single case would be appropriate but committee members insist upon a "more adequate" base.

Arithmetically, enlarging the scope of a study from a case of one to a case of three, four, or five might appear a remarkable enhancement, an increase of 300% to 500%! That assumes, however, that multiple cases produce a corresponding multiplier effect, that a study of five cases is five times more powerful than a study of one. For the in-depth reporting that is the hallmark of qualitative work, I think the effect is just the opposite: Increasing the number of cases serves only to reduce proportionately the attention that can be given to any one of them.

Fieldwork that must be conducted at two sites does not guarantee twice as good a study; rather, it diminishes by half the total attention that can be devoted to either. (Conceivably it might double the time allotted to fieldwork. Except where data collection is to occur for only a brief period, however, I think the argument hypothetical. At most, a novice might be encouraged to do a first site in depth, additional ones more quickly, with the rationale that in subsequent studies the researcher should become more efficient at data collection.) Fieldwork conducted at three sites reduces the total time available for each site to one third, and so on. The risk in conducting fieldwork at multiple sites is to forgo the opportunity to produce one well-contextualized qualitative study in the course of producing an inadequate quantitative one. My argument rests therefore not on objection to comparative study but on forsaking opportunity for the thorough study of individual cases.

The time for collecting data from multiple cases comes with the need to ascertain frequencies and distributions. That is when qualitative approaches must give way to quantitative ones. Each has a contribution to make. Case studies and in-depth fieldwork are designed to shed light on a phenomenon; they are inefficient ways to conduct surveys. The perceptive fieldworker must be able to discern pattern, range, and variation, but distributions are best ascertained in ways other than encouraging qualitative researchers to dabble in comparison or to confuse casual comparisons with controlled ones. (For more on comparison in anthropology, see Eggan, 1954; Goodenough, 1980; Sarana, 1975; for more on comparative methods at the macro-level of cross-national research or global studies, see Øyen, 1990.)

I am discouraged by studies that propose, for a concrete example, to do four cases—one rural male, one rural female, one urban male, and one urban female—for the stated purpose of determining whether there are "any differences" on some dimension. Any one case ought to be enough to learn what can be learned from a single case and to guide that researcher—or the next—to set up a survey or treatment designed to discern important systematic differences. A project involving four minicases seems at once three too many and hopelessly too few to ascertain what one novice researcher sought to learn. The satisfying symmetry of the sample, touching each of four bases, made what she believed to be a foolproof design. As I saw it, however, she somehow managed to thwart the potential of both a qualitative and a quantitative approach.

As with everything else in qualitative work, the final determination as to scope must be made on the basis of the problem to be addressed. My general advice is that a lone qualitative researcher, working with inevitable limitations of time and resources, ordinarily should pursue one case study in depth. I was heartened during a recent rereading of Geertz's (1983) *Local Knowledge* to find him quoting Santayana's "famous dictum" that "one compares only when one is unable to get to the heart of the matter" (p. 233). Perhaps we should restate that idea as our own aphorism: ~~Get to the heart of the matter if possible; if not, compare.~~

Geertz is not reticent about comparison in his own work, however. His comparisons are of the sort that senior and seasoned fieldworkers often indulge in after independent field studies conducted earlier, such as what at first blush appear his unlikely comparisons between the role of colonialism in agricultural development in Japan and Java (Geertz, 1963, pp. 130-143) or religious developments in Morocco and Indonesia (1968). Elsewhere, Geertz offers good counsel about the purpose of comparison, proposing what deserves to become a "famous dictum" of his own: "We need to look for systematic relationships among diverse phenomena, not for substantive identities among similar ones" (1973a, p. 44).

The key to comparison, following this advice, lies in uncovering "systematic relationships." That is the challenge, but that does not seem to be what researchers customarily do. Instead, they endlessly catalogue similarities and differences, meeting the letter but not the spirit of comparison, often leaving the reader with the question we most hope will not be raised about our efforts, "So what?" By way of example, let me quote a passage from a study of British headteachers that I was asked to review:

> Mr King rarely took work home. Mr Dowe loaded his attache case every evening, and accounted for most of his evening work as being related to his examining or on the phone—mostly to parents or to his deputy. Mr Shaw always took work home. Mr Mercer took work home mainly at the weekends. (Hall, Mackay, & Morgan, 1986, p. 118)

The reader does not learn four times as much from this passage surveying the work habits of four individuals. Rather, we forgo the opportunity to learn about any one of them in sufficient depth for this level of detail to have any significance. Given a study with multiple observers and a deliberate attempt at a collective look at headteachers, perhaps a separate chapter describing each individual's work habits in context might have been effective. What we got instead seems to be an example of the constant comparative method gone awry.

That is hardly to insist that comparison and synthesis have no place. Rather, the responsibility for looking after those functions should be placed at another level. Neophyte researchers—and any researcher conducting an inquiry into a totally new domain—ought ordinarily to be allowed and encouraged to focus on a single case, at least in the absence of a compelling reason for comparison. In depth, rather than in breadth, we realize the promise of qualitative research.

Scholars who intend to pursue a line of inquiry in the evolution of a *career* may subsequently do additional cases. Thus the lone fieldworker can gradually build a comparative base, as with the example of Geertz's work cited above. Every field-oriented researcher does this to some degree; neither can we avoid it nor could we proceed without it. As noted, comparison is a hallmark of the anthropological career, with an interesting variation that found British anthropologists inclined to build their comparative base vertically, studying among one group of people over a long period, and American anthropologists typically hopping from group to group to build a comparative base horizontally.

Case studies produced as doctoral dissertations in fields outside the social sciences do not necessarily become integrated into personal research careers, however. What might be done to make better use of them and to better realize their comparative potential?

I feel that responsibility for "doing something" about such efforts should rest not with the authors of individual cases but with academicians like myself who make our living inspiring them, encouraging them, critiquing them, and, yes, even reading them. If anything is to be made of these rapidly accumulating case studies in an aggregating, collective, and comparative way, that task should be ours, not heaped upon students unlikely to have the time, experience, perspective, or incentive for carrying them further. We should take it upon ourselves to ponder whatever "systematic relationships" are being revealed. Those of us who encourage others to do case studies should take responsibility for finding ways to ensure that the good ones in every field of specialization are recognized and synthesized in some cumulative fashion.

And now to two chapters I have chosen to illustrate an emphasis on analysis, each cautiously analyzed, the first through comparison with a case in the classic anthropological literature, the second examining one individual's options as seen from a cultural perspective.

As a personal note, were I pressed here for D-A-I ratings, it would probably be apparent that the two chapters reveal an emphasis on analysis more in a relative sense than in an absolute one. That is, given descriptive accounts that are somewhat limited, the attention to analysis assumes a larger proportion. My monograph-length studies reveal a pattern similar to the account of the Principal Selection Committee in Chapter 4: heavy on description that prompts a concluding interpretation, with analysis playing more of a supportive role than a central one. There are, for example, particular chapters in *The Man in the Principal's Office* (1973) that are analytical, and the entire thrust of *Teachers Versus Technocrats* (1977) revolves around analytical comparison with the moiety form of social organization. But it is also indicative that I had to stretch to find even two examples as illustration here.

## References

Agar, Michael M. (1986). *Independents declared: The dilemmas of independent trucking.* Washington, DC: Smithsonian Institution Press.

Boas, Franz. (1896). The limitations of the comparative method of anthropology: Paper
    read at the meeting of the American Association for the Advancement of Science.
    *Science, 4*, 901-908. (Reprinted in *Perspectives in Cultural Anthropology,* Herbert Apple-
    baum, Ed.; pp. 70-79; Albany: State University of New York Press, 1987)
Charters, W. W., Jr., & Pellegrin, R. J. (1972). Barriers to the innovative process: Four
    cases of differentiated staffing. *Educational Administration Quarterly, 9*(1), 3-14.
Eggan, Fred. (1954). Social anthropology and the method of controlled comparison.
    *American Anthropologist, 56,* 743-763.
Eisner, Elliot W. (1977). Critique. *Anthropology and Education Quarterly, 8*(2), 71-72.
Erickson, Frederick. (1973). What makes school ethnography "ethnographic"? [Council
    on] *Anthropology and Education Newsletter.* (Revised and reprinted in *Anthropology
    and Education Quarterly, 15*(1), 51-66, 1984)
Erickson, Frederick. (1977). Some approaches to inquiry in school-community ethnog-
    raphy. *Anthropology and Education Quarterly, 8*(2), 58-69.
Geertz, Clifford. (1963). *Agricultural involution.* Berkeley: University of California Press.
Geertz, Clifford. (1968). *Islam observed: Religious development in Morocco and Indonesia.*
    Chicago: University of Chicago Press.
Geertz, Clifford. (1973a). The impact of the concept of culture on the concept of man. In
    C. Geertz (Ed.), *The interpretation of cultures* (pp. 33-54). New York: Basic Books.
Geertz, Clifford. (1973b). Thick description. In C. Geertz (Ed.), *The interpretation of
    cultures* (pp. 3-30). New York: Basic Books.
Geertz, Clifford. (1983). *Local knowledge: Further essays in interpretive anthropology.* New
    York: Basic Books.
Glaser, Barney G. (1993). *Basics of grounded theory analysis.* Mill Valley, CA: Sociology
    Press.
Glaser, Barney G., & Strauss, Anselm M. (1967). *The discovery of grounded theory: Strategies
    for qualitative research.* Chicago: Aldine.
Goodenough, Ward H. (1980). *Description and comparison in cultural anthropology.* New
    York: Cambridge University Press. (Original work published 1969 by Aldine)
Hall, Valerie, Mackay, Hugh, & Morgan, Colin. (1986). *Headteachers at work.* Milton
    Keynes, England: Open University Press.
Homans, George C. (1950). *The human group.* New York: Harcourt, Brace and World.
Kluckhohn, Clyde. (1949). *Mirror for man.* New York: McGraw-Hill.
Messerschmidt, Donald A. (Ed.). (1981). *Anthropologists at home in North America.* New
    York: Cambridge University Press.
Øyen, Else. (Ed.). (1990). *Comparative methodology: Theory and practice in international
    social research.* Newbury Park, CA: Sage.
Patton, Michael Q. (1990). *Qualitative evaluation and research methods* (2nd ed.). Newbury
    Park, CA: Sage.
Peshkin, Alan. (1993). The goodness of qualitative research. *Educational Researcher, 22*
    (2), 23-29.
Sarana, Gopala. (1975). *The methodology of anthropological comparisons: An analysis of
    comparative methods in social and cultural anthropology* (Viking Fund Publications in
    Anthropology No. 53). Tucson: University of Arizona Press.
Spindler, George D. (Ed.). (1982). *Doing the ethnography of schooling.* New York: Holt,
    Rinehart & Winston.
Strauss, Anselm, & Corbin, Juliet. (1990). *Basics of qualitative research: Grounded theory
    procedures and techniques.* Newbury Park, CA: Sage.

Wolcott, Harry F. (1973). *The man in the principal's office: An ethnography.* New York: Holt, Rinehart and Winston. (Reissued 1984 with a new Preface by Waveland Press, Prospect Heights, IL.)

Wolcott, Harry F. (1977). *Teachers versus technocrats: An educational innovation in anthropological perspective.* Eugene, OR: University of Oregon, Center for Educational Policy and Management.

Wolcott, Harry F. (1984). Ethnographers sans ethnography: The evaluation compromise. In David M. Fetterman (Ed.), *Ethnography in educational evaluation* (pp. 177-210). Beverly Hills, CA: Sage.

# 6

# A Malay Village That Progress Chose

## Sungai Lui and the Institute of Cultural Affairs

---
P R E F A C E
---

The first of these two illustrative chapters is a one-of-a-kind piece for me, the consequence of an unusual opportunity during a sabbatical year spent in Southeast Asia to study a community development project. I place it here especially to show the use of a comparative framework in analysis.

That comparative basis is hinted at in a play on words in my title, although the clue may be lost on contemporary readers. In 1950 anthropologist Robert Redfield published a follow-up account to an earlier classic coauthored with Alfonso Villa Rojas, *Chan Kom: A Maya Village* (1934). The restudy, destined to become a classic in its own right, was titled *A Village That Chose Progress: Chan Kom Revisited.* I reversed key words in Redfield's title to create a more whimsical one of my own, at once suggesting the parallel nature of the two accounts and a twist in the case I was reporting. In today's world, outsiders sometimes visit progress upon villages to demonstrate what *can* be done without necessarily considering what *needs* to be done. The approach is somewhat reminiscent of the childhood chant, "Ready or not, here I come!" Unlike the Yucatán peninsula's Chan Kom, Malaysia's Sungai Lui seemed to me a village that progress had chosen.

The circumstances of the Institute of Cultural Affairs (ICA) and its presence in the Malay village of Sungai Lui in 1977-1978 intrigued me, just as they seemed to intrigue others familiar with village development in Malaysia at the time. Had anyone suggested that I present this account in the form of a mystery, the suggestion would have posed no problem; to the present day, the ICA remains an enigma to me.

Publication of my article in *Human Organization* in 1983 prompted less than a flurry of correspondence. (Our audiences are usually small, although one can never fully assess what impact an article has had.) I received a few letters from anthropologically oriented observers who shared their reflections and sense of intrigue with an organization that each had encountered elsewhere, and one telephone call from a consultant doing a status report in response to a fund-raising request submitted to a *Fortune* 500 company. In subsequent and rare opportunities to hobnob with the elite of foreign diplomats and officials, to date I have found one other individual who recalled firsthand experience with the ICA. This man, a regional UNICEF director, recalled "a vague sense of having encountered a village project in India" sometime in the recent past. To his surprise, I found the ambiguity of his impressions reassuring.

My previous familiarity with village development work had been limited to reading; I had no firsthand experience. The opportunity to observe a project in action during the year held great promise. Repeated visits to the village and the Project House yielded scant "data," however. What I had for notes dealt mostly with the camaraderie of staff interaction at mealtime, particularly in the evening when everyone— including senior staff whose daily assignments seemed invariably to take them to the city—was present. As with my earlier study of the elementary school principalship, the disparity between ideal and reality—in this case, between project aspirations and project accomplishments— loomed large. There was no end to what villagers allowed project staff to do for them, but nothing seemed to energize villagers to meet the ICA's objective for villagers to "take responsibility" for themselves. ICA notions of progress seemed as foreign to the villagers as the people fostering it. But how does one document—or even assess—reluctance?

I began writing sufficiently early in the fieldwork that I was able to circulate and revise two drafts before returning home. Two ideas from prior reading suggested a framework for organizing and presenting an account of what I was making of all this. One idea, suggested by George Foster in *Applied Anthropology* (1969) and reviewed in Chapter 2, was to focus attention separately on the target group and the donor group, and then show the two groups in motion in their common interaction setting. That analytical separation was especially appropriate for this case in which two distinct social systems seemed to work more effectively to forestall than to enhance effective interaction.

Literally moments before departing for Malaysia on my sabbatical, my monograph resulting from 3 years of fieldwork tracking another effort to produce rapid change had appeared in print (Wolcott, 1977). I found Foster's tripartite scheme useful as a framework in organizing that account, particularly for the way it calls attention to the donor group—the helpers—rather than focusing exclusively on the "helpees." I hoped that my inability to provide an adequate account of "village culture" might partially be offset by a description of "project culture" presented in the broad organizational context of the ICA worldwide.

The second idea was to turn to Robert Redfield's earlier classic about a village that chose progress for comparison with this case in which progress had selected a village. Still, the portrayal promised to be static: village culture, project culture, and an interaction setting with little interaction. Further, I was beginning to wonder whether my understanding of the ICA was any deeper than my understanding of village life. The inner workings of the ICA seemed relatively obscure even to the younger members of the project staff who aired their thoughts—and frustrations—with me. Sharing dinner, hearing accounts of the day's accomplishments, singing a few inspirational songs, and helping afterward with washing and drying the dishes may be part of what participant observation entails, but that was about as "participatory" as I was able to get, barring the full time-and-energy commitment to the project that senior staff "suggested" but that I neither could nor wished to make.

As anthropologist Mariam Slater once noted, it may not be necessary to eat soup with a chicken head floating in it in order to do good fieldwork (Slater, 1976, p. 130). On the other hand, eating soup with a chicken head floating in it, or dropping by a village development project in some regular and predictable manner, is no guarantee of the depth or quality of the field observations one is making. I did what I could under the circumstances. If I wanted to strengthen the anthropological dimension of the account, I realized that I would have to supplement my observational data with other, more accessible data. I turned to the community development literature for context and comparison. In the introductory comments to this part, I have addressed the broad issue of comparison in qualitative work, so let me move immediately to the strategy I employed to compare the circumstances I was observing with an anthropological classic.

Employing a comparison offered a way to introduce the tension the article needed. It provided a broad perspective that drew upon a literature describing development efforts through the years and drew as well on a specific and well-known study from another time and place. The comparison allowed me to raise questions and identify constituent elements appropriate to the account suggested, rather than implicated, by firsthand observation. Raising questions and identifying elements was what I wanted to do, so my purposes were achieved. Tying my new observations back into the literature (and toward the conclusion of the article, where the comparison was needed, rather than at the beginning, where it might have been an interruption) gave me the opportunity to raise as questions the "lessons" I wanted to draw.

I must emphasize that, whether or not I had chosen to compare Sungai Lui and Chan Kom, virtually everything about the Malay village itself was comparative to me as a newcomer to Southeast Asia. My observations were fueled by all that was different, and the differences were so pervasive (dress, food, manner of bathing, religious observations—capped always by language) that I found no common basis for interacting with villagers at all. The experience of a year spent in Malaysia had great potential for further validating me as a "real" anthropologist once I returned home, as most of my career as an educational anthropologist had centered on my own "people"—that is, other white mainstream teachers and administrators in the Pacific Northwest—but for the present I could not overcome the feeling that I not only was, but would forever remain, a total stranger.

Comparatively speaking, everything different about the village and villagers was also striking: beautiful people wearing colorful clothing living in a beautiful setting and speaking a beautiful (sounding) language. Nothing about the project staff seemed striking, except perhaps their striking embodiment of the Protestant ethic of hard work performed either for its own sake or to be rewarded in some Great

Hereafter. Of course, these comparisons were of my own making, essentially the "view from the train window" sort. Only toward the end of my stay did I catch a few glimpses over the top of the rose-tinted glasses worn by the overly sensitive newcomer so appreciative of being allowed a quick look around.

Contrasts posed by reports of cross-cultural differences, as perceived by the researcher, have been a mainstay of traditional anthropological fieldwork. Noting such contrasts was relatively easy to do in such unfamiliar circumstances. But there was another contribution to be made by comparison, far too subtle to notice at the time. Watching the ICA project staff at only one site, I had no way to recognize a telling sameness about their approach worldwide. I did not even recognize their seeming organizational penchant for conceptualizing things in groups of fours rather than threes!

Not until I read ICA "Consult Reports" from other sites did I begin to detect important similarities between a bamboo construction project on one continent, an adobe brick-making factory on a second, and a barrio cheese-making factory on a third. Not until the third time I encountered it did the significance of the phrase "song, sign, and symbol" finally dawn on me as something more than what I perceived initially as a casual discussion about planting flowers at the entrance to the village. Observations conducted at two or more sites would have picked up far more of ICA "culture." Only by the strangest of coincidences did I have the opportunity subsequent to the fieldwork to extend my comparative basis for looking at the ICA itself. Although not alluded to in the text, the additional insight informed my cautious analysis. Subsequently, I have had the opportunity to read a dissertation study by educational anthropologist Alfred Hess (1980) drawing attention to aspects of cultural transmission during an 8-week training program conducted as part of the organization's early efforts at project replication in India.

No one can get all the detail, see all the parts. One's purposes, and a realistic assessment of practical limitations, are the best guide. I remain steadfastly in favor of the thorough study of a single case. Had the ICA as an organization, rather than the village project, been my focus, I would have needed observations at multiple sites. But in so doing, I probably would have missed a telltale tongue-lashing delivered at the project's first "birthday" that was called to my attention by a Malay visitor but, to the best of my knowledge, never revealed to project staff. Depth or breadth—which will best accomplish your own purposes?

I invited feedback to my early drafts from several casual readers and three academicians: a Peace Corps official, an American anthropologist teaching and conducting village research in Malaysia, and a senior anthropologist "reared" in an earlier era of community development. No feedback was offered from any project participant at the time or from a subsequent invitation extended to ICA headquarters in Chicago by the journal editor immediately prior to publication. Recalling the ICA slogan, "Action removes the doubt that theory cannot solve," I wonder whether the draft reports of my observations were dismissed as theoretical rather than practical. To my surprise, I later learned that junior staff were never apprised of the existence of either draft of my manuscript. I had naively assumed that the entire staff not only read but probably dissected every sentence.

After my return home, I developed a final draft of the paper and submitted it for publication. By then my perspective had been expanded through time for reflection and library research. In addition, there were the two unexpected opportunities mentioned above to see the ICA in action in the American Southwest. The first was in a community development project on an Indian reservation. The second was in the ICA's facilitator role as Process Consultants for business and industry, an activity in which it increasingly has focused its effort in recent years, a consequence of "organizational transformations" of its own.

The article almost did not get published, or at least get published in *Human Organization*, although there was never any doubt in my mind that that was the right journal for it. Two successive editors of the journal wrote letters of "encouraging" rejection. At the insistence of International Affairs section editor Peter New, however, one editor did offer a ray of hope if I was willing to pare my long journal-length article to fit format requirements of a feature section limited to relatively brief reports. The original piece never did get published. Colleagues who applauded the shorter version (and report that they continue to have students read it) have never asked to see the full one, so apparently what I regard as the "abridged version" says enough. Although it is not a lesson I originally intended to draw, the brevity of the article is testimony to how much can be compressed by way of both description and analysis to meet rigid format requirements. What at the time seems painful cutting may be recalled later (i.e., after publication) as nothing more than judicious pruning.

Perhaps the article is "underanalyzed," but that was not a ploy on my part. I took the discussion as far as I could in terms of the events I observed and the perspective offered about them. The deeper philosophical issues that I see have to do with the nature of the helping-helped relationship, an issue that is illuminated by the case but is not necessarily informed by it. More recent reading (e.g., Morris, 1991, and a subsequent review by Stevenson, 1992) suggests that problems inherent in development efforts like the one described here continue to outrun solutions.

The analytical/comparative emphasis in the write-up was intended to compensate for a descriptive base that would have to remain "thin." I wanted to understand a village's response to a development effort, but my role as a sometime-visitor who interacted almost exclusively with a few English-speaking project members for a few hours a week largely precluded achieving a deep understanding. The analysis, then, reflects a sort of fallback position, drawing more heavily on subsequent deskwork (or what Plath, 1990, refers to as "filework") to compensate for fieldwork somewhat restricted in time and quite restricted in scope.

# References

Foster, George. (1969). *Applied anthropology.* Boston: Little, Brown.

Hess, G. Alfred, Jr. (1980). *Global development training for village residents: The Maharashtra Village Development Project.* Unpublished doctoral dissertation, Northwestern University, Evanston, IL.

Morris, Timothy. (1991). *The despairing developer: Diary of an aid worker in the Middle East.* London: I. B. Tauris. (Distributed by St. Martin's Press, New York)

Plath, David W. (1990). Fieldnotes, filed notes, and the conferring of note. In Roger Sanjek (Ed.), *Fieldnotes: The makings of anthropology* (pp. 371-384). Ithaca, NY: Cornell University Press.

Redfield, Robert. (1950). *A village that chose progress: Chan Kom revisited.* University of Chicago Press.

Redfield, Robert, & Rojas, Alfonso Villa. (1934). *Chan Kom: A Maya village.* University of Chicago Press.

Slater, Mariam K. (1976). *African odyssey: An anthropological adventure.* Garden City, NY: Anchor.

Stevenson, Thomas B. (1992). Review of *The despairing developer,* by Timothy Morris. *American Anthropologist, 94,* 734-735.

Wolcott, Harry F. (1977). *Teachers versus technocrats: An educational innovation in anthropological perspective.* Eugene: University of Oregon, Center for Educational Policy and Management.

# A MALAY VILLAGE THAT PROGRESS CHOSE

## Sungai Lui and the Institute of Cultural Affairs

In his brilliant Malayan trilogy, *The Long Day Wanes,* author Anthony Burgess pokes fun at "colorless, uxorious men with a taste for . . . writing competent monographs on the more accessible Malay village customs." With that sentence to haunt me, I experienced little temptation to report on contemporary Malay village life based on limited opportunities for observation during a sabbatical leave spent in Malaysia in 1977-78. Nevertheless, the setting for this account is a Malay village, and, not too coincidentally, a village every bit as accessible as many of its customs. Sungai Lui, a village in the district of Ulu Langat and the State of Selangor, is about 25 miles from Malaysia's capital, Kuala Lumpur, and only a bit farther than that from Kuala Lumpur's international airport.[1] In a settlement pattern typical except among coastal fishing villages, the village of Sungai Lui extends 4 miles along a narrow paved road that connects several large clusters of houses

"A Malay Village That Progress Chose: Sungai Lui and the Institute of Cultural Affairs" appeared in *Human Organization,* Volume 42, Number 1, Spring 1983, pages 72-81. It is reprinted here with the permission of the Society for Applied Anthropology and from *Human Organization.*

(*kampung*). These individual clusters constitute the important community unit. Sungai Lui's "villageness" is, for the most part, an administrative convenience.

My attention to Sungai Lui was drawn not to the village itself but to the efforts of a group of self-appointed world helpers who, a few months before I arrived on the scene, had formally initiated a "community development" demonstration project there. These well-meaning outsiders envisioned Sungai Lui not only within its Malaysian network but in an international network of their own, linking the village to a regional office in Singapore, to a host of other villages in Southeast Asia and elsewhere around the world, and ultimately, to headquarters in Chicago. Their efforts were conducted under the auspices of an American-based not-for-profit organization called the Institute of Cultural Affairs. This account describes something of the ICA organization and approach as observed during the early days of the Sungai Lui project.

I endeavored to visit the project site at least once a week during my 8½-month stay in Malaysia. I felt welcome as a regular visitor easily included in routines such as attending staff sessions and meetings with villagers, running brief errands, and sharing cooperatively prepared meals, but my repeated visits revealed little of the inner workings of the project or motivations of its staff. And that, in turn, piqued my curiosity and provided a focus for more extended observations.

What I report here was gleaned essentially as a persistent but marginal observer, both in the village and, especially, among the staff of the ICA project. But I was there, week after week. I could observe (rather than participate, for the most part), and I could talk with anyone willing to talk—in English. My handicap of being unable to converse in *Bahasa Malaysia,* the official language of Malaysia, was shared by all but a few locally recruited project staff as well. Like me, English-speaking staff got along easily in the capital city but were limited in conversational efforts in rural areas.

Although the ICA is based in Chicago, the project was not staffed exclusively by Americans. In addition to local Malays and, especially, Tamils and Hindus of Malaysian citizenship, project associates included individuals from Australia, Indonesia, Singapore, and the United Kingdom. Yet the leadership and organizational know-how—that is, knowing the ICA way of doing things—seemed to reside almost exclusively with middle-aged American males and their wives. While everybody made some decisions, a few people made the decisions that really mattered.

The project's tiny size was noteworthy in terms of vast development projects and "schemes" in contemporary Malaysia. The Peace Corps was there with what was then its second biggest overseas contingent (the Philippines ranked first). American efforts were paralleled by the good works of seven other nations, some (e.g., Japan) weaning their beneficiaries on a high level of technology generously provided by their sponsors. The UN was there with the World Bank, technical advisers, and the World Health Organization. Capping it all were Malaysia's own efforts at national development, the major thrust of the imposing Third Malaysia Plan, 1975-80. One international consultant joked that if Malaysia could still be said to be in the "class" of developing countries, it was surely "about to graduate."

In the face of national and international projects of such magnitude, why did the ICA bother with one little grass-roots effort in community self-help, a project that unsympathetic observers described as "minuscule" or dismissed as a "naive effort of a group of amateurs"? And who, or what, was the ICA?

*The Institute of Cultural Affairs.* "We are what we are and we do what we do" was one answer I received to my perennial but constantly rephrased question about the Institute of Cultural Affairs. "ICA doesn't matter at all," I was also told. "What matters is only the village and that villagers learn how to take responsibility for themselves." At the village, staff self-consciously avoided reference to ICA, drawing attention instead to the village name or to the village's (rather than to the ICA's) Human Development Project. But "ICA" remained the label by which project and staff alike were best known. As predominantly white outsiders dressed predominantly in dark blue field uniforms, ICA staff were rather unconvincing when they failed to acknowledge their obvious presence, their obvious distinctness, or their obvious commitment. Although reference to their collective role as "auxiliary" or as "adjuncts" to the project seemed consistent with their stated mission, in fact they provided not only the project's leadership but most of its vitality as well.

The emphasis on a collective role—everything in the plural, everything emanating from the group, the inevitable reference to The Institute or the good of the Order rather than to oneself—was also apparent during my efforts to learn more about the ICA after returning home. I have never seen an individual's name appearing in connection with any of the organization's printed materials or reports.

From a brief summary in the *Encyclopedia of Associations* (Gale Research Company 1980), I learned as much as I ever learned from repeated questioning of project staff. That document provided the Chicago address, telephone, and name of the organization's president; it also noted that the ICA was founded in 1973, its members number 1,500, and it has 100 international offices. The formal statement of organizational purposes was similar to phrases I had heard in Sungai Lui: a concern with the "human factor in world development," growing out of the belief that "effective human development must be initiated on the local community level." The summary also noted other ICA activities designed principally for use in North America (e.g., a management planning seminar, a community forum, a Human Development Training School, and consultations for corporations) and concluded with a standard entry on affiliation, noting a link between ICA and the Ecumenical Institute of Chicago.

That link provides a sense of history for ICA by tying it to an organization founded almost a quarter of a century earlier as a division of the Church Federation of Greater Chicago. The affiliation provides the basis for ICA to claim "Fifth City," a community revitalization effort in West Chicago, as its earliest project, when in fact Fifth City had preceded the formal establishment of the ICA by a decade. But those strong Protestant ties were hardly the ones that ICA members wished to stress in Malaysia.

In at least some of its global settings, the extent of individual or collective Christian commitment on the part of ICA staff is probably assumed, tolerated, or deemed irrelevant. In Malaysia, Islam is the religion of the politically dominant Malays and it is the official religion. Although Malays constitute what might be termed a "tenuous majority" (the official population figures for Peninsular Malaysia are Malays, 54%; Chinese, 35%; and East Indians, 10%), through a system of inherited sultanates left intact during the era of British colonialism, they control national politics and the national religion. Other faiths are represented among other groups, including Catholicizing efforts of the Portuguese in the Straits of Malacca dating back to the 17th century, but Christians today do not proselytize among Malays, *especially* among rural villagers.

That the ICA was granted access to a rural village was quite remarkable. But to the extent that ICA motivation in any way stemmed from spreading the Good News, opening up hearts to Jesus, or even building "world tolerance," their tenure was precarious. The consequence was what I whimsically came to regard as ICA adherence to a "Peter

Principle" peculiarly their own: inner corps staff avoided the slightest public display of their Christian commitment. Nowhere did I see a cross, a Bible, or a Bible-story illustration. Instead of expressing their fellow-ship in scriptures and hymns, staff pondered secular writings and sang ambiguously inspirational songs like "To Dream the Impossible Dream." The effort at inner glow without telltale sign reminded one observer of the hymn, "They'll Know We Are Christians by Our Love."

The attempt to be "nonmissionary missionaries" was largely but not totally successful. ICA staff were able to acquit themselves before local mosque officials against one outright charge of proselyting, although the accusation itself dealt a blow to morale after they had endeavored to avoid creating any basis for such a claim. But their primary strategy struck many observers as a diversionary one. Instead of addressing the issue of personal motivations that might have helped staff give con-vincing explanations of why they were willing to endure the rigors and uncertainties of their self-appointed roles and to cope (more or less suc-cessfully) with conflicts arising over power and status within the project, staff invariably drew attention to their host's potential for community development rather than to their own motivations for catalyzing that effort.

If this issue of Christian commitment was not critical in all eyes, it did appear critical to the permanent ICA cadre and was of more than passing interest to outsiders most like them—that is, fellow Americans who felt personal misgivings about ICA motives or who needed to examine the professional implications of lending official support. The latter group included Peace Corps officials who had to decide whether it was alright to assign volunteers to the Sungai Lui project (did that constitute an official recognition and endorsement by the U.S. govern-ment?) as well as officers of private companies (e.g., Texas Instruments) and funding agencies (e.g., Asia Foundation) to whom ICA made persistent requests for financial aid. A newly arrived American ambas-sador to Malaysia realized he needed a quick check on the organization before deciding whether he could officially accept an invitation to ICA's celebration of the completion of the first year of the project.

Overseas Americans seemed more intrigued about ICA motives than I think the Malaysian government was. The scope of the project was too modest to command much national attention, and ICA staff had carefully cultivated officials "at the top." No question that there was divided opinion among government officials, but they faced no irreversible decisions. At a moment's notice, formal project approval could be withdrawn and foreign staff asked to leave.

ICA staff had, in fact, devoted such careful attention to getting "right to the top" with officials in the national government that they had largely bypassed lower-level political units of state, district, and *mukim*. They were confronted with a startling reminder of the consequences of bypassing channels during a celebration marking the completion of the project's first year. Amidst laudatory speeches and entertainment before a full complement of villagers and a substantial turnout of interested friends from Kuala Lumpur, the invitation for a few words from the representative of the district office precipitated an angry tirade (delivered in *Bahasa Malaysia* rather than English, so that the initial impact was lost on ICA staff) railing against a project purporting to be a model of community development that ignored every interim level of government. With the American penchant for action, ICA had virtually short-circuited the established political structure and put villagers in direct touch with their federal government, hardly a practical model if many other villages were to follow a similar procedure. At the same time, such seeming violation of protocol was not likely to result in any immediate action against the ICA, even if it was a harbinger of mounting interim-level opposition that in the long run might seriously hamper the project.

The individuals most affected by ICA's effort to dissociate itself from its Christian missionary origins were, I believe, the inner corps of ICA members themselves, a group that included, among those I met, not only a high proportion of active members of Methodist and closely related denominations, but a number of ordained ministers as well. These dedicated staff seemed to me to have a much clearer idea of how they did *not* want to be perceived than what they wished instead to become. They could "let their light shine" but did not want to reveal its source, feel a Presence but not share it, offer help but dare not convert the helped.

To underscore their good intentions, ICA staff emphasized that they were *not trying to bring about culture change,* but only to enhance the lives of the peoples with whom they worked by fostering rapid socio-economic development. And here, I thought, was a fascinating paradox concerning the Sungai Lui Human Development Project: the donor group, the ICA, was making an effort to change in order to accommodate to—rather than produce change among—the target group with whom they worked. Culture change in reverse: would-be changers change themselves and promise to leave the village intact! "Sungai Lui will still be a Malay village, only more so," one staff member explained.

And, of course, villagers would always be Muslims. Possibly "even better ones."

*Sungai Lui's Human Development Project: The vision.* ICA staff served under banners surely designed to inspire and to reassure them that their efforts on behalf of the "awakenment and engagement of mankind" were properly directed toward "local man." Their worldwide network of village demonstration projects was intended to forge the missing link in development, what one ICA member described as the need to stimulate "local man's initiative and self-reliance eliciting a positive response at the local level to broad development programs" (West 1977:73).

Earlier ICA efforts had created a number of centers (houses) in major cities around the world. An ICA house established in 1974 in Kuala Lumpur's industrial satellite, Petaling Jaya, served as a forerunner for ICA activity in Malaysia, just as other "houses" established an ICA presence in Europe, Japan, Africa, Australia, and India. But at an historical annual meeting in Chicago, ICA members were admonished to "pick up the universe and move it," and a massive effort was directed toward village-level projects instead of urban centers. The ICA network already established in Malaysia helped facilitate the new Sungai Lui project. The village, in turn, served as a training site and holding operation for new projects planned for Sabah (East Malaysia) and Indonesia, sites where preliminary negotiations were proceeding more slowly.

"The hopes of a country lie at the village level," villagers were told during a week-long leadership training course. Local villages were the arena, and action was the byword. Action—sometimes seemingly for the sake of motion itself—was part of the ICA style and part of its official liturgy. The universe needed not only to be picked up but to be "moved," imagery constantly reinforced with phrases like "move it," "on the move," "rapid progress." An ICA slogan, "Action removes the doubt that theory cannot solve," was reflected in the fact that virtually every deliberation culminated in some course of immediate action. The regular morning planning session (referred to as the daily Send Out) left no doubt as to exactly what each staff member was expected to do next. Hardly a coincidence that the motto chosen for the project was *Sungai Lui Bergerak Maju*, a reference to the village's newfound progressivism freely translated as Sungai Lui "on the move."

Yet for all the energy to be invested in the village over the ensuing years, Sungai Lui per se was not important to ICA. Sungai Lui would amount to "little more than an interesting experiment," a staff member explained, if it did not serve as a basis for a replication of community development efforts in "a hundred other Malaysian villages just like it." A similar expectation was held for the initial project in every host country.

When ICA members rose to the challenge to "pick up the universe and move it" through global social demonstration, the original goal was to establish 24 village projects by 1977, fulfilling a vague slogan, "Every hour on the hour," with a strategic dispersal that made an impressive display on a world map. The motto itself became obsolete when the number of actual and potential projects exceeded the number of hours in the day. Village involvement within each country reflected an even grander vision: the multiplier effect of project replications. Replication efforts springing from one Human Development Project initiated in the State of Maharashtra, India, were reported to have involved 232 villages! Perhaps the inspirational words spoken to ICA members attending the 1977 meeting in Chicago could become a reality: "You think about the day we, like McDonald's Hamburgers, put upon the marquee out here, 'One Million Villages Underway'." Yet even the possibility of a million villages was but another step in the ICA vision to someday turn attention to the world's urban populations. That slogan, too, was already in place: "The City Is Ahead."

Although the importance of Sungai Lui pales before a world vision of a million projects, villages were not selected in a random or capricious manner. Processes involved in site selection reveal the structure that seems to undergird all ICA activity. A set of formal procedures and processes collectively comprise an ICA "methodology" that prescribes everything from the reckoning of calendar time to the step-by-step sequence for conducting a "consultation" that forms the basis of each new village project.

*Site selection.* ICA's formal "site selection checklist" contains twelve criteria: Visible Suffering, Rapid Change, Symbolic Potential, Easy Access, Local Receptivity, Geographic Design, Physical Organization, Developmental Potential, Unused Resources, Authorization Power, Funding Potential, National Replicability. Each criterion, in turn, reflects a subset of four related "elements and aspects." Elements and aspects for the criterion Geographical Design, for example, include "delimited focus," "natural boundaries," "manageable population," and "public mobility." The criterion Unused Resources includes "natural resources," "technological resources," "leadership capability," and "motivity void."

Sungai Lui offered some advantages over several villages that were serious contenders, certainly including Local Receptivity and Easy Access, but the village also presented problems. By reason of the large population and its ribbonlike distribution along miles of road and river, villagers were widely dispersed, and staff were exasperated by reports that members of any *kampung*, particularly those at either end of the village and thus farthest from the centrally located project house, felt "neglected." An unstated preference for an ethnically representative community had to be waived in the final choice of an exclusively Malay village, although that decision may have been a blessing in disguise. Had ICA members selected an alternative site under consideration they would have had to try to distribute their energy and resources equitably among the three major and often antagonistic groups: Malay, Chinese, and Indian.

Nonetheless, numerous features made Sungai Lui attractive in addition to local receptivity and easy access. The fact that its dominant economic activities included *padi* farming and rubber smallholdings, the latter the single most important form of agriculture in Peninsular Malaysia in terms of both acreage and number of people involved, was especially useful in portraying the village as "typical."

A few villagers commuted daily to work in Kuala Lumpur or to factory-type jobs closer by, creating disparity in terms of income and opportunity. The ICA had estimated average family income at M$210 per month (about US$85 at the time). A young Malay who worked with the project volunteered enthusiastically that Sungai Lui was "one of the most depressed villages in the State of Selangor." Not coincidentally, the criterion Visible Suffering—including "general health," "local housing," "public facilities," and "available employment"— headed the ICA checklist. Though no one argued that the employment of out-of-school youth, in the village as elsewhere, posed a serious problem, critics of the ICA were not impressed with the idea that Sungai Lui was either "forgotten," "depressed," or truly "needy." Seemingly quite independent of the ICA presence, two new bridges were under completion along the road to the village and a national program of rural electrification was extending service to the farthest village reaches.

The site selection checklist can also be examined as an implicit statement of some of ICA's own "needs"—in addition to being needed, or at least "allowed," to initiate human development projects. Criteria like Authorization Power, Funding Potential (including "foundations appeal," "corporations interest," "potential patrons," and "government support," all of which ICA staff were able to garner) and Unused Resources, including natural, human, and technological resources, suggest that selection decisions were made with an eye toward a broad support base. The criterion National Replicability drew attention not only to the element of "local spinoffs" but to "international appeal" as well, an appeal reflected among the exotic names on the worldwide Human Development Project roster (e.g., Inyan Wakagapi, Isle of Dogs, Kelapa Dua, Kwangware, Lorne de l'Acadie, Nam Wai, Oombulgurri, Sudtonggan).

Most important for ICA was the need to distinguish a good risk from an impossible challenge. Though the checklist probably overplayed the criterion of Developmental Potential, including "forgotten people" and "unplanned future," the idea was clearly recognized and frequently stated that villages were selected on the basis of "demonstration power." It was, after all, the ICA, not villagers in Sungai Lui, who were bent on demonstrating in Malaysia what they were simultaneously trying to demonstrate at numerous sites around the world: that villagers can (must?) learn to take responsibility for making a better life for themselves and then set others in motion to do likewise.

There are, of course, elements of tentativeness, negotiation, and personal judgment in the site selection process. Conducting programs in such varied settings as they do, the ICA recognizes that "field judgments" play a critical role in all their work. To outside observers, however, ICA approaches and procedures usually appear highly regimented. An Australian official on assignment in Malaysia and familiar with the ICA's efforts among Aborigines in his own country characterized the organization and its "methodology" as "rigid and doctrinaire, but in a benign sort of way."

*The consult.* Of all formal ICA activities, probably none better reflects ICA methodology than the procedures followed in conducting the formal "consult" held at each new Human Development Project site. The consult itself is a highly structured effort at group process reported in widely distributed consultation summary statements available in both English and local language versions.

The consultation summary statement for Sungai Lui is a 115-page document describing the analysis and plans for a village project resulting from a one-week meeting (April 3-9, 1977) that involved 423 villagers,

80 outside consultants, and a constant flow of visitors and observers. However, the document is not a record of conference proceedings; it is a carefully written proposal describing the village, the problems identified, and the plan for the future. There is no question that its (unidentified) corporate authors were knowledgeable about the village but were also conversant with the ICA approach to "comprehensive community reformulation."

Nested within a week-long schedule of activities necessary to create a mood of excitement and involvement are the five critical tasks of a consult. A full day is given to each task. The summary of those deliberations, with the addition of a Prolegomena, provides the basis for the five-part table of contents in the consultation report.

*Day One* was devoted to identifying the "operating vision" of the village, an activity neatly consolidated into an operating vision chart that showed villager concern for strengthening their economic support base, revitalizing their "engagement" (employment, basic services, community identity), and instituting practical training. As the consultation report explains:

> It was only when the subjectivity of the local residents of Sungai Lui was confronted by the objectivity of the guest consultants that the Operating Vision of the community emerged. . . . In order to discern this local vision, the consultants were divided into five teams and spent a whole day in the field becoming generally familiar with the community. In addition to an overall survey, each team was assigned to investigate closely a specific aspect of community life (ICA Consultants 1977:11).

*Day Two* was spent examining goals and objectives already identified in terms of obstacles or "underlying contradictions" to achieving them. As one consultant noted, "Finding the contradictions," a process referred to as contradictional analysis, "is one of the different things we do and one of the most important." ICA members express preference for the term "contradiction" rather than "problem" because they believe that looking for contradictions leads naturally to the next step, identifying "practical proposals" for coping with contradictions. Like the operating vision, the underlying contradictions in Sungai Lui could be neatly summarized in chart form. The summary listed ten major contradictions: narrow scope of practical training, diminishing engagement of village population, fragmented development of basic services, unopened channels of financial capital, unstable pattern of employment opportunities, underdeveloped usage of local resources, subsistence approach of modern economy, unfocused direction of village youth, unrealized potential of village products, limited access to educational resources.

*Day Three* marked the crossing of a watershed as attention was directed to practical proposals, the examination of what needed to be done. Here again, ICA members gave their own special meanings to terms; their practical proposals were neither practical nor proposals in the ordinary sense of those words. They represented instead the identification of grand designs that constituted "decisions about the future" or "the image of the direction in which the community needs to move in relation to contradictions" (ICA Consultants 1977:29).

*Day Four.* Although a proposal is "never something which is performed," the proposals identified on day three pointed to "crucial arenas of action within which tactics are forged and implemented" (p. 29). Identification of those "tactical systems" became the work of day four. At this point, a recognition of action leading to "social change" appears in the consultation summary, with change defined as anything to help villagers bring about the outcomes they have identified: "social change occurs through tactical implementation rather than by simply grasping the vision or forging the proposals" (p. 45). Again reducible to a one-page summary, the accompanying prose description of the "tactical systems chart" suggests the level of detail and rapidly compounding complexity of the overall design for the village: "The Tactical Systems Chart . . . is comprised of four tactical arenas, seven paratactics, thirty basic tactics and 200 sub-tactics" (p. 45). The 30 tactics displayed on the chart ranged from broad themes like "providing effective public media" and "increasing useful domestic skills" to specific projects like "establishing local community kindergarten" (successfully implemented) or "farming commercial fish ponds" (summarily abandoned on the recommendation of a Peace Corps technician).

*Day Five.* The fifth and final task of the consult, and its corresponding section of the summary report, was devoted to giving form and structure to make the tactical systems operative through a set of "actuating programs." Fourteen such programs were identified for the village, six each in social and economic development and two additional ones (village construction; essential services) under the rubric of environmental development. Critical functions served by the careful specification of the actuating programs included not only a cost analysis for the project, a "phasing design" for planning the sequence of so many activities, and a means for coordinating "local forces who implement the project and the extended forces who form the support network," but also the release of an "imaginal power that motivates the local people, the project patrons and the public at large by reflecting the possibility, the inclusiveness and the unity of the Human Development Project" (p. 69).

*Budget.* Budget estimates for the 14 programs provided a "four-year phasing of the model" (p. 104) designed to make the project self-sufficient as quickly as possible. Overall cost estimates for the four years amounted to US$300,000, with almost two-thirds of that amount budgeted for the first year (fiscal year 1977) and dramatic reductions in years two, three, and four. The estimated budget for the essential services complex, four times greater than any other program budget in year one, included anticipated purchases of items of heavy equipment intended to "provide a full line of tractors, vehicles and equipment to support the agricultural, industrial and business development of Sungai Lui" (p. 88).

Staff expenses written into various program budgets provided for initiating the project with the equivalent of ten full-time ICA staff at M$4,800, slightly under US$2,000 per person. Year two projections reduced the staff to seven and one-half equivalent full-time positions. Beyond year two, no provision was made for ICA subsidy of auxiliary staff.

In the formal history of such projects, an event like the consult is typically described as initiating the work. In fact, the consult marked the completion of a phase that began years earlier by establishing an ICA house in Petaling Jaya and had now culminated in the widely feted and officially sanctioned commitment to make Sungai Lui a pilot project in community development. The consultation summary noted that Sungai Lui was ICA's nineteenth Human Development Project and the eleventh project launched in the first four months of 1977.

In the course of the consult, particularly in conceiving the 14 "actuating programs" that represented the action plan for local staff, 56 specific tasks had been identified. The list of tasks provided numerous points for initiating action programs. Staff endeavored to have at least one active project in each of the 14 major areas at all times. Although emphasis and accomplishments among the programs varied according to changing leadership, the talents and interests of available personnel, villager response, and simple practicality, the 14 program areas served as the guideline for directing staff efforts and provided a checklist for systematic review.

*Sungai Lui's Human Development Project in action.* One important consequence of the consult was to set the project dramatically in motion. Though villagers were accustomed to cooperative community efforts, such as hosting wedding celebrations that included serving a meal for invited guests who might easily number one or two hundred, those efforts did not require cooperation among all the *kampungs* or provision for hosting so many strangers. Even brief visitors had to be fed, and local and regional ICA staff were on hand long before and after the formal consult. By the completion of the consult, the ICA was firmly established in the village. From that time on, villagers witnessed a steady parade of project-related visitors. Resident staff and long-term visitors present at any one time ranged from as few as 7 to more than 20. To serve as combined living quarters, office, meeting place, and kitchen-dining area, the ICA rented a village dwelling officially designated "Rumah ICA" (ICA House). Rented houses nearby provided additional sleeping quarters.

As one would expect, the day-to-day activities of the project were of more modest scope than the vision outlined in the consult report might suggest. During occasional periods when few people were actually in residence at the village, staff voiced concern over the lack of tangible evidence of accomplishment and self-consciously renewed efforts to maintain their visible "presence," perhaps by calling a special meeting to launch a new facet of the project or by organizing some conspicuous group activity.

"Celebration," a conscious part of ICA strategy, served the dual functions of public relations and maintaining staff morale. Publicly, attention was called to any newsworthy project event (as, for example, when members of an urban Lions Club devoted a day to helping villagers with a construction project). When a village meeting was scheduled, the director often suggested that the modest array of machinery actually acquired for the project be washed and conspicuously displayed. Within project routines, a weekly "celebrative meal" was held when dinner itself was deemed, sometimes by a considerable stretch of imagination, to be "special" and when attention was given to reviewing the week's accomplishments.

For the birthday celebration, ICA staff catalyzed village preparation for an all-day affair that began with a procession and formal program of speech making and entertainment, included a generous meal prepared in village houses and served at the schoolhouse, provided opportunity to review the year's accomplishments, and concluded with an evening of traditional dancing. Except for the note of discord discussed earlier, the speeches were flattering, the guests—including the American ambassador—seemingly impressed, and the villagers pleased with the turnout and response.

Words and photographs had to tell most of the project's history, since the art and craft items actually on display posed marketing problems that seemed insurmountable. (The world's markets can absorb just so many bamboo napkin rings.) Among the first-year accomplishments, in addition to the new sign of welcome at the village entrance, a new marketplace, and five new bus shelters, and in addition to the new Sungai Lui T-shirts worn by the preschoolers while performing a dance, there were new badminton courts, evidence of villagewide efforts at cleanup, a "glove industry" providing income for some village women, and 90 acres of reclaimed padi land growing rice for home use for the first time in several years. There was a village newspaper. There was the new hillside dam and gravity-flow system bringing water directly to five dozen houses in Kampung Bahru. Superimposed on the traditional *kampung* organization were also new guild organizations and a geographical reorganization of the village into five "stakes." ICA staff also expressed satisfaction about watching villager leadership emerge within this new superstructure.

It was the tangible evidence of accomplishment, rather than their faith in emerging village leadership or self-reliance, that the ICA exhibited at the birthday celebration. It was my impression that these tangible results and material accomplishments also engaged villagers. What ICA saw as opportunities for villagers to demonstrate leadership or self-reliance may for the most part have been perceived as hurdles among villagers who already had rather clear ideas about what they needed and wanted. Although a few young adult villagers were frequent visitors to the ICA house and staff, most villagers kept their distance unless specifically invited to confer or engage in some clearly beneficial activity such as construction of the new water system. The attitude of "wait and see" was nicely illustrated in a comment attributed to an elderly villager attending one of the numerous meetings called (but not necessarily conducted) by ICA staff: "Why do you keep calling all these meetings? We already gave you a list of the things we want you to do. When that is finished, we should all meet again and make another list." Thus, in addition to an impressive set of accomplishments, the project also continued to face problems of receptivity and resistance as it began its second year. Such problems could be masked for a brief public display, but in the long run they posed a threat to project welfare and staff morale.

Villagers seemed to have evolved a strategy of their own for dealing with the incessant ICA call to action: they simply disengaged themselves from activities deemed not to be of direct concern (i.e., benefit) to them. This was especially true of older males, whose very presence lent credibility to most enterprises. ICA meetings and events scheduled for "all the village" were often attended only by older women and a small but loyal group of enthusiastic young people. ICA staff cheerfully interpreted this as evidence that village women were particularly receptive to new ideas.[2]

Villagers discovered another tactic for coping with project staff. They learned not only to express their visions for the future, but to "out-envision" their mentors by suggesting highly improbable ideas or objectives. For example, responding to the (translated) question, "Five years from now, what industry and agriculture do you see here?" villagers promptly volunteered a list of nine potential industries— bamboo, ratan, food processing, wood processing, repair shops, bakery, plastic, shoe manufacturing, and sewing—that they estimated would provide jobs for 1,250 people!

Although I found no evidence of the use of anthropological sources concerning either social change or the specific peoples with whom they were working, staff members seemed to have enlightened views of culture and culture change and often pointed with interest to cultural differences perceived between themselves (referring to the ICA inner corps of white middle-class Americans on the scene) and their village hosts. Problems that arose dealt not so much with the fact of cultural differences as with what to do about resolving differences that might hinder the project and thus hinder "progress" itself. Task and work oriented as core project members were, nicely reflecting their own middle-class American values, enlisting their hosts' recognition of and commitment to the importance of local initiative and self-reliance was critical.

In their efforts neither to preach nor to moralize, project staff attempted to demonstrate through exemplary behavior what local initiative and hard work could achieve. That effort, however, may have produced an outward pose of grim intent rather than of rich fulfillment. Few project staff gave evidence of being able to overcome that grimness with any visible demonstration of personal joy. An observer commented that

ICA members created the impression not just of being earnest but of being *too* earnest. The pervasive work ethic of the project also fed intrastaff tension. The ethic led easily to a call for moment-by-moment accountability for everyone's time and energy, consistent with an ICA tenet that "All time is assigned time." The whereabouts and activities of every staff member were regularly reviewed at mealtimes. As one disgruntled junior staff member who later left the project reflected, "We are treated like children." Junior staff frequently and visibly "tuned out" of a project atmosphere they sometimes regarded as "Sunday schoolish."

Coupled with the close time-and-effort accountability was another tension-creating problem among staff, the division of labor. Kitchen details and routine chores were allocated on an egalitarian basis, but on major assignments equity, rather than equality, was the guiding ICA principle. In the eyes of junior project members (and that usually included all nonwhite staff as well), inner corps staff were more interested in garnering outside support for the project or probing the possibilities for ICA activities elsewhere, tasks that took them from the village almost daily and sometimes for weeks at a time. In the absence of souls to convert, the solicitation of dollars, in-kind donations, and high-level government and corporate support served as a tacit measure of individual prowess on the project's behalf. Junior staff were left behind to do what they disparagingly described as "coolie work." Theoretically, all assignments were voluntary, but as one staffer put it, "The finger always pointed."

An observer suggested that ICA staff seemed to live "at" the village but not "in" it. Confounded by a language barrier and the obligations of hosting a continual parade of short-term visitors, even those who remained "behind" could be characterized as existing "at" rather than "in" the village. Confined to a ghetto of their own making, staff found it almost impossible to create a casual basis for venturing out among villagers other than to go to a nearby store or to have a cold bottle of pop at a coffee shop. Older staff also kept a worrisome eye on young unmarried staff. Thus staff-villager interaction was restricted largely to formal instructions and meetings or to formally organized "work parties" initiated through the project but following a widespread tradition of cooperative community work known by the Javanese term *gotong royong* (see Wilson 1967:99n). In consequence, an ever-changing staff made up of volunteers from a worldwide army of dedicated inner corps ICA members and casual field recruits often worked in semi-isolation. They sometimes seemed to share little in common except for their engagement with tasks immediately at hand and their cramped, stoic, communal, and very public lifestyle.

*Sungai Lui's Human Development Project: Reflections.* Although I credit the ICA with generating a keen sense of purpose among its members and associates, I could never escape the feeling of something more coldly institutional than warmly humane about the whole enterprise. Project staff seemed to do things "by the numbers," more concerned with displaying visible activity than with attempting to measure the pulse of village life or to learn how villagers themselves perceived either the project or the world about them. In armylike fashion, platoons were dispatched hither and thither on missions they themselves did not design, following procedures applicable worldwide but not necessarily appropriate for any society in particular. Privates and field commanders alike (ranging, in ICA terminology, from "soujourners" and "interns" to "member of the order" and "prior of the house"), were assigned to and from the village with little apparent concern for what was occurring at the village. Good soldiers that they were, ICA staff complied with "requests" made of them. The project operated as though it did not have particular human beings in it or a particular population to serve, it had only a mission to accomplish and a standard set of procedures for accomplishing it. Somewhere in the ICA's massive efforts of the late 1970s at global social demonstration and its concern for the "human factor in world development," those "people who care" may have fallen into the trap of relying on their institution to do their caring for them while their attention was diverted toward institutional maintenance that assigns top priority to the good of the order. Perhaps that problem began when putting pins on a world map became an end in itself and visions of "One Million Villages Underway" loomed as a genuine possibility.

Although the Sungai Lui project raised questions like these for me, I do not mean to diminish the sincerity, integrity, or accomplishments I observed there. And although such efforts as these, when associated in even the remotest way with missionary overtones, seem invariably to raise suspicion in the minds of secular sponsors and social scientists alike, it is worth recalling that others, including social scientists, have acted on behalf of goals similar to those expressed by the Institute of Cultural Affairs.

To illustrate, let me cite a case well known in the anthropological literature, the "Vicos" or "Cornell-Peru" Project. The Vicos Project was conceived by Allan Holmberg in 1949. Reflecting on the project 30 years later, William Mangin, another anthropologist associated with the project from 1951, its first year in the field, described Holmberg's motivation in terms strikingly similar to ICA concerns today:

> Genuine as Holmberg's interests in research were, I think his interest in improving the lives of the Vicosinos was even more important to him. He wanted the anticipated results of the Vicos project diffused throughout Peru and the world, for he felt he was developing a model that would aid greatly in solving universal problems of poverty, exploitation, and racism. Basically, the project represented to him the opportunity to demonstrate the capacity of the "common man" to assume responsibility for his own life and well-being, given the opportunity to do so (Mangin 1979:67).

Until the occasion of an almost chance encounter with the ICA's Human Development Project in rural Malaysia, I had regarded cultural missions and community revitalization schemes as romantic relics of an era of village reform that began about half a century ago and ended before the 1960s. The title of a book epitomizing that era came to mind during one of my early visits to Sungai Lui, Robert Redfield's account of Chan Kom, described in his widely circulated 1950 monograph *A Village That Chose Progress*. My opportunity to observe a small, essentially American, essentially Christian group engaged in community revitalization in a totally Malay, totally Muslim village in the late 1970s confronted me with the fact that similar visions and efforts continue apace today. In Sungai Lui, however, the ICA, rather than the village, had made the critical choice, and I adapted Redfield's title accordingly.

I must again emphasize the numerous agencies and the magnitude of the international programs augmenting Malaysia's own efforts at development. Malaysia seemed almost overserved by a coterie of international helpers. Similarly, much as ICA would have liked to find a village of "forgotten people," Sungai Lui was something less than a neglected village. The government maintained a local primary school for grades 1-6 with a staff of 12 teachers, none of whom resided in the village. Bus transportation was provided daily to the government secondary school 8 miles away. The government also provided teachers for the separate and state operated Religious School in which village children received Koran lessons each afternoon, and it maintained a health center occupied by a resident (but not local) community nurse-midwife. Villagers were even participating in a long-term parasitology study conducted by their own government but cosponsored by the University of California at Berkeley. The director of a home economics program at the not-too-distant agricultural university told me she wanted to find a different village where her students could practice their food and health demonstrations because so many agencies were already serving Sungai Lui. One might wonder when it will be underdeveloped villages themselves—especially the well-situated ones like Sungai Lui —that will be in short supply.

Compared to the vast resources available as international aid, as well as to Malaysia's own development, replanting, and relocation projects, the efforts of the ICA in one small village did indeed seem "minuscule." Yet the romantic, ambitious ICA effort at Global Social Demonstration provides a contemporary example of how, in terms of the nationality and humanitarian orientation of their membership, the political climate, and the current views of the period, there are always people among the "haves" ready, willing, even insistent on accepting assignments and "doing good" among those they deem to be in less advantaged circumstances.[3] "Whatever else he may be," Ward Good-enough has reminded us, "Man is also a reformer" (1963:15). That is lesson number one.

A second lesson, corollary to the first, is to appreciate how deeply some people feel this commitment and how much personal sacrifice they will endure for it. The ICA presence in a Muslim village, with the clearly understood proviso that staff refrain from celebrating the faith that directed most of them there in the first place, illustrates the depth of the commitment. Although the material resources and level of expertise of their project were dwarfed by virtually every other development project in Malaysia, the extent of personal energy and commitment exhibited by most staff were second to none.

Commitment was not only their major resource, it was virtually their only one. The ICA had neither funds nor expertise to bring about major changes in local technology. The ICA goal was to get villagers to appreciate what they could do for themselves and then set them in motion helping other villages to a similar realization. Institutionally, inner corps ICA staff were so deeply committed to this vision that they were willing to make the profoundest of changes in their own customary style of behaving, refraining from the least hint of sharing their "Good News" in order not to appear to be imposing ideological change on their host group. Thus, and to me this is the most incredible aspect of the ICA effort, would-be changers changed themselves instead in order to ensure that their target group remain unchanged.

One major consequence of this remarkable effort at demissionizing the missionaries was quite apparent: the fact that ICA was allowed access to the village. The costs may not be so apparent within the ranks of the organization as to an outside observer: ICA members seemed much clearer about how *not* to act than about how to act, about what *not* to talk (or sing, or give thanks) about than what to talk (or sing, or give thanks) about. The only clear role model they had for personal behavior was the missionary one they were trying to discard, and that created ambiguity. Outsiders frequently commented that they thought they detected "missionaries in disguise"; neither ICA as institution nor ICA members individually seem yet to be convincing as the "secular order" they are trying to become.

A third lesson, and for a different audience, is that while the sensitivity expressed toward, and respect expressed for, the host culture seemed to reflect anthropology's message of cultural relativism, anthropology as a resource about either the world's peoples or about processes of community development and change was totally ignored.[4] This is a lesson for anthropologists themselves. In a day when they voice concern for demonstrating the relevance of their discipline, anthropologists might ponder what they would have to do (and whether they are willing to do it) to make their resources and counsel useful to a group like the ICA.

A fourth lesson, of potential interest both to social scientists and to an action-oriented organization like the ICA, revolves around the process of effective "helping." ICA staff tended to substitute hard work and self-sacrifice for expertise (accompanied by a well-rationalized view that it was more useful to show villagers how to seek help than simply to provide it). The vision described in the consult summary included an exhaustive list of projects and tasks. But I saw no evidence that project members ever considered the issue of what, in addition to sheer energy, is necessary to make a success of a village-level project. Working to the point of exhaustion might assuage personal concerns over whether one has done enough, but villagers provided less-than-subtle reminders that ICA staff could never really do enough for them. What other measures might be considered in examining issues of staff size, type and duration of projects undertaken, and the speed at which new activities are introduced?

One could seriously question whether the project's all-work-and-no-play atmosphere might inadvertently have shown the outsiders to be virtually humorless, lacking in customary social grace. Was a "worker commune" the best model for demonstrating how villagers might improve their individual circumstances? Or will villagers some years hence remember the endless procession of ICA staff and associates only for the sometimes unwieldy size of the group; their penchant for activity, meetings, and blue uniforms; and strange customs such as bathing indoors (rather than in the river), loud singing at mealtimes, and having adult men help do the dishes?

*Long-term consequences.* Finally, there is the issue of long-term versus short-term consequences of the help efforts. To the extent that the project serves as a model for a comprehensive world effort at "social demonstration," what will be demonstrated, and to whom? Let me point to some reasons why I believe the long-term consequences of the project, what will remain after ICA ceases to maintain its "presence," will be rather minimal. I turn again to Redfield's account *A Village That Chose Progress.*

In 1944, Redfield reports, a cultural mission was assigned to Chan Kom for a period of 16 months, part of a national effort by the Mexican government to raise the standard of life in rural villages. In summarizing the effects of that effort, Redfield made a distinction between activity during the life of the project and what he termed its "residue":

> While the mission was there . . . the village was a lively place. The mere presence of so many loud and active people, with the manners of the town, changed for a time the general tone of the community. . . . Nevertheless, the residue of accomplished change in the ways of Chan Kom from this cultural flood is not impressive (1950:146).

There is at least one critical difference between the approach of the cultural mission in its Mayan setting almost 40 years ago and the Institute of Cultural Affairs in its global mission today. Redfield makes particular note of the absence of "any indication that the mission had an interest in learning what the policy and goals of the village were and might be made to be" (p. 147). This absence is in seeming contrast with the ICA's explicit and formal procedures for identifying community objectives and analyzing the barriers to achieving them. But I am skeptical whether the rigid ICA approach exemplified by the Consult really gets at basic village concerns—other than an obvious upgrading of physical facilities—or merely provides a format for ICA's own conception of progress, oriented around such satisfyingly American preferences and values as speed, efficiency, the accumulation of material resources, and "self-reliance." Did villagers really want new roles in leadership and a new posture of self-reliance, or did they see a way to obtain some extra assistance by acquiescing in the face of what I imagine was a rather persistent wooing by early ICA emissaries?

Redfield's observations about Chan Kom seem applicable in anticipating long-term effects in Sungai Lui: "Before progress came to Chan Kom, Chan Kom had a life-view of its own . . . and Chan Kom has shaped the progress it has won in conformity with this ethos" (p. 154).

Life view! Ethos! It is hardly surprising that anthropologist Redfield devoted the final chapter of *A Village That Chose Progress* to reviewing Chan Kom's transformation in terms of its "ethos," the quality and style of life of its villagers. Ethos may prove as well to be central in the final chapter of the saga of Sungai Lui and the ICA. In fact, ethos may prove to be the project's Achilles' heel, not in the sense of its downfall—there was already evidence enough of accomplishment, new friendships, and new experiences for staff and villagers alike not to judge the project as a failure—but in the sense of a crucial oversight that will keep it from achieving the deep and lasting impact on village life originally envisioned.

A senior project member reflected, "You never really know what these people are thinking." As a recognition of the complexity of understanding others, especially across differences of language, culture, and setting, such a statement might appear admirable. In that context, however, I took it to mean that if anything was to be accomplished, one had best get on with it rather than waste a lot of time trying to "figure out" the villagers. Another senior staff member stated candidly, "If we did 'business as usual,' we would be here ten years just getting the project off the ground."

Action oriented as they were, ICA's strategies did not invite attention to the ethos of its village hosts. ICA staff might well insist that they were not attempting to change that ethos. To try to induce people to accept more responsibility for their own plight *is* a change of ethos, nonetheless. And by ignoring the ethos of their hosts, ICA also failed to examine the meanings that villagers assigned to the project. Inner corps ICA staff were awakened to a sense of meaning in their own lives but failed to be sufficiently attentive to "meanings" in the lives of others.

It is not a lack of goals and objectives that will prove to be the project's undoing but rather, I believe, a case of the ICA having its own institutional purposes so clearly in mind that local staff feel no need to review systematically how their hosts might organize their lives around different purposes that are not less important simply because they are less explicitly stated. Staff were preoccupied with their own carefully prescribed procedures and traditions. The ICA format for human development did not call for staff to come to know villagers in other roles than the one that they themselves exercised so fully, the role of worker, to learn how villagers felt about "progress," or to understand what villagers perceived as worthy of celebration in their lifestyle before being chosen by the ICA. Staff heard the words but, I think, missed the message when villagers, expressing delight with a bountiful first harvest from padi fields previously idle for several years, noted that with such a surfeit there seemed little need for going to all that work again in the next growing season.

## Notes

**Acknowledgments.** Appreciation is expressed to Robert Bonnin, A. Terry Rambo, and the late Shirley M. Kennedy for help in preparing the original draft of a longer, unpublished paper and for the constructive suggestions of editors H. Russell Bernard, John Poggie, Jr., and Peter New in preparing this abridged version. Institutional support was provided through a sabbatical leave from the University of Oregon and the courtesy of an appointment as Research Associate in the Fakulti Pendidikan, Universiti Malaya, during 1977-78.

1. Following the Malaysian practice of marking road distances with milestones and using milestone designations as place names (e.g., "18th mile"), distances are given here in miles rather than in kilometers.

2. This same observation appears frequently in the literature on change. It is difficult to sort out fact from interpretation. In Sungai Lui, ICA staff perceived the support and participation of the adult males to bc critical for project success but found the women more available and receptive. (For a study of "tradition and transition" among rural Malay women, see Strange 1981.)

3. As Mangin notes, Holmberg's thinking also "conformed closely to that of other social reformers of the time, especially those concerned with community development" (Mangin 1979: 67).

4. See, for example, classics like the casebook *Human Problems in Technological Change* edited by Edward Spicer in 1952, or Ward Goodenough's *Cooperation in Change*, 1963.

## References

Note: Not all references listed are cited in this abridged version. They have been included here as a resource for readers interested in rural Malaysia.

Burgess, Anthony
    1977 [1964] The Long Day Wanes: A Malayan Trilogy. New York: W. W. Norton.
Downs, Richard
    1967 A Kelantanese Village in Malaya. In Contemporary Change in Traditional Societies, Vol. 2. J. Steward, ed. Urbana, IL: University of Illinois Press.

Gale Research Company
  1980 Encyclopedia of Associations, 14th Ed., Vol. 1. Entry under "Institute of Cultural Affairs."
Goodenough, Ward H.
  1963 Cooperation in Change. New York: Russell Sage Foundation.
Husin Ali, Syed
  1975 Malay Peasant Society and Leadership. Kuala Lumpur: Oxford University Press.
ICA Consultants
  1977 Sungai Lui Human Development Project: Consultation Summary Statement. Chicago, IL: Institute of Cultural Affairs.
Kuchiba, Masuo, Yoshihiro Tsubouchi, and Marifumi Maeda, eds.
  1979 Three Malay Villages: A Sociology of Paddy Growers in West Malaysia. (Transl. by Peter and Stephanie Hawkes.) Honolulu: University of Hawaii Press.
Malaysia Federal Government
  1976 Third Malaysia Plan 1976-1980. Kuala Lumpur: Government Printer.
Mangin, William
  1979 Thoughts on Twenty-Four Years of Work in Peru: The Vicos Project and Me. *In* Long-Term Field Research in Social Anthropology. George M. Foster, Thayer Scudder, Elizabeth Colson, and Robert V. Kemper, eds. New York: Academic Press.
Provencher, Ronald
  1971 Two Malay Worlds: Interaction in Urban and Rural Settings. Research Monograph No. 4. Berkeley, CA: Center for South and Southeast Asia Studies.
Redfield, Robert
  1950 A Village That Chose Progress: Chan Kom Revisited. University of Chicago Press. (Phoenix edition 1962.)
Spicer, Edward H., ed.
  1952 Human Problems in Technological Change. New York: Russell Sage Foundation.
Strange, Heather
  1981 Rural Malay Women in Tradition and Transformation. New York: Praeger.
Swift, Michael G.
  1965 Malay Peasant Society in Jelabu. London: Athlone Press.
West, Richard
  1977 Human Development, A New Future for Local Man. The Planter 53(611):71-75.
Wilson, Peter J.
  1967 A Malay Village and Malaysia. New Haven, CT: HRAF Press.

# 7

# Life's Not Working

## Cultural Alternatives to Career Alternatives

---

### PREFACE

---

The second example illustrating an emphasis on analysis is also the second installment in what has become the Brad trilogy ("Sneaky Kid," Chapter 3, was the first). This writing grew out of a need to try to discern for myself what I had learned and understood from more than 2 years of conversation with Brad, a dialogue that had come to an end with his abrupt departure.

The questions I was left with seemed to get farther and farther ahead of my "data." The original report and subsequent "Sneaky Kid" article had already been published. I had little additional information to work with except for Brad's anguish surrounding his sudden decision to leave (in spring of the previous year) and the discussion and events prompted by that decision. But I had gained new insight into Brad's worldview as a result of his very self-conscious introspection into his prospects for the future. An examination of those alternatives became the focus for this writing.

There is a heavy emphasis here on the activities of a single week, in contrast to my earlier effort to encapsulate Brad's whole life in less than 30 pages. As with the proceedings of the Principal Selection Committee (recounted in Chapter 4), a small subset of activities is described and analyzed here as revealing of the whole, although these events reflect a far more critical "turning" in Brad's life than did the deliberations of committee members in theirs.

I first drafted "Life's Not Working: Cultural Alternatives to Career Alternatives" in 1983, without any particular audience in mind and without a clear idea of whether I was preparing a publishable article. My perspective, however, is always cultural, consistent with my anthropological preoccupation with culture and culture acquisition. Although I did not attempt to write especially for an anthropologically oriented audience, I pressed heavily on cultural analysis to see what insight my professional orientation could offer to my personal one in thinking through issues that had begun to occupy a great deal of my thought. Neither did the account seem a likely candidate for a psychological journal (nowhere near rigorous enough) or a pedagogical one (implications for the classroom not all that clear). But these factors were not a primary concern; the Brad story was becoming increasingly personal and conjectural, and I wrote because I felt compelled to do so, to try quite literally to figure things out on paper.

The story is still Brad's. The life history account published earlier had to be repeated, at least in synopsis form, for readers unfamiliar with the Sneaky Kid article. The emphasis, of course, is mine, both in the telling and in the analysis: Brad as the reluctant student but intrepid learner, Brad as the reluctant employee but consummate survivalist.

My analysis consisted primarily of identifying and examining, as a set of "cultural alternatives," the choices that Brad either explored or contemplated (e.g., join up, stay put, be crazy) in thinking through what to do next, once he decided that the time had come for "hitting the road." It did not occur to me at the time how the alternatives that he posed differed so markedly from those I would have identified for myself. That difference, a comparative one between observer and observed, provided the basis for the article, a systematic and reflective review of events that at the time seemed random and disconnected.

With those events labeled, reordered, and reported in the narrative part of the account, I then offer some interpretation. I attempted a broad cultural perspective to focus on what Brad *did* seem to be doing, rather than a narrow and prescriptive one that might have seen him as simply avoiding work at all costs. That interpretation is raised cautiously through questions posed and an effort to provide readers with sufficient information for drawing their own conclusions. More by default than by design, the chapter offers about equal parts description, analysis, and interpretation, with analysis given a heavier role as I endeavored to make do with the meager additional data at hand.

As noted in the chapter itself, only reluctantly did I raise the issue of "sanity," as reluctantly as I had first embraced it myself while interacting with Brad during his final weeks at the cabin. Initially I resisted the idea for both our sakes, his for negative stereotypes that questions of sanity call forth, mine for the realization that, if Brad was crazy, my efforts to describe and understand his social behavior might be rendered largely inconsequential: Crazy people do crazy things.

Sue Estroff's remarkable book *Making It Crazy* (1981) offered an anthropological perspective (and corrective) to my thinking. Brad had pretty well figured out for himself how to go about "making it crazy" as a set of social behaviors accommodating of the mental state to which he had so quickly succumbed. I needed to be analytical about that element of the story. I also welcomed the perspective from Estroff's work—another observer in another setting—for gaining my own perspective. In this case, the literature served not so much in a comparative way as to provide a sense of detachment that I seemed unable to achieve by myself.

The publication history of this chapter has a strange turn. Earlier, I had declined an invitation to write a Foreword for a volume of new descriptively oriented educational studies being assembled by George Noblit and William Pink for Ablex. At the time of our initial correspondence, the editors had not settled on a title. When the book was finally published in 1987 (note again the slow process of publishing in edited collections), it bore the title *Schooling in Social Context: Qualitative Studies.* They agreed that the title was something less than eye catching, but they wanted it to be accurate. It was no coincidence that their title included a new magic word in educational research, *qualitative.*

I applauded their effort, in part, as I have noted, because I feel that we need to focus on the results and lessons of these studies rather than remain so preoccupied with how to go about doing more of them. Nevertheless, I declined their invitation to write the Foreword. That kind of writing presupposes a certain laudatory bias that does not come easily to me. I would rather be free as an outside reviewer to say what I really think of a book than be co-opted as an insider obliged to make more of it than may seem warranted. Furthermore, as best I can recall now, the editors were also toying with the idea of using another magic word, *ethnography,* in their title. Looking at the earliest list of possible contributors and topics gave me pause. I was concerned that too few of the proposed chapters would support a claim for "ethnography" in the title, although the collection promised a substantial contribution to the broad genre of qualitative inquiry.

(Ray Rist, who subsequently prepared the invited Foreword, avoided both the question of ethnography and the problem of commenting on individual chapters, noting instead how the volume marked the crossing of a threshold that had finally given qualitative inquiry the critical mass necessary for expanded influence among educational policymakers.)

Months after that brief initial correspondence, I heard that another invited contributor, Kathryn Borman, was preparing a chapter for the book's final section, "Moving From School to Work." I had forgotten the internal structure proposed for the book. I realized that my article might be appropriate for that section and would offer another perspective on the nexus between school and work. I rushed off a copy of my latest draft and found the editors receptive to the idea. In turn, they offered suggestions incorporated into the final version.

## References

Borman, Kathryn M. (1987). Fitting into a job: Learning the pace of work. In George W. Noblit & William T. Pink (Eds.), *Schooling in social context: Qualitative studies* (pp. 265-283). Norwood, NJ: Ablex.

Estroff, Sue E. (1981). *Making it crazy: An ethnography of psychiatric clients in an American community.* Berkeley: University of California Press. (Reissued 1985 with the addition of an epilogue.)

# LIFE'S NOT WORKING

## Cultural Alternatives to Career Alternatives

Life's productive years and efforts, at least as perceived by North American educators who take responsibility for talking and writing about such things, are properly directed toward two complementary and all-consuming activities, school and work. Because entry into school ordinarily precedes entry into the work force by at least 10 years—and up to twice that long in the professions—school is regarded as both antecedent to and prerequisite for work. This common acceptance of schooling as prerequisite for work (and virtually no question that work is what human life in the contemporary social order is all about) provides a comforting raison d'être whenever educators entertain self-doubts about their vital role and contribution to the common good.

My purpose here is to serve reminder that *school and work are not the only options perceived by today's youth.* The seemingly invariable sequence of school then work, reflected in titles such as Eli Ginzberg's (1980) *The*

This is the article as it appeared on pages 303-324 in *Schooling in Social Context: Qualitative Studies*, edited by George W. Noblit and William T. Pink and published in 1987 by the Ablex Publishing Corporation. Used by permission.

*School/Work Nexus: Transition of Youth From School to Work,* is not so invariable after all. Preoccupation with issues of employment, vocation, career, and the necessary transition from school place to workplace leads us to perceive everyone as falling into one of two critical categories, the already employed and the to-be-employed. With a few categories for the convenient labeling of exceptions (e.g., the retired, "preemployeds" still in school, the physically incapacitated) we dismiss from immediate purview those who detract from the implicit message: After school comes work. Even housewives (and, more recently, househusbands) have been redefined to be counted among the economically productive rather than to be viewed as nonworkers.

Through the use of life history data from a 22-year-old male, and from his perspective, I want to illustrate the obvious, but often ignored, fact that school and work are *not* the only alternatives. Stated more strongly, the case study presented here raises a question of whether, at least for some individuals—including white, middle-class, mainstream American youth—school and work offer realistic alternatives at all.[1] Minority status and inner-city lifestyles only confound the problems further for other youth for whom schooling opens no doors.

My case study is drawn from a young man whom I refer to here as Brad. I have written elsewhere about Brad in an account contrasting *schooling* and *education* and in which I discuss how, although Brad's schooling had stopped several years earlier, his education had continued apace (Wolcott, 1983). As in that earlier account, this one draws on an extensive dialogue with Brad held over a 2-year period, although comments concerning events subsequent to those conversations are of necessity more speculative.

Brad was not part of a systematic research effort on my behalf to collect life histories in order to examine alternatives to school and work as young people in similar straits perceive them. To the contrary, I cannot imagine that I would have written this account had I not happened to encounter Brad, for my own everyday existence comprises that very world of school and world of work of the sort already mentioned. Those two worlds dovetail nicely for me in the career of a professor who is at once an educator and an anthropological observer of educators and the educational process.

Nor do I write about Brad because he is "typical" or "average." It will become apparent to anyone who has read the earlier account, as it has become increasingly apparent to me, that Brad is not typical or average at all. Nevertheless, there are many like him; if he is not typical, neither is he one of a kind (for another firsthand account see, for example,

Brown, 1983). I think his story is worth relating, because its implications extend far beyond the case of one seemingly "screwed-up" kid.

I first came to know Brad through what ethnographers doing fieldwork refer to as serendipity. Literally as well as figuratively, I discovered Brad in my own backyard several weeks after he had managed, unannounced and uninvited, to construct a 10- by 12-foot cabin at a far corner of the 20-acre, densely wooded slope on which my own home stands. At the moment of our first and unexpected meeting, I felt hesitant about allowing him to remain on my land; yet I felt even greater reluctance in insisting that he leave, especially when he affirmed what was already quite obvious: He had no money, no job, and no place to go. Food stamps provided his major source of income, and most of what he needed in order to build and live in his rather hastily constructed sapling cabin he either found or stole. I did not expect or encourage him to stay, but as time went on and he continued to make improvements (a sturdy roof, wooden floor, windows, shelves, plastered walls, a wood stove, kerosene lamps), he gradually became as much a fixture about the place as was his cabin.

Although Brad "wished" for a regular job, he made no effort to find one. At one point, his failure to engage in ritual employment-seeking— during a period of staggering local recession and unemployment— cost him the previously dependable source of welfare dole that he had found in food stamps. I tried to underwrite his modest but recurring need for cash by letting him work for me whenever he needed a few dollars. Several large projects he undertook earned him sums adequate to allow major purchases.

Brad's early life, as revealed first through bits and pieces of conversation and later through formal taped interviews, had many elements familiar in contemporary middle-class American life. After his parents' divorce, Brad's mother moved to southern California, and Brad was shunted back and forth between his parents and their new spouses, a "hassle" in one household usually resulting in his being dispatched to the other. He was no longer welcome (i.e., allowed) in either parent's home; however, in the course of the two years he spent at the cabin, both parents did visit his homestead, his mother making a special trip from California to see him for the first time in several years.

Brad was proud of the cabin and of having done virtually everything on his own to get his life together. As his material circumstances improved, however, his social orientation seemed to deteriorate. An impending and once eagerly anticipated 21st birthday that would mark the completion of two full years "on the mountain" found him instead growing despondent and increasingly preoccupied with events and people largely the creation of his imagination. Through a casual acquaintance he found what he described as "the best job I ever had" working as an occasional helper for a gardener-landscaper. Yet after a few weeks he convinced himself that he was no longer wanted on the job, and he stopped reporting for work. Following several days of aimless wandering and musing, he announced abruptly (but after what appeared to have been an agonizing decision), "I'm hitting the road. Something's gotta happen. There's nothing for me here."

Knowing Brad's impulsive nature, and realizing that he had been preoccupied with the decision to leave but probably had given little thought to where he would go or what he would do, I urged him to postpone his departure for a few days while he considered his alternatives. Reluctantly, he agreed.

There were several things I hoped might be accomplished by the delay. First, I wanted Brad to have time to renege, if his thoughts of departing were merely an ill-considered whim. Although he had stated more than once his intent to stay at the cabin "as long as two years," and two full years had come to a close just 10 days earlier, this was the first time he had actually mentioned leaving. (As well, I suddenly realized that, in spite of our sometimes stormy relationship in resolving what he could and could not do as an unofficial tenant, I would greatly miss this unexpected intruder into my life and thought.)

Second, although there was little doubt that someday Brad would leave, I felt grave reservation about seeing him depart just then. His recent behavior had become uncharacteristically frenetic. He had begun "hearing voices" and he complained of psychological stress that he described as "a sledgehammer to the brain." I had asked earlier whether he thought talking to a counselor at a local mental health office would help, and I felt he might be willing to go there now. Acknowledging his own concern, he conceded that he "might try talking to them," although he insisted that it wouldn't really help.

Third, if some new precipitating event had occurred in Brad's wide wanderings or limited social contacts during the previous few days, there had not been time to talk it out. Over the course of two years we had communicated with what seemed a good deal of candor. If something specific was bothering him, I hoped eventually he would be able to talk about it.[2]

Fourth, if Brad was going to leave, here was an opportune time for him to take stock of his options and to review what he hoped to accomplish by the move. I suspected that he would identify fewer options than he really had, and I thought I could help him review his choices. "After all," I argued, "once you get to the freeway, at least you have to decide whether you'll head north or south."

"South," Brad replied, without a pause. Then he added, "Yeah, staying awhile will give me time to get my story, too." If you're going to be hitchhiking, it seems, people want to know why you are traveling. You've got to be ready for them. Deep inside my customarily reticent young friend lurked a practiced storyteller.

## Approved Career Alternatives: School or Work

The remainder of this account deals with a review of the options that Brad saw as he set out, deliberately and self-consciously, to take the next major step in his life. Some of these options were considered explicitly during the ensuing five days before Brad "hit the road." Other options had been pondered over the course of the preceding months. There was, of course, no systematic review in the sequenced array in which I now discuss the options, but the essential range of alternatives as Brad perceived them are the substance of what follows.

As my title suggests, Brad's quest was not undertaken in search of a career. Let me begin by discussing the two alternatives that reflect mainstream society's orderly world but that now seemed of little consequence in Brad's life: school and work.

In brief, school had not "worked" for Brad and work had not "schooled" him, in the sense of teaching him or socializing him. If experiences of both schooling and working were inevitable at some point in his life, neither had given him any sense of satisfaction or accomplishment. They may be society's alternatives, but they had not become his.

Brad's earliest recollection of schooling was of a kindergarten teacher's threat to wash his mouth with soap for using objectionable language. Things seem to have gone downhill from there. Even in his early school years he was frequently excluded from class for disciplinary reasons. While still in the primary grades, he and a pal found themselves in serious trouble after a weekend break-in to their school.

After his parents' divorce, Brad bounced between families and states and was constantly being re-enrolled in different schools. Apparently lacking any other sense of school achievement, and forever feeling "behind the rest of the class," he boasted that in his upper elementary grades he "must have had the world's record for ditching school."

That was his only accomplishment and his only recollection of grades 5 and 6.

Brad recalled "a pretty good year" after he enrolled in junior high school and earned marks that assured him he was not stupid. Relatively speaking, that may have been a good year from Brad's point of view, but a school counselor remembered Brad as a somewhat troubled seventh grader who had spent most of his time either in a counselor's office or "seeing the vice principal," the school disciplinarian.

Grades 8 and 9 were spent in southern California. Though little seems to have resulted other than the performance of the ritual itself, school personnel were forever testing him. He was eventually assigned to what he described as "an EH [educationally handicapped] class with the other stonies." He preferred that assignment to otherwise big and boring classes, but psychologically he had already dropped out of school. Even *during* school he regularly left the rest of the class; while they went for physical education, he enjoyed a daily respite in a nearby orange grove:

> I wasn't interested in sports. So I'd go get stoned. I'd take a walk during that class, go kick back in an orange grove, maybe eat an orange, get high, smoke a cigarette, and by the time I'd walk back, it was time for another class. I did it for a long time and never got caught. Anyhow, then I switched schools.

Another family hassle during grade 10 found Brad again "on a bus back to Oregon." He had no intention of re-enrolling in school, but this time his parental hassle resulted in a sentence to reform school. Once more, his "work" was school. Recognizing that his lack of diligence at classroom assignments was prolonging his stay, Brad finally "started to speed up and do the stuff, and then I got out."

At age 20, reflecting over his academic achievement, Brad claimed, "I was doing ninth grade work. I probably did some tenth- and eleventh-grade stuff, but not a lot." In voluntary testing he underwent as part of my collecting his life history, Brad's reading level tested at grade 9. His grade-level achievement at spelling and arithmetic was about 3 years below that. He was remarkable in his phonetic spelling of a language that is not, unfortunately, all that phonetic: *edgucate, beleve, preshious, angsiaty, conchens, phisithion, egsagurate;* yet he was sufficiently intrigued with words he wanted to understand or to spell that he would try patiently to locate them in an old dictionary he procured for the cabin. Hunting for unfamiliar words proved no easy task for a phonetic speller who had to recite the alphabet as his first step.

Brad was proud and confident of his ability to read, and he shrugged off poor performance at other school skills such as multiplication facts "kind of forgotten." When he once expressed interest in looking for a job as a waiter, I asked how he expected to write an order the cook could read. "That's easy," he explained. "I'll just write down what they say, good enough for me. Then I'll go around the corner and copy the words off the menu."

Clearly Brad had gotten something out of 10 sporadic years spent at school, but equally important to him, he had gotten out of school itself. It was barely conceivable to him that he would ever again subject himself to the frustrations of a classroom, to didactic instruction (he hated being told *anything* by *anybody*), or to having to display in public his marginal spelling or computation skills or slow reading speed.

If Brad is a classic case of a school underachiever, a kid whom the schools simply could not reach, he was a learner, nonetheless. As he himself summarized, "I've always liked learning. I just didn't like school." He would pore over instruction manuals, disassemble and reassemble machine parts to see how they worked, devise and refine improvements for the cabin, and, in the evening, select among the more educational and informative programs to view on his battery-operated TV. In his fiercely independent mode, learning, like everything else, had to be something that occurred strictly at his own pace, in his own time, for his own purposes.

Brad's experiences as an employee ran afoul of similar considerations: He could not find work that he could do at his own pace, in his own time, and subject to whether or not he was in the mood to work. He reported having worked briefly at a number of jobs, all of which entailed hard physical labor, required no special skills or previous experience, and offered no future. The pattern at each job seemed to have been the same, whether planting trees, washing dishes, doing yard work, or working for his father in light construction: at the beginning, high hopes, a clean slate, and a fresh burst of energy; at the end, reduced hours and take-home pay, "misunderstandings" about what was to be done or when he was next expected to work, and, usually, a final verbal confrontation in which the job was lost but pride regained. Against a real world of jobs he had done or might possibly get, Brad had a vision of jobs he would like, such as waiter at a fancy restaurant making big tips (although he had never worked as a bus boy) or driver of heavy equipment (although his driver's license had been revoked). "Just any job" would not do. Furthermore, Brad abhorred the fruitless ritual of job hunting. He disliked having to ask for anything and the likelihood of being refused.

If in my own experience I have become less than euphoric about the intrinsic value of work, in conversations with Brad I nonetheless found myself arguing on behalf of very traditional views; e.g., everyone should work, you have no self-respect without work, you should take whatever work you can get. I felt that I was helping Brad "build character" by doggedly insisting that he earn every penny I gave him. He avoided the lesson by working for me only as a last resort.[3] True, the security of being able to earn ready cash did help him. He was well paid; in turn, he worked hard for his money. But I was less altruistic than I thought; there was no future for Brad in working for me, so he worked only for the present. He liked to goad me with his conviction that it was easier to steal what little he needed than to put in the time and effort necessary to earn it. If he had more than a dollar or two in his pocket, he usually chose not to work at all.

On an escalated scale, Brad expressed the same antipathy toward holding a regular full-time job that he felt about working occasionally for me. Before he "took to the woods" he experienced what he described as "having a second-class job so you can live in a second-class apartment and lead a second-class life." Having reduced his cash outlay to under $100 a month, he did not need to put himself in bondage to ensure survival. The possibility of a regular job also posed a threat to his new-found security. Living in a cabin at the edge of town made getting to and from work difficult, requiring either a long walk to public transportation or a bicycle ride of several miles with a strenuous uphill return. His semi-outdoor lifestyle, as well as tramping through the perennial northwest rains and along a network of muddy trails, also created difficulties in keeping himself presentable, should a job demand it. A dependable income meant not only the loss of food stamps, but also dedicated his earnings either to purchase and operate a motorcycle or an automobile or to a move back to town and thus back to the second-rate life style again.

I thought I would be able to present Brad with a convincing argument on behalf of work, but I never succeeded. The best argument I could muster had virtually nothing to do with work itself: A job might help him become socially involved and therefore reduce his self-imposed alienation. Yet the thought of working with others, particularly in a job where "everybody sees you," was another of Brad's expressed concerns (as well as a cue that his publicly stated reasons for not working were not necessarily his only reasons).

As a consequence of conversations with Brad, I now pay more attention to menial jobs and to the people performing them. I am far less certain that being a bus boy, clerk, waiter or waitress, maid, usher, counter person at a fast-food chain, or gardener's helper really builds character or warrants a lifetime of occupational commitment. There are a lot of dull jobs, and employment projections are that dull jobs will increase in number in the years ahead. Because many working-class and middle-class youth have the skills, connections, or social savvy to make the leap from early experience at menial jobs to the opportunity of better ones, work "works" for them, but it does not work for everyone. Without skills or connections or savvy, it takes grim determination and great faith to start at the bottom, dutifully to put in one's time day after day, year after year, and to sustain a belief that someday it will prove worth the effort. Brad had watched his parents engage in that struggle. He was not sure what it got them; he had rejected it as a worthwhile goal for himself. As he said of his father, "He's worked hard all his life, but he doesn't have any fun."

What Brad quite consciously had set out to do in heading for the hills and "hiding out from life" was to learn something about life's minimal essentials, an exploration that led him away from customary and (to him) unattractive alternatives. As he summarized, "I don't have to work my life away just to survive." The material aspects needed for survival, particularly for a stoic 19-year-old, were surprisingly few: food and water, either on a meal-to-meal basis or with ways to get, keep, and prepare meals for himself; clothes enough to keep warm, dry, and presentable; satisfactory places for sleeping, for toileting, and for washing himself, his utensils, and his clothes; a sleeping bag or blanket; and—the pervasive problem of accumulating even so modest an inventory as this—places for the safe storage of any possession that he did not wish to carry everywhere with him.[4]

Armed with little more than determination, an old sleeping bag, and a handful of tools and nails, the immediate essentials in Brad's new lifestyle were not hard to discern. The location he selected for his cabin, a site discovered in earlier wanderings, was fortuitous. Young trees for building a cabin were there for the cutting. Within a radius of two miles were new house constructions, several shopping centers, and hundreds of unlocked cars and well-stocked sheds and garages. Such resources, coupled with years of successfully "being sneaky" and acquiring what he could not or would not purchase, hastened the initial construction and provisioning of an adequate shelter. Food stamps underwrote his basic menu.

Primal needs adequately attended to, humans look for ways to make life more satisfying, if infinitely more complex. In that quest they are guided by cultural norms so embracing that they even tell us how to go about being alienated or different or socially marginal. For Brad, first-order luxuries such as cigarettes, "pot," being able to listen to rock music on the radio, a camp stove, or a sturdy pair of boots soon became second-order necessities. In turn, new items like the stove entailed procuring additional items such as fuel and containers. The young hermit, at first hiding his every movement lest he be discovered, grows proud of his homestead and wants others to see what he has built. A painfully shy teenager-cum-adult now "showers," shampoos, and carefully combs his hair, dons a clean shirt, and sets aside one pair of shoes exclusively for wearing to town (rather than walking on muddy trails) before making even the quickest trip to the store, ever alert to the possibility of a brief exchange with "someone my own age" and the remote possibility of meeting the girl of his dreams.

Socially ill at ease as he was, I think Brad was nonetheless responding to social impulses he could no longer contain when he decided to "hit the road" and give up the security of the cabin. If his departure was not people-centered, he himself probably would subscribe to the idea that the time had come to embark upon a new experience. Brad measured his life in "experiences" the way others mark periods of their lives through promotions or the social events of birth, marriage, and death:

> I've lived in a lot of different places. Like going to California. Living out in the country. Living different places in town. Dealing with people. Living at the reform school. Living in Portland. Living here. I've definitely had more experiences than some of the people I went to school with and I've had my ears opened more than they have. In some things, I'm wiser than other kids my age.

Although Brad needed money while hitchhiking, his quest was neither for work nor riches. Nor was it an ideological search for an alternative lifestyle. Brad held "hippies" in low regard, observing categorically: "They are dirty." In the same breath that he once wondered aloud if he ought to try living in a commune (there are many such groups on the backroads of western Oregon), he dismissed the idea because of the social involvement he anticipated: "They'd never just let you be by yourself." Brad was too antisocial to become part of a socially inspired counterculture movement. Nor was he really at odds with his own middle-class background. He was not making a social statement in his decision to leave. His problem, simply stated, was that neither of the two traditional alternatives—going "back" to school or going on to a job—appeared as a realistic possibility to him.

## Cultural Alternatives to Career Alternatives

In what follows I have tried to portray options that Brad saw, in the way he saw them, during the days after his sudden announcement about leaving. The categories themselves are mine. Wherever possible, I have expanded the discussion to include related thoughts Brad had shared during earlier conversations.

### Join Up

For Brad, the idea of enlisting was not new but neither was it his own. More than four years earlier, his father had "encouraged" him to join the army, to the point of virtually insisting on it. Brad took and passed the necessary paper tests, including the G.E.D. (General Equivalency Diploma) exam attesting to his acquisition of basic literacy. Overnight in a Portland hotel as a guest of the government prior to undergoing the routines of the regional military processing station, he had second thoughts; in the morning, he was gone. His view since that time was that he would go into the military only if drafted; he would never volunteer.

Now, on impulse but also older, stronger, and wiser, he was willing to reconsider enlistment, on one condition: They had to take him immediately. Like a flash, he was off to the local recruiting station, only to discover to his surprise that the U.S. Army had a minimum waiting time of 6 months, the Navy even longer. Only the Marines offered the prospect of quick processing. Brad made a formal appointment with a Marine recruiter for the following day, elated by easy questions asked during a screening interview and bolstered by an overheard comment definitely intended for his ears, "That looks like officer material."

Back at the Marine recruiting office next day, the military option suddenly vanished. High school graduates were preferred; tenth grade was the absolute minimum, at least without the delay of undergoing an entire battery of tests. The G.E.D. test was no longer sufficient. At reform school, his last "school of record," Brad had been classified a ninth grader. School had failed him one more time! Eventually, the reasons that had gotten him into reform school would also have been subject to review, but for now, his lack of formal education was enough. Brad was not acceptable.

## Stay Put

"If you just had a job now, you'd be all set," Brad's mother told him during her visit 6 months earlier. Even without a job or close friends, however, he did seem to have succeeded in his goal of getting his life together. In a rare display of contentment, he once summarized his circumstances with the observation, "For me, it's great." Later he found a "perfect job" working as a landscape gardener's helper. He voiced little objection to the facts that the job demanded hard work, had more days off than on, was slow to pay, and, as often happens to people who must take such jobs if they want to work at all, part of each hour's earnings were withheld—without receipt—for purported tax purposes. Nevertheless, the job provided the prospect of at least part-time work. Brad also liked the young man he worked for: "I can relate to him," he said in the argot of his generation.

After Brad failed to appear for several days, his new employer made a special trip to the cabin to see what was wrong and to disabuse Brad of his illusion that he was no longer wanted on the job. But it was too late: As he had done before, Brad had decided to run away. For once, he was not in trouble with anyone else; this time the trouble was within. Nonetheless, the dearly gained lifestyle and security of the cabin were not enough to hold him.

## Be Crazy

The months immediately prior to his 21st birthday became a time of emotional stress and increasing personal anguish for Brad. His wanderings in town seemed to lack their earlier purposefulness, and his activities at the cabin often appeared aimless and repetitive. On dreary, rainy days he sometimes sat for hours gazing into the flames of his wood stove, interrupting his reveries only to roll a cigarette or joint or to prepare a snack. Not only was it an exceedingly difficult time for him (his food stamps had been summarily cut off, job searches seemed futile, and he was penniless) but he began to brood over his "hard life" and things that seemed forever beyond his reach: job, car, friends, a girlfriend.

With the approach of spring, the weather gradually improved, and so did Brad's luck (with the new part-time job), but his outlook did not. Momentary highs (several consecutive days of work; payday and the purchase of a new cook stove; the birthday itself, which did get celebrated) were eroded by days of brooding. Distant "voices," usually approving and just within Brad's hearing ("Boy, look at that guy—how strong he is—I wouldn't want to mess with him") were reported more often, along with occasional headaches, and finally Brad's acknowledgment of the incessant "sledgehammer to the brain."

For at least a year I had noticed Brad's tendency to preoccupy himself with one—and only one—major purpose or thought at a time, seeming virtually to get "stuck" on any problem until it was resolved. I hoped— but with a rapidly diminishing basis for such hope—that his persisting state of mental turmoil centered on some new and unresolved question, but I also broached with him the idea that perhaps we could—and should—find someone in addition to me for him to talk with, someone who might provide more help than my patient listening seemed now to accomplish. I doubted that Brad would be receptive to the idea—and he was not—but I laid part of the problem to my own seeming inability to be of help, and he did not appear to take offense at my concern for his mental state. On my own, and anonymously, I contacted a local mental health office to learn what resources were available either to me or to Brad should we want to use them. Having overcome my reluctance to consider "professional help," I inquired how I could ever hope to get an even more reluctant youth to talk to a counselor. I received what I thought was reasonable advice that subsequently proved effective: "You might ask whether the things bothering him seem to be making him uncomfortable. Maybe we can get him some help so he won't feel so uncomfortable."

Brad operated at or near a level of constant mental "discomfort" during the days leading to his decision to leave. He was so distraught on the day he announced the decision that he agreed at least to a telephone conversation with a counselor, but his guarded revelations provided little basis for anything more than encouraging him to come in for a visit. Brad took the unsatisfactory exchange as proof that counselors "don't do anything but talk."

Two days later, following the crushing announcement that his educational attainment did not satisfy the required minimum for joining the Marines, Brad was so distraught that he agreed (or at least acquiesced) to my suggestion that now might be the time to talk to someone at the mental health agency.

Responding to my tone of urgency, a counselor set an appointment for that afternoon. After a short consultation, Brad was asked to return the following morning to meet with a staff doctor. As we drove away, Brad reviewed the kinds of questions he had been asked. "Dumb questions," he related, like "Do you know what day of the week it is?" "Today's date?" "What month?" Brad knew it was Wednesday and probably was still April; cabin life does not give priority to such information. He said that the two options offered him were to receive outpatient attention (their preferred alternative) or to commit himself to a mental institution until he could "get things straightened out." He was adamantly opposed to medication and outpatient care, but he seemed intrigued with going to a mental hospital where he would be clean, comfortable, and cared for. "Hmmm," he mused aloud as we drove home, "Crazy Brad." In that moment, a new alternative seemed to be forming in his mind.

In order to ride to town with me to keep his appointment, Brad was at the house bright and early the next morning, but his demeanor was anything but bright. He had not washed his face or combed his hair, and I wondered whether he had slept. He summed up his strategy in one sentence: "I'll tell them whatever I have to tell them to make them think I'm crazy." He appeared convincing enough as Crazy Brad that I wondered whether I would see him again that day. It seemed thinkable he might get them to commit him straightaway.

Returning home that afternoon, I set out immediately on the steep trail to the cabin to see whether Brad was there. He was—along with a new sleeping bag and a new backpack. He had already packed his personal gear. He announced that he might start hitchhiking that very evening. His mood seemed lighthearted, although with the actuality of his departure now virtually assured, his ambivalence was even more apparent.

And what had been the outcome of his visit to the mental health office, I asked? "They wouldn't help me," he announced, and the subject was dropped. But he *had* been offered help; instead, he had experienced a change of heart. He was not ready to be Crazy Brad after all. He had been given the choices outlined the previous day: drugs and therapy as an outpatient or voluntary commitment, if he so chose. He declined both options. As if to punctuate his decision, he had "acquired" the new sleeping bag and backpack along the route of his return to the cabin.

Brad did not deny that he was still experiencing a great deal of mental stress. He assured me he would find a mental health clinic or seek out a halfway house if he needed help.

## Suicide

I am reluctant to include suicide among Brad's alternatives, but I am equally reluctant to ignore it. My intuitive sense was that Brad was not a suicide risk. Even if it is at the outermost periphery of alternatives for him, however, it was not entirely unthinkable. For many youth, middle-class whites as well as young people (males especially) in certain ethnic groups, suicide offers a patterned response for coping with the unmanageable; Brad's own pattern was to run rather than to give up.

From my conservative, middle-aged perspective, Brad was an impulsive risk-taker. He liked to impress me with stories of street drugs he had tried and of dangerous (or at least foolish) things he had done, ranging from driving a motorcycle "115 miles an hour" to creeping out with his companions on the runway of a busy southern California airport at night when jets were landing. His high-climbing and high-swinging antics in towering fir trees near the cabin were enough to convince me of his youthful daring, but I came as well to appreciate that he was not as foolhardy as he sometimes appeared.

I never felt that this risk-taking reflected suicidal tendencies. Moreover, at the time of his greatest stress, there was not the slightest hint that "ending it all" was an option he was considering. Nevertheless, he did use the phrase, "I'd kill myself first," to underscore circumstances that to him seemed beyond the pale. And on one occasion, finally talking through a problem that had weighed heavily upon him, he confided, "I even thought of pulling myself up by a rope, and when you came up here looking for me you'd be staring at my feet swinging from a tree."

## Welfare

Brad once offered the opinion, "Food stamps are society's way of paying me to drop out." He was first-generation welfare; I doubt that either of his parents had ever sought it; most likely they would meet an emergency in some other way should an occasion arise where welfare was an option. For some people, seeking welfare is virtually unthinkable. Brad held strong feelings against begging—as he said (and did), "I'd steal before I'd ever beg." But welfare was different.

Even at 19, Brad had been down and out often enough that he saw welfare—particularly the receiving of food stamps—as one of his rights, albeit a capriciously or conditionally given one. He also knew he could count on handouts any time in a big city. All he had to do was to locate its missions or meal stations, something he often had done before. In Brad's experience, it was all right to go for a free meal if you needed one, but in general you were better off keeping to yourself. For him, a mission handout was a last resort: Missions were places where too many people congregated, and they were not Brad's kind of people. That type of charity was the emergency solution; government welfare was preferable.

## Getting Locked Up

In just three days of pondering, Brad's options seemed at first to increase, only to narrow again to his original idea to "hit the road." Adamant in his feeling that he had to move on (thus excluding consideration of the possibility of remaining at the cabin), his two most attractive long-term alternatives appeared to be the institutional ones that had now been ruled out: military enlistment or mental hospital.

Strikingly different in my perspective, to Brad these two institutions shared common and even appealing properties (regular meals; a warm, dry place to sleep; clothing; opportunity to keep oneself and one's clothes washed; things to do and other people to do them with) that compensated in large part for some obvious drawbacks (regimentation, everyone telling you what to do, large groups of people, lack of privacy or autonomy). The military rejected Brad, at least on his "now or never" terms; he, in turn, rejected institutionalization in a mental hospital. One additional institution was also a possibility: jail, leading perhaps even to prison. Brad had no qualms about going to jail; he had been there before and had no fear of it. Even prison was not unthinkable to someone who had already spent the better part of a year in reform school.

I recognize my inclination to focus on differences among institutions; Brad tended to see their similarities. From his perspective, jail had certain attractions over other institutions, provided one's presence was not for anything too serious. Going to jail offers a chance to clean up, to sleep, and to be fed, and one does not have to stay as long as in the army or a mental hospital. In Brad's view, born of experience: "They have to let you out sometime."

With jail as his most likely risk, the idea of simply "moving on," living by his own resourcefulness and cunning, came around again not only as a good alternative but as the only realistic one for a young man in a hurry to be on his way but with no particular place to go. Easily acquiring a new sleeping bag and backpack for his anticipated travels served to reassure Brad that his skill as a shoplifter—seldom used in the past year—remained intact for the adventure ahead. As always, he would take only what he needed; he emphatically had explained that he was not a "super thief" who made a living by stealing, he was merely resourceful in obtaining necessary items he could not afford. He could get by. The mixed blessing of a few days in jail was the most likely consequence of getting caught at petty theft.

## Hustling

As for the long-term future, Brad's strategy was simply to "see what happens and not worry too much about it." On the streets, he would remain alert to whatever possibilities came up. "Dealing" drugs, for example—particularly to younger kids, just as older kids once had sold drugs to him—was a likely possibility.

Brad recognized a new sexuality and physical prowess in himself, only recently having outgrown an adolescent agony over what he had regarded as his youthful puniness (another of his personal reasons for deciding originally to take to the woods and live by himself, a topic broached only after months of discussing less personal issues). He now remarked casually about the possibility of marketing his body. His ideal sex-for-hire scenario was, predictably, to have a "beautiful woman" offer him a ride and immediately take him home with her, where he would enjoy the good life as a handsome young consort.

Brad also acknowledged that at his age and with his physique he would be attractive to males as well, and the idea of easy money and no work had its appeal. Along certain well-known boulevards of the metropolitan areas where Brad was headed, "San Francisco, maybe even as far south as Los Angeles," young males regularly hustle customers under the guise of hustling rides. Brad had caught glimpses of the hustler's role in exposés on television and may have experienced them firsthand on the streets of the larger cities in which he had lived or traveled. The moral issue was not particularly at stake: "I can drop my morals whenever I want." Brad doubted that he would try it—but the issue was largely academic until a real occasion presented itself. One had to be open to any possibility. After all, if he got to Hollywood, he might end up as a rock star *or* a hustler.[5]

## Going Home

Brad's world was confined essentially to the West Coast, from Portland to southern California. He told me he might go as far south as Los Angeles, so I asked whether he would return to the community where he had spent several years as a youth and where his mother resided. Currently expressing feelings of deep alienation from both parents, he insisted that he had no intention of going near his mother's home, reminding me that he was neither welcome nor allowed in his stepfather's house. Brad seemed to regard his departure more like *leaving* home than heading there. More than once while growing up he had run away from both his father's and his mother's homes. Once again he was resolving his problems by running away, but this time it was from a literal as well as a figurative home—and life—of his own making.

That Brad felt utterly rootless was evident in a new and poignant concern expressed during the brief interim when he was considering the military: "When everyone else goes home on leave, like at Christmas, I won't have any place to go to." I reminded him that the cabin would still be standing, and that he could return there (or to my home, if in the semi-stoicism of the peacetime military he had grown used to such creature comforts as hot and cold running water).

Underscoring that the cabin did now represent home, Brad sorted through his assortment of tools, parts, and utensils, carrying rubbish to an accessible pick-up point and storing valued items in cartons packed safely in my basement. Moments before his departure he suddenly changed his mind and, in the bizarre fashion that had come to characterize his behavior, he began sorting through his possessions looking for anything that might bring a few dollars at a pawnshop. (I hadn't realized our town had a pawnshop.) Then he was off.

Prior to that formal, dramatic, and seemingly defiant act ("These are my things; I can do whatever I want with them"), I thought Brad might return after a few weeks or even a few days. But as of this writing I have not seen him again.[6]

## Epilogue to the Story

The range of alternatives as Brad saw them serves to make the point of this writing in the way that attention to individual cases makes its impact. Here is a young man for whom neither school nor work held much attraction and who saw and reviewed his options in rather different light from his mainstream middle-class cohorts. Like all human stories, his is, in its specifics, unique, the combination of body chemistry, social experience, local circumstances, and the particular sense he made of the world as he perceived it. But Brad is also part of the story of all humankind as each of us goes about defining and locating himself or herself in a social world. In particular, Brad's story speaks for those of similar age and circumstance who fail to get caught up in the work ethos dominant in our society and who therefore seem oblivious to the forced choice they are given between school and work.

Our attention is more often drawn to highly visible and less transient groups in this "neither school nor work" population such as unwed welfare mothers, the job-seeking unemployed, or identifiable groups like "inner-city black youth." Young people like Brad ordinarily do not show up on official rosters until they are in trouble. But that does not mean they are not there. Like Brad, they may regard themselves as essentially alone, facing a "tough life" (Brad's phrase), largely forgotten or even unwanted, and, as they perceive it, entirely dependent on their own resources to survive in a social system that constantly threatens that very survival. For Brad, the solution offered by those about him—myself included—was apparent and simple: "Why not get a job?"

Brad's story—at least to the 22nd year of his life and to the extent I was able to piece it together—had not taken a course I might have predicted, yet it is intriguing how well it accommodated many of the seemingly disparate strands among his alternatives and underlying motives.

Almost from the moment Brad left, I expected either to see him reappear at the cabin—hale, hearty, and resigned, if not content, with his lot—or to receive a long-distance telephone call from (or about) him, informing me that he was in serious trouble. Instead, more than 2 months after he departed, I received a call from his mother. By a circuitous route that had included "waking up in Phoenix," hustling on the boulevards of West Hollywood, and spending several days in jail in a suburb of Los Angeles on a shoplifting charge, and following a series of increasingly frequent collect calls from localities throughout southern

California that gave his mother her first hint of Brad's current mental state, he had finally gone home.

Brad's mother reported that she found a motel room for him, but as she listened to him drift between fact and fancy in relating events, she began to realize that Brad was home to stay. She rented a small place where he could live, and discussed with him the idea of seeking professional help. Shortly after arriving home Brad voluntarily committed himself to the County Mental Institution for 16 days, but a steadfast refusal to join therapy groups or regularly take medicine left everyone, Brad included, feeling that institutionalization was not likely to be any more helpful than it was necessary. In response to a letter sent in care of his mother, Brad telephoned me once from the institution, the conversation seemed forced and aimless; he concluded it by saying, "Send me money."

Distraught and, I suspect, somewhat guilt ridden, for several weeks Brad's mother cooked and delivered a hot meal to him daily, did his laundry, and resumed the "mothering" that she had given up years earlier. Dissuaded by a mental health worker (as well as Brad's stepfather) who insisted that Brad was not all that helpless, she subsequently reduced her visits to about three a week.

As soon as he was formally diagnosed as a mental health patient—and thus a disabled member *within* society rather than a renegade from it—Brad became eligible not only for welfare benefits but for additional SSI (Supplemental Security Income) payments as well. In his mother's opinion, given Brad's moodiness, constant daydreaming, and short interest span, it seemed unlikely that he would ever be able to hold a job. She resigned herself to the fact that he was "insane" and to the likelihood that she would have to look after him the rest of his life.

Although Brad purportedly started taking an antidepressant prescribed for him and, in his mother's words (and in *her* meaning of the term rather than in Brad's) eventually became "mellow," he continued to refuse counseling or to attend voluntary vocational therapy sessions. She said he occasionally rode his bicycle, mostly sat in his room listening to rock music, and was leading what she described as a "very boring life."

Perhaps it was boring. It appeared so to his mother. It sounded incredibly boring to me when I reflected on the energy and sense of accomplishment once demonstrated by a fiercely independent youth who now waited for the government to send him money and for his mother to bring his supper and wash his clothes. But from Brad's perspective, compared to the lifetime he could envision as a dishwasher, tree planter, or day laborer, life may have been no less boring as he was living it. He would be the first to admit it was easier. Words once spoken at the cabin could be echoed again: "I don't have to work my life away just to survive."

## Life's Not Working: Some Final Comments

Although this case is necessarily incomplete, in part because it examines a young life still in the making, and also because I am no longer privy to Brad's thoughts or actions, I feel the data are sufficient to illustrate that for Brad—and for others like him with similar stories to tell—the "school/work nexus" represents neither *realistic* alternatives nor the full *range* of alternatives that they perceive. For many youths, school represents their first task-related failure; the neat and orderly progression from school success to work success is broken at the first step. Brad failed at school (or, stated more accurately, school and Brad repeatedly failed each other) and seemed now to have failed at work. He had taken a roundabout way to locate himself in a world in which he had nonetheless achieved some modicum of security and control.

As noted in my introduction, I did not seek Brad out as part of a systematic effort to investigate cultural alternatives to career alternatives. That opportunity arose in the course of events of Brad's life, the result of an unanticipated (though perhaps impending) crisis that precipitated an explicit review and choice of a course of action. The anthropologist in me is reluctant to dismiss Brad as (a) an isolated case, of (b) an alienated dropout, who (c) began exhibiting psychotic tendencies and therefore could not do what all normal people do, which is (d) hold a job. There are other possible interpretations—cultural ones—that invite us to examine the social circumstances of such a case and to raise other questions and speculations. Let me conclude by suggesting a few of them.

First, it is difficult for those of us reared under a strict ethos of the propriety of work, and who have in turn subscribed to that ethos in the ordering of our own lives, to fathom that *all* individuals capable of doing so would not choose either to work or at least occupy themselves with some moral equivalent of it. We need to recognize our own deep-seated and unexamined assumptions regarding the inviolability of work. The dignity we associate romantically with "work" is not equally apparent in each of the jobs that comprises the work force;

young people appear well aware of the distinction (see Sherman, 1983, chap. 3). Brad could get jobs, but they do not lead to careers.

My own role as an educator is ipso facto evidence of having bought into the work ethic. The same holds true of any of the formal role-occupiers with whom a young person like Brad comes in contact: welfare worker, psychiatric counselor, personnel manager, police officer, probation officer, employed staff member at an unemployment office. Brad's encounters of record were held entirely among the comfortable and diligent, the standard-bearers of mainstream American society. They surrounded him in every official role to serve simultaneously as his judges, teachers, counselors, and benefactors. They provide living testimony to the fact that the system "works," because it works for them.

But a dominant ethos is not a universal one. Brad stood not so much in opposition to the work ethos as disengaged from it. He did not seek his identity in work any more than he had sought it earlier at school. He had tailored his hopes and ambitions. He had a keen sense of what for him constituted the essentials: obtaining them provided his driving force. His attention was on what he needed, rather than what he might become. Survival was his challenge and his work, and he worked full time at it. But work for its own sake cast no compelling spell over him; it was no more than a ready trap back into the second-class life he had already tried and rejected.[7]

*Second,* Brad's case reveals a far stronger institutional "pull" in our society than I had been aware of, a pull toward compliance and dependency. Yet the case also illustrates both how powerful and how few are those institutional alternatives. The three "total institutions" that beckoned—the military, jail, or a mental institution—seemed in his assessment to provide roughly the same amenities in exchange for a full-time commitment.[8] Second-order institutional support—welfare, outpatient mental health services, meals at some mission—required less commitment but offered less in return.

I do not regard these institutions as providing alternative ways to order *my* life, and perhaps that is why it astounded me to hear Brad review them in inventorying possible resolutions for what to do with *his* life. It proved even more astounding to recognize how limited his choices were and the social cost of making them; the commitments are not casual. To me, each of his choices represents what I would take to be at best an interruption in life's work; to Brad, they represented genuine alternatives to it.

Although I have sensed growing disenchantment with the dominance of the role that work heretofore has played in our lives, some lessening of the dignity or pride associated with it, more tolerance for people who retire early even if they are *not* technologically displaced or under doctor's orders, I assume that gainful employment will continue to reflect an American core value, one of the realities of contemporary life. But we might attend more closely to the possibility of providing institutional options to help individuals like Brad find their way and to deal more directly with the social fact that we do not need—and cannot accommodate—every able-bodied person in the work force. One would think that we could come up with more creative primary institutional options than jail, mental institutions, or a reluctant stint in the armed forces.

Rather than foster alternatives that build or nurture institutional dependence, perhaps we should examine the ways we currently provide secondary institutional support. With Brad's problems conveniently "medicalized," he received two government checks, one (welfare) rewarding his acknowledged dependency, the other (SSI) rewarding his acknowledged incompetence.[9] During his years at the cabin, Brad was able to live on far less, maintaining his independence through the modest subsidy of food stamps that neither encouraged continued dependence nor (initially) punished him for it. Coincidence or not, it was in the weeks immediately after his food stamps were "cut off" that Brad began to show dramatic signs of the stress that eventually consumed him. He needed immediate financial help; instead, he received an appointment for a hearing. With his newfound and medically validated social status as "mentally disabled," he became eligible for subsidies that may last for a lifetime, as well as a life, of not working.

*Third and last,* I want to comment on the totally unexpected alternative that Brad followed, an alternative that anthropologist Sue Estroff (1981) described as "making it crazy." I am inclined to think that Brad "chose" to make it crazy. Viewed not only as a psychological response but also as a social solution that simultaneously resolved several important problems in his life, he could hardly have chosen better.

I do not mean to imply that Brad was faking a psychosis. He was rapidly losing touch with reality during his last few weeks at the cabin, and he steadfastly ignored my suggestions of ways to test whether the things he had begun to hear and to believe were true. Nevertheless, there are important cultural dimensions in the resolution of his problems.

Much as I agreed that enlisting in the military offered Brad a possible option, I breathed a sigh of relief when the Marines turned him down. Given his mental state and his natural antipathy toward being ordered about, I doubted that he was ready for the psychological abuse of initiation into the military even though he would have reveled—and excelled—in its physical rigors.

Similarly, a customary wariness that heretofore had served him well "on the streets" seemed to have escalated into a dysfunctional paranoia. Whatever actually occurred during his brief escapade as a street hustler, Brad subsequently confided to his mother that he was being followed and that the "Hollywood Mafia" was after him. The streets had become too dangerous. It was time to go home.

Originally, Brad dismissed the idea of going home. As part of his assertion of independence, he prided himself on not having (and therefore not being dependent upon) a home or family he could turn to, faltering in his pose of self-reliance only at the realization that even Marines go home at Christmas. Because he had been banished from the home of his stepfather as a result of unruly past behavior, all his mother could have done had he come to visit would have been to "go out for pizza" and give him money or buy him clothes. She had steadfastly refused his demands for a car or another motorcycle until he could demonstrate responsibility; turning up jobless and penniless would hardly have provided a basis for appeal on that decision.

But turning up as a son now deeply disturbed and obviously in need of help provided a point of entrée that made it all right for him to go home, all right for his mother to assume responsibility for him, all right for him to cast aside all thoughts of a job, and all right to accept a new status as a helpless dependent, the very antithesis of the qualities on which he had so prided himself the previous two years. The physiological basis was there; social circumstances called for everyone to play it to the hilt.

With Brad-the-social-problem now reinterpreted as Brad-the-medical-problem, the state was willing to assume the economic burden and provide professional help that Brad could not find earlier. The only condition attached to his new status was that he continue to be crazy, or, more accurately, to act crazy enough to be convincing. That became  his work. It is relatively permanent, relatively secure; it requires only physical presence, not physical effort. One can, more or less, choose one's own hours. The role requires a certain amount of acquiescence but tolerates a great deal of aberration as well; indeed, as Estroff (1981, p. 190) pointed out, it is important not to become *too* compliant or *too* cooperative.

There is some sacrifice of self-esteem, but since one may remain in relative isolation, the loss of self-esteem is probably no greater than one would find in many demeaning jobs. The only thing one must be careful to do is to demonstrate one's continuing inadequacy at some—but not all—social roles, including "work" in particular. As Estroff (1981) noted in what she identified as "Rules for Making It Crazy," it is all right to "try new things, like working, every once in a while," but you must assume you are going to fail, and when you do, you offer it as proof to yourself and to those about you that you are sick and cannot manage" (p. 189). Brad had been rehearsing appropriate behaviors for years.

In anthropological fashion, Estroff (1981) explored paradoxes in the lives of American psychiatric clients, focusing particularly on the seductive pull of income maintenance programs that "may perpetuate the crazy life not only by making it attractive as a source of income but also by rewarding the continuation of inadequacy demonstrated by not working" (p. 171). Estroff (1981) concluded with a broad generalization amply demonstrated in Brad's case:

> Being a full-time crazy person is becoming an occupation among a certain population in our midst. If we as a society continue to subsidize this career, I do not think it humane or justifiable to persist in negatively perceiving those who take us up on the offer and become employed in this way. (pp. 255-256)

I realize that, given the slightest hint that an individual has been professionally diagnosed as mentally disturbed, there is the likelihood that the individual is then regarded *only* in those terms. Thus I run the risk that my efforts to present a study illustrating a range of cultural alternatives to career alternatives can be dismissed on the grounds that crazy people do crazy things and the case demonstrates nothing more.

I hope that readers will feel, as I do, that the case does illustrate something more: that school and work are not the only alternatives, that the school/work nexus is not the only nexus, and that the realistic alternatives for eking out a living—that is, for sheer *survival*—as today's youth perceive them, may vary considerably from the ideal world we like to think has been created for them. Schools and social agencies oriented to a world of a-job-for-everyone-and-everyone-in-a-job address only part of the population and part of the problem of the transition that every human must make to adulthood. That is the message, or at least the reminder, of this case.

If the case is diminished because its young protagonist crossed a psychological threshold and lost some touch with reality, there is still something to be learned.

As noted, being a paid and full-time crazy person is becoming an "occupation" for a discernible portion of our population, a social group

whose distinguishing economic characteristic is that they are remuner-
ated on the basis of their *incompetence* rather than their competence.
Further, no one is crazy all the time. Even during the moments when
they do act crazily, the cultural repertoire from which so-called crazy
people draw remains essentially the same as it is for those around
them. Even inappropriateness must be exercised in culturally appropriate ways. In his paranoia, Brad did not bury his fingernail clippings,
cast a magic spell over his cabin and belongings, stick pins in voodoo
dolls, or run amok: rather, he hitchhiked a thousand miles, cast about for
several weeks, and then suddenly began making collect telephone calls
to his mother from freeway points conveniently accessible from her
home, insisting that he was broke, hungry, and lost.

Against such alternatives as being in jail, joining the military (out of
desperation rather than preference), or holding a menial job—and
taking into account the dependable income he now "earned"—Brad
had opted for what seemed at the moment to be society's best offer. I did
not envy his solution to the "school or work" dilemma; nor, apparently,
did he envy mine.

## Notes

**Acknowledgments.** Collection of the original life history data upon which this account is based was inspired and in part supported pursuant to Contract Number NIE-P-
81-0271 of the National Institute of Education. However, the focus of the present article
is different and is based largely on events that transpired following submission of the
original commissioned paper. A version of that report, to which the present article is
sequel, appeared in Wolcott (1983). Numerous readers have offered encouragement or
insight on early drafts including C. H. Edson, Sue E. Estroff, Bryce Johnson, William
Pink, John Singleton, and George Spindler.

1. I have not sought to document my observation that "school or work" is generally
accepted as the normal order of things; volumes and professional lifetimes have been
made out of the problems of career education, youth employment and training, and the
school's role in preparing young people for "the marketplace." In 1983 the National
Commission on Excellence in Education released a widely circulated report, *A Nation
at Risk: The Imperative for Educational Reform*, that presents the "school or work" option
in classic form: "More and more young people emerge from high school ready neither
for college nor for work" (p. 12).

The point of the present article is that college and work may be the most apparent
options for young people—and they are certainly perceived so both by educators and by
their critics—but they are not the only options. The specific reference to Ginzberg's work
is included because I find the phrase "school/work nexus" a convenient way to underscore
the pervasiveness of our work-focused view of the world, not to any particular issue I
take with Ginzberg. For an illustrative bibliography on the school-work transition and
interviews with high school juniors relating their views of its inevitability, see Sherman

(1983). For a historical review of the circumstances that so firmly established the relationship between work and school in American education, see, e.g., Edson (1982). For contemporary views of that relationship, see, e.g., LeCompte (1978) and Wirth (1983).

2. To forestall anticipation: If there was a single precipitating event, I never learned what it was. On reflection, I also wonder whether we had the level of candor that I once perceived. Brad did reveal a great deal of himself—but he kept a great deal to himself as well.

3. I am intrigued here with word choices that make me appear as benefactor: I *gave* Brad jobs; I *offered* or *provided* him work; I let / allowed him to work for me. From Brad's point of view, my seeming "generosity" went unremarked, particularly because I let him work anytime but steadfastly refused to let him draw money in advance.

4. It is the need to carry some sort of bedroll that makes the self-sufficient wanderer in temperate climates so conspicuous, be it student traveler, mountain backpacker, or transient hobo.

5. I have used the term *hustler* here to refer specifically to young males hustling sexual partners. In Bettylou Valentine's (1978) *Hustling and Other Hard Work: Life Styles in the Ghetto*, hustling constituted a major category of activity in what she presented as a threefold solution to the hard work of making a living in the ghetto: jobs, welfare (perceived as the *effort* required to obtain what one could, rather than the dole itself), and hustling.

I am unaware of any systematic anthropological attention to young male hustlers. Such studies would seem rife with possibilities for examining the rapid transmission and acquisition of culture as well as with the balancing of paradoxical norms and self-sustaining belief systems that assure people that they are not *really* doing what they are in fact doing (see, e.g., Reiss, 1961). A journalistic account by Lloyd (1976) provided some perspective into the sociological *role* but not into the fuller human context of its young and transient occupants; see also a perceptive "novel" and subsequent writings by John Rechy (1963) and a study by Weisberg (1985).

Brad was aware that the same youthful attractiveness he might "hustle" casually on the streets would not be a casual commodity were he to find himself in prison. In the fewest possible words, a wise jailbird had conveyed to Brad how quickly the decisions might be made. The scenario as Brad related it: "Hey, kid, wanna smoke a joint? You'll be *my* 'punk' now." Ironically, the same qualities of self-reliance and independence exhibited by young white males like Brad so culturally appropriate outside prison walls, are the qualities that make them more susceptible than members of minority groups to victimization once inside them (see, Wooden & Parker, 1982, especially chap. 6, "The Punks in Prison").

6. In the interim between completion of the manuscript and publication of the book, Brad did return, just as several readers of early drafts predicted. Within hours of his arrival he provided sufficient evidence of "craziness" to be incarcerated. Long beyond the moment for timely help, the state's resources for dealing with him punitively seemed limitless.

I do not yet understand those events or their meaning in terms of Brad's life or my own well enough to relate them; I am not sure I ever will. Bizarre as they are, the ensuing events do not change what I have written. In retrospect, my comments seem almost prophetic. But Brad had been equally prophetic years earlier when he reflected on what had been and what was yet to be: "I always seem to screw things up at the end."

7. Valentine's (1978) black ghetto residents who include *hustling* and *obtaining welfare* as forms of "hard work" appear to have adopted the ideal of the work ethic even though the jobs actually available to them are "scarce, poorly paid, unreliable, and often degrading" (p. 2). Here, consistent with both Brad's and my middle-class view of things, I have used "work" in the more restricted sense of holding a regular job and have regarded other income-producing activities as alternatives *to* work rather than alternative forms *of* it. It is interesting to realize that a restricted definition of work excludes much ghetto activity, thereby denying external legitimization of ghetto residents as "industrious." Their own interpretation of their activities suggests that because black ghetto residents do embrace the work ethic, they include as "hard work" certain activities that outsiders consider the very antithesis of it.

8. I have portrayed "the military" as Brad perceived it, an alternative to getting a job, a one-time-only choice with no thought of a lifetime career; at best, "time out," at worst, time wasted. Prior to his reconsideration about enlisting, Brad had characterized individuals who join the service as "mostly black and not very smart." When thinking about enlisting, Brad showed little interest in the branch or term of enlistment; his only concern was which one of the armed forces would take him the earliest.

9. As Estroff noted (1981; chap. 6) the SSI check that rewards incompetence paradoxically weds one to it.

# References

Brown, W. K. (1983). *The other side of delinquency.* New Brunswick, NJ: Rutgers University Press.

Edson, C. H. (1982). Schooling for work and working at school. Perspectives on immigrant and working-class education in urban America, 1880-1920. In R. B. Everhart (Ed.), *The public school monopoly.* Cambridge, MA: Ballinger.

Estroff, S. E. (1981). *Making it crazy: An ethnography of psychiatric clients in an American community.* Berkeley, CA: University of California Press.

Ginzberg, E. (1980). *The school/work nexus: Transition of youth from school to work.* Bloomington, IN: Phi Delta Kappa Educational Foundation.

LeCompte, M. (1978). Learning to work: The hidden curriculum of the classroom. *Anthropology and Education Quarterly, 9*(1), 22-37.

Lloyd, R. (1976). *For money or love.* New York: Vanguard Press.

National Commission on Excellence in Education. (1983). *A nation at risk: The imperative for educational reform.* Washington, DC: U.S. Department of Education.

Rechy, J. (1963). *City of night.* New York: Grove Press.

Reiss, A. J., Jr. (1961). The social integration of queers and peers. *Social Problems, 9*(2), 102-120.

Sherman, D. F. (1983). *Views of school and work: Interviews with high school juniors.* Unpublished doctoral dissertation, Division of Educational Policy and Management, College of Education, University of Oregon, Eugene.

Valentine, B. (1978). *Hustling and other hard work: Life styles in the ghetto.* New York: Free Press.

Weisberg, D. K. (1985). *Children of the night: A study of adolescent prostitution.* Lexington, MA: Heath.

Wirth, G. (1983). *Productive work—In industry and schools: Becoming persons again*. Washington, DC: University Press of America.

Wolcott, H. F. (1983). Adequate schools and inadequate education: The life history of a sneaky kid. *Anthropology and Education Quarterly, 14*, 3-32.

Wooden, W. S., & Parker, J. (1982). *Men behind bars: Sexual exploitation in prison*. New York: Plenum Press.

PART III

# Emphasis on Interpretation

*Like all scientific propositions, anthropological interpretations must be tested against the material they are designed to interpret; it is not their origins that recommend them.*
—Clifford Geertz, *Islam Observed*, p. vii

*Anthropology has shifted from questions of the accuracy of the data in the notes to matters of how one interprets them as text. Now everything is interpretation: culture is a text to be interpreted; fieldnotes are a text; we are in a world of hermeneutics, symbolic and metaphoric analysis, and there is a strong turn to examining the self as anthropologist.*
—Simon Ottenberg, *Thirty Years of Fieldnotes*, p. 156

The four chapters in this part represent my more interpretive efforts. I must repeat that what makes one article more descriptive, analytical, or interpretive than another is not only a matter of degree but also a matter of opinion. When I initiated the project that became this book, I felt that my articles could be sorted easily into the three proposed categories. As I have read and reread them with the categories in mind, the categories themselves seem to serve their intended purpose, but the sorting has not proved as neat as expected.

In part, any effort to categorize qualitative studies exacerbates the very problems that categorizing is designed to resolve. It is not so much a question of where description stops and analysis or interpretation begins as a question of whether description itself can ever be free of the analytical or interpretive frameworks that drive it. As one interpretively oriented researcher stated flatly when queried about the suitability of my three categories, "There has to be an interpretive framework guiding the research before it can even begin." I have heard the same argument put forth on behalf of theory, of concepts, of analytical models, of a solid disciplinary base, of a problem, of a foreshadowed notion—you name it. Researchers who insist on interpretive frameworks to orient their fieldwork are pretty likely to come up with accounts that emphasize interpretation as a result. That does not mean that description and/or analysis will necessarily be slighted but that interpretation is sure to shine through as raison d'être for the effort.

Interpretation has hardly been slighted in recent years. Indeed, as Simon Ottenberg observes in one of the opening quotes for this part, the anthropology of the 1970s and 1980s seemed to mark a moment of excess in which interpretation was everything and everything was interpretation. It has been suggested that, as ethnographers came to a public recognition—consistent with the critical mood of the era—that they could never really know the people among whom they studied, they began to turn their sights more introspectively on themselves. A new "reflexivity" became part of the interpretive act.

As fad, the excesses of that new reflexivity may have passed, but the way has been cleared for researchers to express more of their own voice in their accounts. If the art and act of interpretation have not been correspondingly enhanced, at least the personal reflections of the researcher as interpreter have come not only to be allowed but expected.

But these are lofty thoughts. The interpretive dimensions of the essays before you are of modest scope, although in each example they transcend the data that prompted them, and they are definitely reflexive. They represent my efforts to extend beyond the boundaries of a particular case to find broader application or meaning. They are my answers, tentative but not timid, to the nagging question faced by everyone who conducts research in the qualitative/descriptive or, for that matter, any other mode: "So what?"

I mention the overall "degree" to which researchers consciously set out to be analytical or interpretive, but each and every shift back and forth between what is offered as analysis and what is offered as interpretation should be clearly evident as an account unfolds. That is why I settled upon a teeter-totter rather than, say, a ladder, as analogy for the relationship between analysis and interpretation. Neither is "higher" than the other; neither necessarily must come first. In the interpretive mode, both the reach and the risks constitute more of a "dare" as researcher-turned-author enters the realm of how things *mean*. To come "down" fully on the side of plausible interpretation is to give "up" some of the comforting undeniability of analysis. Or, following the cautious tactics characteristic of early-career researchers, what one has to offer by way of bold interpretation is often preceded (and thus "counterbalanced") by a prior weighting given to cautious analysis.

Yet there is a potential for interaction between analysis and interpretation. Just as a teeter-totter can be as much (or more) fun out of balance as in, kept in motion by coordinated give-and-take, so analysis and interpretation can be played off against each other. If analysis sometimes serves as a conservative counterweight to lofty interpretation, the latter may also offset the sometimes formidable "weight" associated with analytical procedures.

To illustrate: A colleague whose academic specialization is higher education administration invited me to critique a paper he was preparing based on interviews with several "old-time" community college presidents. His research focus had to do with decision-making strategies, and so he had asked his interviewees to recall their strategies in that regard. What had they done, he asked them, to "make things happen"?

Although the only "data" for the reader were brief interview excerpts selected for their seeming relevance to decision making, the selections prompted me to propose quite a different interpretation of their content. These seasoned survivors of college administration did not seem to me to be saying much of anything! Whatever their success as pragmatic decision makers on a day-to-day basis, they had little to offer in response to an abstract question except through cliché and nostalgic reminiscing (e.g., "Build step by step. Don't get too high and mighty"). Easy talkers all, easy talk seemed to be the way they had approached their interviews, talking around the researcher's questions without really answering them. That may have been an important clue to their success as administrators, but that was not how the questions had been posed. In this case, a plausible alternative interpretation cast doubts on what at first seemed a tight analytic framework. The researcher had assumed that his respondents had *answered* his queries, and he took his analysis from there. I suggested that, although they "talked," they had found themselves unable to answer. Adequate descriptive data and a skeptical outsider uncommitted to the analytic framework guiding the research proved antidote to a topic that needed to be broached in other ways.

Another element, largely unrecognized, creeps into the interpretively oriented account: a self-consciousness about audience. When we address issues of how things mean, we examine those meanings in terms of readers like ourselves. And with readers like ourselves, we share a common academic language—those common bodies of theories, concepts, paradigms, and the like that link us closely with some audiences and preclude our ever reaching others. When we *describe,* we hope and intend that those in the setting will applaud our results or will, at the least, find them acceptable. When we *analyze,* we carefully select a few factors for scrutiny; we rely on the weight of evidence and the systematic nature of our procedures to be convincing. But when we *interpret,* it is our colleagues' presence we feel over our shoulders; our interpretive "rightness" is judged within traditions, not in the correspondence between our accounts and Truth or a strict adherence to procedures.

Under what conditions do we take the risks and challenges of the interpretive mode? I think we do it to demonstrate to others (and to reassure ourselves) that, in spite of their undistinguished origins, our works and the implications to be drawn from them are socially significant. Thus we do it to be profound. To accomplish that, we must not only transform our data, we must *transcend* them. If our goal is to contribute to knowledge, our own knowing is not enough: We must recruit other "knowers" as well. Knowledge is a matter of agreement. Field observations alone, data largely of our own making, cannot achieve status as knowledge. Our analyses reside safely because we carefully link them to the claims-making of others. Our interpretations are our claims to the independent creation of new knowledge. Arrogant work, indeed.

I have not held back on interpretation in my own work, but neither have I crossed the line to give an interpretive *emphasis* to much of it. The advice I give to others is the same that I follow myself: I would rather err on the side of too little interpretation than too much. I strive first to present an adequate descriptive account and then—marking the threshold—suggest what I make of it. The following chapters are among my boldest efforts to transcend the original case or problem that inspired them, yet even here description remains the heavy.

It is not mere coincidence that with each of these illustrative chapters the time between my initial encounter with the topic and the subsequent publication of an interpretive statement is at least a decade, or that for each of these selections a separate and earlier descriptive account preceded the more interpretive one presented here. Having thus "paid my dues" by providing the obligatory descriptive account, I felt not only free but, in a self-righteous kind of way, professionally obliged to say anything more I could to address bigger underlying issues. That implies "going a next step." Under optimum circumstances, one has the *option* to take it but is not required to do so.

Where to draw that line is problematic, particularly for authors trying to respond to journal editors and publishers or for doctoral students who must satisfy a committee's insistence on "more" by way of interpretation. Researchers who find themselves in such a predicament might be encouraged either to convey to the reader the nature of their impasse or to suggest alternative plausible interpretations, avoiding their own declaration on behalf of any particular one. These strategies were among several discussed in Chapter 2.

One of the biggest traps in interpretation—beckoning us to say just a bit more or to reach just a bit beyond a plausible conclusion—comes from stylistic rather than research concerns. It is the ever-present urge to go just a bit too far, to finish with a flourish in order to achieve what Margery Wolf calls "a tidy first-world ending" (1992, p. 55). Many a carefully conducted and reported study has caught readers off guard, and thrown them off track, with an irrelevant, illogical, or tangential ending that raises doubts about the credibility of the entire study. I urge you to make doubly certain that what you say in the final paragraphs of a study follows from and relates to the argument of the rest of the text. Do not sell out at the end or allow yourself to be pressured into writing something that satisfies conditions imposed by someone else but overextends or overstates your case.

I did not have to face such dilemmas while preparing these chapters. For one thing, time was on my side. Although each was an invited piece, I did not *have to* write. When I did write, my interpretation was consistent with my inquiry style, to open things up rather than seal them up. Each essay builds upon previous work, not so much by introducing new data as by offering a new perspective gained after extended reflection. It is, of course, gaining the perspective that counts, not merely the passing of some fashionably acceptable period of time. For most of us, however, interpretation comes about as a result of an ongoing, reflective process. The process can be stimulated and nurtured but, as I caution, it cannot be rushed. Perhaps we fail to realize that the depth we sometimes find lacking in accounts rendered by our students and colleagues comes from a perspective emerging only slowly in our own.

## References

Geertz, Clifford. (1968). *Islam observed: Religious development in Morocco and Indonesia.* Chicago: University of Chicago Press.

Ottenberg, Simon. (1990). Thirty years of fieldnotes: Changing relationships to the text. In Roger Sanjek (Ed.), *Fieldnotes: The makings of anthropology* (pp. 139-160). Ithaca, NY: Cornell University Press.

Wolf, Margery. (1992). *A thrice-told tale: Feminism, postmodernism, and ethnographic responsibility.* Stanford, CA: Stanford University Press.

# 8

# The Teacher as an Enemy

PREFACE

Although it does not warrant a capital letter when printed in upper- and lowercase type, the tiny word *as* plays a key role in my title by indicating that the interpretive thrust of this article is in the form of an analogy.

As I so often have had to do in the past, it was again necessary to look up the terms *analogy, metaphor,* and *simile* rather than trust a memory never quite clear about how to distinguish among the three in the first place. I was informed by my dictionary search that readers who recall my title and message as "The Teacher Is an Enemy" rather than "The Teacher as an Enemy" are transforming my direct comparison, a simile, into the indirect but more powerful comparison of a metaphor. I was also reminded of the expression and practice of "arguing by analogy." In qualitative research, however, the practice of employing analogy in any form seems designed more to lend perspective than to overwhelm with rhetoric, for analogies only clarify, they never prove. They draw attention to similarities among unlike things, one of which is assumed to be known to the reader. That makes it easy for the author to turn attention to particular features, and to ignore others, after a brief review intended to establish the basis for the comparison.

The excesses of analogy are humorously related in John Godfrey Saxe's poem, "The Blind Men and the Elephant," in which each blind man assumes that the entire elephant is like the part to which he has been directed. The danger of excesses in our work is the failure to recognize when to stop pressing an analogy. The merit of analogies lies in the depth of insight that can be achieved with analogies rather than in the lengths to which they can be extended.

In "Confessions of a 'Trained' Observer" (Chapter 5), I discussed how observers may identify paradoxes when they observe people behaving in ways antithetical to the purposes they are trying to achieve. Analogies can serve in like manner, sometimes suggesting a rather startling and not altogether unflattering perspective. One might expect, for example, to read about teachers as friends or, more austerely, about teachers as strangers. Here the suggestion that the teacher be viewed as an *enemy* is met head-on in the title. The perspective is introduced as a literary technique, however. The players in this account—the Kwakiutl Indian children in my classroom on the British Columbia coast —were not really my enemies, nor was I theirs. But as my pupils, they were what virtually every adult observer—village resident and outsider alike—would have described as "misbehaved."

A good analogy ought to enhance interpretation; a weak one is not worth risking, lest it detract from the study itself. Mixed metaphors, and mixed-up analogies, do a similar disservice. As you will discover, the enemy analogy introduced here is not strengthened by my unexpected (and unnecessary) reference to having "a tiger by the tail." And if I am forgiven for introducing *that* metaphor, I should have been satisfied just to hang on to the tiger. I did not have to stretch the metaphor to "crossing some kind of symbolic finish line together." Granted, those thoughts—and metaphors—did cross my mind; minds are like that. Our formal accounts are not supposed to be like that; my inadvertent meander into Metaphor Land did not enhance the essay.

Developing the enemy analogy did open dimensions I had not anticipated as I reflected further on what my pupils were trying to convey whenever they said—or acted as though—they hated me. My search for alternative ways of thinking about the role of teacher in a cross-cultural setting was itself a breakthrough. I had to recognize that not every classroom, even in the early grades, is a friendly place for pupils or for teacher, all of whom may find themselves acting out predetermined statuses established without regard for personalities or particular settings.

My first afternoon at the village, I knew something was wrong when I looked out the window to see two preschoolers throwing stones at the walls of the school building. By village grapevine they had heard that the new teacher had arrived, and although they had never seen me and had never attended school themselves, they were expressing in their own way the antagonism most village children had learned to feel toward school and teacher.

In search of a different perspective, I turned things around in this writing to suggest that teachers in comparable cross-cultural settings might think about their own culture, rather than the "target" one, as alien. From that viewpoint, a teacher might better understand how students could remain resistant, required by law to be present but determined not to be persuaded. The enemy analogy, however, conjuring up as it does a pitched battle, seemed inappropriate for a sustained encounter of the classroom kind. A better parallel was drawn by comparing my young charges with long-term prisoners of war, suggesting that the repercussions of battles being waged elsewhere filtered down to affect every facet of village life.

In just a few pages, the article moves from its basis in a descriptive account of one teacher and his pupils in one remote village to offer a broad perspective for looking at *any* classroom where differing cultural orientations between teacher and students provide unresolved and seemingly irreconcilable differences. The suggested "resolution" neither derives from the data themselves nor resolves anything. It offers a perspective, a way for a teacher to think about what is (and is not) happening as a social phenomenon rather than a personal failure. It is an interpretation, my interpretation; an old problem, a different way to think about it.

The chapter is practitioner oriented, so much so that I doubt whether a social science journal would have considered publishing it. Having written a largely descriptive dissertation, then subsequently having revised it for publication, I felt I had made sufficient academic use of the data—or, viewed another way, that I had validated my work sufficiently through prerequisite description and analysis—to justify turning my efforts now to interpretation. Did I have anything to say directly to teachers, something indicative as well of the kinds of things to come from the newly evolving "anthropology of education"?

What resulted from that effort is testimony to the greater freedom allowed in interpretation. Descriptive accounts must by definition be well grounded in observational data. The researcher's presence is already assumed (if not made explicit) in the organization and presentation of data. *Analysis,* in the restricted sense in which I use the term here, must also be tethered to its data base; it can float above but must not drift far away. Links to the data must be apparent and strong.

Interpretation can soar high overhead, mere threads connecting it to its origins. It is far more susceptible to theoretical or ethical fads, and thus its path is not all that predictable. (Case in point: The final and less well known stanza of "The Blind Men and the Elephant" draws the lesson of the poem to the comparable lack of a larger vision among disputants in "theologic wars.") Interpretations may clearly demonstrate their links between the research at hand, exemplifying data-in-use. Sometimes, however, they attempt so valiantly to rise above it all that a presumed data base seems to provide little more than a launchpad. The point at which data-driven interpretations become free-floating conjecture may be difficult for researchers themselves to discern but all too evident for readers who cannot help but wonder: "How did we get here from there?" The temptations of interpretive excess can be held in check with careful stocktaking: Is there a basis in this research (and/or in the work of others) for the interpretation I offer? Am I trying to rise above my data to gain perspective, or have I cut myself loose from the data to free myself to say whatever I want? If the latter, is this the place and way to do it?

Different audiences have different expectations as to whether an adequate research base is critically important. There is nothing objectionable about interpretation "for its own sake," the interpretive essay. There is nothing objectionable about drawing upon research, even casually, for apt illustration or example. There is something objectionable in failing to distinguish between transcending data and being totally oblivious to it in work advanced as research based.

Analytically inclined readers, and qualitative researchers more interested in method than results, will expect connections to be apparent in interpretive studies, with interpretations linked to reported observations rather than taken on faith. Practitioners, on the other hand, may be impatient with description, already painfully aware of how things are. Their burning questions have to do with how to change or improve them. The prescriptions they seek cannot be drawn from the data themselves: *How things are never points to how they should be.* The "shoulds" and "oughts" that grace our studies come from the researcher's reading of the data, the context in which the data were gathered, and embedded questions of values of right and wrong, or good, better, and best.

Years ago, anthropologist Solon Kimball noted that a great deal of what passes for educational research is really educational reform in disguise. I think his statement applies to social research in general. The reformer element can lead interpretive efforts astray when researchers fail to recognize the circumstances that influence their interpretations, influences often unrelated to the settings and data at hand. A totally subjective reader will probably judge an interpretation in terms of his or her agreement with it. A more objectively inclined one will also consider whether the data base supports the interpretation and the interpretation makes sense of the data.

I don't think "Teacher as an Enemy" pushes any limits. It offers perspective rather than remedy. It does rather blithely accept the status quo, but that is an inherent aspect of descriptive work. It also locates the heart of both problem and solution somewhere else (the adult community rather than the young children in school), conveniently citing a recognized authority for saying so—a study of social adjustment among the Indians of British Columbia conducted by Canadian anthropologists (Hawthorn, Belshaw, & Jamieson, 1960). If it is a call for reform, it is muted. It invites—rather than insists on—another way of thinking, to help—rather than castigate—teachers.

Nevertheless, the idea of teacher as enemy is not inherent in the data, explicitly or implicitly. It was imposed on, or "attached to," the descriptive account. There are no widely agreed upon criteria for judging such interpretations. As with any interpretive effort, this one might appear incidental to the case yet prove sufficiently provocative or satisfying that some readers would find it acceptable anyway. Ironically, that is where good writing is both an asset and a potential liability in qualitative inquiry, and why good writing requires critical reading as well as satisfied readers. My personal reaction to any unduly high praise for my writing ("You write *so* well") is always one of ambivalence, even when clearly intended as a compliment. I must weigh the possibility that I have said too well something not necessarily worth saying, or that a weak idea was too well camouflaged to be recognized for what it really was. As in the case of all my writing, I endeavored here to create a chapter engagingly written without letting the writing get in the way of the message. We are researchers who write, not gifted writers who can indulge in writing for its own sake.

The fieldwork on which "The Teacher as an Enemy" is based began as doctoral dissertation research in 1962. I prepared a brief paper for presentation in a symposium at the American Educational Research Association 6 years later (1968), after completing both the dissertation (1964) and its subsequent rewrite as a monograph, *A Kwakiutl Village and School* (1967).

As part of a symposium, my paper had to fit one of those narrow time slots assigned at national meetings; even with a 12-page, double-spaced document, I exceeded my time limit. That short paper was titled "Classroom Learning—Kwakiutl Style." Embedded in it was the idea and subtitle of the teacher as an enemy, which I subsequently developed into this chapter-length article. The invitation to do so had come from George Spindler, who was then planning a revision of his edited collection *Education and Culture* (1963) to become his (1974) volume, *Education and Cultural Process*, the same volume in which the discussion of the Principal Selection Committee (Chapter 4 here) originally appeared.

In the Preface to Chapter 4, I discussed the practical reason for accepting Spindler's invitation to prepare the article (in addition to the fact that I don't recall that he gave me much choice): to help publicize both my new monograph and the new series in which it had appeared, the Spindler-edited Case Studies in Education and Culture. Here was a chance, and a challenge, to go beyond the carefully descriptive course I had chosen in writing the dissertation—and followed again in revising it for publication—to try to say something both more helpful and more provocative. At that time (the late 1960s), educators were just beginning to grapple with issues of "minorities" in ways that now included a growing sensitivity toward cultural differences. (For more recent contributions on issues of minority education, see, for example, Gibson & Ogbu, 1991; Jacob & Jordan, 1993; Spindler & Spindler, 1993.)

Until I prepared the new Afterword for *A Kwakiutl Village and School* (the selection that immediately follows as Chapter 9), this was the only other writing I had done based upon my Kwakiutl experience. I have always been glad that I wrote it, and pleased to hear from others who have remarked on its impact on themselves or their students, especially students preparing to teach in cross-cultural settings. In retrospect, my only reservation about the article's impact is with the number of people who did later recall—as title or message—that the teacher *is* an enemy. That is not the message I intended. But one's written words go on to a life of their own. I console myself that readers who concluded, "Wolcott says that teachers are enemies" heard the message they were prepared to receive.

The chapter is grounded in descriptive data, yet the writer assumes an authoritative voice. He is no longer merely a guide calling things to the reader's attention; instead, he assumes the role of interpreter, suggesting parallels between the words and actions in a particular setting and the broader issues of communication and education across cultural boundaries anywhere. In this role, the researcher now tells us—or at least invites us to ponder with him—how things mean. This is the part of qualitative/descriptive work that readers often anticipate most keenly, but it can put author and reader at cross-purposes as each waits for the other to reveal what it all means. It is not a time when researchers must remain silent, but it is the time for an appropriate tentativeness as the researcher *proposes* what one might make of it all.

# References

Gibson, Margaret, & Ogbu, John. (Eds.). (1991). *Minority status and schooling: A comparative study of immigrant and involuntary minorities.* New York: Garland.

Hawthorn, Harry B., Belshaw, C. S., & Jamieson, S. M. (1960). *The Indians of British Columbia: A study of contemporary social adjustment.* Berkeley: University of California Press.

Jacob, Evelyn, & Jordan, Cathie. (Eds.). (1993). *Minority education: Anthropological perspectives.* Norwood, NJ: Ablex.

Spindler, George D. (Ed.). (1963). *Education and culture: Anthropological approaches.* New York: Holt, Rinehart & Winston.

Spindler, George D. (1974). *Education and cultural process: Toward an anthropology of education.* New York: Holt, Rinehart & Winston.

Spindler, George D. (1987). *Education and cultural process: Anthropological approaches* (2nd ed.). Prospect Heights, IL: Waveland.

Spindler, G. & Spindler, L. (Eds.). (1993). *Pathways to cultural awareness.* Thousand Oaks, CA: Corwin Press.

Wolcott, Harry F. (1964). *A Kwakiutl village and its school: Cultural barriers to classroom performance.* Unpublished doctoral dissertation, Stanford University.

Wolcott, Harry F. (1967). *A Kwakiutl village and school.* New York: Holt, Rinehart & Winston.

Wolcott, Harry F. (1968, February 9). *Classroom learning—Kwakiutl style.* Paper presented at a symposium, "Cross-Cultural Cognitive Studies," American Educational Research Association.

Wolcott, Harry F. (1972). The teacher as an enemy [abridged]. *Practical Anthropology, 19*(5), 226-230.

# THE TEACHER AS AN ENEMY

I don't like Mr. Wolcott
he always make me work
I hate Mr. Wolcott

A Kwakiutl Indian boy directed these written words to me while he was attending school in his native village on the coast of British Columbia, Canada. At the time I was the teacher at the village school. My purpose in living in the village and teaching at the school was to study the relationship between village life and the formal education of village pupils. An account of my year as teacher and ethnographer at Blackfish Village is contained in *A Kwakiutl Village and School*, which is a case study of the problems of Western education in a contemporary cross-cultural setting (Wolcott 1967).

"The Teacher as an Enemy" first appeared in 1974 and was subsequently retained in Spindler's second edition of *Education and Cultural Process* published by Waveland Press in 1987. It is reprinted here with the permission of Waveland Press. It also appeared in an abridged version in *Practical Anthropology* in 1972, a curious circumstance in which the abridged version of a "published" article actually appeared 2 years before the original found its way into print. The wording of the original has been left intact, including now outdated "gender language," an issue discussed briefly in the next chapter. I beg forgiveness from today's readers and remind them that at the time such usage was proper; ambiguous plurals were considered poor form. There is further ambiguity in this instance because many preferences to the teacher are specific references to myself. In contemporary usage, one also finds Canadian references to First Nations or First Peoples in preference to "Indian" as used here.

As the village teacher I had the responsibility for conducting a one-room school for all the resident village children between the ages of six and sixteen. As an ethnographer, I wanted to identify and assess the influence of cultural barriers to classroom performance as a way of studying why Indian pupils have so often seemed refractive to the formal educative efforts of the school.

Although I had taught previously in public schools, I was not prepared for the classroom problems that confronted me at the village school. I found there a firmly entrenched pattern of pupil hostility toward the teacher and toward nearly every nonmaterial aspect of the way of life the teacher represented. In the time that has elapsed since the original fieldwork in 1962-1963, I have had the opportunity to reflect upon the experiences of that year and to return for several brief periods of subsequent study. I have been seeking alternative ways of thinking about the role of the teacher in a cross-cultural setting like Blackfish Village.

In a setting in which critical differences between a teacher and his pupils are rooted in antagonisms of cultural rather than classroom origins, I believe that the teacher might succeed in coping more effectively with conflict and in capitalizing on his instructional efforts if he were to recognize and to analyze his ascribed role as "enemy" rather than attempt to ignore or deny it. To those educators who insist that a teacher must always present a façade of cheery optimism in the classroom, the notion of the teacher as an enemy may seem unacceptable, overly negative, perhaps even dangerous. One might question, however, whether cheery optimism and a determination to accomplish "good" inevitably serve the best interests of culturally different pupils, especially pupils from socially and economically depressed or deprived sectors of the population. Any teacher who has faced such pupils in the classroom may have recognized that one alternative for him is to try to do less harm rather than more good. Even with so modest a goal, any strategy that may minimize psychological harm either to pupils or to their teachers merits consideration. The strategy of regarding the teacher as an enemy is explored here as it relates to formal education in antagonistic cross-cultural settings.

## Antagonistic Acculturation

Anthropologists refer to the modification of one culture through continuous contact with another as acculturation. Often one of the contact cultures is dominant, regardless of whether such dominance is intended. Not infrequently, the situation of dominance leads to a relationship that breeds antagonism on the part of the dominated group.

Antagonism rises rather expectedly out of feelings that one's own cherished ways are being eroded and lost or that one's ethnic group belongs to a have-not class. Antagonistic feelings may be aggravated by the attempts of members of the dominant society to hasten the process of assimilation. Frequently antagonisms are aggravated by a contradiction between the ideal of assimilation and the reality of prejudicial treatment accorded to minority groups within the dominant society. This was the case at Blackfish Village, not because of any problem unique to the village but because there had been a concerted, although not very successful, effort by both the Canadian and U.S. governments to hasten and even to complete the assimilation of North American Indian groups. Indian schools run by the federal governments of both countries consciously directed their efforts toward replacing Indian ways with ways more acceptable to and characteristic of the dominant white middle class, although the respective societies have at the same time responded prejudicially to the Indian who attempted to assimilate.

Contemporary social commentary describing the relation of pupils to their schools among the Sioux Indians, along the Mexican-American border, in Harlem and in Puerto Rican East Harlem, in the Deep South, in Boston, in Washington, D.C., or in the inner city everywhere suggests that cultural barriers to classroom performance are not unique to my confrontation with Blackfish pupils. However, I shall relate my discussion to that specific setting. I will describe how the stresses resulting from "antagonistic acculturation" were manifested in microcosm in the behavior of the village children in the classroom. First, I shall describe how I perceived the classroom to be organized to thwart my instructional efforts. A rather different picture of the classroom follows as written accounts from some of the older Blackfish pupils suggest how the classroom looked to them.

## Classroom Learning Kwakiutl Style— as Seen by the Teacher

Here are seven important characteristics of the classroom at the Blackfish Indian Day School as I saw it:

1.  The pupils set their own pace, not in the ideal sense of an individualized program with each child working independently at an optimum rate, but rather with doing little in lots of time. My inclination, having found them "behind" in their work, was to get them "caught up." Their inclination was, generally, to let the school day slip by without having expended too much—or perhaps any—effort in the direction I was so anxious to push them. Their whole orientation to school, I believe, was one of patiently enduring. What my pupils wanted most to get out of school was to get out of school. Since maturity provided the only means to achieve that goal, the amount of school work accomplished in a day had no meaning unless one's peers wanted to engage in a self-imposed competition or one really valued the praise of the teacher. But neither the rewards the teacher had to give nor the manner in which he gave them were likely to warrant the effort necessary to attain them or the risk of incurring the displeasure of one's fellow pupils for having done so.

2.  Classroom assignments were frequently perceived as a group task. My worksheets and practice papers were treated as though my class was a secretarial pool—older or brighter pupils did papers for younger or slower ones, sometimes because the assignments were difficult, sometimes because they were fun. My pupils, as a class, were organized to cope with me collectively, while I was trying to cope with them individually. The nature of this mutual classroom help among pupils had several concomitant aspects described below.

3.  Almost invariably students collaborated as partners in electing to complete or to ignore classroom assignments, in deciding whether to write long diary entries about their day, in making choices when alternative activities were offered, or in preparing answers to my questions. My "divide and conquer" tactic was constantly subverted. I had great difficulty assessing the progress of any given pupil because pupils so frequently teamed up to write daily entries for each other and to work each other's assignments.

One of the most successful classroom activities of the year was the exchange of a series of letters between the older pupils and a sixth-grade class in a California school. As the exchange of letters progressed, some members of the class began receiving more letters than others. Those who received many letters farmed out the excess and had other pupils write the replies. At another time, I gave eight older pupils a sentence-completion test. I later discovered that instead of eight sets of answers I had received four sets of paired answers in return. Before beginning to complete the sentences each pupil chose a partner with whom he worked out a tentative answer, and then both partners wrote comparable—or identical—responses for each sentence.

4. Teasing and bullying were very disruptive elements in class. Often the teasing was related to inter- or intra-family squabbles which had their origin outside of school. Included in the teasing, however, was a process of pupil socialization in which children learned not to outperform their peers. Particularly, I observed change in the behavior of two children, a fourth-grade girl and a first-grade boy, who came to the village after the school year had begun and who seemed to be particularly capable students. Both underwent continual taunting in class, and both learned to display less overt enthusiasm for school and to restrict their academic prowess to tasks on which they could work alone, while they performed only minimally at those tasks on which greater achievement was apparent to their peers. The boy had come from a provincial school where he was one of few Indian pupils: the girl had been attending a day school in another village, one in which school achievement was more acceptable and school success more frequent. Whether the socialization of these children was due to their ability in school, their being outsiders to the village, or a combination of both, I have never been certain. That the quality and quantity of their academic performance diminished, I am sure. The girl traveled to her parents' village for Christmas and never returned to Blackfish Village; the boy survived the year by learning to perform more like other village boys in school, which meant doing very little on group assignment, although he usually worked well alone. He outperformed all the other pupils in the seclusion of two intelligence tests I administered.

5. At the same time that overperformance was restrained through socialization, there was some tendency to help the slower children of one's age or ability group. Such help differs from the help given to younger pupils, because that assistance seemed to be used to get the tasks completed (if the teacher was going to insist on them) while the helping to which I now refer served to keep a pupil from appearing too inadequate in the eyes of the teacher. For the teacher, this "equalizing" behavior among the pupils made the task of finding suitable material or diagnosing individual learning difficulties almost impossible.

The most glaring instance was that of a fifteen-year-old boy who was almost a nonreader. In September I assigned to him a fourth-grade basal reader which was being read by several other boys. It was some time before I realized that he was so used to having difficult words whispered to him by his reading mates that during my limited opportunity to hear the children read aloud he did not necessarily look at the pages to appear to be reading from them. Eventually I realized he could read independently only at grade-one level, and as late as May I recorded in my notes, "He gets so much help from other kids that I still doubt that I know his own capabilities."

As a social phenomenon, the cooperative efforts of my pupils may appear both remarkable and praiseworthy. In each case, however, the extent of their cooperation and organization inevitably thwarted my efforts in both assessing and instructing them, according to the expectations which I held for myself as a teacher. Further, to whatever extent I was able to see the positive aspects of pupil cooperation rather than to feel threatened by it, I was still unable to mobilize the cooperative potential of the pupils to accomplish *my* purposes. I could not make them help each other, be patient toward each other, or socialize each other toward such teacher-approved purposes as keeping the classroom quiet so pupils could read, working quickly enough to allow time for other activities, or letting younger pupils join in the recess play of the older ones.

6.  Antagonistic as they were toward so many aspects of school, my pupils nevertheless held very rigid expectations about the activities they considered appropriate for school work. Insistence on attention to the three R's constituted the only legitimate kind of demand which the pupils both expected and accepted on the part of their teacher. Their notion of an ideal classroom was one in which pupils were busily engaged in highly repetitive but relatively easy assignments for long periods of time, uninterrupted by the teacher. Their notion of an ideal teacher, consistent with this, was of a person who meted out assignments but not explanations, a person who had an infinite supply of worksheets and tasks but who never asked a pupil to engage in an exercise he could not already perform. The only favors or rewards expected of a teacher were in the distribution of coveted materials (crayons, water colors, compasses, scissors, puzzles, athletic equipment), the allocation of prestige positions (attendance monitor, bell ringer), and the rationing of school "fun" ("free" time, art periods, extended recesses, classroom parties).

Given their narrow expectations for proper classroom activities, it is not surprising that the pupils responded most favorably to assignments at the specific tasks required in arithmetic and spelling. Occasionally they requested an assignment to repeat a page of arithmetic drill or requested my validation of a self-imposed assignment to write each spelling word three, five, or ten times.

Weeks passed before the older pupils grew accustomed to my daily assignment—making at least a brief entry in a diarylike notebook. Even when they had grown used to this activity as part of our daily program, they were uneasy that I did not "teach" language arts because I did not often use the language arts texts. Although their basal readers and the accompanying workbooks were difficult, dull, and pedantic, the pupils were never satisfied that they were "having reading" unless these readers were before them. They never completely accepted my progressive idea that reading a book of one's own choice was also a legitimate type of classroom reading. Patiently, and sometimes impatiently, they endured my reading aloud to them, because they had been subjected by their teachers to that dubious pleasure for years, but I could seldom induce them to any kind of classroom discussion subsequent to hearing a story. My attempts to relate social studies to their own lives made them uncomfortable both because they perceived this as prying and because I did not depend on textbooks in my approach. They were generally impatient with instruction in concepts that were not included in their texts (for example, notions from the new math). In short, my pupils had very specific expectations for the formal purposes of school, they generally hated school as defined by these expectations, and they refused to have their expectations modified. They disliked school and that is just how they liked it.

7. Let me conclude this description of the classroom as seen by the teacher with one final pattern of pupil behavior, the attempts of the pupils to socialize their teacher. It is misleading to refer to this socialization as "attempts," for my pupils were good teachers and their techniques were effective. The methods they used to socialize me included giving slow, reluctant responses to my directions, ignoring my comments (by not "hearing" them or occasionally by putting their hands to their ears), mimicking my words or actions, constantly requesting to leave the classroom to go to the toilet, and making me the target of spoken or written expletives. To illustrate, the following note was written to me during the daily writing period by a twelve-year-old boy the day after I took a partially eaten apple away from him and inadvertently forgot to return it:

We were packing wood yesterday me and Raymond were packing lots of wood. Oh, you little monkey, little asshole you got my apple why don't you mind your own business you think you smart little asshole. Goodbye, that's all I can say now. Goodbye, no more writing because you throw my apple.

The most direct and telling comments were those that identified me as "White man," the outsider, or drew attention to our different cultural origins: "Just like a White man," "That's the trouble with you White guys," or, twice during the year, an angry stare and the comment, "What's the matter; haven't you ever seen an Indian before?" With such a statement as: "We don't have to tell *you* anything," I was at a loss to know whether my distinguishing attribute was that I was white, the teacher, or a cranky adult, or all of them.

## Classroom Learning Kwakiutl Style—as Seen by the Pupils

Although I have referred frequently to the pupils in the class, the classroom picture presented above is entirely a construct of a teacher's perception. Consequently, it is cast primarily in terms of the teacher's instructional goals and how the subculture of the pupils seemed to be organized to thwart them. Written comments of the older pupils provide some insight into how the class and teacher looked to them.

1. This response was written by a fifteen-year-old girl to an assigned topic, "If I Were the Teacher." Note how she relates her concept of the role of a teacher to perpetuating such middle-class values so revered by teachers as cleanliness, quiet, punctuality, and obedience. Note also the emphasis she gives to discipline and punishment. The classroom is an orderly, severe, and punishing place.

> If I were the teacher. When I first get here I'd like to meet all the children here. The first day in school I'd tell the pupils what to do. First thing we do is clean the school up then clean the desk and the cupboards. Then straighten the cupboard up for the books. When the school is cleaned up, then I'll give out the books. And ask what grade they're in. And ask how old are they. And give the rules for school. The school starts at 9:00 A.M. recess at 10:30 A.M., dinner at 12:00 P.M., come back in the afternoon at 1:00 P.M., recess at 2:30 P.M. and after school 3:30 P.M. And if anybody's late they have to write hundred lines.[1] And keep the toilet clean. Their clothes clean and comb hair. First thing they'd do in the morning is Arithmetic, spelling, language, Reading. And the afternoon Science, Social Studies, Health, and free time. And if nobody works they get a strapping. If I had a fourteen year old in my class she or he would take care of grade one and two. And I'd take care of three to eight. If I had a class all in one grade that'll be nice. Then I won't have to bother about other grades except the class I have. And if they get the room dirty they'll sweep the whole classroom. I'd get a monitor for the

bath room to be clean and swept. And if anybody talks back. They'd get a strapping. If they get out of their desk they'll have to write lines. If they don't ask permission to sharpen their pencil they'll get a strapping. If they wear hats and kerchiefs in class they'll have to stand in the corner for one hour with their hands on their heads. I'd tell the children to draw Indian Design for the room. If they make a noise in class, they all stay in for half an hour. If anybody talks in class they write lines about a hundred lines. If anybody's absent they have lots of homework for the next day. And if anybody fights they get a strapping. And I'd have a monitor for the books so nobody touch it except the monitor. Dust the shelves. And on Christmas they'd have to play or sing. And on Halloween they have to dress up for the party.

2. Here is the response of another pupil, a fourteen-year-old girl, to my request for a theme on the same topic, "If I Were the Teacher." Note the contrast she makes between discipline and scholarship. If one of her pupils were to fail to be on time, she would strap him. If he were to fail a comprehensive examination, she would have a talk with him.

If I were the teacher for Blackfish Village, or someplace else, I'd like my class to be very quiet. If not, they would get a straping from me. They would get a straping if they are late.

They would come to school at nine A.M. No sooner nor later. They would have one recess in the morning and one in the afternoon. In the afternoon they would go home at 3:30 P.M.

The subjects I'd give them in the morning are Math, Spelling, Reading. If they do not get it finished they would have it for homework, same in the afternoon. They would have a story, Language, then Library or drawing.

I'd like my class to be very neat, clothes clean, hair neat. In the morning they could sing "God Save the Queen." In the afternoon they would sing "Oh Canada."

I would choose Monitors for toilets, paints and for blackboards. But of course I would do the Attendance myself. I would give them tests before Christmas, Easter, and the final tests at June. After the tests if anyone fails, I would ask them to tell me why. For example if one of my pupils did fail I'd tell that child to write a on paper to tell me why. If that child has a good excuse, I'd tell that child to "smarten up" and pay attention to his or her work more.

I would go to see their parents to see if they have a normal living, like if they go to sleep before nine o'clock, have good meals every day.

Yes sir! If I were the teacher a lot of changes would be made around here at Blackfish Village. The children would have to listen even if I were a girl teacher.

But I didn't plan the future yet. That's for sure I'm not sticking around here in the future.

3. In most cases where the hostility of the children toward the teacher flared up over a specific incident at school, the pupils did not record their perceptions of the event in their classroom writing. Typically at such times they refrained from performing any task that might please the teacher, and writing in their notebooks did win teacher approval. The following excerpt reveals one instance where a pupil did record anger which she shared with several other pupils. I had refused to admit a group of the older pupils into class when they were late in returning from morning recess, and at least for this fourteen-year-old, trouble at school had precipitated more trouble at home.

> Today is a very horrible day for Norma and me. Of course we would be treaten as babies. When we are late in this dump the teacher would [i.e., *did*] tell us to come back in the afternoon. There was Larry, Joseph, Norma, Tommy, Jack, Herman and me. Norma got in trouble too, of course. My brother would tell on me that brat. This is a strict world for some of us. I thought this was a free world. Norma and me can't even go on Larry's boat and for me I'm not aloud to go to their house! My brother said I was in my aunties house. I guess thats why I ain't aloud in their. All the time I was in Sarah's house. The teacher is so lazy to ring the bell I guess he expects us to hear him when he calls us. That's all!!

4. Two final examples suggest the contrast between the pseudowork and satisfaction of the classroom and the real work and real rewards of adult life. Here is a written comment, in the form of a note to the teacher, from a twelve-year-old boy who recognized that although he was required to attend school, he had a more important contribution to make to his family when he could assist with the work of the men:

> I am going to go halibut fishing with my father and Raymond. That's why I asked you is there going to be school tomorrow because I want to go with my father. He always has a tough time when he catches halibut [alone]. We got one halibut yesterday.

In a similar vein, the following was written in November by a fifteen-year-old boy. The note mentions only a week's leave, but it was in fact the boy's last classroom assignment forever, because he never returned to school:

> We are going to Gilford Island tomorrow. I'm going to stay there one week. I'm going to dig clams. There is a big tide this week. I'm not coming to school next week.

## The Teacher as an Enemy

In the school at Blackfish Village, or for teachers in any number of comparable settings, I believe there would be real utility in having more than one way of perceiving the reciprocal roles of teacher and pupil. In my own case, experience in both roles prior to my year at Blackfish Village had been within the confines of a middle-class setting of which I am very much part and product. Sometimes, in my twenty years as a student, I had experienced antagonism toward teachers and occasionally I had generated antagonism among my students as a public school and university teacher. Such antagonism, however, was a consequence of immediate psychological or personal incompatibility, never an antagonism rooted in social forces outside the classroom. I had never encountered teachers or pupils with whom I did not share relatively similar expectations regarding behaviors, values, and attitudes.

At Blackfish Village my pupils and I shared few mutual expectations regarding our formal role relationship. Those expectations we did share tended to provide pacts that enabled individual survival in a situation beyond our making, rather than opening avenues for trust or understanding. No one, teacher or pupils, ever let his guard down very far. If we were not at any one moment actually engaged in a classroom skirmish, it was only because we were recovering from a prior one or preparing for the next. On the last day of school I reflected that I had not won a battle; instead I felt that all year long I had had a tiger by the tail, and we had merely crossed some kind of symbolic finish line together.

I had anticipated that one of my major problems of the year would be to induce my pupils to come regularly to school. Except for the fact that pupils expected to leave school at about age sixteen, however, my pupils and I did not have to do battle regarding school attendance. Economic sanctions could be taken against families who failed to send their children regularly to school, but in fact attendance (other than a perennial problem in getting pupils from certain families to school on time) was not a major concern. Indeed, parents not only sent their children off to school each day but also ritually endorsed the benefits of formal education with such comments as "Education is the only answer."

I had mistakenly assumed that once the pupils were inside the classroom they could be led to a host of new learnings under the guidance of their dedicated teacher. Ever since my year as a teacher at the Blackfish Indian Day School I have been seeking an alternative teaching perspective, one that would have enabled me to present an instructional program without such personal frustration at my lack of success and without nurturing an atmosphere of hostility where I had intended to create an atmosphere of help.

The direction my quest has taken is *not* to ponder how to "outpsych" or outmaneuver my pupils. Training in anthropology had convinced me of the fact that differences exist among groups of human beings and that the differences may touch every facet of human life from household composition to cognition. But I was not assigned to the village to teach villagers their way of life; I was assigned to teach them something about mine.

I think that I might have been a more effective teacher if I had taken the perspective of regarding the *teacher*, me, *as an enemy*. By effective I mean that I would have remained more objective about my lack of success, and I would have been more sensitive to the high cost for each pupil of accepting me or my instructional program. The "enemy" relationship I use here as my analogy does not refer to entering into combat, although on the worst days we may not have been far from it. More appropriate to antagonistic acculturation as manifested in school might be an analogy to a prisoner-of-war camp. Prisoners of war—inmates and captors alike—are faced with the probability that a long period of time may ensue during which their statuses remain unchanged. While a great hostility on the part of either group might be present in the relationship, it is not essential to it, because the enmity is not derived from individual or personal antagonism. Nonetheless, the captors, representing one cultural group, are not expected to convert the prisoners to their way of life, and the prisoners are not expected to acculturate the captors.

So far, a teacher in an instructional role has no place in the analogy. Let us extend the analogy one step further. Suppose that along with the usual cadre of overseers the captors have also provided teachers charged with instructing the prisoners in the ways of, and particularly in the merits of, their culture. The purpose of instruction is to recruit new members into their society by encouraging prisoners to defect, and achieving this by giving them the skills so that they can do so effectively. The teachers are expected to provide information about the captors' way of life and about the skills that this way entails. It has been established that prisoners will attend the classes and that they will not be allowed to disrupt classroom proceedings, but beyond these strictures the teacher is not expected to dwell on the negative aspects that have brought his pupils to him. The teacher is not unaware of the probability, however, that since he is perceived as an enemy, his pupils may not see him playing a very functional role in their lives other than as a representative of the enemy culture.

What purposes might be served in cross-cultural education if a teacher were to draw an analogy between himself and an enemy captor in trying to understand his relationship with his pupils? There are several potential advantages one might anticipate.

First, the teacher who can imagine how pupils might feel toward him as a member of a captor society recognizes a distinction between having pupils physically present in class and having them psychologically receptive to instruction. Cognizance of the pervasive hostile and suspicious influence of the enemy relationship helps the teacher maintain realistic expectations for what he can accomplish in the classroom. Despite his most valiant efforts to make his instruction effective, he is never overcome by feelings of personal inadequacy at a lack of response to his lessons. He realizes that under certain conditions the energy and resources of prisoners are utilized in a desperate struggle to survive and to maintain their own identity in the face of overwhelming odds. The teacher recognizes that the antagonism of his pupils may be addressed to the whole cultural milieu in which they find themselves captive rather than to him as an individual. He understands that any attempt on his part to alter or to ameliorate the basis for antagonism may be met with suspicion. He is not personally disappointed when his pupils show tendencies toward recidivism when they feel themselves being seduced by the constant attention and encouragement of their mentor-enemies. If this is how things seem to the prisoners, the teacher realizes that a modification of a lesson plan or an ingenious new teaching technique is not going to make any important difference to them. Taking the point of view of his pupils, the teacher can ask himself, "Just what is it that a prisoner would ever want to learn from an enemy?"

Second, the teacher who can entertain a perspective that regards himself and his pupils as belonging to enemy cultures acknowledges the possibility that there could be important and systematic differences in life styles and in value-orientation characterizing each group. He is not inclined to share a perception, common among teachers, that if a pupil does not have the same cultural background as the teacher he does not have any cultural heritage at all. Granted, the teacher can be expected to believe that his own life style is right, but he also recognizes that he is not likely to achieve his purposes by insisting that all other life styles are therefore wrong. Anthropologist Ruth Landes has written cogently in this regard, "The educator, or other authority, can advance his inquiries and explanations by taking the position that he represents one culture talking to another. This minimizes personal and emotional involvements by focusing on the grand designs of each tradition. . . . " (Landes 1965:47).

The teacher's instructional objectives are to try to make his own way of life appear sufficiently manageable to his "enemy" pupils that they may choose to explore it further, and, for those pupils who do make this choice, to provide them with a set of survival skills for living in a different culture and having access to its rewards. Children growing up in Blackfish Village, for example, will have to be able to demonstrate the skill aspects of specific middle-class manners and values such as cleanliness, courtesy, responsibility, punctuality, or how to take orders from a white boss in order to survive in the dominant society. They do not, however, need a teacher who insists that such skills are necessary steps on the road to nirvana. They need a teacher who can identify and instruct them in certain specific behaviors which an individual *must* exhibit if he is going to move successfully in a society that heretofore has been regarded as an alien one.

We would hardly expect the teacher to engage in much "correction" of pupils except for what was essential to the maintenance of an orderly classroom. The language or dialect used by prisoners need not be singled out for ridicule, correction, or extermination. What the teacher might do, however, is to teach a standard dialect of his own language to prisoner-pupils who entertained an intellectual curiosity about it or, especially, to those pupils interested in learning the enemy culture well enough to see if they can survive in it.

Most important, the teacher realizes the meaning that accepting his teaching may have for those prisoners who do accept it. It may mean selling out, defecting, turning traitor, ignoring the succorance and values and pressures of one's peers, one's family, one's own people. It can require terrible and anxious decisions for the prisoner, and it may even require him to sever his most deeply rooted human ties. The teacher needs constantly to review what these costs mean to any human. As a consequence, the teacher interested in his enemy pupils as humans may find himself less inclined to act as a cultural brainwasher and more inclined to weigh both the difficulties of cultural transition and the ultimate consequences of change. In the latter regard a proverb quoted in Robert Ruark's novel *Something of Value* seems particularly appropriate: "If a man does away with his traditional way of living and throws away his good customs, he had better first make certain he has something of value to replace them" (Basuto proverb).

The teacher may feel a greater need to alert his pupils to the fact that he has *not* been able to provide them with all the prerequisite skills for successfully "passing" in the teacher's own society than to fill them with hopes and promises which few may ever realize. His pupils need to know how much information they actually have, what problems they must anticipate, and which vestiges of their earlier heritage may present almost insurmountable handicaps.

Through the exercise of examining his *own* culture as the alien one, the teacher-enemy may be less aggressive about forcing his lessons on his prisoner-pupils. He may not accept so unhesitatingly the belief that what he is doing is necessarily "good" for them. He may be more inclined to think of teaching as an offer of help to members of the dominated group who seek it rather than as an imposition of help from members of the dominant group who insist on giving it. Pausing to consider the possibility of being regarded by his pupils as a member of an enemy culture offers the teacher a perspective for understanding why pupils might sometimes appear able but unwilling to accept his teaching. This perspective also encourages the teacher to give more help to the potential defectors who seek it, rather than to spend his time bemoaning the lack of defection by the prisoner generation of today.

## Conclusion

Cultural systems provide us with practical answers to questions of how we should act and what to think about how we act. But no "culture" ever provides its members with a perfect and complete blueprint of how to act in every situation. If cultures accomplished that, they might never change, and we know that change is inherent in human life and human organization. We do not often pause to examine our own behavior, and it can be with a real sense of surprise that in a new role we suddenly discover that we already know exactly how to act; we may even feel we have "known it all the time." Student teachers, as a case in point, provide themselves and observers with remarkable examples of how well they have internalized the teacher behavior associated with the teacher-pupil role relationship even if they have never formally taken the teacher role before.

When circumstances bring us into contact with others who do not share the same cultural orientation, particularly if our "proper" behavior invites inappropriate responses or no response at all, we become more self-consciously aware of our own patterns of behavior. Initially this may result only in our speaking or gesticulating a bit more emphatically, in a manner characteristic of the American tourist abroad. Under conditions of prolonged contact, one might want to do better than simply wave his hands more or talk louder. Regardless of how much effort he makes at understanding those who are different from him, however, it is from his own repertoire of cultural behaviors that the individual must choose. If he has no perfectly appropriate pattern of behavior, then he has to look for relevant analogous situations. The choice of analogies is crucial.

The teacher working with culturally different pupils exhibits a natural inclination to draw upon a single analogy, that of the idealized teacher-pupil relationship suitable for the monolithic transmission of culture. I do not imagine that teachers will ever escape from drawing upon this analogy. Their very identity as teachers requires that they have specific notions about teacher behavior. Teachers should not be asked perfunctorily to discard their own "good customs."

I have suggested here that the teacher seek out alternative behavior analogs rather than depend solely on the not-always-appropriate model of the ideal teacher in the ideal setting. Like the role relationship between teacher and pupil, the relationship between enemies is also a culturally based one. The enemy relationship may actually draw more heavily upon universal aspects of behavior than does the teacher-pupil role which has tended to become so crystallized in Western civilization. In spite of the negative implications of an enemy role, and barring extremes of physical cruelty, there are certain ways in which pupils equated with captive prisoners might get better treatment than pupils regarded as allies. For example, in thinking of antagonistic pupils as prisoners of war, one comes to recognize that the classroom is neither the underlying source of intercultural antagonism nor the site of its critical campaigns. Such a realization may also help the reform-oriented teacher to recognize that the proper target for his efforts at community reform is the adult community rather than young children in school (Hawthorn et al. 1960:303).

One last dimension of the enemy perspective is that few demands are made of enemy prisoners. Demands are made explicitly; they are not based on assumptions of shared values about fair play, individual rights, ultimate purposes, or the dignity of office. In a sense, the behavior between enemies gives more overt evidence of respecting the other person's cultural ways than does that between friendly groups. Based as it is upon the recognition of vital differences rather than on the recognition of underlying similarities, the perspective of thinking about teachers and their culturally different pupils as enemies invites teachers to examine the kinds of differences cherished by enemies just as they have in the past addressed themselves, at least ritually, to what they and their pupils share in common.

## Note

1. By "write lines" she refers to the practice of repeatedly writing a sentence like "I will not talk out in class" to the satisfaction of a teacher. In my defense I should add that none of the assortment of disciplinary measures she refers to was used in my classroom, although I did have children put their heads down on their desks as a mild disciplinary measure and sent them out of the classroom for a variety of infractions, including that exquisite pupil weapon, sullenness.

## References and Further Reading

Goffman, Erving, 1969, "The Characteristics of Total Institutions." In Amitai Etzioni, ed., *A Sociological Reader on Complex Organizations*. 2d ed. New York: Holt, Rinehart and Winston, Inc. Readers interested in exploring the analogy between pupils and prisoners will find a number of strategies which "inmates" pursue suggested in this essay.

Hawthorn, Harry B., C. S. Belshaw, and S. M. Jamieson, 1960, *The Indians of British Columbia: A Study of Contemporary Social Adjustment*. Berkeley: University of California Press, especially Chap. 23, "Schools and Education."

Henry, Jules, 1955, "Docility, or Giving Teacher What She Wants," *Journal of Social Issues* 11:33-41.

King, A. Richard, 1967, *The School at Mopass: A Problem of Identity*. New York: Holt, Rinehart and Winston, Inc.

Landes, Ruth, 1965, *Culture in American Education: Anthropological Approaches to Minority and Dominant Groups in the School*. New York: John Wiley & Sons, Inc.

Rohner, Ronald P., 1965, "Factors Influencing the Academic Performance of Kwakiutl Indian Children in Canada," *Comparative Education Review* 9:331-340.

———, 1967, *The People of Gilford. A Contemporary Kwakiutl Village*, National Museum of Canada, Bulletin 225. Ottawa, Ontario: the Queen's Printer.

———, and Evelyn C. Rohner, 1970, *The Kwakiutl Indians of British Columbia*. New York: Holt, Rinehart and Winston, Inc. especially Chap. 4, "Growing Up Kwakiutl."

Ruark, Robert C., 1955, *Something of Value*. New York: Doubleday & Company, Inc.

Smith, Alfred G., 1968, "Communication and Inter-cultural Conflict." In Carl E. Larson and Frank E. X. Dance, eds., *Perspectives on Communication*. Milwaukee: University of Wisconsin Press.

Wax, Murray, L. Rosalie H. Wax, and Robert V. Dumont, Jr., 1964, Formal Education in an American Indian Community. *Social Problems, Monograph #1*. Society for the Study of Social Problems.

Wolcott, Harry F., 1967, *A Kwakiutl Village and School*. New York: Holt, Rinehart and Winston, Inc.

# 9

# Afterword, 1989

## A Kwakiutl Village and School 25 Years Later

---

### PREFACE

---

After serving on dissertation committees and advising doctoral students for three decades, I realize that "Afterword, 1989" is the kind of final chapter my own dissertation committee was probably hoping to receive from me—in 1964! That is not to say they really expected it, but I now know that hope springs eternal among university faculty who guide dissertation research and writing. Maybe this time . . .

I am not chagrined that it took so long for these thoughts to form. I am satisfied that I was finally able to recast the study as I have done in the chapter here. I was especially fortunate to have the opportunity to include this material in a reissue of the original work. The lesson is clear: It may be years before one brings closure to a study. Even then, one simply lays a work aside for what is *perhaps* the last time. Paraphrasing Paul Valéry, Clifford Geertz reminds us that we never really complete our studies, we only abandon them (Geertz, 1983, p. 6).

Except for those rare flashes of insight sometimes reported by others, interpretation is essentially a process and product of mulling. One can nurture the process but, I repeat, I do not believe it can be forced. When time does not allow for adequate reflection, we have no choice but to say what we can and let it go at that. I was not pressed for a more substantial "So what?" chapter in the dissertation, perhaps because it was already long, even for a descriptive account (512 pages). What I did at the time was address the topic promised by its subtitle, "Cultural Barriers to Classroom Performance," by identifying 14 dimensions on which cultural differences seemed to play a critical role.

Although merely suggestive, my 14 points of cautious interpretation were the seeds of my subsequent thinking and writing, first about education across cultural barriers (resulting in the "Teacher as an Enemy" chapter) and eventually about enculturation and culture acquisition itself. The points I outlined are uneven, ranging from pupil "nonlistening" to the lack of any observable advantage accruing from formal education. Nonetheless, they were a beginning, a tentative identification of underlying issues that seemed worthy of further deliberation. Regardless of where it might all end, this was a starting point. As well, I now realize, the points reflected the thinking of the day, a period when "assimilation" was the goal and "acculturative status" was regarded not only as a label but as an explanation and/or implied remedy for social ills. (I think Appropriate Technology became the next panacea; today's buzzword seems to be Infrastructure.)

In his new role as general editor of the Case Studies in Education and Culture, overseeing the transformation of my dissertation to become one of the first studies published in that series, my dissertation adviser George Spindler did not spare me. I was directed to add a final section drawing the lessons of the study together more tightly. Identifying "barriers," as I had done in the original reporting, was no longer enough.

I found the writing difficult. I did not know what to say, and dissertation writing had hardly emboldened me as a creative or interpretative writer. Until I came across the idea in Simon Ottenberg's essay, "Thirty Years of Fieldnotes," it never occurred to me that a field-based dissertation can be viewed as merely another iteration in a series of transformations from headnotes to handwritten notes to typed notes to dissertation to published account (Ottenberg, 1990, p. 148). If such a realization brings any comfort, it comes only later in a career. At the time, nothing is more formidable than writing a dissertation substantial enough to pass the scrutiny of "the committee." Doctoral students may find little solace in realizing that the dissertation is supposed to mark the beginning of a writing career rather than the culmination of a writing chore.

Nevertheless, my dissertation did become exactly what Ottenberg describes, a reinterpretation of typed fieldnotes that was to be reinterpreted again for a monograph published 3 years later. A still brief but slightly more interpretive final chapter would be followed years later by the material that appears here as "Afterword, 1989."

During those intervening years, the case study itself did not change, and I did not for a moment consider revising it for the 1984 reissue. The only aspect to change was any further insight I could bring to the study. My changed perspective was related to rethinking issues of cultural transmission and acquisition, a topic broached in this chapter and developed more fully in the next (Chapter 10). I came to realize that what I had described as my pupils' "lack of commitment to the acquisition of knowledge" (1964, p. 491) reflected a realistic educator assessment but not an enlightened anthropological one. An anthropological perspective invites a closer look at the question: Who is defining knowledge, and for whom?

The mulling process meant putting the entire experience into perspective, pulling a multitude of little problems into some larger context than one tiny village during one brief year of fieldwork. As a classroom teacher, I was aghast at all my Indian pupils did not know, measured against what I felt responsible for teaching them. I was too preoccupied to consider what they did know, what knowledge—and which "knowers"—they themselves considered of most worth. The shift in my thinking ultimately turned on a point implicit in a focus on culture acquisition: to attend as an anthropologist to what people *do* know, rather than to attend as an educator to what they do *not* know—that is, to what they do not know and are therefore in need of being taught!

That basis for a new interpretive framework turns back upon the need for and value of careful description, the business of looking at what *is* rather than looking for what is *supposed to be* or bemoaning what is not. Therein lies the genius of the great naturalist observers like Charles Darwin who serve as our models for descriptive research. Darwin was well aware of what he was supposed to see and even what he wanted to see; in his role as observer, however, he recorded and pondered what he did see.

Prior to the recent era of fieldwork reflexivity, perhaps the least touted feature of field research has been its potential for involving researchers so totally that it has profound effect on their lives. My fieldwork experience among the Kwakiutl had a profound influence on me. It left me with questions to ponder forever regarding the role of culture, the processes of cultural transmission and acquisition, and the nature and purposes of "helping" across cultures. Those are the issues that, at long last, I was ready to address in the Afterword, together with bringing a brief history of the school, the village, and the villagers up to date. The events themselves remain as originally chronicled; the interpretation—and interpreter—had matured.

If it is gratifying to have a monograph remain in print so long—*Kwakiutl Village and School* was available almost continuously for 25 years—it is even more gratifying to be able years later to append a postscript that becomes part of the work itself. This "Afterword" was included in the 1989 Waveland Press reissue. It was added without fanfare. Waveland did not want to advertise a "new" edition on the basis of some minor changes and 15 pages added to the old one. Even today the Afterword remains something of an unexpected dividend: First-time readers don't recognize anything new and earlier readers remain unaware that a new section has been added. More than one faithful adopter of the case study as a college text discovered the existence of the Afterword through student comments leading to the realization that something had been added in the edition students had purchased that was not in the instructor's well-worn desk copy.

By way of summary and advice, I underscore two points related to the interpretive emphasis, ideas that have already been noted in this preface. First is to allow time. Do not become impatient when you realize that you have not achieved the all-encompassing conclusion toward which you have been working and striving. The second and related point is to keep circling back over your earlier experiences, your personal as well as your professional life, in order to keep *all* your experience under review. Develop the potential for integrating elements in your life as researcher and scholar with your "lived" life in other roles. In making writing part of your life, entertain possibilities for making your life part of your writing. The interpretive mode allows and invites you to do just that.

The American penchant for the new and novel tends to keep us from looking back, from reconceptualizing and, in our lives as researchers, from making sure that we ourselves have made the most not only of our data but also of our experience. Brace yourself for whisperings that you are not doing anything new when your writing reflects upon what has gone before, but do not get caught up forever churning out new studies rather than endeavoring at least occasionally to make something more of what you understand of earlier ones. You can always hit them with the quote from Blaise Pascal (the opening epigraph) if necessary. The arrangement *is* new, isn't it?

# References

Geertz, Clifford. (1983). *Local knowledge*. New York: Basic Books.

Ottenberg, Simon. (1990). Thirty years of fieldnotes: Changing relationships to the text. In Roger Sanjek (Ed.), *Fieldnotes: The makings of anthropology* (pp. 139-160). Ithaca, NY: Cornell University Press.

Wolcott, Harry F. (1964). *A Kwakiutl village and its school: Cultural barriers to classroom performance*. Unpublished doctoral dissertation, Stanford University.

Wolcott, Harry F. (1967). *A Kwakiutl village and school*. New York: Holt, Rinehart & Winston. (Reissued 1989 by Waveland Press, Prospect Heights, IL, with a new Afterword)

# AFTERWORD, 1989

## A Kwakiutl Village and School 25 Years Later

"The old Indian ways are just going to die out," my host reflected, adding, with characteristic Kwakiutl panache, "I'm the only one in the family that's even interested in them any more."

For an instant, I was swayed by the familiar lament. I nodded sympathetically, just as I had when I heard essentially that same message of seeming despair a quarter-of-a-century earlier. My thoughts on this hearing were anything but the same, however. During the intervening years I have lived enough of a lifetime to know that things never remain the same: not for a society, not for a community, not for a family, not for any individual. With all honesty, I could nod assent: the old ways are dying out, or, stated less dramatically, are undergoing continual modification.

Those words once heard from Reggie's grandfather were being spoken now by Reggie himself, during the course of a reunion in 1984 after

This is "Afterword, 1989," reprinted with minor revisions from *A Kwakiutl Village and School*, second printing 1989, pages 133-147, by Waveland Press, Prospect Heights, Illinois. The material is used by courtesy of Waveland Press, with copyright retained by the author.

a lapse of many years. My first-grade pupil of 1962 proudly paraded his own young children before me, the eldest "about ready to start school." Self-consciously intent on raising his children as Indian members of contemporary Canadian society ("I'm the only one who married an Indian. My sisters all married white guys"), Reggie himself is the answer today to the same question his grandfather pondered in days gone by: "Who is going to keep Indian ways alive?"

The form in which Reggie lives out and attempts to transmit "his" culture will be less recognizably Kwakiutl than the tradition his grandfather sought to pass to him. Yet I think that "the Old Man," as we all (and for the most part affectionately) called him 25 years ago, would be pleased to know that Reggie and others of his generation do feel that they have a heritage worth preserving to counterbalance the inevitable forces of change.

"There's no use giving a potlatch anymore," the Old Man had grumbled in the mid-1960s. "The old people don't pay it back, and the young people don't even know what it means!" I took him too literally. I believed he really had given up all hope for keeping vestiges of Kwakiutl tradition alive. We both saw evidence during the ensuing years to convince ourselves that Kwakiutl customs in general were headed for the same fate as the Kwakiutl village and school of my study: deteriorated, deserted, and ultimately destroyed. Village Island as residence and the Mamalilikala (or Mamaleleqala) as its residents, a readily identifiable village group among the Kwakiutl people, are gone. Reggie's grandfather, like most old men, and Reggie's grandmother, "the Old Lady," prior to her death a few years before her husband's, mourned the passing of good old days and good old ways and often portrayed themselves as helpless victims of a slow but inevitable extinction of everything Indian.

What a surprise to get a long-distance telephone call in the mid-1970s from one of Reggie's aunts living at the north end of Vancouver Island informing me, "We've been trying and trying to reach you. The Old Man says you better get up here next month. He's giving another big potlatch. He says if you want to see it, you better come now, because this is his third one and it's *definitely* going to be the last!" Three major potlatches given by the very individual who had convinced me the custom was dead! By failing to remain in closer touch, I had failed to realize that the Old Man's resignation to the inevitable demise of Kwakiutl ways was mitigated by a recognition of his own potential to alter that course. Reggie, in turn, represents *his* generation's answer to how to keep Indian ways "alive." They are alive in two ways. First,

they remain in living memory. Second, they remain adequately dynamic to provide cultural templates for coping within Canadian society in a manner sufficiently stereotyped to be recognizable as "Indian."

At best, Reggie can maintain only traces of a discernibly *Kwakiutl*
life-style. Reggie's father is Indian but not Kwakiutl; he was seldom
home and never really "at home" in his father-in-law's family or village.
Reggie himself never again stayed as long at the village as he did that
year I first met him, the year I served as village teacher. By the end of
that year, Reggie's parents had made their more-or-less permanent
move back to Vancouver Island, resolved never to return for more than
a brief visit. Reggie has lived in the cities and towns of Vancouver Island
from its northern tip at rough-hewn Port Hardy to its southern tip at
genteel Victoria ever since. He and his wife have a network of immediate kin and casually extended family ties that encompass much of
the island.

During the rapid demise of the village precipitated by the closing of
its school, Reggie's grandfather moved his household belongings and
relocated at Port Hardy. During adolescence, Reggie often stayed with
his grandfather, and he regularly joined him during each summer's
salmon run until his grandfather finally "hung up his nets for the last
time," deciding that with failing vision and failed hearing he was too
old to be out fishing. Reggie was in grade 10 at Port Hardy when he quit
school and took a job with an auto parts company.

 Today, Reggie expresses the same ambivalence about commercial
fishing that his father expressed a generation earlier. But, like his father,
Reggie seems to "have fishing in his blood." Summer earnings account
for the major portion of his annual income, and fishing is the dominant
activity in his working and wage-earning life. Qualities that made
Reggie something of an anomaly in the village as a six-year-old help
him today to negotiate jobs and play his Indianness up or down as
social or bureaucratic circumstances demand.

I have lost contact with some village families. What once would have
been a relatively easy task through casual conversation or tracing Band
Lists readily accessible at the Kwawkewlth Indian Agency at Alert Bay
now must be done by locating people in widely dispersed networks,
although Port Hardy and "The Bay" have continued to serve as the
locus of activity for many of them. The Canadian government provided housing assistance for outlying villagers during efforts at band
amalgamation in the mid-1960s, and when several village families
relocated along one Alert Bay road someone remarked that it "ought to
be nicknamed Little Mamalilikala." But once-critical band and village

identities have proven difficult to maintain in the absence of such natural boundary markers as remote locations, not always navigable waters, and villagers not always hospitable to outsiders—even those from neighboring islands. Everyone's name must be on some band list, but precisely which band seems not all that important, especially to younger adults.

The completion of a highway system that now links the northern tip of Vancouver Island with its better-developed southern region has greatly reduced dependency on slow and often unreliable travel by ferryboat. Local travel is easy, but with it has come the paradox that anthropologist Ernestine Friedl describes as lagging emulation: during the same period when outlying villagers were challenged to be "progressive" by relocating at once-thriving Alert Bay, non-Indian residents and many government services formerly housed there were relocating elsewhere on Vancouver Island at nearby Port McNeill and Port Hardy or in the larger island communities of Campbell River, Nanaimo, or Victoria.

Surviving villagers whose offspring attended my classroom are becoming today's new generation of elders. For the most part they are an undistinguished group except for the very fact of their survival in the face of endless stories of personal hardship, "all these years of sickness and sorrow" as one village woman reflected. Accidents and violence continue to account for a large portion of their woes, and alcohol problems are at the root of most of those. Of the roster of pupils in my classroom, fewer than half were still living 25 years later. Those who did survive, however, started families of their own at comparatively young ages. Dorothy found it amusing to think of herself as "a very young grandmother" at age 38.

As in the past, economically successful villagers have "kept the distance" between themselves and other former villagers. They maintain family ties but live apart from Indian ghettoes, self-consciously maintaining middle-class life-styles. They accumulate and display contemporary Western appliances, appurtenances, friends, and often non-Indian spouses as well. Nonetheless, they neither deny their Indian origins nor ignore obligations to participate within and contribute to the larger Indian community.

My impression is that to whatever extent Indian people in Canada continue to be accorded second-class status, less opprobrium attaches to "being Indian" today than 25 years ago. Advantaged by the abundant resources of the region, Indians of the Northwest Coast have always lived within grasp of a relatively prosperous life-style. Official policy and platitudes are not what really matter; the critical element is how Indian people regard themselves and the extent to which they believe they are systematically denied responsibility in, or access to, aspects of mainstream society on the basis of ethnicity. Complaints are still legion, but their impact and significance are diffused, in part because complaining itself is ritualized in the Indian-white dialogue, in part because Indian people have become more vocal about matters that affect them. A new *band directed* elementary school operating in the shadow of St. Mike's in the 1980s, and that includes instruction in Kwakwala in its daily program, is an example of the impact from that growing voice.

## Reflections on Doing the Study

Not more than a month or two had passed after I completed the doctoral dissertation upon which *A Kwakiutl Village and School* is based when George and Louise Spindler raised the question of how to bring the study before a wider audience. Louise offered the suggestion that not only prompted me to rewrite the dissertation but launched the Spindlers on another major undertaking, editing the Case Studies in Education and Culture.

*A Kwakiutl Village and School* was one of the four monographs with which the Spindlers introduced the series in 1967. That introductory material was part of the format of the new series. Eventually the collection grew to 17 monographs. Although the series never enjoyed the wide distribution of its predecessor, the Case Studies in Cultural Anthropology, many of the titles in the Education and Culture series became well-known and remain so even today.

Contrary to expectations that the more exotic cases, or those in which the influence of formal schooling was new or minimal, would be the most sought after, the monographs that actually "caught on" described settings in North America and circumstances teachers were likely to meet in their own experience. Problems related to poor school performance of young Native Americans fit well with growing concern for Indian education as well as with burgeoning interest in the 1960s and 1970s with problems of minority group education in general.

In spite of aggregate sales of about 20,000 copies and the fact that the original edition remained in print almost 15 years, *A Kwakiutl Village and School* was not considered a commercial success. My royalties started at 19½ cents for copies sold in the U.S. and half that amount for copies sold in Canada. This was my first book, and I was quickly disabused of the notion that authors get rich, although the publication marked a critical step in my academic career. On the other hand, that the study has been well received, is widely known, and continues to be available has been not only rewarding but a bit baffling. I would like to elaborate on this point.

One source of bafflement is that the study appears to be well-known—among educators and anthropologists alike—in spite of the fact that it does not deal at length with the process of ethnographic research. Reflecting customary practice of the day, I paid scant attention to fieldwork procedures in the text, and there are no references on method in the bibliography. Nor were there many references I might have made. In those days there was no tradition among anthropologists of belaboring what was to them obvious: if you wanted to learn about the way of life of some group of people, you went to live among them to whatever extent was appropriate and possible. Educational researchers, with their heavy borrowing of measurement techniques and experimental design from psychology, recognized no "method" at all in the approach of the field ethnographer.

In that climate we hardly imagined "anthropology and education" would gain recognition in either its discipline of orientation or its arena of practice. Who would have guessed that ethnographic research (which increasingly came to be called ethnographic "method" once educators started talking about it) would be so central in the influence of anthropology upon educational researchers? Careful explication of my study as method would have been timely and might help to account for the book's popularity, *if* I had anticipated that potential interest in the ethnographic approach.

A second source of bafflement is that although the book admirably catalogs problems, it offers little in the way of solutions. Even at that, the book goes farther than I originally intended. The six pages comprising the final chapter, "In Retrospect and Prospect," were added at the insistence of publisher's reviewers who felt that readers would expect more and that, with three years for further reflection, there must be more I could say about educating minority group children. Those three years have now lengthened to 25, and once again I am struggling to identify whatever insight I have achieved that might prove helpful, but neither have the problems receded into the past nor the solutions become more apparent. . . .

As my comments no doubt reveal, even today I will be satisfied if I am able to offer provocative and constructive ways to think about the *problems*. At the time I was writing, I felt a responsibility to present the case without yielding to the urge to offer facile solutions or to suggest that there were "answers" if we could just find them. I seriously doubted that a book laden with problems-without-solutions would find an audience among educators already aware of what is wrong and frustrated in their call for help with what to do about it. However, some teacher readers have mentioned how refreshing it is to find an author grappling with problems in his own classroom rather than indicting them for problems assumed to exist in theirs.

Admittedly, I do not know who the book's readers have been; perhaps I am correct in my suspicions that its audience included few experienced teachers. But somewhere—perhaps in teacher preparation programs addressing issues of multicultural education—one must account for thousands of readers (those 20,000 copies sold and often resold; library copies read and re-read) who should have recognized—at the conclusion of their reading, if not at the beginning—that in their chosen profession, problems related to the social context of schooling far outstrip the magnitude of our understanding.

Another source of bafflement was my feeling that the negative cast of the account would turn readers off—and possibly turn them away—rather than engage them with the complexity of the issue. I have never spent another year, before or since, as intense as my year at Blackfish Village. I felt an obligation to portray that experience candidly, rather than to whitewash it or to hide behind a facade of scientific objectivity. My strong and positive feelings toward many of the people individually were offset by an uneasiness while living at the village that was nurtured by acts and accusations of petty and sometimes not-so-petty theft, petty and sometimes not-so-petty violence and crime.

An official of the Indian Affairs Branch, in those days the unit that staffed and operated Canada's Indian schools, reacted strongly to the newly published monograph, admonishing me for preparing so negative an account. "How will we ever recruit teachers for these schools once they read a book like yours?" he queried. I was so taken aback that I do not recall offering a reply, but since that moment I have frequently quoted him to make a counterpoint: in terms of teacher recruitment alone, my efforts seem worthwhile if I headed off even one or two of the disastrous placements that continue to occur in comparable outpost schools in parts of Alaska and Canada (to name two places within my own experience). Teachers who seek and accept such assignments are often totally unprepared for the potential physical *and* *social* duress of rural living under extreme environmental conditions, compounded by difficulties of cross-cultural misunderstanding and the inevitability of village factionalism. Happily, the reaction of that one official was not the majority reaction.

My portrayal of village life was intended to be neither complimentary nor defamatory. I sought to be objective but discrete. In the interest of the latter, my discretion necessarily goes unremarked, while questions of possible indiscretion may arise for each reader anew.

My choice of whether and how to report the vocabulary of certain villagers, particularly after drinking parties, was critical. I decided to quote speech as I heard it, in a day when vernacular language was treated daintily, especially in texts or scholarly works. (To illustrate: In the original galley proofs sent to me, all expletives had been deleted, the result of overzealous copyediting that replaced them with equally telltale dashes. The margins of the author's proofs that I returned made for rather startling reading in themselves!) In turn, language reported in the book distressed some of my most valued Kwakiutl friends, giving me second thoughts long after the deed was done.

On the other hand, the straightforwardness of the account proved to be one its strengths. Even my directness with language drew unexpected support from Reggie's grandfather, the one individual whose judgment of the completed work was most critical to me personally. Discussing the book shortly after its publication, another prominent elder expressed dismay to Reggie's grandfather at the "poor image" created of Kwakiutl people, noting particular concern for the drunken comportment and "bad language" I had so meticulously chronicled. " 'But Jimmy,' I said to him," the Old Man related when next we met, " 'you know that Harry's book tells about the village just the way it is.' "

Were I to initiate the study today, pursuing the same problem orientation—to investigate why Indian pupils so often fail in school—most likely I would follow a similar course in conducting the research. Accepting a position as classroom teacher—a role in which I was both qualified and experienced—gave me a legitimate status in the village and was virtually the only full-time role available to an outsider. Although the children represented much of what was lively about the village, I chafed at being isolated day after day with them in the schoolhouse, thereby having to miss aspects of everyday village life. Only later did I realize that I might (and should) have attended *more* rather than less to these young Kwakiutl, as I will discuss below.

With my overriding concern for education, I would again give particular attention to schooling, although in organizing the presentation I would begin with a description of the community before introducing the topic of formal education, just as I did earlier. At Blackfish Village, differences in the cultural systems underlying community and school were nicely accommodated by presenting the account in two major sections.

Nevertheless, I would make several changes if I were repeating the study. First, I would make more extensive use of case studies of individual children, focusing the village and classroom accounts even more closely on the same five (or perhaps only one or two) school-age children. In part that reflects my growing interest in life history approaches in ethnography as well as in drawing upon anthropology to expand the scope of our inquiries in education. I draw a general maxim inspired by Alfred North Whitehead that we should do less more thoroughly, and an anthropological one from Clifford Geertz, who cautions that there is no ascent to truth without a corresponding descent to cases.

I did not approach the original fieldwork with studies of individual children in mind. Working in so small a village, efforts to preserve anonymity might make such focused study impractical, but in rethinking how to conduct and present the fieldwork I certainly would explore the possibility. For example, I might have made Reggie's story central to the school, perhaps contrasting it with his grandfather's story in portraying the village. The Old Man made it clear that he would have enjoyed a more central role in my account (or in a sequel in which he recounted his life story to me), similar to the role he played in my well-being at the village and my eventually achieving new insight about humans in general and the integrity of "being Indian" in particular.

Another stylistic change would be to write almost entirely in the past tense rather than employ the "ethnographic present" still popular among anthropologists. True, the past tense seems to "kill off" everybody as soon as an action is completed, but present quickly becomes past, and I wish I had not left my pupils in eternal youth, trudging up the path to a school that no longer exists in a village that has been totally deserted for 20 years.

There are other changes, also editorial, that have come with the times. Students in my classes today are quick (and correct) to point out that my preoccupation with the preferred usage of "that" and "which" must have begun *after* I wrote this study. On the other hand, it was correct in those days to use the masculine pronoun for indefinite references to people, and preferable to write in the singular to avoid ambiguities of "they" and "their." Today it is not correct. Even language does not remain the same! Indeed, if a small but vocal group, particularly individuals active in the U'mista Cultural Society centered at Alert Bay, can exert enough influence, the term Kwakiutl itself that anthropologists assigned long ago, as well as the parallel term Kwawkewlth used by government agencies, may give way to Kwakwaka'wakw, a term referring to all Kwak'wala speakers rather than only to one village group (Fort Rupert, the Kwagu'ł) where it was spoken.

## Reconceptualizing the Study

I cannot imagine, however, that I would take the same problem orientation. My approach to the fieldwork would be similar and, had I not aged by these same 25 years, I would *probably* be willing to assume again the dual (and in some ways antithetical) roles of teacher and anthropologist. But in the intervening years, "anthropology and education" has taken form and substance as an interdisciplinary inquiry and I have found a niche for myself as a shaper of that form and a contributor to that substance. Following the direction set by George Spindler, my mentor and colleague of almost 3 decades, today I would give far more attention to cultural transmission. Even more specifically, my efforts would focus on *cultural acquisition*: how each child acquires his or her particular version of what the world is about.

In that earlier day, the educator part of me was totally preoccupied with what my pupils did *not* know. Like village teachers before and since, I found the pupils, "behind" and saw a mandate in trying to get them "caught up." Today, the anthropologist part of me would pose the problem differently: granted these pupils do not know many (most?) of the things I, as teacher, want them to know (e.g., to speak standard English, to be able to "read, write, and do arithmetic"), what is it that they *do* know? If they are inattentive to what is accepted as important in *my* world, then to what do they attend in theirs?

What, for example, is the underlying structure of language as each of them individually has worked it out? Just think what an incredible laboratory I had: a multilingual classroom where some children heard only Kwakwala at home, most heard a mixture of Kwakwala and English, a few heard essentially English (because their parents had made a conscious linguistic choice for the presumed benefit of their children, or because English was the language the parents themselves had in common). How and when do children code-switch to accommodate multiple dialects and different listeners? I have heard experienced teachers in similar village settings argue that their pupils, caught between dying native languages and nonstandard English, have "no language at all." Linguists insist this cannot be the case; teachers insist that it is. A linguist would have had a field day in my Kwakiutl classroom. With how much training might I have been a more linguistically sensitive observer?

Conversely, might even a bit more thinking about language acquisition, and efforts and accomplishments in studying it, have provided an analog for looking at cultural acquisition? Even preschool village children made distinctions between things Indian and things white. Where did they draw the line between these two cultural influences? What does a contemporary 6-year-old or 16-year-old Kwakiutl know? They were all in my classroom—hour upon hour every day—yet how little I learned of what *they* knew in my penchant to get them to learn more of what I knew. How I discounted the value of their knowledge and inflated the worth of my own.

*Cultural acquisition would be my focus today*: an anthropological inquiry into what children *do* know, rather than an educator preoccupation with what they *do not* know.

At first blush, it might seem the teacher role would not be well served by that orientation. Teachers, after all, should be teaching their pupils, not learning from them! Or should they? What might result if learners felt that their own knowledge was valued, their interests deemed interesting, their ability to survive day-to-day under possibly adverse conditions respected, their ways of figuring things out regarded as reasonable, even if they might lack the elegance of the teacher's practiced solutions? What might happen in a classroom that celebrated how much its participants knew rather than doted only on their deficiencies? Or a classroom that helped individuals look introspectively into their lives to discover how and why some things they "know" vary from the versions that others, including neighbors and even siblings with seemingly identical backgrounds, carry about in their heads?

This focus on cultural acquisition might seem to imply particular interest on my part in two topics: how children sort between elements of white culture and elements of Indian culture, and a preoccupation with "things learned at school." Although those topics are of more than passing interest, neither seems an appropriate starting (or ending) place for the line of inquiry I am proposing. Let me explain.

My anthropologist colleague Malcolm McFee cautioned years ago that if there was going to be an anthropology of education, there should be something distinctly anthropological about it. By commitment and training, educators have their work cut out for them in defining what it is that teachers should be trying to put into the heads of students and assessing the extent to which it actually gets there. The anthropological complement to that well-intended effort might be to help teachers understand and appreciate what is *already* in the heads of their students, the existing mass to which new knowledge must be linked if it is to become personal knowledge. School learning is of interest to the anthropologist's concern for cultural acquisition only as an aspect of a far more comprehensive question: What is it that any particular child, of a particular age and as a member of a particular social group, knows?

As to sorting ideas and behaviors into two distinct and mutually exclusive categories, things "Indian" and things "white," it strikes me as more important for the anthropological observer to try to discern *whether* and *how* individuals at different ages accomplish any such sorting than to assume that macrocultural distinctions so axiomatic to government officials, educators, and even anthropologists, are necessarily even recognized. Imposing rigid Indian-culture, white-culture taxonomies leads to drawing a conclusion similar to the one teachers in cross-cultural settings sometimes draw about student proficiency in the prevailing languages: that their students are deficient in both. With old Indian ways dying out and new white ways inadequately learned, villagers are denied "culture" on the same basis they are denied language. The terms "linguistic deprivation" and "cultural deprivation" were frequently employed in the 1960s to explain school failure.

I should not be one to scoff at such explanations: I came perilously close to laying part of the blame for the failure of Indian pupils on "linguistic deprivation." Fortunately, I qualified my observation by locating it in terms of one setting where it does hold, "for the purposes of the school." What I might have done as teacher, given a realistic appraisal of the language facility and language needs of my pupils (at least for successful interaction in mainstream Canadian society), would have been to encourage classroom conversation and to see whether I could gradually increase the ratio of English. But anyone who has managed a classroom of as many as 29 elementary school children (not to mention a one-room school with a ten year age span) probably can guess that my class was organized toward exactly the opposite goal: obedient silence. Indeed, as the year progressed, there was less and less classroom talk, even on my part.

In spite of the fact that I recognized the phrase itself as "inadequate and misleading," I was more vulnerable to "cultural deprivation" explanations of school failure. I yielded to a way of thinking about culture strongly influenced by the origins of the term as a social science concept, comparable to contemporary ways of thinking about human intelligence—that there is one optimal form of it and that not everyone enjoys the full measure achieved by those preoccupied with assessing it. Transitional ("marginal" was another popular term then) peoples like those of Blackfish Village were viewed as having lost most of the elements of their former culture without having replaced them with comparable elements from the newly dominant one. I leaned on explanations that saw villagers exhibiting a "truncated" or "partial" culture in my effort to account for what I perceived as cultural inadequacy, although I resisted the idea that they were "cultureless."

What I now take to be a more instructive way of viewing culture has been suggested by anthropologist Ward Goodenough in a paper first published in 1976 (in the forerunner of today's *Anthropology and Education Quarterly*) entitled "Multiculturalism as the Normal Human Experience." Goodenough urges us to regard human beings individually as the locus of what *collectively* can be regarded as the "culture" of some interacting group of humans, when standards of behavior are held sufficiently in common by its members to allow satisfactory social intercourse. Goodenough has proposed the term "propriospect" to label this "private, subjective view of the world and its contents" that each of us acquires out of the totality of our personal experience (see his *Culture, Language, and Society*, Benjamin/Cummings, 1981, p. 98 ff.).

No functioning human ever lacks a propriospect or has only a partial, or truncated, or "inadequate" one. Each human has a unique propriospect. Every human's propriospect includes versions of appropriate roles within at least one macrocultural system, together with a version of all the particular roles in all the attendant microcultural systems in which he or she is expected to exhibit competence.

The propriospect of each village child included, therefore, his or her age-and-gender-specific working conception of western Canadian mainstream culture, in a coastal logging-and-fishing-community form appropriate for the Alert Bay region of the early 1960s. To some extent each child's propriospect had been modified by intentionally educative influences (like the school or Indian Health Service or missionaries of the day) as well as a constant barrage of casual influences ranging from visitors and visits, cinema and radio, reading, and the sporadic but critical interaction of family members and themselves with a host of seen and unseen agents that virtually controlled their social and economic lives as Canadian citizens.

Their propriospects also included their age-and-gender-specific working conceptions of Canadian Indian culture, in a 1960s, Kwakwala-speaking, Blackfish Village variety. Each child's propriospect also had been modified by intentionally educative influences (like important potlatches or inter-village sports and social events) and a constant barrage of casual influences, particularly with visits and visitors that provided opportunity to experience, both firsthand and through the accounts of others, a sense of (a sometimes cohesive) Indian community among neighboring villages, among Kwakwala-speaking people of the region, and a pan-Indianism that allied them with other unseen agents of their own on both sides of the Canadian border.

As village teacher, I nicely illustrated Goodenough's point that every human acquires competence in at least one macro- or national cultural system: My competence was in (and remains limited essentially to) mainstream North American culture, particularly its male, white, middle-class, English-speaking, West Coast variety. My teacher role neither required nor assumed competence in Kwakiutl culture. Had it not been for anthropological interests, I would not necessarily have known anything about the Kwakiutl or about North American Indians at all: such knowledge was not part of the job description. The only important question was whether I knew how to "run" a school, a competence acquired in *my* cultural system, not in that of the villagers.

Reggie's grandfather, on the other hand, illustrates Goodenough's complementary point: humans often acquire competence in two or more macrocultural systems. Born and raised in an earlier day when Indian and white differences in western Canada were more readily distinguishable, the Old Man had acquired competence in two recognizably different cultural systems. He could "talk Indian," had experienced many of the old ways of his people firsthand, and could manipulate (and be manipulated) within Kwakiutl social systems of family, *numima*, community, and "people." But he could also speak, read, and write English, had acquired many of the "new ways" of mainstream western North America (his was the family with the highest average grade-level attainment in school, his the village home with two-way radio communication to Alert Bay, his among the seine boats with the latest technological equipment) and he could manipulate (and be manipulated) within mainstream Canadian social and economic systems that included government benefits and regulations, commercial business negotiations, seine boat skippers and their fish packing companies, and the Anglican church.

Anthropologist Goodenough reminds us that even for those of us whose competence is limited essentially to one macroculture—as in my own case—we are *all* multicultural. All humans acquire competence in myriad microcultures and their subcultural variants within at least one macrocultural system. At the same time, we do not need to acquire complete mastery of other social systems in order to interact with individuals in them. I did not have to be competent in Kwakiutl culture to be able to manage a one-room school in a rural Canadian community. It did not even matter that I was American rather than Canadian: At least I said "with" rather than "mit," and I could hum "God Save the Queen" even if I didn't have the words quite right at first.

Similarly, Reggie's grandfather did not need competence in all the nuances of social interaction for individuals from all the various social systems with whom he came into occasional contact: Chinese shopkeepers of Alert Bay, Finnish settlers of nearby Sointula, crews of the "Yugoslav" fishing boats, Indian people from different Northwest Coast groups. As they did with their verbal discourse, members of these diverse groups could switch to their common orientation in mainstream western Canadian *culture* to conduct their mutual affairs. For all the diversity of their individual propriospects, there was sufficient recognition of and competence in a National Culture that they could interact, intermarry, and even (rather begrudgingly, it often seems to outsiders) admit to some common purposes and identity in being Canadian.

Today, Reggie has acquired and continues to acquire the competence *he* needs in conducting his life. He moves even more easily than his grandfather did among and between Indian and non-Indian associates. But he does not have to surrender a measure of "Indian" competence for each measure of non-Indian competence he acquires: cultural competencies are not mutually exclusive, to be acquired as if in a zero-sum game where each competence gained necessitates a corresponding competence lost.

I assume that Reggie will continue to add to his repertory of cultural competencies both in Indian *and* non-Indian ways—as he had learned to do even before I first met him as a six-year-old—to seek self-consciously to have and to be "the best" in both societies. That is how he was raised by parents and grandparents whose ambitions for themselves are now vested in him. Because he sets his marks so high, personal ambition itself may prove his undoing. On the other hand, maybe he is one of those individuals who sees himself poised rather than caught between two cultures, inclined to see opportunity where many find only cause for despair. If such individuals are relatively rare, at least they are not a romantic fiction. I have known them personally among the Kwakiutl, and they did not all "die out" with Reggie's grandfather's generation. It's simply easier to acknowledge those who succeeded during bygone eras than to recognize with certainty their counterparts in the process of trying to make it today.

## Teaching Across Cultures

Formal education is predicated on the notion of learner incompetence. Education across cultures exacerbates the magnitude of that incompetence by identifying worthy knowledge as something located entirely outside the cultural system of the student. We continue to perceive multicultural education as a problem of the student, a problem to which teachers and schools supposedly are the answer. We are correct with this approach often enough. Education frequently "takes," and we witness wave upon wave of refugee and immigrant and minority groups successfully incorporated into new communities and nations.

But sometimes the lines are drawn differently, especially in cases where indigenous minorities see themselves as overrun, dislocated, or threatened with involuntary assimilation. In such settings, resistance to "the system," or to the teacher as its spokesperson, may become an entrenched student strategy, a posture readily adopted as appropriate behavior within one's group even though the underlying basis for antagonism is not well understood, especially among its youngest antagonists. Such was the case at Blackfish Village.

I did not set out to find the roots of that antagonism or attempt to eradicate it. I do not recommend that teachers individually adopt such goals as their professional mission or personal crusade. I did not create the tensions between white and Indian groups, nor did I see as my role the responsibility to singlehandedly resolve them. I could not help wishing I could make things "better," although I felt a clearer (and more realistic) sense of purpose in trying to keep them from becoming worse. But what about considering that different perspective suggested in the closing sentences of the original monograph, looking at the school as the problem and pondering whether in any way students might be viewed as the answer?

Were I faced today with the Kwakiutl classroom that I met in 1962, as both teacher and researcher I would attempt to approach the setting differently. I would devote my major *intellectual* effort to trying to discern what the children already knew and knew about (individually, collectively) and how they had gone about acquiring that knowledge, even if my major *physical* effort went to "running" the school. My strategy would be to learn from and about my students and, in the process, to try to make them self-conscious "knowers" about the processes of knowing. By no means would this be as easy as it may sound: my interest in virtually anything to do with the lives of village pupils usually had the effect of causing them to "clam up," perhaps preceded by a hostilely delivered, "What do *you* want to know for?" They did show interest in aspects of my personal life, however, particularly my family upbringing and childhood experiences—me as person, rather than me as teacher. Swapping stories, comparing settings, looking for universals, might be the way to get a dialogue going.

In time, I think even recalcitrant pupils *might* be encouraged to share glimpses into their world as they have come to understand it. That understanding—their understanding—of the universe would provide my orienting focus. One might begin by inventorying the skills and recipes young people have for doing things and making choices, discerning the maps in their heads that provide routes connecting persons and places in their known world. Eventually we might be able to examine their ways of sorting and categorizing elements identified in that world and some attendant attitudes and beliefs. And that might open the way for inquiry into how and why other people in other places organize and categorize their "worlds," on similar or different bases. The approach seems worth a try in a classroom where nothing else appears to be working. I am not the only teacher to observe the difference between silent, sullen Indian children in the classroom and talkative, even bossy ones outside it.

I would not abdicate my role as teacher, but I would soften its pedantic aspects and strengthen its inquiring ones. On reflection, my rigid curricular preoccupation of those days seems a bit misguided. Such rigor might have been tempered had the thought crossed my mind that I would outlive the majority of my young pupils. Although it flies quite in the face of the back-to-basics educational mood of the 1980s, I continue to wonder if I might have identified, or created, more teachable moments through an "inquiring" approach than a formal, traditional scope and sequence ever can generate.

Through three decades of teaching I have become less and less concerned or content with merely doling out knowledge. That is not to say that I object to curriculum efforts at scope and sequence; my very use of the phrase "teachable moments" implies that there are things I expect to teach and that I have some sense of what I might want 12- or 20-year-old students to learn beyond what I would want 8-year-olds to learn. The scope and sequence of North American schools, incredibly uniform as it is, might be viewed as a common "experience" to which all children are subjected—perhaps with a bit more abandon than we customarily see in schools, but a shared experience, nonetheless.

I have never been one to insist that schooling must be relevant. School experience is probably at its best—and maybe is most effective as well—when it is wildly irrelevant, particularly in terms of the classroom's own well-ordered routines. Given the years and years we devote to "schooling" our youth, the skills-and-training aspects can be tightly packaged and efficiently taught with plenty of time left for wonderment, even in the least permissive of educational climates. We can all speed up the lesson when we have to. Cultural repertories consist of far more than techniques and recipes.

The important difference, however, would not be in teaching style but in teacher stance—to recognize every pupil as a profound knower-and-wonderer-about-certain-things (but not about everything, and not necessarily what I wonder about). As both researcher and teacher, I would dwell more on the already known of their way of life rather than be preoccupied solely with what they did not know of mine. Before we try as educators to "catch people up," we need to have a better idea of the anthropologist's concern for where they already have been and what they already understand that enables them to cope, just as we do, one day at a time. And then educator and parent, and maybe even anthropologist, can attempt to address the difficult issues of where they are headed, what they seek for the next generation, the social costs and risks that may be involved, and the extent to which the school *possibly* may be of help.

## Postscript

In the interim between first drafting these words and mailing a final version to the publisher many months later, I received the sad news that Reggie, at age 31, had taken his own life, apparently despondent over a pending separation and the thought of losing custody of his beloved children. Only ten days earlier we had the opportunity of a good visit, made possible by an extended closure during the 1986 fall fishing season reminiscent of the problems about which fishermen were complaining 25 years ago. Although Reggie remained unimpressed with the book ("It's so out-of-date"), his reaction to the new Waveland edition was, "That should have been me on the cover."

I had intended originally to conclude this Afterword by honoring the memory of Reggie's grandfather, *Kla-kli-li-tla,* not only for the full and rich four score years of his life but in recognition of the influence he continues to exert even today through words and deeds well remembered and carefully recounted. As a younger member of the family reflected, "No one thought I paid any attention. But everything he said, I can still hear now, and I listen to him."

Without that same sense of celebration, I mark Reggie's tragic death as well, a young life still in the making. But during that recent visit to Kwakiutl country I heard and saw evidence of other young adults assuming responsibility for maintaining links with the past and making appropriate adaptations for the present, and of mature adults assuming the mantle of elder to offer guidance and encouragement.

Reggie's concern was that Indian ways are dying out. Watching today as Kwakiutl pupils bring home computerized report cards or navigate local shopping malls can buttress that impression. Still, my sense is that although personal circumstances may alter dramatically, the underlying interpersonal rhythms and patterned ways of coping that I attribute to "being Kwakiutl" seem to endure. Indian *people* do the dying; figuratively, so can entire villages. Yet Indian *ways* are faring pretty well. Kwakiutl culture most certainly has changed through time, not only in the 100 years since Franz Boas began systematically to describe it, but even in the quarter century of my own firsthand experience. As long traditions must, however, it is also proving remarkably resilient.

# 10

# The Acquisition of Culture

## Notes on a Working Paper

---

### PREFACE

---

After putting the finishing touches on my dissertation at Stanford in June 1964, I loaded my worldly possessions into my automobile (with plenty of room to spare) and headed north to Eugene, where I had accepted a position at the University of Oregon's newly funded R&D (research and development) Center for the Advanced Study of Educational Administration. I planned to stay a couple of years. Instead, I stayed forever.

The organizational structure of the university kept evolving through changing but never radically different assignments that found me shuffling from Educational Administration and the R&D Center, to Sociocultural Foundations of Education, to Educational Policy, to Curriculum and Instruction, finally winding up as Professor Emeritus in the Department of Anthropology. Through it all, I remained intellectually linked with colleagues across North America and throughout the world in the emerging interdisciplinary field of "anthropology and education." As ethnographic and other qualitative approaches became better known and appreciated beyond the fields of cultural anthropology and Chicago School sociology, I was in the company of those who had been there all along.

The times grew increasingly favorable not only for qualitative inquiry in general but for ethnographic research in particular. If anything, they were almost too favorable, given the tendency of researchers and their graduate students in professional fields such as education to become preoccupied with method. As the years, and my own career, progressed, I felt drawn more and more into questions of method. As a consequence, I was drawn away from an interest in teaching-learning processes that had prompted my decision to enter the teaching field and my subsequent decision to pursue advanced graduate studies.

Under Spindler's influence at Stanford, my classroom-oriented interest in teaching and learning had been expanded and redefined to become an anthropological interest in socialization, enculturation, and, especially, cultural transmission. Early in 1979, taking my 50th birthday as turning point, I made a conscious decision to redirect my intellectual focus, or at least to modify its emphasis, to allow more attention to an earlier interest in learning viewed as cultural process. Tentatively I dubbed this the "anthropology of learning" and invited colleagues to join in presenting a symposium on the topic (Wolcott, 1982).

In a nutshell, that explains how the first article in the Brad trilogy (Chapter 3) came to have a life history approach and a learner-centered interpretation. I had heeded Frederick Erickson's advice, having previously sought his counsel on how one might go about developing an anthropology of learning. "First of all," he had replied succinctly, "get yourself a learner!" My "learner" was Brad. This also explains why, in "Afterword, 1989" (Chapter 9), I reintroduced anthropologist Ward Goodenough's concept "propriospect" and discussed how culture acquisition would be the focus of that study were I initiating it today.

The chapter presented here, "The Acquisition of Culture: Notes on a Working Paper," follows in that vein. It is not my formal statement on the topic, which has been published separately as "Propriospect and the Acquisition of Culture" (Wolcott, 1991b). This piece is a complement to that one. It includes an earlier and shorter version of the now-published article, but it goes beyond that by letting the reader in on the dialogue that accompanied the development of the formal paper.

My "data" for this discussion consist of the original paper together with comments and written reactions from invited and anonymous reviewers. For these data, I didn't have to venture even as far as my backyard; they were already on my desk. And although I am author of the paper, the interpretations exceed my ability at interpretation, at least to the point of satisfying all my critics. The result is an interpretive essay treated as the descriptive data base that calls forth further interpretation provided by others.

The article that appears here was originally presented as a Keynote Address to the Fourth Annual Conference of the Qualitative Research Group at the University of Georgia. At the time I presented the talk, the formal paper was still undergoing revision and review. As I remark in my opening comments, after working on draft after draft of the paper during 4 previous years, I had begun to wonder if its "time" would ever come. I did not *really* doubt that the paper would eventually be published, however; I kept the *Anthropology and Education Quarterly* as my ace-in-the-hole while first submitting drafts to journals that reach other audiences.

I was intrigued by the responses and reactions I was receiving to successive iterations of the paper, and I wondered how I might weave this ongoing dialogue into it. Unfortunately, the original paper had grown too long, and the revised version seemed in danger of heading the same way. The informality of an invited talk to an audience of qualitatively oriented researchers offered an opportunity to share reviewer comments in the form of a working paper about a working paper. My "talk" appears here as it did in the published conference proceedings.

As a substantive issue, I hope the content of the paper raises intriguing questions about the relationship between culture and the individual. In terms of process, I included the paper to illustrate how the interpretive process itself can be approached descriptively. In terms of the D-A-I formulation, description and interpretation are the heavies, another illustration (comparable to Chapter 5) in which inquiry processes themselves provide the descriptive base.

Interpretation need be neither lonely nor risky business; it can be that part of an otherwise individual and independent venture in which we not only engage our colleagues but make colleagues of our students. My approach here suggests one format for doing so; seminars and symposia provide others.

The original drafts of my paper provided a baseline for interpretation; my invited critics took it from there. Here I use "original" only in the sense of "initial." I had been mulling these ideas ever since Spindler sparked my interest in them more than 30 years earlier, and

I drew the key term *propriospect* from a paper by Ward Goodenough published in 1971. ("Originality," Howard Becker recalls being told by Louis Wirth, is "the product of a faulty memory"—Becker, 1986, p. 136.)

As critics so often do, mine were inclined to carry the discussion off in directions different from the one in which I was attempting to go. I did not feel obligated to respond in the formal manuscript to every issue raised. The differing views were instructive and worthy of being heard, however, and I realized that the cautions and concerns already expressed would be raised by other readers as well.

In the process of seeking feedback, keep in mind that virtually anyone you invite to give critical comment will have critical comment to offer, regardless of how satisfied you yourself feel with your efforts. Further, the direction such comments take will lean toward each reviewer's frame of reference, vested interests, or presentation style. Except perhaps in dealing with an adamant dissertation committee, I think that the advice one receives as to the direction of interpretation can be regarded as just that: advice. Authors need to remain open to suggestion and, as noted in Chapter 2, careful not to gain a reputation for seeking advice they never follow, but the author always remains final judge of how an interpretation will stand, how many competing views to try to present or attempt to silence. Seeking still further opinions (or trying other journals, as I did here) may seem an obvious resolution, but my experience is that reviewers have a tendency to want to stamp a manuscript with their own imprint. Thus the review process is potentially endless. In cases where reviewers act in common to identify something that needs reworking, the problem is more likely to be one of style or organization than of interpretation.

Of the reviewer reactions reported here, only one—that of Spindler himself—resulted in a *major* modification in my thinking and my draft. Spindler objected strongly to my treatment of cultural transmission as the "old" anthropology and education, culture acquisition as the "new" one. Out of courtesy and respect, I would have softened that point anyway, but I realized during the rewriting (and so, perhaps, did he) that in recent years he had been redefining cultural transmission, particularly his view of formal education. I felt that his own evolving views deserved to be heard more widely. Certainly it was not necessary for me to "kill off" cultural transmission to make way for culture acquisition.

We perform a useful service whenever we open up, rather than close up, important issues. Even when identified with no more than a brief parenthetical comment or footnote, important questions raised by colleagues and early reviewers can be incorporated into final drafts, perhaps as topics to be addressed at another time. To help keep things "open," we probably should regard *all* our writing as interim or progress reporting. Those Grand Finales we are tempted to employ in closing ought to be rationed one to a career, not one to each separate report. That might help us to interpret interpretation itself as an ongoing process rather than a task to be completed. This paper illustrates interpretation viewed that way. It is also another example of "circling back" over one's prior experience. The Afterword of the previous chapter took a long look back; the present chapter focuses narrowly on the evolution of a single article.

I do not mean to suggest that every article we write warrants a parallel article recounting its history and critical reception. But I do believe that the candid treatment offered here may be every bit as informative as the major conceptual paper that inspired it, particularly for students ordinarily privy only to polished final works rather than to multiple drafts rewritten along the way.

## References

Becker, Howard S. (1986). *Writing for social scientists*. Chicago: University of Chicago Press.

Goodenough, Ward H. (1971). *Culture, language, and society* (McCaleb Module in Anthropology). Reading, MA: Addison-Wesley.

Wolcott, Harry F. (1982). The anthropology of learning. *Anthropology and Education Quarterly, 13*(2), 83-108.

Wolcott, Harry F. (1991a). The acquisition of culture: Notes on a working paper. In Mary Jo McGee-Brown (Ed.), *Diversity and design: Studying culture and the individual. Proceedings of the Fourth Annual Qualitative Research in Education Conference* (pp. 22-46). Athens: University of Georgia, College of Education.

Wolcott, Harry F. (1991b). Propriospect and the acquisition of culture. *Anthropology and Education Quarterly, 22*(3), 251-273.

# THE ACQUISITION OF CULTURE

## Notes on a Working Paper

### Opening Remarks

In April, 1987, I began preparing a handwritten draft of the paper I am going to discuss with you here. That paper, and to a large extent these comments as well, deals with the topic of culture acquisition, a topic that has come to assume a central place in my academic thinking.

My first draft of the paper ran to 53 pages and was titled, "The Acquisition of Propriospect." It began with the words, "Propriospect may be an idea whose time has come." In the second draft completed two months later, I note that I changed the opening sentence to read a bit more tentatively: "Might 'propriospect' be an idea whose time has come?"

This selection was originally presented as a Keynote Address delivered January 3, 1991. The conference proceedings that contain this address were published by the College of Education, University of Georgia, under the editorship of Mary Jo McGee-Brown. The title of the volume reflects the theme of the 1991 conference: *Diversity and Design: Studying Culture and the Individual.* This copyright for this version is retained by the author.

Almost four years have elapsed. I'm still working on that paper. The title was the first to go; by the second word, "acquisition," I was already in trouble. The paper now starts at a different point, the storyteller's art only part of the problem. The original first sentence has disappeared, but I continue to ponder, "Might propriospect be an idea whose time has come?"

What follows is an account of the *evolution of that paper*, rather than the paper itself; one story has become two. In its final form, the full paper will have to account for, or blatantly ignore, many of the issues I raise in this telling. Because I believe that these issues are instructive for the continuing dialogue about studying culture and the individual —a topic of critical interest to those of us in anthropology and education, and the theme selected for your qualitative research conference this year—I would like to share them with you in their rough, unpolished form.

I am going to read an early version of the paper, but not the original 53-page tome. Rather, this will be a slightly revised version of the paper as adapted for presentation in an invited symposium at the American Anthropological Association meetings in Phoenix, November 1988. The session was sponsored by the Council on Anthropology and Education and convened by John Chilcott. My rambling original version had to go by the boards in order for my comments to fit within one of those 15-minute time slots into which we condense professional careers at national meetings. I present the briefer paper here, admittedly without quite the same restraint imposed by the 900 seconds allocated for its first hearing. For my purposes now, the original comments serve as a point of departure. As to topic and content, the paper must speak for itself, as it had to do in a symposium with the title "Anthropological Theory and Education Research."

## "The Acquisition of Propriospect" as Presented November 17, 1988

One of the most salutary chapters ever written in culture and personality—a chapter in the literal as well as the figurative sense—was penned by A. F. C. Wallace in the second edition of his essay on that topic, *Culture and Personality* (Wallace 1970: Chapter 1). In the short run, Wallace's words and ideas came too late to save the field of culture and personality by redefining its core concern. It was probably too late in

1961, when the first edition appeared (Wallace 1961a), and his reconceptualization did not appear until the second edition, nine years later. By then, "Culture and Personality" studies, books, and courses were "on the wane" (Watson and Watson-Franke 1985:10).

That is not to say that anthropologists no longer look at issues of culture and the individual, but they do so differently today, and the orientation differs radically from studies of the 40s and 50s that spawned them.

Perhaps there was no way out of the dead-end that gave us National Character studies, and concepts like "basic personality structure" and "modal personality," other than to forget it all and start over. But cultural anthropologists were reoriented, and the word "shared" has been used more gingerly in the perpetual efforts to define and explain that elusive mantra "culture" ever since.

In just six words, Wallace identified what he described as "two major, and to a degree antithetical, conceptions of the nature of the relation between cultural and personality systems. . . . These conceptions may be construed, respectively, as emphasizing the *replication of uniformity* and the *organization of diversity*" (1970:22).

Under the *replication of uniformity* conception, Wallace explains,

> the anthropologist . . . is primarily interested in the extent to which members of a social group . . . behave in the same way under the same circumstances. For the sake of convenience in discourse, they may even be considered to have learned the "same things" in the "same cultural environment." Under such circumstances, the society may be regarded as culturally homogeneous and the individuals will be expected to share a uniform nuclear character. (Wallace 1970:22)

By contrast, the *organization of diversity* conception considers "the actual diversity of habits, of motives, of personalities, of customs that do, in fact, coexist within the boundaries of any culturally organized society" (p. 23). Attending to that "actual diversity," Wallace observes, immediately raises a critical question:

> How do such various individuals organize themselves culturally into orderly, expanding, changing societies? When the process of socialization is examined closely, it becomes apparent that, within the limits of practical human control and observation, it is not a perfectly reliable mechanism for replication. (p. 23)

Wallace's nicely chosen phrases may have created a dichotomy that he did not intend: It was easy to remember two seemingly opposite phrases of three words each, easy to ignore qualifying terms such as "to a degree antithetical" or cautions that uniformity and diversity are to be variously "emphasized" rather than regarded as mutually exclusive.

I recall being particularly taken with the phrase "organization of diversity" as a way of understanding and explaining how there was any room for personality or possibility for culture change if culture really exerted the influence I liked to claim for it. Whether or not Wallace intended it, I have always regarded "replication of uniformity" as the *old* culture and personality school, and "organization of diversity" as the *new* one—or what the new one might have become, had culture and personality studies not been transformed altogether into studies in cognitive anthropology, psychological anthropology, culture and cognition, and the like.

I go back to Wallace's 1970 publication, and to an issue seldom discussed in those same terms these days, because I think they offer a perspective on the development of another subfield, anthropology and education, including not only what we *have* attended to, but what we *might* attend to.

## The "Cultural Transmission" Era

"Anthropology and education" was evolving when culture and personality studies were in their heyday almost 40 years ago. There was nothing to read that specifically linked education and anthropology except George Spindler's edited volume reporting the proceedings from the Stanford conference held in 1954 (Spindler 1955). We took our readings largely from the culture and personality literature, augmented by those few ethnographic accounts where the anthropologist happened to say something (anything, really) about child-rearing that we could examine for implications about processes contributing toward cultural continuity. The literature of the day reflected the replication of uniformity school. Culture was assumed to be strong and pervasive. The new perspective we brought to it—especially those of us under Spindler's influence at Stanford University—was *cultural transmission*.

As long as we held the assumption that people in a society "behave in the same way under the same circumstances" (Wallace 1970:22), then our focus was appropriately on the *transmitters* of culture, whether "mother's brother or Miss Humboldt of Peavey Falls," to quote one of my favorite Spindlerisms (Spindler 1955:14). Convincing ourselves that anthropologists were "just like children learning a culture," we directed our attention to those transmitters of culture—especially the adult ones like ourselves who could explain to us what they were up to. That gave us lots of good material to observe and report. We directed little attention to how children actually went about *acquiring* culture. We felt we could do that for them, and much more efficiently. I still recall how I chafed at being isolated in a classroom with my Kwakiutl pupils almost 30 years ago when I might instead have been out in the village really learning how it is to grow up Kwakiutl.

Disenchantment with, and criticism of, culture and personality studies also dates back at least to the 50s. We realized that cultures weren't as monolithic as often portrayed, especially as anthropologists began studying among groups closer to home, where ideal types were not so easily confused with reality, and where fieldworkers understood more of what was going on than they had sometimes understood.

Nor could we continue to ignore work being done and questions being raised by language-learning theorists pondering universals in the sequence of language acquisition. They were beginning to recognize that each individual learner has the ultimate responsibility for putting it all together. Language learning and language-learning sequences were proving somewhat independent of the efforts of caregivers. Toddlers do not reinvent language or culture, but neither do they learn quite the same things, no matter how similar the cultural environment.

## The "Culture Acquisition" Era

Perhaps we precipitated another major shift, from an emphasis on cultural *transmission* to cultural *acquisition*—in a symposium, "The Anthropology of Learning," presented at the American Anthropological Association meetings in December 1980 (subsequently reported in the summer 1982 issue of the *Anthropology and Education Quarterly*). If the shift did not occur precisely at that moment, it nonetheless was during those times, and the times were right. Today the phrase "cultural transmission" is ordinarily joined with its complement, "cultural acquisition." I find my own interests better described by the phrase *cultural acquisition*, which I take to be the more inclusive of the two. For the past decade, some of us have been stumping to boost "cultural acquisition" (or "culture acquisition," as more often written these days) into prominence as the core concept in anthropology and education.

In our professional dialogue, however, the phrase culture acquisition warrants scrutiny. While communicating a broad locus of interest to people outside our field, it remains conceptually ambiguous. It can lead back to the "old" culture and personality school, with the replication of uniformity a logical consequence of culture perceived monolithically, its acquisition a collective phenomenon, a common set of experiences through which we all pass and from which we all derive comparable lessons. We must avoid the trap of taking culture to be a well-specified body of knowledge, a common core of information that every member of a group not only knows but knows in exactly the same way. (Trap though it may be, those who set it with their public outcries at collective ignorance or bait it with handy guides to cultural literacy have always done rather well.)

## Enculturation

Culture acquisition has moved us a step forward, although the step may be a small one. For the past four decades our dialogue has benefitted from—but also been restricted by—the term "enculturation," first proposed in 1948 by Melville Herskovits in *Man and His Works*. Herskovits felt we needed a term that extended beyond *socialization*, which he defined as adaptation to the group and was, therefore, behavior seen in animal as well as human aggregates (Herskovits 1948:38). He wanted a concept that would account for "the aspects of the learning experience which mark off man from other creatures, and by means of which, initially and in later life, he achieves competence in his culture" (p. 39). Enculturation, the term he proposed, refers to the processes involved when an individual "learns the customary ways of thinking and acting that make up the culture that distinguishes his society from other human groupings" (p. 38).

As his definition of enculturation suggests, and consistent with the times, Herskovits appears to have meted out culture on a convenient one-to-a-customer basis. And although he acknowledged that the enculturation process is continuous throughout every individual's life, he saw the early years as most critical. "The enculturative experience of later life," he noted, "is only intermittent" (p. 41).

Because anthropologists have been preoccupied with the *content* of culture far more than with processes of *acquiring* it, the important phrase nested within Herskovits' definition about achieving "competence" in one's culture seems to have gone unnoticed. Anthropological concern has always been for the urgent and seemingly endless task of inventorying those "customary ways of thinking and acting."

In the course of being human, every individual grows up into a social world and acquires competence in at least some of the cultural systems of his or her immediate environment. But it is equally true, and critically important to recognize, that no two humans ever experience the world in the same way. No one gets it all; no one needs it all. Even ethnographers, who seek fame and fortune in trying, are forgiven responsibility for providing the total inventory of any particular group's "culture."

In every sense of the word, culture is an abstraction. Culture acquisition, regarded as a human process in which we are all engaged from first breath (and earlier) to last, is quite real as a *process*. But the idea that anyone ever accomplishes the task is patently absurd. No one can possibly "acquire" culture! What, then, do we acquire, if we do not acquire culture itself?

## Enter Propriospect

What we need is a term that points clearly and unambiguously to the sum total of *all* the cultural content that any *one* individual accumulates, a term that effectively sorts out, from all that can be known, what any one human—you or me, for instance—actually knows.

Tempting as it is to coin a new word, there is no great need to do so. Others have thought about these concerns and suggested possible terms—such as "propriospect," in the title of this paper—although the terms have not caught on, as you yourself may attest if you do not recall ever seeing or hearing the word before.

The term propriospect was proposed by Ward Goodenough in 1971 in an Addison-Wesley Module titled "Culture, Language, and Society." The roots of the idea in his writing go back even further, to *Cooperation in Change* (Goodenough 1963:260), where he makes reference to the sum of the cultural knowledge known by any one individual, but offers only a descriptive title, "private culture." In 1971, Goodenough substituted *propriospect* and offered a definition that remained unchanged in his elaborated second edition of *Culture, Language, and Society* published a decade later (cf. 1971:31; 1981:98).

Goodenough defines *propriospect* as the totality of the private, subjective view of the world and its contents that every human develops out of his or her personal experience (1971:36). Propriospect does not describe "culture" per se; rather, propriospect refers to any *particular* individual's unique *version* of a culture. More than that, as I believe Goodenough intended it, propriospect refers to the aggregated versions of all the cultural settings or activities of which any particular human is aware.

In Goodenough's conception, it is critical to understand that individuals employ their own criteria, however implicit (or explicit, in the case of anthropologists), for identifying the culture-sharing groups significant in their own lives, and for identifying the individuals whose actions locate them within those groups. As a homely example—a set of individuals to whom I personally attribute behavior that distinguishes them as a culture-sharing group—I identify drivers heading north on Oregon's Interstate 5 in automobiles with Washington (state) license plates. I perceive them as driving 10 miles an hour faster than anyone else in their perennial haste to get through Oregon on their return home from California. Whether in fact they have all visited California, all drive 10 miles faster than the flow of traffic, or even really exceed the speed limit, is quite immaterial; I *attribute* this behavior to them. As I understand Goodenough, they would, therefore, constitute a culture-sharing group, a point to which I shall return.

*Idiolect.* Not surprising, given his interest in language and culture, Goodenough develops propriospect as comparable to a better known and somewhat equivalent term from linguistics, *idiolect.* The concept of idiolect underscores that, just as with culture, no two humans ever experience or engage in *language* in exactly the same way, either. "There are as many versions of a language," Goodenough reminds us, "as there are speakers of it" (1971:14). Unfortunately for the analogy, however, idiolect is defined as "the individual's own version of what he perceives to be a *particular* dialect or language" (Goodenough 1971:8, emphasis added). Since speakers of a language not only recognize but often can speak more than one dialect of it as well, speakers may be competent in multiple idiolects, just as some speakers may be competent in multiple languages. One language or many, however, each of us has but one propriospect.

*Idioverse.* Anthropologist Theodore Schwartz has proposed an alternative term to propriospect: *idioverse.* Schwartz discusses idioverse at some length in a 1978 chapter in Spindler's edited volume, *The Making of Psychological Anthropology*, tracing its first use to psychologist Saul Rosenzweig more than 25 years earlier. Schwartz defines idioverse as "the total set of implicit constructs of each individual in a cultural system" (Schwartz 1978:424), constructs derived from that individual's experience "in all the events making up his life history" (p. 425).

Whether "propriospect" or "idioverse" is more suitable for referring to the total content of culture known by any one human seems a toss-up. We might coin yet another term, such as "idiospect," combining the elements of something personal, private, separate, and distinct—from the Greek *idios*—and the "view" or "outlook" of *spectus* from the Latin. My inclination is to follow Goodenough, on the assumption that with two editions of *Culture, Language, and Society* extending through two decades, more people probably have been exposed to that term and have access to it in the original, although the monograph itself is no longer in print. Readers familiar with both concepts will recognize that Goodenough's conceptualization takes more cognizance of culture, Schwartz's of personality.

## Drawing Attention to Propriospect

Propriospect draws attention to a critical distinction Goodenough makes between a society's culture pool, defined as "the sum of the contents of all of the propriospects of all of the society's members" (1971:42) and what each of those members knows individually. The concept is well suited to convey the complex notion of cultures (like languages) as something known partly in common, yet susceptible to endless variation and reinterpretation. It also offers a refreshing and alternative way to think about issues like multiculturalism, which some educators appear to regard as a zero-sum game in which knowledge or competence gained for one set of cultural circumstances necessitates competence surrendered in another. Adding new cultural competencies does not require abandoning old ones. The capacity of propriospect is infinite; we are limited only by the extent of our personal experience. "We all begin with the natural equipment to live a thousand kinds of life," Clifford Geertz observes, "but end in the end having lived only one" (1973:45).

To date, my unbridled enthusiasm for propriospect seems to have gone largely unchallenged and totally unmatched. Goodenough wrote about it only briefly when he introduced the concept in 1971 and added nothing in the slightly expanded version of his essay published a decade later. A simple model he included seems to have lent rigidity to what otherwise might have been perceived as an interesting, if somewhat freewheeling, idea.

In trying to represent aspects of their own propriospects, my students sometimes get lost as we search for an adequate level of detail to be able to view propriospect comparatively. If we try partially to represent the propriospects of class members from overseas who must acquire critical competencies in some aspects of our culture as well as (presumed) competence in their own, students sometimes get a wrongheaded notion that foreign visitors acquire two propriospects, while stay-at-homes are limited to one. Instead of regarding propriospect as unique to each human being, they perceive it as a property of individual societies, to be issued like the entry permits stamped into passports by officials at international borders. Such misperceptions are revealed in proposed term paper titles like "My Two Propriospects."

We work to overcome these obstacles, so that students become comfortable with Goodenough's model of propriospect as a shorthand way to represent and compare what different humans have come to know. Once we achieve that, we can delve into some profound issues about cultural knowledge. One question that arises is whether humans ever know anything that is "outside" of culture. Goodenough (and others before him) argues yes, there are things about which individuals have knowledge "gained from private experience" not attributed to others (1971:42); so do some of my students. We find ourselves in good company looking more closely at just what we mean by culture  and whether knowledge can ever be "culture-less" or "beyond culture."

By far the most complex questions arise over issues raised by the idea of cultural competence. Following Goodenough again (and literally, in this case) we begin by defining propriospect in terms of all the "versions" of culture an individual has—these being of his or her own perception, as already noted—but we find ourselves drawn toward a redefined notion limited to cultural systems in which an individual actually *exhibits* competence (cf. p. 36, p. 42). From "knows about," we narrow our scope to those cultural systems, and, more precisely, to aspects of those systems—*traditions* within a culture, as Goodenough calls them—in which an individual actually "knows how." With the introduction of a criterion of competence, propriospect becomes infinitely more manageable. Further, the analogy with language is strengthened. Linguistic competence is not all that elusive to assess, at least in everyday behavior. At the same time, we find ourselves transforming propriospect from a seemingly passive view (or version, or "outlook")

developed out of personal experience, to an ability to engage in that
experience ourselves. This is not inconsistent with Goodenough, who
observes:

> A person may not only attribute different systems of standards to different
> sets of others, he may also be competent in more than one of them—be
> competent, that is, in more than one culture. (1971:37)

Restricting propriospect to *displayed competence* seems to provide a
better way to talk about the cultural stuff in people's heads and to
facilitate comparisons among different individuals. We are drawn into
the question of *assessing cultural competence*. Given our interest in cultural
acquisition, we find ourselves wondering how to distinguish—and
how to represent in a model—competencies *acquired* from competencies in the *process of being acquired*. How, for example, can we distinguish
various levels of competence with the English language, and North
American customs, among foreign students who argue that although
they can get by in English, they would never describe themselves as
competent in it?

Similarly, can competencies once acquired later be "lost," or are they
filed deep in memory? The idea of regarding ourselves as TABs,
"temporarily able bodies"—borrowed, I think, from the mental health
field—is reminder that our competencies are ephemeral, changing
with our physical capabilities and social circumstances. The enculturative experience of later life is not so "intermittent" as Herskovits
might lead us to believe, although as time passes we may, as he
suggests, give it "little thought" (1948:41).

My purpose in sharing these thoughts is to encourage dialogue
about the term and concept behind "propriospect." I would like to see
it employed in life histories and in studies of culture acquisition—can
it add precision to that work? I would like to hear discussion about
ways of introducing it so that students better understand the sense in
which Goodenough argued years ago that we are all multicultural

(Goodenough 1976), able to navigate within myriad *microcultural* systems in *one* macrocultural system, even for those whose experience
does not extend to other *macrocultures*.

I also believe that propriospect might help wean us from almost
invariably equating cultural differences with ethnic ones, to the virtual
exclusion of all the other bases on which culture can be attributed. When
we speak of an individual's competence within a macro- or national
cultural system, we are acknowledging that cultural competence means

being able to engage appropriately in appropriate activities in particular social settings.

I must emphasize that competence is not a function of membership. As Goodenough reminds, we cannot "belong" to cultures any more than we can "belong" to languages (1971:38n). Our propriospects catalog our competencies, not our memberships.

As antidote to the concern of the educator for how little students know, anthropologists might provide a valuable service in reminding teachers how very much every human "knows." Viewed in terms of competencies rather than deficiencies, propriospect is a step toward positive thinking, not only about human potential but also about human accomplishment. In turn, that astounding amount pales by comparison with how very little of the great "all of it" any one individual ever knows or ever needs to know. *Nobody has ever acquired culture and no one ever will.* What we are talking about when we talk about the individual in society is a particular version of cultural knowledge that each of us is acquiring: propriospect. I suggest that the *acquisition of propriospect* should be the focal concern in anthropology and education.

## Notes on a Working Paper: The Keynote Continues

The session in which the previous remarks were delivered was well attended, the applause gratifying. However, I may have been premature in thinking about film rights or wondering whether Robert Redford would be right for the lead. The applause from Margaret LeCompte, Judith Goetz [Preissle], and Jacquetta Hill was the polite applause of fellow presenters. Symposium organizer John Chilcott probably applauded because I stayed within the time limit. My own students comprised a substantial part of the audience.

By the time we got around to the comments sent by our invited but absent discussant Charles Harrington, difficulties already were beginning to mount, in spite of the fact that I had sent Harrington the longer paper (the 53-page one) that was supposed to explain everything. He raised three issues, lightheartedly beginning by dissociating himself from my apparent obituary for his own field of psychological anthropology, another of those deaths, he noted, that had been "greatly exaggerated."

For his second point, although he agreed that Wallace's distinction between the replication of uniformity and the organization of diversity marked an important turning point, and that the replication of uniformity model was "inappropriately reductionistic—that is, culture is not simply replicated in each individual, and therefore personality is not simply culture 'writ small,' " he felt that, in accepting Goodenough's idea that multiple propriospects comprise a culture pool, I had come "close to the reverse logical error, that culture is simply the individual writ large—that is, culture as nothing more than the sum of individual propriospects." Harrington pointed out that Wallace's intent was *to distinguish personality from culture,* and thus was a more dynamic model than I had implied.

Finally, Harrington lamented that the concept of propriospect may fill a hole in theory, but since it is lodged in the heads of individuals, it "may not be a useful construct because it cannot be directly researched." He felt it necessary to distinguish between calling attention to the theoretical necessity for explaining how diversity works, which I had done, and introducing a concept to guide future investigations, which I had not done.

I hadn't left the podium and already three major criticisms had been aired. I might have headed off the first of those by being sensitive to the fact that the field of our invited discussant is psychological anthropology. Had I graciously noted that "culture and personality" is often viewed today as a historical era in the development of psychological anthropology, I would have been off to a better start.

That I stumbled in portraying the nexus between personality and culture, or between individual and society, was disappointing but hardly surprising—I've almost come to believe that the resolution lies in one's perspective: personality becomes the dominant feature when viewed from within cultural settings, culture the dominant feature when looking across them. But I am fascinated with Goodenough's notion of the culture pool and have come to realize with this very writing that I regard a *culture pool* as far more vast and complex—and interesting—than culture itself. That is, culture is better regarded as less, not more, than the collective action of individuals as they engage in it. Culture is the common denominator, the centripetal force; personality is the centrifugal one, forever trying to wrest itself free from that pull. The trajectory of the two forces, working in tandem, is the one we plot as observers of our fellow humans who at once insist that they exert free will on their every action, yet must know the day of the week in order to decide when to arise, what to wear, and probably what to prepare for breakfast, as well.

The discussant's third criticism caught me by surprise—for a moment I must have forgotten that there are different kinds of anthropologists, too. To be faulted because the concept of propriospect cannot be "directly researched" left me wondering how the concept of culture ever fared as well as it did. Then again, not all psychological anthropologists are that taken with it.

Another colleague, also a psychological anthropologist, had already  raised the same issue in response to my original paper:

> I worry that maybe you've been away from kids too long when you give yourself the unachievable (in my opinion) task of figuring out "how each child acquires his or her particular version of what the world is about." You're right, it sounds easy, but to my knowledge no one has yet found a way to do it in any practical (i.e., doable) way, except in small, delimited and well-defined domains.
>
> Are you derailing a whole generation of young upcoming professionals by suggesting that this is an achievable goal? Your assignment for yourself (and, by implication, for the next generation of educational anthropologists) is much like the dream of the ethnoscience crowd at Stanford during our days there—to write ("rigorous" for them) ethnographies solely from people's own points of view and using their own conceptual categories, etc. That dream, I think, turned into a nightmare for some and was given up by most. But if you can figure out how to do it, you will have assured yourself a place among the greats, not only in your field, but in mine (Ronald P. Rohner, personal communication 26 June 1987).

In case I still hadn't heard the message, here is the reaction I received to my manuscript from another seasoned anthropological editor:

> I guess I have to pass on this one. The journal hardly ever publishes programmatic articles. I understand your enthusiasm for the propriospect concept, but it needs to be showcased in the results of empirical research if it's to catch on, I'm afraid.

My former student Jean Campbell raised the next critical issue while we were sitting at the Phoenix airport having a beer and waiting for flights home. How could I reject the idea that people "acquire" culture, she wondered, and then proceed in my paper to insist that they "acquire" propriospect? Culture is not acquired, it is *constructed* out of social experience. Shouldn't propriospect be regarded in parallel fashion? We acquire the *experience* out of which propriospect is constructed; we do not acquire propriospect itself, which is a capacity for action. Had I not glossed a two-step process with too slick a phrase, "acquisition of propriospect?"

For awhile, I reduced the working title of the paper to the single word "Propriospect." But that label lacked context, and I found it necessary to bring back into the title the very phrase I was trying to redefine. The working title now is "Propriospect and the Acquisition of Culture." However, I take pains to point out not only that no one acquires culture, but also that no one acquires propriospect, either. (Do we make the same mistake in speaking of the "acquisition" of language, glossing a staged sequence with a single term?) Granted, the banners "Acquisition of Culture" and "Acquisition of Language" are handy for pointing in a general way to spheres of interest. The refinements I propose need to be understood, but they need not get in the way of everyday discourse. I will continue to announce my interest as culture acquisition—but I will add for any discerning audience, "Of course, technically, there's no such thing."

Some time later I was pleased to find this observation by W. Penn Handwerker in the pages of the *American Anthropologist* (1989:324):

> It follows that the system of concepts and behavior we commonly call "culture" cannot constitute an "inheritance system," for there is nothing about culture that can be passed from one person to another, except metaphorically.

Before I made copies of the original 900-second wonder, I began to flesh the paper out in roughly the form presented above. Initial feedback from students and invited colleagues indicated that the paper was likely to become a "permanent working draft" unless I was willing to risk editorial rejection for the benefit of critical outside review. So, along with finding opportunities to present current drafts in seminars, and finding colleagues who hadn't yet been burdened with reading the paper in one of its many iterations, I decided to send copies for review on a "submit, revise, submit elsewhere" basis. You have already been privy to my first formal rejection by an editor who decided not even to bother reviewers.

With the next rejection, another editor took the opposite tack, letting a reviewer do the dirty work and adding only the obvious "We have decided to pass . . ." Excerpts from the review:

> The author knows that his readers will think that he is engaging with the ideas and frameworks of yesterday's fashions in anthropology (obviously, though, he still sees much value in the work of Goodenough, Wallace, et al., and in another venue would probably be critical of all that has happened since

then—to which there is no reference at all in this piece, that is, to the cultural anthropology of the 1980s).

Theoretically, this paper knows nothing of semiotics, hermeneutics, or theories of interpretation which have been influential, and rich ways of exploring the "organization of diversity/uniformity" distinction made by Wallace. It does not seem possible to take this distinction up again without at least some attention to more recent developments in theory and approaches in cultural anthropology.

The paper is governed by the methodological individualism of classic culture-and-personality concerns through Goodenough and Wallace. The neologizing just pursues cultural knowledge at the level of the individual more extreme. [I had to look up the word new to me, "neologizing." The dictionary informed me it refers to making up new words!]

. . . the neologism that the author rather cagily plays with has little use in research. It is rather an effective teaching tool. The author's forte is indeed in presenting certain concepts about learning culture to students new to anthropology . . . This paper could be published if it took the anthropology since the early 1970s into account, and if it more explicitly explored the teaching of anthropology as its purpose.

It was a relief to have a sympathetic senior colleague in anthropology read this last review and dismiss it as "typical of the bullshit anthropology of the 80s," but it is unnerving to hear the suggestion, no matter how muted, that one may not be keeping up with the field. Admittedly, however, having a paper and topic like this "in the works" does alert an author to attending more closely to recent, relevant sources that lend insight or fresh perspective. Three books that have proven especially helpful are two edited collections—Jordan and Swartz, *Personality and the Cultural Construction of Society*, 1990; and Dougherty, *Directions in Cognitive Anthropology*, 1985—and the scholarly yet delightful "story of linguistic anthropology" as told by "John Doe," *Speak into the Mirror*, 1988.

My counter-strategy was a new one to me, and one I recommend, although in this case it did not pan out: after another revision (but no attempt to remedy my datedness), I sent the new draft off to a journal that I considered *more* rather than less prestigious. And I made no effort to mask its shortcomings, noting in a cover letter:

The article speaks to an old issue rather than a new one. One reviewer informed me that the paper knows nothing of semiotics or hermeneutics, which I took to be a compliment.

"Sincere regrets" once again, this time accompanied by a longer explanation and the usual encouragement, noting that reviewers "found much of interest but uniformly argue for substantial further development." Two well-honed critiques were enclosed; I quote a bit from each, drawing in particular on comments relevant to issues of culture and the individual.

> [First reviewer] I think the author must make much clearer *why* pro-priospect is needed to better understand the relationship between culture and the individual and *how* the concept meets that need. . . . A related problem is that almost no attempt is made to define "culture" in a collective sense. Given that the paper is purportedly about the relationship between the individual *and* culture, I don't think the author can leave culture so under-theorized.

> [Second reviewer] Does the author mean to use "culture" in something like a Geertzian way—an abstract pattern of symbols and meanings—or in a more Goodenoughian way—culture pool, i.e., the concrete total of what everyone knows? At one point he suggests the latter; elsewhere he seems more inclined toward the former. More generally, it would be good to refer to something of the intellectual background of this debate, one in which it is generally felt that Goodenough lost and Geertz won. To propose a revival of a Good-enoughian approach is potentially very important, and the significance of this for anthropological theory should be stressed.

Both reviewers called attention to authors with whom they are familiar and I am not, and one chastised me for "the lack of attention to other recent work on the relationship between culture and the individual in anthropology, including educational anthropology, such as interpretive anthropologists' work with life histories, autobiographies, and personal narratives; cognitive anthropologists' applications of Vygotskian theory; and school ethnographers' reformulations of cultural reproduction theory. It seems to me that the author could benefit from consideration of these theoretical developments."

Well, no doubt he could. I can only add, "Thank goodness this isn't the author's tenure year, with his professional life depending on publication of this paper." A reviewer cited earlier had noted, "The preference for Goodenough seems mainly nostalgic," but one of these later reviewers criticizes me for reopening an issue seemingly resolved long ago in Geertz's favor.

During one of several helpful written exchanges we have had about the developing paper, should Goodenough have revealed his defeat at Geertz's hands? True, his emphasis on cultural rules is different from

Geertz's emphasis on hermeneutical forms of interpretation, but others (e.g., Basso 1979:105) noted long ago that these differences did not necessarily make their positions incompatible.

In correspondence, Goodenough has seemed preoccupied more with making sure I understand that propriospect encompasses all the things of which a person has knowledge, including not only versions of various cultures but also one or more idiolects as well, thus, as he notes, making idiolect "a part of propriospect and not something analogous to it" (Ward Goodenough, personal communication, 18 April, 1989).

Goodenough also has expressed interest in the issue of cultural competence, and whether competence can be lost as well as gained. He writes,

> What kinds of things, once learned, stick, and what kinds of things have to be kept in constant use in order not to get lost? Information gets forgotten, some, but not all. Some skills go for lack of use, but not all. Can you still take a square root? What are the things you learned in school that have stayed with you, and what are the kinds of things that have not? As you see, your paper has set me to thinking about these things again, for which I am grateful (Ward Goodenough, personal communication, 19 June 1990).

Taking a cue from my critics, I, too, could go on and on, but I think I have shared enough to accomplish my purpose—to take you behind the scenes of a working paper and an author who has sometimes sensed an uphill struggle. Clifford Geertz has commented that our academic lives can be viewed as "vexing each other with profit," but I wonder if sometimes we go on vexing simply out of habit. To the extent that my critics seem to pull in different directions, I feel relatively free to go my own way. I get a better sense of direction at those points where critics' reactions seem to overlap, except that the overlap leads invariably back to the complexities of studying culture and the individual, to the press for empirical illustration, and to resistance to the term "propriospect" itself.

There is one other dimension to the critiques that I want to emphasize before closing. It deals with my depiction of cultural transmission as the *earlier era* in anthropology and education, and culture acquisition as the *current* one (see also Wolcott 1990 in this regard). It is hardly surprising that my mentor and colleague George Spindler has taken umbrage at that aspect of the paper. His name—along with others like Fred Gearing—is closely associated with cultural transmission, and he is no more going to allow me to prepare its obituary than he or Charles

Harrington was going to let me prepare an obituary for psychological anthropology.

Spindler has probably read more drafts of the developing paper than anyone—and been more annoyed by it, in spite of the encouragement with which he has always greeted my every scholarly effort. (The paper "keeps getting better," he reassured me after draft number three.) An unintended lambasting of culture-and-personality studies, and my originally curt dismissal of concepts like modal personality and basic personality structure, have softened in later versions of the paper, but while some critics were nudging me into the current decade, Spindler suggested point blank that maybe it was time for me to read his 1955 monograph on Menomini acculturation.

Spindler's reflections on the development of anthropology and education have proven instructive, and it is those comments that I want to report here in conclusion, for Spindler has been rethinking cultural transmission in a new and provocative manner. I am *almost* tempted to take some credit for helping him realize it was time to do so. Here is how he summarized his reaction:

> The only thing I *object* to is the Cultural Transmission Era, juxtaposed with the Cultural Acquisition Era. What you say by this is that the former era is over and the latter is now the thing. That is probably what you mean, but I think it is wrong. Cultural transmission—as calculated intervention in learning, to serve the interests of society—will continue to be the major rationale for studying schools and other formal or explicit interventions. Setting up a dichotomy in this fashion is unnecessary. Surely cultural acquisition has been underplayed and needs to be emphasized, and you make a good argument for it. . . . The conceptualization of a focus on cultural transmission as *calculated intervention in the learning process* has just begun and is quite unfinished (George D. Spindler, personal communication, 31 May 1990).

In an earlier note, Spindler offered a fuller description of his reconceptualization of the educational processes as calculated intervention:

> What is important about transmission is that some part of the community organizes forces to *intervene* in the individual's learning. Education and cultural transmission become a *purposeful intervention* (or *interference*) in learning. (This is the definition I now use for education.) To contrast the two (learning and cultural transmission) seems almost irrelevant, since they are conceptually and practically quite unlike (George D. Spindler, personal communication, 24 March 1990).

What I have reviewed here is something of a project report, a working paper about a working paper. There is no logical stopping point unless, or until, I can report that my formal paper has been accepted for publication or abandoned forever. The current revision is once again out for review, informally to a couple of invited colleagues and formally to a journal that notified me by form letter not to expect a response in less than 4 to 6 months. (Alas, will propriospect's time ever come?) Since Spindler was the last reviewer to have the floor, I'll let him close the paper for me with prophetic words from his note of 31 May 1990:

> Good luck with publication. I'm afraid that starting with Wallace 30 years ago and discovering Goodenough 20 years ago is not going to turn on all the editors, postmodernist or not.

So far, he's absolutely right!

## Afterword [Spring 1991]

Some time after delivering the preceding remarks I received word that my paper had been accepted for publication in the *Anthropology and Education Quarterly* [22(3): 251-273]. Not only is that a "right" journal for it, I must admit that the editor had been urging me to send the article for review from the moment he first heard of my topic. However, I have also been reminded that, like other focused interest groups, those of us in anthropology and education talk mostly to each other rather than make an effort to reach other audiences. I made an attempt to reach out.

Both the costs (repeated rejections) and the benefits (thoughtful critiques) of going "outside" are evident in this telling. Needless to say, I did not burden the *AEQ* editorial office with the barrage of comments I have reported here, although the final version submitted for review incorporated or clarified many points raised by previous reviewers. That is not to suggest that I necessarily have resolved them as much as I have tried to address them in some forthright manner. I've always been a fan of heady candor.

# References

Basso, Keith H.

1979 Portraits of "The Whiteman": Linguistic Play and Cultural Symbols Among the Western Apache. New York: Cambridge University Press.

Doe, John

1988 Speak into the Mirror: A Story of Linguistic Anthropology. Lanham, MD: University Press of America.

Dougherty, Janet W. D., ed.

1985 Directions in Cognitive Anthropology. Urbana: University of Illinois Press.

Geertz, Clifford

1973 The Impact of the Concept of Culture on the Concept of Man. *In* The Interpretation of Cultures. New York: Basic Books.

Goodenough, Ward H.

1963 Cooperation in Change. New York: Russell Sage Foundation.

1971 Culture, Language, and Society. McCaleb Module in Anthropology. Reading, MA: Addison-Wesley.

1976 Multiculturalism as the Normal Human Experience. [Council on] Anthropology and Education Quarterly 7(4):4-7.

1981 Culture, Language, and Society. 2nd ed. Menlo Park, CA: Benjamin/Cummings.

Handwerker, W. Penn

1989 The Origins and Evolution of Culture. American Anthropologist 91(2):313-326.

Herskovits, Melville J.

1948 Man and His Works: The Science of Cultural Anthropology. New York: Alfred A. Knopf.

Jordan, David K., and Marc J. Swartz, eds.

1990 Personality and the Cultural Construction of Society. Papers in Honor of Melford E. Spiro. Tuscaloosa: University of Alabama Press.

Schwartz, Theodore

1978 Where Is the Culture? Personality as the Distributive Locus of Culture. *In* The Making of Psychological Anthropology. George D. Spindler, ed. Pp. 419-441. Berkeley: University of California Press.

Spindler, George, ed.

1955 Education and Anthropology. Stanford, CA: Stanford University Press.

Wallace, Anthony F. C.

1961a Culture and Personality. New York: Random House.

1961b Schools in Revolutionary and Conservative Societies. *In* Anthropology and Education: The Martin G. Brumbaugh Lectures. Frederick G. Gruber, ed. Pp. 25-54. Philadelphia: University of Pennsylvania Press. (Reprinted in Cultural Relevance and Educational Issues. Francis A. J. Ianni and Edward Storey, eds. Pp. 230-249. Boston: Little Brown, 1973.)

1970 Culture and Personality. 2nd ed. New York: Random House.

Watson, Lawrence, and Maria-Barbara Watson-Franke

1985 Interpreting Life Histories: An Anthropological Inquiry. New Brunswick, NJ: Rutgers University Press.

Wolcott, Harry F.

1990 Review of Culture Acquisition: A Holistic Approach to Human Learning, by M. A. Pitman, R. Eisikovits, and M. L. Dobbert. Educational Studies 21(3):367-371.

# 11

# On Seeking—and Rejecting—
# Validity in Qualitative Research

---

### PREFACE

---

This final illustrative chapter is also the final essay in the Brad trilogy. The Brad story emerges in the latter half of the chapter, where I present an argument as to why validity does not seem a useful criterion for guiding or assessing qualitative research.

In the opening paragraph, I announce that I was assigned the topic for this chapter. At the time, Elliot Eisner and Alan Peshkin, two distinguished qualitative researchers in the field of education, were organizing a conference to be held at Stanford University in June 1988. They identified a set of topics to be addressed including—in addition to validity—subjectivity and objectivity, generalizability, ethics, and the uses of qualitative inquiry. Each topic was to be addressed independently by two different authors, the two papers in each set to be critiqued by a third scholar who would receive them in advance. With minor revisions and the addition of some author responses, the papers were to eventuate in an edited volume. The book, published by Teachers College Press, appeared 2 years later.

My initial insistence that I seemed an unlikely choice to write about validity fell on deaf ears. On the other hand, being *assigned* to write on a topic by someone else, instead of having to generate it entirely on one's own—coupled with a guaranteed audience to hear it and an almost-guaranteed publication to follow—is somewhat akin to being a new laboratory student instructed to observe a fish in a pan: I knew what I was supposed to do and could get right at it. I delved into the recent history of validity in psychological and educational research and then, as the editors had requested, proceeded to describe what I do—or think I do—to achieve validity in my work. That constitutes the methodological review of the first part of the chapter, at once descriptive in style and analytical in structure. I then go on to discuss—and illustrate— why validity does not seem to be an appropriate concept for judging the results of qualitative inquiry.

The continuing "Brad story" serves as my vehicle for raising doubts about validity, although the story takes such an unexpected turn and raises so many new questions that readers have wondered whether validity itself gets lost. That was an author's choice, a risk I was willing to take. I had something to say; this seemed the time and opportunity to say it. Once again it was necessary to recount earlier events that are by now familiar to readers here; like each of the illustrative chapters, this one had to stand entirely on its own.

In this writing, as in all my writing, I found myself drawing upon my professional work and perspective for insight into my lived world, just as my lived world serves as a reality check for what I say and write as an academic researcher and author. To whatever extent I succeed in that resolution of personal and professional careers, I achieve that "heady candor" to which I aspire. But striving for it has its cost in the tensions between an ideal world and a lived one, coupled with the academic dread of self-contradiction. Nothing is more personally discouraging than to find myself writing something on one page that is just the opposite of something already written on another (except, of course, to have someone *else* point it out first) or that appears to trap me into taking a position I do not support. This "strain for consistency" weighs heavily in academic writing. I wish we could write with more abandon and live with (and be instructed by) our contradictions. In *Song of Myself*, Walt Whitman pointed a way: "I contradict myself? Very well, then, I contradict myself. (I am large—I contain multitudes)." In any case, the fear of contradiction probably stiffens far more of our interpretive writing than does the concern for validity.

Whether the editors could live with so personal an account from one of their contributors was quite up to them. That the connection between the assigned topic and the account as I originally wrote it appeared a bit tenuous surfaced quickly when I read a working draft of the paper to a graduate seminar. One of my doctoral students asked afterward, in a quote repeated in the body of the paper, "Had you been given one of the other conference topics, would this still be the paper you would have written?" I had to admit that it was. I remember thinking to myself, "Just be thankful they didn't assign me subjectivity or ethics!"

By its very location in the present volume—the final illustrative chapter in this part emphasizing interpretation, and the final illustrative selection in the book—I present this as the "most interpretive" example of my academic writing. Recall that my first selection was also a Brad story, the "Sneaky Kid" of Chapter 3. A comparison between that one and this provides something of a yardstick for assessing the contrast (and personal preferences as well) between a more descriptively oriented and a more interpretively oriented account, at least within the scope of one researcher's work. Both should evince a solid descriptive base, but this chapter goes further in an analytical dimension to examine the concept of validity and further still in an interpretive and deeply personal one to probe meanings.

Most recently I've been toying with the idea of taking the Brad story—now as a story about us both, as you will discover—in a new direction, putting it in the form of a short novel or play. Whether I can overcome the strictures of these many years of academic writing seems unlikely, though it is interesting to note how academic authors do make occasional forays into other literary genres, particularly poetry. As anthropologist Margery Wolf describes it, "Some of us will gradually drift off into writing fiction" (1992, p. 139). If I ever feel ready, I have a title rife with interpretive possibility and double entendre for relating the story from the moment of my first encounter with Brad through the events recounted below: "Finding My Place."

In terms of those events and the questions they raise, you may find yourself wondering what happened next, where Brad is now, even whether the trilogy seems destined someday to become a quartet. At the moment of this writing—make that at the moment when this volume actually goes to press, for I have already remarked on how long it usually takes to get edited collections published—there was nothing more to add. That will be apparent in the reading. The method review of the first part of the chapter, and the recounting of the initial Brad story, are largely descriptive. Once attention turns to Brad, the description is limited to reporting a few well-publicized events. The focus shifts to interpretation and my own effort to make sense of what we all are up to in the collective effort to make sense through qualitative inquiry.

As for Brad himself, for a brief period during late 1991, he started making telephone calls, long distance, collect. Then he stopped. We have not forgotten him. And in spite of his firm and repeated insistence to the contrary, we know for certain that he still thinks about us. Alas, sometimes even to know with certainty can prove a mixed blessing!

I trust that the fine irony is not lost here: In a professional lifetime devoted to teaching, research, and writing, I know little and understand even less about this case, the one that has affected me the most and that continues to haunt me for answers I doubt that I will ever find. Yet readers seem to forgive me for failing to understand more, noting instead their appreciation (if not always their admiration) for rendering a straightforward account and adding what insight I could. The experience has not lessened my faith in the power of the descriptive account, accompanied by a careful—and not too extended—explication of what one believes one has understood. Whether that entails an interpretation of the descriptive process or a description of the interpretive process seems, once again, to be a matter of emphasis.

## References

Wolcott, Harry F. (1990). On seeking—and rejecting—validity in qualitative research. In Elliot W. Eisner & Alan Peshkin (Eds.), *Qualitative inquiry in education: The continuing debate* (pp. 121-152). New York: Teachers College Press.

Wolf, Margery. (1992). *A thrice-told tale: Feminism, postmodernism, and ethnographic responsibility.* Stanford, CA: Stanford University Press.

# ON SEEKING—AND REJECTING—
# VALIDITY IN QUALITATIVE RESEARCH

The topic of this paper is validity in qualitative research in education. The topic was assigned. I would not have thought of myself as one to address this question, while certain other names came immediately to mind (e.g., Dobbert, 1982; Goetz & LeCompte, 1984). "Of all people, why me?" I asked. "I'll have to look up the term just to make sure I don't have it confused with reliability!"

No sooner had I voiced my concern, however, than it became part of the rationale for inviting me. "No, don't do that," Alan Peshkin quickly reassured. "We don't want a literature review. We are inviting you as someone who has done research and who deals with the issue *implicitly* in your work. How do you deal with validity if you are *not* self-conscious about it?"

Had he said "oblivious to it," I would have kept my guard up. But Alan is a gentle man, and, contrary to the old saying, flattery will get

you everywhere. Assured that I was the right person for the assignment and (tacitly, at least) that whatever validity is, I apparently "have"
or "get" or "satisfy" or "demonstrate" or "establish" it, I accepted the
challenge.

Like other ethnographers—and qualitative researchers in general—
there are strategies I follow to "strengthen the validity" (which, according
to word roots, is something of a redundancy) of my work. I offer them
here for consideration by anyone contemplating fieldwork, as well as
to subject them to review by others. As a result of these reflections, I
am no longer quite so un-self-conscious about validity. On the other
hand, I am even less concerned with it than previously.

I have responded to the assignment in the manner suggested by my
title, first by inventorying some procedures for achieving validity and
then by raising the central issue of whether validity serves us well as
a criterion measure or objective for qualitative research.

## Validity: Early Encounters

Although it is not recorded in the annals of science, I first confronted
the issue underlying validity by an act of independent discovery almost
half a century ago. For about two years after I was given a Swiftset
Printing Press one Christmas, the kids in our neighborhood published
a usually weekly "newspaper." (To help you locate this in time, the only
edition we ever printed early—but, alas, never delivered as the surprise Extra we planned—carried the headlines, "Willkie Wins! Roosevelt
Out, So Is Eleanor and the New Deal!") Our source of paper was a huge
roll that could be cut into long strips so the tiny rotary press would
actually "roll" at press time. When one of the "little kids" in the neighborhood received a gift of toy electric scissors, we decided to award
her the position of paper cutter on the newspaper staff. However, we
felt she should demonstrate her qualifications for the job. We designed
a convoluted test pattern and watched with approval as she swiftly
and adroitly cut along our meandering line.

Our measurement error was classic. She cut the paper for the printing press the same way she cut the test pattern, with jagged and curvy
margins of such uneven widths that about half the time the paper
jammed between the edges of the press and the rest of the time was in
strips too narrow to reach both drive wheels. In our penchant for
rigorous testing, we had overlooked the only critical skill involved:
precision in cutting along an extended straight line.

More than a cautionary tale about the excesses of testing (as well as an interesting reflection on how as children we had acquired a sense of the cultural ethos surrounding it), my story also serves two other purposes. First, it points to the essence of validity, which asks whether one is measuring whatever it is that is supposed to be measured. Obviously, we were not.

Second, it points to the arena in which the concept has acquired its formidable status: tests and measurement. It is my distinct recollection that in the 1950s (and actually much earlier) the terms *validity* and *reliability* were associated almost exclusively with testing. Validity has not been totally ignored as an issue in field research, however. Through the years there have been discussions on questions of validity in its general sense of obtaining accurate data (e.g., Becker, 1958), on assessing the validity of data already collected (e.g., Vidich & Bensman, 1954), on drawing valid meaning from data (e.g., Miles & Huberman, 1984), and on validating theoretical ideas (e.g., McEwen, 1963).

Virtually everyone who has ever addressed the issue, quantitatively and qualitatively oriented researcher alike, seems to have written on its behalf. Every source I consulted takes a position contrary to my validity-rejecting one, whether claiming that everybody is doing it ("Most anthropologists rank informants for validity and reliability, at least in their own minds," Dobbert, 1982, p. 263); we already have it (our "major strength," Goetz & LeCompte, 1984, p. 221); we desperately need it (external validity identified as the single greatest weakness in case studies, Campbell, 1975); we are nowhere without it ("In order to be believed . . . it is absolutely necessary to have the property of being true or false," Phillips, 1987, p. 10); or that all roads lead to it—if you can follow the directions:

> What I join him [Habermas] in rejecting is the currently fashionable hermeneutic nihilism, in which validity of interpretation is rejected as a goal. Like the nihilists, I applaud the achievement of radical interpretations, but only because I see these as the inevitably wasteful route to a potential future consensus on a more valid interpretation. (Campbell, 1986, p. 109)

My effort to catalogue various "types" of validity and clarify the relationships among them—on the assumption that to be forgiven the assignment of a literature review did not give me license to ignore the literature itself—has revealed a proliferation of qualifying adjectives that may enhance validity for those who set store by it but often confuses those who do not. Validity is variously presented as a twosome:

external and internal; as a threesome: instrumental (pragmatic, crite-rion; also predictive, concurrent) theoretical (construct), and apparent (face); and as a foursome: content (face, apparent; also sampling), predic-tive, concurrent, and construct (or theoretical). If I have correctly situated these major terms, there are still others not easily placed—conclusion validity, ontological validity, overall validity, and practical validity. One also finds references to consensual validation (Phillips, 1987, p. 19), cross-validation, final validation, self-validation (Geertz, 1973, p. 24), validity coefficient, and even "validity-seeking hermeneutics," as Campbell (1986, p. 109) characterizes the position of Habermas.

Two recent sources that attempt conceptual clarification about va-lidity and thus help differentiate among critical nuances are Brinberg and McGrath (1982) and Weber (1985). Educational psychologist Lee Cronbach's 1971 article "Test Validation" stands as a definitive state-ment. His opening sentence provides an intentionally narrow defini-tion of validation: "The process of examining the accuracy of a specific prediction or inference made from a test score" (p. 443). A footnote addendum on the same page suggests that Cronbach might have preferred to see validity applied in a broader context, although his own efforts produced the opposite result. Limiting his discussion to tests, Cronbach nonetheless noted that validation refers to the "soundness of *all* the interpretations of a test—descriptive and explanatory inter-pretations as well as situation-bound predictions":

> For simplicity, I refer to tests and test scores throughout the chapter. The statements, however, apply to all procedures for collecting data, including observations, questionnaires, ratings of artistic products, etc. Most state-ments apply to protocols and qualitative summaries as well as to numerical scores. For some writers, *to validate* means to demonstrate the worth of, but I intend to stress the openness of the process—i.e., *to validate is to investigate*. (p. 443n; emphasis in original)

Perhaps it is ironic that the "enshrinement" of construct validation—as Cronbach himself describes it (1986, p. 86)—occurred with publica-tion of his own co-authored article "Construct Validity in Psychologi-cal Tests" (Cronbach & Meehl, 1955). At the time, as Sandy Charters has observed (personal communication, April 21, 1988), validity became "irretrievably ensconced in the positivistic tradition and the hypothetico-deductive mode of explanation." If the word *test* did not appear at every mention of validity, it was nonetheless implied. Consider, for example, this explanation from Roger Brown's *Social Psychology* (1965), an authoritative source in its day:

> The problem of validity is the problem of what the data *indicate*. Have we measured what we have undertaken to measure? In one very limited sphere the notion of test validity has a precise meaning. If a psychologist has devised a test for the purpose of selecting men who will be able to do well on some job or task then the validity of the test is the correlation between test scores and the quality of job performance. The job is the *criterion* for the test and the test's validity is measured against its criterion. (p. 438; emphasis in original)

Somewhere between then and now—and I refer specifically to three decades when I thought I had been paying attention to such things—the word *test* seems to have been eased out. In an age of growing self-consciousness and sophistication about scientific measurement, the evolution of validity as a desirable but ambiguously defined criterion for *all* research may have been something like this:

Test validity
Validity of test data
Validity of test and measurement data
Validity of research data on tests and measurements
Validity of research data
Validity of research

Today one finds enthusiastic endorsements for validity easily at hand. This one is from anthropologists Pertti and Gretel Pelto (1978):

> "Validity" refers to the degree to which scientific observations actually measure or record what they purport to measure. . . . In their field research anthropologists have invested much effort to achieve validity, for we generally assume that a long-term stay in a community facilitates the differentiation of what is valid from what is not, and the assembling of contextual supporting information to buttress claims to validity. (p. 33)

An adaptation of this definition for educational research appears in Goetz and LeCompte (1984):

> Validity is concerned with the accuracy of scientific findings. Establishing validity requires (1) determining the extent to which conclusions effectively represent empirical reality and (2) assessing whether constructs devised by

researchers represent or measure the categories of human experience that occur. (p. 210)

Who would have dreamed that educational researchers in any number might someday pay heed to so-called qualitative approaches or comprise a ready audience for books with titles such as *Doing the Ethnography of Schooling* (Spindler, 1982) or *Ethnography and Qualitative Design in Educational Research* (Goetz & LeCompte, 1984)? Even twenty-five years ago, who would have believed that quantities-oriented educational researchers would make room for and eventually begin a dialogue with qualities-oriented ones? We should hardly be surprised or offended by the assumption that the vocabulary of *their* perceived world would constitute the language of the dialogue. Questions they addressed to us were the ones they pondered among themselves. For example, "How do you deal with the issue of validity?"

And instead of replying, "That's your problem," we too hastily replied, "We've got it." From whatever moment concern for formal validity was first expressed, qualitative researchers in education appear to have been defending and, for the most part, successfully demonstrating claims about validity. Perhaps we wanted to divert attention from uneasy anticipation about a parallel question concerning reliability, the extent to which studies can be replicated, which, as Goetz and LeCompte (1984) note, poses a "herculean problem for researchers concerned with naturalistic behavior or unique phenomena" (p. 211). Given the choice, we've steered the conversation toward validity: "Reliability poses serious threats to the credibility of much ethnographic work. However, validity may be its major strength" (p. 221).

The reason I tend to confuse the two terms is that for me their esoteric meanings among researchers are the very opposite of their everyday ones. The synonyms and "related words" given for *validity* in my thesaurus include *cogency* (appealing, convincing), *efficacy* (power to produce an effect), *force, punch, persuasiveness,* and *potency.* For me, these terms conjure up a "might makes right" approach. Among the qualities I seek in research, I would rather my work be regarded as *provocative* than as *persuasive.* On the other hand, I feel honored when someone describes me (as observer) or one of my accounts as *reliable.*

I suspect that claims about validity reveal a similar kind of confusion—the consequence of taking a term overspecified in one domain and reassigning it a more satisfying, intuitive, and global definition in another. Validity has a technical set of microdefinitions relating to correspondence (Brinberg & McGrath, 1982). It can point to critically focused macrodefinitions as well, relating at one extreme to truth value and, at the other, to external validity as implied in such terms as *dependability, generalizability,* or "robustness" (p. 12). But my sense is that except for those hypothetico-deductive types mentioned earlier, validity serves most often as a gloss for *scientific accuracy* among those who identify closely with science and for *correctness* or *credibility* among those who do not.

What is it about ethnographic and other qualitative approaches to research that leads us to boast that validity may well be our "major strength"? Let me address that issue before turning to the broader one: whether validity is well suited as a criterion, guideline, or objective for qualitative approaches to research.


## Seeking Validity, or on Not Getting It All Wrong

I have quoted the following words from Clifford Geertz's (1973) essay "Thick Description" so often that I am coming to think of them as my own:

> Cultural analysis is intrinsically incomplete. And, worse than that, the more deeply it goes the less complete it is. It is strange science whose most telling assertions are its most tremulously based, in which to get somewhere with the matter at hand is to intensify the suspicion, both your own and that of others, that you are not quite getting it right. (p. 29)

I assume that by "cultural analysis" Geertz refers both to what one is attempting to describe and how one interprets it. Thus we can say of field studies in general that "to get somewhere with the matter at hand is to intensify the suspicion . . . that you are not quite getting it right."

But I also go to considerable pains not to get it all wrong. At least in its broad sense of scientific accuracy or correctness, validity haunts qualitative researchers as a specter, even if it may not be precisely the quality we seek. Others have offered arguments to show why validity can be claimed, either in their work or on behalf of qualitative researchers in general (e.g., Goetz & LeCompte, 1984, p. 221), and I take this opportunity to do the same.

In nine points that I follow, I have described what I do, try to do, or think I do to satisfy the implicit challenge of validity. I hasten to add that I probably do some of these things to keep the question from being raised at all, since it can be one of those accusations not lightly dismissed even if subsequently refuted. There is no particular order to the points as presented, although I more or less follow a progression from early stages of fieldwork, devoted primarily to getting information, through later stages given more fully to analysis and writing.

### Talk Little, Listen a Lot

Like any fieldworker, I have some personal qualities that I believe serve me well in research. A seemingly unlikely one (about which others may disagree) is that I regard myself as neither particularly talkative nor particularly gregarious. I am basically a loner in thought and work; I do not like to be lonely, but I enjoy and need solitude when pursuing my academic tasks. It requires great patience under any circumstances for me to "sit and visit." A rather inevitable consequence of being inquisitive without being a talker is that my conversational queries usually prompt others to do the talking. During fieldwork, I make a conscious effort to be sociable, thus providing opportunities for people to talk to me. My work ethic takes over to help me become not only more social but more attentive and responsive, and out pour the informants' stories and explanations so essential to good fieldwork.

(Parenthetically, I note my suspicion that many fieldworkers talk too much and hear too little. They become their own worst enemy by becoming their own best informant. This is especially serious in school research, where we often presume to "know" what is supposed to be happening and consequently may never ask the kinds of questions we would ordinarily ask in any other research setting. I have suggested elsewhere (Wolcott, 1984) that educational researchers need to be wary of this "ethnography minus one" approach.)

Since no one ever can say everything about anything, in virtually any conversation, and especially during fieldwork, I find myself pondering what part of the whole story is being told and what part of that I am actually understanding. Like most of us, I *think* I sense when I am getting a straight story, when I am getting a story straight, and when I am on a detour of my own or another's making. If the latter, I usually try to swing by that way another time. I never confront informants with contradictions, blatant disbelief, or shock, but I do not mind presenting myself as a bit dense, someone who does not catch on too quickly and has to have things repeated or explained—what Kirk and Miller (1986) describe as "willing to look a fool for the sake of science" (p. 49).

## Record Accurately ⌒

Whenever I engage in fieldwork I try to record as accurately as possible, and in precisely their words, what I judge to be important of what people do and say. I note that this occurs during formal fieldwork because, unlike some ethnographers, I am not a regular diary keeper. Rather, like most of them, I detest notetaking, in part because I tend to be so meticulous about it. I record field notes only when my work ethic demands. When I do take notes, I endeavor to make them as soon as possible after an event, if not at that moment. I prefer to make notes *during* observations or interviews—including written notes to supplement mechanically recorded ones. (It is not a bad idea to remind people of one's research presence and purposes.) By recording as soon as possible, to capture words and events as observed, I try to minimize the potential influence of some line of interpretation or analysis that might have me remembering and recording too selectively or reinterpreting behavior prior to recording it.

## Begin Writing Early ⌐

Since I do not work quickly anyway, I make something of a fetish of taking my time at fieldwork. In seeming contrast, however—because I have come to regard writing as an integral part of fieldwork rather than as a separate stage initiated after fieldwork is completed—I often begin preparing a rough draft soon after fieldwork begins. Most recently I have suggested that qualitative researchers consider writing a preliminary draft of a descriptively oriented study before even venturing into the field (Wolcott, 1990). The intent is twofold: to make a record of what one already knows or suspects and to identify obvious gaps where more information will be needed.

In every study in which I have begun writing early, I have been able to share a draft (but not that first one, by any means) with others knowledgeable about the setting. Thus I obtain valuable feedback for myself and sometimes provide welcome feedback for others who may have expressed curiosity or concern about what I was observing and what kind of story I would tell.

To borrow a phrase from linguistics, my accounts move forward by "successive approximations." It would be nice if that meant they became successively more accurate; I suspect they only become successively better contextualized (i.e., more complex). But I try to "stick around" long enough, and keep in touch long afterward, so that events observed can be reviewed from the perspective of time—for observer and observed alike. Twenty-seven years after beginning fieldwork, I am still in contact with Kwakiutl families I met in 1962 (Wolcott, 1989). Twenty years after initiating a study of the principalship in 1966, I sat down with "Ed Bell" to record his reflections on that study and his now completed career as an educational administrator. And in neither of those studies—nor in any of my others—does it seem that I have ever quite gotten it right.

In spite of extending one's fieldwork and one's subsequent reflections over time, I begin making detailed notes immediately upon initiating fieldwork, as I pointed out before. Right or wrong as first impressions may be, I feel they should be carefully recorded as a baseline from which the work proceeds. First impressions also serve as a useful resource in subsequent writing. Through them, researchers can introduce readers to settings the way they themselves first encountered them, rather than in the presumably more discerning way they have come to see them through extended time for observation and reflection.

## Let Readers "See" for Themselves

I make a conscious effort to include primary data in my final accounts, not only to give readers an idea of what my data are like but to give access to the data themselves. In striking the delicate balance between providing too much detail and too little, I would rather err on the side of too much; conversely, between overanalyzing and underanalyzing data, I would rather say too little. Accordingly, my accounts are often lengthy; informants are given a forum for presenting their own case to whatever extent possible and reasonable. This poses a dilemma: In reading the descriptive accounts of others, I confess that I often skip over the quoted material in my haste to "get right at it" and see what the researcher made of it all; yet I knowingly risk boring my readers with potentially tedious detail.

More subtly, my growing bias toward letting informants speak for themselves is exactly that—a bias in favor of trying to capture the expressed thoughts of others rather than relying too singularly on what I have observed and interpreted. The extent to which participant observation and interviewing are a natural complement or get at quite different aspects of thought and action has always vexed experienced fieldworkers (see, for example, Bernard, Killworth, Kronenfeld, & Sailer, 1984; Dean & Whyte, 1958; Freeman & Romney, 1988). Terms like *triangulation* and *multi-instrument approach* may strike neophytes as ample safeguard against error in qualitative research, but anyone who has done fieldwork knows that if you address a question of any consequence to more than one informant, you may as well prepare for more than one answer. I try to report what I observe and to offer an informed interpretation of those observations, my own or someone else's. Only the most central of issues in one's research warrant the thorough probing implied by triangulation. We are better off reminding readers that our data sources are limited, and that our informants have not necessarily gotten things right either, than implying that we would never dream of reporting an unchecked fact or underverified claim.

## Report Fully 5

I am not disconcerted by data that do not fit the developing account or my interpretation of it. That does not mean I report every discrepant detail, but I do keep such bits and pieces in front of me (often quite literally on 5" × 8" cards) as a way of testing my efforts at making sense of things. Sometimes a comment or observation can be introduced via brackets or footnote to flag an issue that is not as well resolved as the prose implies, or not developed more fully, because my data are "thin" or certain events never occurred during the period of fieldwork.

When I can do so without seeming too obtuse, I also include comments and observations that I do not understand or for which I feel I have no better basis for discerning meanings than might the reader. To illustrate: A Kwakiutl parent commented during a discussion about the kind of teacher best suited to a village assignment, "I think what we need here is a teacher who isn't *too* smart" (Wolcott, 1967, p. 85). I did not know exactly what he meant, and I still do not (although I have a hunch). I included it without comment—and today it continues to provoke *possible* interpretations every bit as plausible as my own.

## Be Candid 6

I opt for subjectivity as a strength of qualitative approaches rather than attempt to establish a detached objectivity that I am not sure I want or need. As I am doing here, I have always put myself squarely into the settings or situations being described to whatever extent seemed warranted for the purpose at hand. With some fear and trepidation, I introduced that strategy in my doctoral dissertation, and committee members raised no concern except for the question of excess. I decided that if I could get away with it there, I certainly could be as forthright in the future when writing to satisfy myself.

To the extent that my feelings and personal reactions seem relevant to a case, I try to reveal them: The greater their possible influence, the more attention they receive and the earlier they appear in the account. In writing *Teachers Versus Technocrats* (1977), I was distressed both by the nature of a project designed to impose greater accountability on public education and by the heavy-handed manner by which it was being implemented. As a result, I began the monograph with a chapter titled "Caution—Bias at Work" to bare my feelings and objections.

How far to go with personal revelation? I see no easy resolution. The issue has become of more immediate concern than I could have imagined, as will become apparent in the course of this essay. Qualitative research has brought researchers self-consciously back into the research setting. That has been healthy for all, including those quantitative types who wanted everyone to believe that they were not part of their own investigations. Yet when someone remarks, often charitably, "I learned as much about you in your study as I did about the people you were studying," I feel dismay at the likelihood of having taken more light than I have shed.

I try to draw a distinction between revealing my feelings and imposing my judgments, however. If circumstances call for me to draw implications or suggest possible remedies, I try to "change hats" conspicuously. There is simply no way one can get from a descriptive account of what is to a prescriptive account of what should be done about it. Those are value judgments. Granted, such judgments are critical to the work of practicing educators. It is appropriate for them to seek whatever help they can, and for us to be prepared to offer help, but we need to clearly mark the boundaries where research stops and reform begins. A different set of principles must be employed to validate our personal or professional authority to offer pronouncements about what needs improving and how to go about it.

The big value judgments are easy to spot because words like *should* and *ought* abound in sentences containing them. There are opportunities for eliminating little judgments as well, simply by careful use of the editing pencil. Little words of judgment creep into all kinds of sentences but can be rounded up and marched right off the page again. Consider the difference between reporting, "Only one villager had ever graduated from high school" versus "One villager had graduated from high school," or "Few pupils were at task" versus "Five pupils appeared to be engaged in the assignment."

## Seek Feedback  7

I share my developing manuscripts with informed readers as part of the process of analyzing and writing. Rather than a mass distribution of a manuscript in next-to-last draft, what I have in mind is a continuous process of asking one or more individuals to read the current version. Academic colleagues are usually good for one careful reading at most; there is little point in pressing busy people for more, but no excuse for not asking at all.

Accuracy of reported information is one critical dimension, and  readers close to the setting provide yeoman service by checking for correctness and completeness. Further, their reactions sometimes help me recognize where the reporting or the interpretation (or both) seems overblown or underdeveloped. Readers not so closely involved can also be helpful in assessing the suitability of my analytical concepts, my sensitivity to the people involved, or the adequacy and appropriateness of interpretations made and lessons drawn. Readers who disavow their expertise or their familiarity with protocol in qualitative research may offer valuable suggestions about style and sequence, may question inadequate explanations or definitions, or may express straightforward but intuitive reactions conveyed in such statements as, "I just don't see what you are getting at here." I also like to circulate working drafts among my graduate students. In terms of providing feedback, they are not necessarily one's severest critics, but even when they are not, they keep me mindful of my audience. In addition, it is valuable for them to have a glimpse of manuscripts in process rather than to have access only to polished final accounts.

Am I straying from validity? I believe not. I am describing a constellation of activities intended not only to help *me* get things right (or keep me from getting them all wrong) but to convey ideas in such a way that the *reader*, who is also not quite getting it right, is not getting it all wrong, either. I am willing to admit that some of this activity is image building, intended to create the *impression* that my accounts are credible. To the extent that is true, I can only add that having gone to great lengths to make such an impression, there is no particular reason not to work to live up to it.

## Try to Achieve Balance

At some particular point or points in the writing/revision process, I take time either to return to the field setting or, second best, to read entirely through my field notes one more time (why do I find that so onerous a chore?). Then I reread my current draft to assess the extent to which the account I have created squares with the setting and individuals on which it is based. Objectivity is not my criterion as much as what might be termed *rigorous subjectivity* (or "disciplined subjectivity," following Erickson, 1973, p. 15). It is I who must be satisfied now, with elusive criteria like balance, fairness, completeness, sensitivity.

Ed Bell raised the question of balance in reacting to my study of him in his role as principal (Wolcott, 1973), but the issue exists in every study I have conducted. He found my reporting sufficiently accurate but nonetheless expressed dismay that the recounting of his problems (e.g., teacher evaluation, parent complaints, disagreements with the central office about his "leadership style") received a disproportionate amount of attention. Ed literally worked day and night to smooth out problems and to create a positive, constructive atmosphere. I meticulously uncovered and examined every little malfunction to show what a principal must contend with.

Had I conveyed the minute-by-minute routine of Taft School during those 2 years, I think I would have fallen asleep writing about it long before anyone could have fallen asleep reading about it. Somehow I had to communicate the customary "hum" of a smoothly functioning elementary school while also assuring readers that the account would probe beneath the surface. Now, years later, Ed insists that my study helped him because it enabled him to see things that "needed improving." Even he has forgotten what he once expressed as "real disappointment" at the perceived lack of balance in my account.

## Write Accurately

As a parallel activity to the field check just described, at one or more points during the rewriting process I read through a manuscript with an eye for what might be called technical accuracy. This stage usually comes rather late, prompted by feelings that the content and interpretation are pretty well in place but that I still need to make an almost word-by-word assessment of the manuscript. One such check is for coherence or internal consistency. Much as coherence may appear to be a concession to the strictures of validity, I think of it more as an element of style. I accept as a compliment that something I have written appears to have "internal validity," but frankly I regard consistency (which I think is implied) as much an author's trick as it is revealing of research acumen. That our studies are so free of inner contradiction ought really to set us wondering how they can be describing human behavior. As long as we employ consistency as a criterion, however, we will continue to find it in full measure.

There is another kind of internal review that seems more critical. I have no better term for it than a "word check." I mean a literal sentence-by-sentence examination to check that the verbs are appropriate, the generalizations have real referents in what I have seen or heard, and the points of conjecture are marked with appropriate tentativeness. Admittedly, some part of this task is also a kind of window-dressing. At a minimum I strive to make every sentence technically correct. I confess to having written sentences that virtually defy editing because they cannot be changed and still retain their truth element. (I give my own special meaning to "technical writing"—sentences that are correct as written but actually reveal how little, rather than how much, I know.) Still, in attempting to satisfy canons of technical accuracy, I try as well to be forthright (or sometimes just more modest, if that is what the circumstances warrant). The fact that a sentence needs fine honing serves notice that maybe it should not remain in the manuscript.

If such intentional wordsmithing seems unbecoming in scholarly work, it seems better dealt with head-on than by wishing it away from so human an undertaking as the human reporting of human social life. Qualitatively oriented studies of what goes on in laboratory life, the bastion of true science, do more than hint that comparable efforts at the social construction of facts are not unknown among so-called hard scientists as well (see, for example, Gould, 1981; LaTour & Woolgar, 1986).

Wordsmithing also has its complementary and lighter side in sometimes allowing researchers to convey more, rather than less, information or to keep confidences. Let me illustrate with two sentences from *A Kwakiutl Village and School* (1967) describing tensions that arose over thefts of teachers' personal property in outlying villages:

> During the year, five teachers in local day schools suffered losses by theft either of personal property taken from the teacherages or of skiffs and kickers (small outboard motors). Two thefts were privately resolved between teachers and villagers, two were reported to the RCMP, and no action was taken on the fifth. (p. 87)

Over the Christmas holiday, someone literally had "taken the fifth," a bottle of liquor hidden among the belongings of an older female teacher concerned as to whether she was breaking the law by bringing liquor onto the reserve in the first place. She dared not report the loss. She also felt some personal awkwardness, recognizing that the theft implicated a particular villager. Those of us who knew about her missing liquor had our chuckle and felt vindicated because all the thefts—with their demoralizing impact on everyone involved—had been reported accurately without exacerbating hard feelings.

Having reviewed some of the procedures I follow that provide the basis on which I would claim validity—were I pressed to claim it—I have come to the end of this part of my paper. These activities are my "answer" to validity, but reviewing them has only confirmed my feelings that the more important issue before us is to examine whether validity is the right question.

## When It Really Matters, Does Validity Really Matter?

The points developed in the preceding discussion of validity-enhancing procedures were extracted from my own experience and my complete studies. Four monographs constitute the major evidence I can present on behalf of validity or any other criterion on which qualitative research may be judged: *A Kwakiutl Village and School* (1967), *The Man in the Principal's Office: An Ethnography* (1973), *The African Beer Gardens of Bulawayo: Integrated Drinking in a Segregated Society* (1974), and *Teachers Versus Technocrats: An Educational Innovation in Anthropological Perspective* (1977). Two modest field-based studies have been reported in shorter articles, one describing efforts at community development (1983b), another dealing with the introduction of a program for instructional television (1984).

Although I would be loathe to dissect the studies of others in a critical essay on validity, neither would I ordinarily have put my own works forward on its behalf. As already noted, validity neither guides nor informs my work. What I seek is not unrelated to validity, but "validity" does not capture its essence and is not the right term. I am hard pressed to identify the expression that is.

To support my position, let me turn from cases concluded and published to some personal experience coupled with ongoing research that currently occupies some of my time and much of my thought—a study begun but not completed. In this current preoccupation, I am not the least preoccupied with validity. By describing these circumstances, I hope to raise valid questions about validity for you as reader. Be forewarned: The account may also raise some question for you about me.

The case has its origins in three rather independent events. (There are similar "event chains" in all our work.) One was an effort I made at "fine-tuning" my professional career. Coinciding with my fiftieth birthday, I made a self-conscious decision to focus my teaching and research more on how culture is acquired—a social process in which humans engage individually—and less on schools and what is done in their efforts to transmit it. Originally I referred to this as "the anthropology of learning" (Wolcott, 1982a), although "culture acquisition," the phrase I use today, points more accurately to my particular interest. I raised the idea of an "anthropology of learning" in conversation with colleagues and asked what they felt it should embrace and how we might approach it. Frederick Erickson's personal counsel was direct and to the point, "First of all, get yourself a learner." I was on the lookout for a learner.

The second event was an invitation from the director of a federally funded project at the U.S. Department of Education to prepare an essay on educational adequacy. The intent of the project, as I understood it, was to explore ways of assessing whether each state was providing "adequate" education and to suggest how state efforts might be subsidized with federal funds, were they to become available. It sounded like a task for economists, and apparently a number of them had been commissioned to write papers. The project now sought broader perspectives, I was told, "such as you might provide as a sociologist." Wrong discipline, I realized, but the project officer seemed undaunted when I asked whether I could prepare an anthropologically oriented case study of one individual rather than take on so ambitious a topic as an equitable way to allocate federal dollars. I was assured that I was free to approach the topic as I wished, provided that I addressed the issue of educational adequacy. I sensed an opportunity to dramatize the useful but often overlooked distinction between schooling and education by presenting a case contrasting adequate schools and inadequate education.

The third element of this story had its beginning about a year earlier, in the kind of circumstance ethnographers often refer to as serendipity, although in retrospect I am not sure that is the right term. In a remote part of the hilly and densely wooded twenty-acre tract on which I live, a young man, then aged nineteen, had been constructing a crude but sturdy cabin and was also attempting to construct an independent survival-style life of his own. He had freed himself from most of the trappings of the workaday world, eking out a living on food stamps, reducing cash expenses to the minimum, scrounging what he could, and taking whatever else he felt he needed. Although he had roamed this countryside as a youth, he did not know on whose property he had built his cabin, perhaps hoping he had chosen public land adjacent to mine. His first question when I discovered him and his cabin after several weeks was, "Can I stay?" Belligerence seemed just beneath the  surface, but I could not see how I could claim to be any kind of humanitarian and throw him off the property. I allowed him to remain.

I seldom saw him in the next few months, although I did stop by from time to time to see how he was getting on and occasionally hired him to work for me. The following winter he asked if I would let him dig a 700-foot trench for a new water line to the house rather than contract the work out as I had planned. Together we installed the line, a major undertaking. In the course of a year of casual contact, then working together on an ambitious project, he became more talkative and revealing about himself. We found ourselves becoming more intimately involved, psychologically at first, and, in time, physically. After that there seemed no topic that we could not discuss, no aspects of his (or my) life about which we did not talk freely.

 On the basis of the long-term and now candid nature of our relationship, I began thinking about doing a life history with him, recognizing that he seemed willing, even eager, to discuss his "experiences," his outlook, and his deliberate effort to put his life together. He presented an unusual opportunity to learn about a life dramatically different from my own or those of the people I ordinarily meet as a university professor. About this time I received the invitation from Washington, D.C., giving me both impetus and focus to proceed more systematically on a project that until then was only a gradual realization that I had found my "learner"—literally in my own backyard.

He agreed to the study, estimating that it would take him about six hours to narrate his life story into a tape recorder. To start, we planned to record in sessions of up to an hour. On the day we began, he spoke quickly and uninterruptedly for about twelve minutes, concluding with "So here I am up at the cabin." Then he announced, "That's it!" His account was finished.

From that moment, getting his life story in more detail and putting it together into a cohesive narrative was up to me. He was paid for his interview time, the dollars providing adequate motivation once initial enthusiasm waned. He also was paid to review the manuscript, and at his request I deleted minor portions that sounded "dumb" to him. "If only to please me," I noted in a subsequent footnote, "he even commented that he hoped his story might 'help people understand.' "

I felt that his story did reveal a different lifestyle, presented in an integrated fashion, in contrast to the bits and pieces of most newspaper articles or educator and sociological accounts of dropouts, drifters, or the young alienated-and-unemployed. I received encouragement to make the case more widely available. I retained the title but changed the subtitle of the original report (Wolcott, 1982b) when it appeared in slightly revised and elaborated form in the *Anthropology and Education Quarterly* as "Adequate Schools and Inadequate Education: The Life History of a Sneaky Kid" (Wolcott, 1983a). "Sneaky Kid" was a reference he once made to himself; I assigned him the pseudonym Brad.

By that pseudonym, Brad is on his way to becoming fairly well known in educator circles, particularly among qualitative researchers. In spite of the intrigue and events subsequent to publication of "Sneaky Kid," methodologically I think the piece offers a good model for life history in educational research, and I unabashedly point to it as such. Subsequently, when I was asked to identify an illustrative example to accompany my chapter, "Ethnographic Research in Education" (Wolcott, 1988), for an edited volume describing several "alternative" approaches to research in education, the Sneaky Kid article was my choice, for several reasons. It is journal length. It is told largely in the (edited) words of a key informant. It is well focused. And it attempts to offer some insight at the same time that it raises a host of provocative questions.

(Needless to say, eyebrows have been raised about becoming intimately involved with an informant, even for those who recognize the ways humans become involved with each other—physically and emotionally—far exceed the prescriptions our various societies endeavor so diligently to impose. I note emphatically that our mutual involvement *preceded* the life history project and in a sense opened the way for another dimension in our relationship and dialogue. It was during our long conversations—or, more accurately, innumerable short conversations over what was becoming an extended period of time—that I realized how, with a host of personal concerns now an open topic between us, Brad talked fairly easily about everything that comprised his "world." Here, at last, was one time I would finally get it right.)

A few days after celebrating a twenty-first birthday that marked his second full year at the cabin, Brad abruptly announced that he had decided to leave. The previous weeks had been a time of terrible mental turmoil for him, coupled with strange behavior and increasingly longer periods when he appeared depressed and disoriented. As he tearfully announced his decision, he consoled me with, "I'm sorry; I know you liked me." By this time, with the exception of occasional and almost rib-crushing hugs, our physical relationship had ended, but the dialogue had not. He insisted that he had to "hit the road," although he seemed to have no corresponding idea about where he would go or what he would do. I urged him to take a few days to review his options, which he agreed to do. He became more distraught with each passing day. I was able to get him to talk to counselors at the county mental health office but they offered no dramatic action and he was impatient for something—anything, really—to happen. By the end of the week, he was gone.

Several weeks later I received an unexpected telephone call from Brad's mother in southern California. Contrary to his stated intentions, Brad had returned to the community (but not the home—he was not welcome in the home of either of his estranged parents) where his mother had relocated after divorce and where he himself had briefly attended high school before dropping out. She succeeded in getting him under psychiatric review and county outpatient care. Brad made one telephone call to me shortly after arriving in southern California, during a brief period when he voluntarily committed himself to a mental institution. After that, I did not hear from him again. He did not respond to my letters.

I had scant information about his current status. In reflecting about his final days at the cabin, however, I realized that I had gained considerable insight into a whole new set of alternatives facing young people like Brad—options quite different from any that ever would occur to me. Without any particular audience in mind, I began drafting a sequel to the Sneaky Kid article focused on events precipitated during that final week. ("What does the ethnographer do?" Geertz asks rhetorically. "He writes" [1973, p. 19].) I hoped that the process of writing would help me sort out complex and conflicting feelings of personal loss and social responsibility and provide a genuine test for the power of cultural explanation.

The writing did not come easily, and I felt that for the most part I was writing to and for myself. When eventually completed, however, the account seemed to fit with a collection of qualitative studies being planned and edited by George Noblit and William Pink as *Schooling in Social Context*. My paper "Life's Not Working: Cultural Alternatives to Career Alternatives" (Wolcott, 1987) was accepted for that volume.

In the body of the chapter, I reported that after his departure, I never saw Brad again. But in that always-interminable delay between rushing off a contributed chapter and waiting to see the final copy-edited version of it, Brad did come back, unexpectedly and unannounced. With him came tragedy. At that point all I could do was add a long footnote recording events recently past and presaging others yet to come:

> In the interim between completion of the manuscript and publication of the book, Brad did return, just as several readers of early drafts predicted. Within hours of his arrival he provided sufficient evidence of "craziness" to be incarcerated. Long beyond the moment for timely help, the state's resources for dealing with him punitively seemed limitless.
>
> I do not yet understand those events or their meaning in terms of Brad's life or my own well enough to relate them; I am not sure I ever will. Bizarre as they are, the ensuing events do not change what I have written. In retrospect, my comments seem almost prophetic. But Brad had been equally prophetic years earlier when he reflected on what had been and what was yet to be: "I always seem to screw things up at the end." (Wolcott, 1987, p. 317n)

Initially, Brad was charged with attempted murder. I was the principal victim. The district attorney's office decided not to press that charge ("Too hard to prove," they explained), opting for assault and battery instead. But the major crime for which he was charged was arson. Hours before my return home from the campus one evening in November 1984, Brad had broken into the house, siphoned 500 gallons of stove oil onto the floors from a storage tank on the hillside above, taken my chainsaw to cut holes in the ceilings and roof, and trashed the house, so that the instant he poured on gasoline and ignited it, the place would become an inferno. Then he waited until I walked into his deadly ambush.

My long-time companion, Norman, returned home during the course of Brad's maniacal attack and interrupted what had to that moment seemed my quick and inevitable demise. Norman's arrival lent an element of distraction that provided opportunity for me to escape only seconds before Brad "torched" the house. The arson inspector described it as the hottest fire he had ever investigated. The destruction was total.

While still in the emergency room being stitched back together, I realized that my worldly possessions now numbered three: an old Chevrolet and two Bic pens. Even the clothing I had worn—blood and oil soaked—was confiscated for evidence. Neither did anything of

Norman's survive, except the clothes he was wearing. Our losses included my entire professional library—a devastating loss to me—as well as field notes from my studies, all my lecture and reading notes, and, for each of us, a lifetime accumulation of family memorabilia and household goods, as well as slide photography, recorded music, art and artifacts from all over the world. (Except in latest revision, however, working manuscripts were spared—from my first days in the field, I have always kept backup copies of manuscripts at my campus office.)

Brad was quickly apprehended. By morning he had confessed to the arson and assault, basing his rationale on damage I had caused his delusional "Hollywood career" and insisting that everything about our relationship had been anathema to him. He left unexplained the haunting phrase he repeated while battering and attempting to subdue me. "You hate me. You hate me." He voluntarily gave an oral confession to the police, but when formally charged he changed his plea to the frequently heard "guilty but insane."

That plea tripped a whole new host of events. Each side, prosecution and defense, got the psychiatric opinion they sought (or bought?) and the case headed into court for a jury vote as to Brad's sanity. Technically the verdict turned on whether he was assumed able to "conform" his actions while planning and carrying out the arson and assault. The consulting psychiatrists were in agreement with each other (and with written reports forwarded from people working with Brad during the previous two and a half years) that his symptoms exhibited what is known as a paranoid schizophrenic disorder.

The trial proved a professional as well as a personal nightmare. Although I was "allegedly" (to use court terminology) the victim, for the first four days of the trial I became the defendant while a carping public defender built a case to suggest I had gotten what I deserved. The Sneaky Kid article was introduced and leveled against us both, destroying intended confidentiality and revealing Brad to have been often at odds with school and society, dating back long before his reform school days. At the same time, the article was turned against me to show both how gullible and how ruthless I was. Under oath, Brad's mother insisted he had made up most of it—this, the story I felt I had finally gotten right—simply to impress me. A further implication was that I had extracted the story in order to enhance my career and thus had exploited Brad not only sexually but professionally as well.

Eventually the drawn-out trial turned to the issue of Brad's sanity, each psychiatrist having a literal "day in court" as expert witness. (The courtroom approach to validity is a different game entirely. The essence seems not to attempt to validate one's own position but to discredit [impugn] all others.) Three weeks after the jury was convened, they returned the guilty verdict, rejecting the insanity plea. The pre-sentence investigation recommended that Brad be sentenced to a *minimum* of ten years. The judge commented on the severity of the crime, ritually imposed a "severe" twenty-year sentence, and urged that Brad be considered for psychiatric assessment and assistance in prison. However, he imposed no minimum sentence: The bets were that Brad would be released in thirty months. (My next social "cause" may be for truth-in-sentencing!)

Brad's tentative parole date was set for the three-year anniversary of the crime. When he did not do well on a prerelease psychological assessment, his tentative release date was postponed for twelve months.

New victims' rights laws in effect since the trial now allow limited access to parole information at the time of such hearings (and would have allowed me to be present during the trial, from which I was then excluded except when testifying). Other than at formal hearings, however, the prison walls effectively barred me from all information about Brad except whether he was actually in custody. For most of the time he was assigned to a special voluntary program for emotionally and mentally disturbed inmates.

Long before this chapter appears in print, Brad will have been released. Unless the risk to society could be shown to be clear and substantial, detaining him longer had to be weighed against the negative effects of the prison environment and, more critically, chronic overcrowding in the state's institutions.

I cannot predict how all this will end: Prediction is not the long suit in social science. The probabilities would be difficult enough to estimate even with all available information at hand, and I have been able to glean virtually no information at all. My own sense is that when he has the opportunity, Brad is likely to return to do more harm. It does not seem unthinkable that he might attempt to kill me or to destroy what Norman and I have attempted to rebuild of our lives.

I make that statement somewhat dispassionately. My last encounter with Brad pretty well eliminated any thoughts I had about immortality. Had Norman not returned at the moment he did, my chances of surviving that evening would not have been good. As I see it, my fate at Brad's hands turns on whether he still nurtures the hatred and convoluted ideas that rationalized his violence in the first place. A psychiatrist whom I consulted—who also expressed surprise at my lack of awareness that April and October are particularly stressful months for mental patients and that the attack had occurred during a period of full moon—suggested that the critical unknown is what triggered Brad's violent response and under what circumstances a similar reaction might be precipitated again. That, in turn, will depend on his mental health and—more unknowns—the extent and consequences of any current medication or new interpersonal involvement. I assume Brad has been well coached as to appropriate responses in this regard for he stated in my presence at his earlier parole hearing, "I don't even think about Harry Wolcott any more." How comforting it would be were I able to assess the validity of his claim.

## The Absurdity of Validity

Let me return summarily to my academic purpose. Although there are aspects of all this about which valued colleagues may not be informed, I am not trying to engage in "confessional" anthropology. Furthermore, should this account suddenly seem to have taken a confessional turn, it is the earlier how-I-really-go-about-fieldwork section to which that label properly applies, at least according to the typology suggested by John Van Maanen (1988) distinguishing among realist, confessional, and impressionist styles for writing ethnography. To the extent I can lay claim to be acting as ethnographer in a case in which I have become so centrally involved, I exemplify Van Maanen's "impressionist" mode. The ethnographer's intention in the impressionist mode, he explains, "is not to tell readers what to think of an experience but to show them the experience from beginning to end and thus draw them immediately into the story to work out its problems and puzzles as they unfold" (p. 103).

I might note here a critical but instructive reaction of my students to an earlier and even more highly personal version of this account: "Had you been given one of the other conference topics, would this still be the paper you would have written?" they asked. My answer had to be "Probably yes," at least to the extent of seeing the opportunity to clarify certain matters and to write about problems of genuine—and in this case personal and pressing—concern rather than of only "professional" interest. I hasten to add, however, that I *always* try to present issues in terms of concrete and complex illustrations, guided by Geertz's maxim that there is no ascent to truth without a corresponding descent to cases. I also think it instructive and provocative to examine cases that are open, confounding, and of immediate consequence, rather than to retreat always to cases where known outcomes make us appear so much wiser in our ability to explain. (See Kaplan's [1964] distinction between reconstructed logic and logic-in-use.) My long-held suspicion that validity does not serve well as a criterion or goal for qualitative research seems to me to find firm ground in examining how I am trying to understand the circumstances I have described.

My mind swirls constantly with questions and concerns about the events and circumstances I have related, not only as a personal matter but in terms of a multiplicity of social issues on which they touch. Mental health, justice, social responsibility, morality, mortality, ethics—they are all here. As qualitatively oriented researchers portraying and reflecting upon them, what can we bring to or take from this case? What is the nature of the contribution we can make? And what criteria are most helpful in guiding our efforts or evaluating our results?

For my personal health, safety, and sanity, this time more than ever I need to get things as "right" as possible, and I feel a certain urgency  about it. I do not compartmentalize my personal and professional lives: I personalize the world I research and intellectualize the world of my experience. I have presented this case—and, to the extent possible, given its immediacy and my deep involvement, suggested what I can by way of interpretation—in substantially the same manner that I outlined for my previous studies.

I can state unequivocally that I find no counsel or direction in questions prompted by a concern for validity. There is no exact set of circumstances here, no single and "correct" interpretation, nothing scientific to measure that tells us anything important. (The arson inspector could estimate with a high degree of scientific accuracy the relatively inconsequential fact of the heat of the fire; on the pivotal issue of sanity, a lay jury had to decide because the psychiatrists could not.) For every actor in these events there are multiple meanings. In spite of seemingly direct access, I have never been able to sort out even my own thoughts and feelings, for Brad is a person about whom I cared and whom I believed I had not only reached but also "helped." Which are the errors of judgment? Does validity help with that? Will anyone, even Brad, ever know whether I am really antagonist or fall guy?

To the extent that Brad did undergo a dramatic mental breakdown, I was both the caring human and the detached observer closest to him during the time when it became manifest. Yet I did not have access to his mind, and I am certain he himself could not always find reason in it. When, subsequently, he was formally diagnosed, I was astounded to learn that problems related to getting and holding a job are accepted as major symptoms and social indicators in the mental health field. I had no idea of the ambiguity (flexibility?) of mental health diagnoses or their narrow prescriptions for "proper" cultural behavior.[2]

Also, despite whatever physiological basis there was—and Brad as a young male in his early twenties was statistically right on schedule as a candidate for a diagnosis of paranoid schizophrenia—I was aware of his own volition in embracing the social role offered him to be "crazy." I will never know the extent to which his words revealed a reluctant acquiescence or a bold new strategy when he announced after his first visit to the local mental health office, "Crazy Brad! OK, if that's what they want me to be, that's what I'll be." But I could and did share his frustration at systems of schooling that forever tested someone they could not teach and systems of welfare that eventually denied the assistance of less than $100 a month in food stamps (enough to sustain him when he had the freedom of life at the cabin yet could not face more employment refusals) but spent thousands upon thousand of dollars a year to confine and treat (?) him in what I trust was the most restrictive, and assume to be the worst possible, environment for regaining personal equilibrium.

At the same time, I will never, never be convinced that Brad can be depended on to maintain self-control. I am entitled to personal opinion: In fieldwork, I am guided by the maxim that you do not have to be neutral to try to be objective. Although I did not wish him sent to prison in the first place, neither do I relish the idea of his ever being without immediate supervision. I felt "safe" only as long as Brad remained institutionalized. My freedom was placed in jeopardy the moment he regained his.

Has Brad now forgotten about me, as he has learned (correctly) to insist? Can anyone ever discern the true genesis of his hate? Why did it get transformed into his insistence that I hated *him* in the final intimacy of the life-and-death struggle between us? What part did I really play in wreaking all this destruction, what part is Brad's (and of his, how much is real, how much delusional?), what part properly should be attributed to family and peers? How many more ways are there to tell the story than the one Brad originally volunteered, the one I have related here, and what was extracted or extrapolated in three weeks of courthouse antics? Is one of these accounts the "valid" one?

A concern for validity in the story of Brad's life and its intersection with mine seems not only an unfortunate choice of objectives but a dangerous distraction. What I seek is something else, a quality that points more to identifying critical elements and wringing plausible interpretations from them, something one can pursue without becoming obsessed with finding the right or ultimate answer, the correct version, the Truth.

Perhaps someone will find or coin qualitative research's appropriate equivalent for "validity"; we have no esoteric term now. For the present, *understanding* seems to encapsulate the idea as well as any other everyday term. Among the definitions offered in *Webster's New Collegiate Dictionary* is the following, in addition to others like "harmony in opinion or feeling" or "kindly tolerance," neither of which I seek at present:

> *understanding*: the power to make experience intelligible by applying concepts and categories

I do not for a minute believe that validity points the way to saving my life or my soul or suggests how to come to grips intellectually with a case study that really matters. Perhaps *understanding* can do little more. But as a human who happens also to be a qualitative researcher, I feel that it sets a more heuristic course than does validity.

Let me hasten to add, as should be evident from the case I have used in illustration, that I do not restrict myself to the phenomenologist's sense of understanding social phenomena from the actor's perspective or, especially, from *an* actor's perspective. That was the goal in my original and focused effort to understand something of Brad. My present concern grows out of events closely linked with individual perspectives that now include my own (and it seems strange to acknowledge that I am not sorting out my "meanings" with much more success than I had with Brad's), but it is system qualities I seek to describe and understand. To attempt to understand a social system is not to claim to understand or be able to predict the actions of particular individuals in it, oneself included.

In a thoughtful essay titled "Understanding People," philosopher Zeno Vendler (1984) contrasts *knowing* and *understanding*, the latter a more ambitious activity requiring one to be able to interpret and explain (e.g., distinctions implied between claiming to know, and claiming to understand, a poem or person). "To understand," he posits, "it may not be enough to know" (p. 204).

Perhaps that is the critical point of departure between quantities- and qualities-oriented research. We cannot "know" with the former's satisfying levels of certainty; our efforts at understanding are neither underwritten with, nor guaranteed by, the accumulation of some predetermined level of verified facts. For us, again quoting Vendler, "There is no 'ready-made world,' a realm of virginal noumena, immaculately perceived and untainted by the perceptual patterns and conceptual network imposed upon it by the human observer" (p. 202.)

I do not go about trying to discover a ready-made world; rather, I seek to understand a social world we are continuously in the process of constructing. (For a "constructionist" perspective on culture, see Peacock, 1986.) Validity stands to lure me from my purpose by inviting me to attend to facts capable of verification, ignoring the fact that for the most part the facts are already in. My present reality includes a case study in which any understanding I may achieve will occur largely in answer to questions that are *not* matters of fact.

Encouraged by Geertz's (1973) reminder that "it is not necessary to know everything in order to understand something" (p. 20), I struggle to understand complex facets of my own everyday, American, middle-class social life that seem almost to defy understanding: ambiguities of mental health definitions and treatments; the social "boundary-maintaining" function of the courts (and the seeming absence of judicial wisdom in them); social welfare systems that do too little until too late; schools that test their problem students with the same zeal they exhibit toward their promising ones—but have little idea and even less authority about what to do with the information they collect; prison systems that lock away information but release inmates; and always and ultimately, nagging questions about what might be done to check the human waste of young people like Brad in those brief interludes when they signal for help. What interventions might be effective, in what situations? How might we allocate help, recognizing there will never be enough to go around?

I also struggle with questions of the role of research in all this, particularly qualitative research. What contribution can we make to complement what other researchers already do and what (little?) we already understand? If cases like this are "powerful," to what extent is that because they touch a note of reality we ordinarily avoid in setting our research problems? What criteria are relevant to guide and judge our work so that its unique contribution can be retained and nurtured rather than reformed and assessed according to standards developed within and appropriate to other approaches?

Paradoxically, I think that a slippery old chestnut like "understanding" also reminds us that we sometimes learn from poorly reported studies and poorly analyzed ones, while seemingly truthful, or correct, or neatly analyzed accounts may have no impact or provoke no further thought. A preoccupation with validity may be as much a distraction to our collective efforts at qualitative research as it most certainly would be for me individually were I to set my course by it. That is not to dismiss validity but to attempt to put it into some broader perspective. What a surprise to discover that Cronbach concluded his carefully analytical and now-classic discussion of test validation in 1971 with the same words I might have chosen here: "Everything said in this chapter has returned to a concern with understanding" (p. 503).

## Last Words

What I have attempted here is to inventory some of the things I (and other fieldworkers) do to achieve and even "enhance" validity and at the same time raise the question of whether validity itself points to a quality about which we should concern ourselves. In an often-cited article written more than thirty years ago and addressed to researchers interested in participant observation, Howard Becker (1958) wrote, "The researcher faces the problem of how . . . to present his conclusions so as to convince other scientists of their validity" (p. 653).[4] The invitation to write this paper is testimony that "the problem" has not gone away, but I am not convinced it must be addressed in such singular fashion. I do not have conclusions to present. I try to understand, rather than to convince. I do not write to an audience of "other scientists." I do not accept validity as a valid criterion for guiding or judging my work. I think we have labored too long under the burden of this concept (are there others as well?) that might have been better left where it began, a not-quite-so-singular-or-precise criterion as I once believed it to be for matters related essentially to tests and measurement.[5] I suggest we look elsewhere in our continuing search for and dialogue about criteria appropriate to qualitative researchers' approaches and purposes.

If I have succeeded in making a case for cutting the concept of validity down to size, let me note with fine irony that even in restricting it to  its original locus, the concept offers cold comfort. Brad's parole originally was delayed twelve months on the basis of a brief interview and his performance on three tests (Rorschach Psychodiagnostic Technique with Palo Alto Destructiveness Scales, Bender Visual-Motor Gestalt Test, and Draw-a-Person) administered by a consulting psychologist. Once his paper-and-pencil test scores demonstrated a "positive" psychological evaluation, he was reevaluated and, on the basis of his "potential for improvement," was recommended for parole to harried board members eager for that message. I do not envy professional careers built on that kind of validity. I wish even more that I did not feel henceforth my own life may be hanging in the balance. Under such circumstances, how valid is "valid enough"?

## Notes

**Acknowledgments.** I appreciate the invitation extended by Alan Peshkin and Elliot Eisner to prepare this account and the challenge it might have posed for Philip W. Jackson, who was assigned responsibility to react to it. My own earlier critics included, at various stages in the writing, W. W. Charters, Jr., C. H. Edson, and Sakre Edson, all of whom also helped me live through and think through the "Brad" years, as well as Robert Everhart, David Flinders, David C. Potter, Philip D. Young, and editors Susan Liddicoat and Karen Osborne at Teachers College Press. I am particularly grateful to Sandy Charters for his caution that although it was clear that I was not using the term *validity* in the technical manner indicative of its origins, he was not clear about the sense(s) in which I *was* using it. I hope that is now more apparent as the point of the paper: It is not that clear to me how any of us uses the term. Or why.

1. Anthropologist Philip Young reminds me that by training and inclination he does just the opposite, that is, he carefully goes through informants' accounts to see what *he* can make of it all. Our difference, I think, lies not in personal styles but in what we read. In anthropologically oriented accounts, one expects to come to know one or a few informants rather well. The quoted material one finds in much of the descriptive research in education, on the other hand, often reads more like conversational snippets than informant accounts.

2. Anthropologist Stephen Tyler (1986) refers to DSM III, the *Diagnostic and Statistical Manual* (third edition) that serves as sourcebook for mental health diagnosis, as "that terrorist bludgeon of the psychiatrist" (p. 139).

3. Egon Guba (1981) is among those who have pioneered the effort to identify criteria for judging adequacy within naturalistic research paradigms that parallel rather than replicate those of the rationalistic tradition. I am not much taken with his early choice of *trustworthiness* as a global term. However, the four "aspects" of trustworthiness that he identifies seem to hold promise. Perhaps the parallels he draws with their quantitative ("scientific") counterparts do not need to be as tight as those he has proposed, in which internal validity is equated with credibility; external validity/generalizability with transferability; reliability with dependability; and objectivity with confirmability.

4. I admit to some initial disappointment at discovering Becker's seeming endorsement of validity in this early statement. I had opportunity to discuss it with him when these papers were presented. As he intended the sentence, he explained, the emphasis was on "convince" rather than on "validity." "And that," he noted, "is still the problem."

5. Substituting *valid measure* might help foster this distinction, consistent with Bernard's (1988) observation, "Valid measurement makes valid data, but validity itself depends on the collective opinion of researchers" (p. 54).

# References

Becker, H. S. (1958). Problems of inference and proof in participant observation. *American Sociological Review, 23,* 652-660.

Bernard, H. R. (1988). *Research methods in cultural anthropology.* Beverly Hills, CA: Sage.

Bernard, H. R., Killworth, P. D., Kronenfeld, D., & Sailer, L. (1984). The problem of informant accuracy: The validity of retrospective data. *Annual Review of Anthropology, 13,* 495-517.

Brinberg, D., & McGrath, J. E. (1982). A network of validity concepts within the research process. In D. Brinberg & L. H. Kidder (Eds.), *Forms of validity in research* (pp. 5-21). San Francisco: Jossey-Bass.

Brown, R. (1965). *Social psychology.* New York: Free Press.

Campbell, D. T. (1975). "Degrees of freedom" and the case study. *Comparative Political Studies, 8*(2), 178-193.

Campbell, D. T. (1986). Science's social system of validity-enhancing collective belief change and the problems of the social sciences. In D. W. Fiske & R. A. Shweder (Eds.), *Metatheory in social science: Pluralisms and subjectivities* (pp. 108-135). Chicago: University of Chicago Press.

Cronbach, L. J. (1971). Test validation. In R. L. Thorndike (Ed.), *Educational measurement* (2nd ed., pp. 443-507). Washington, DC: American Council on Education.

Cronbach, L. J. (1986). Social inquiry by and for earthlings. In D. W. Fiske & R. A. Shweder (Eds.), *Metatheory in social science: Pluralisms and subjectivities* (pp. 83-107). Chicago: University of Chicago Press.

Cronbach, L. J., & Meehl, P. E. (1955). Construct validity in psychological tests. *Psychological Bulletin, 52,* 281-302.

Dean, J., & Whyte, W. F. (1958). How do you know if the informant is telling the truth? *Human Organization, 17*(2), 34-38.

Dobbert, M. L. (1982). *Ethnographic research: Theory and applications for modern schools and societies.* New York: Praeger.

Erickson, F. (1973). What makes school ethnography 'ethnographic'? *Council on Anthropology and Education Newsletter, 4*(2), 10-19. [Revised and reprinted in *Anthropology and Education Quarterly, 15*(1984), 51-66.]

Freeman, L. C., & Romney, A. K. (1988). Words, deeds and social structure: A preliminary study of the reliability of informants. *Human Organization, 46*(4), 330-334.

Geertz, C. (1973). Thick description. In C. Geertz (Ed.), *The interpretation of cultures* (pp. 3-30). New York: Basic Books.

Goetz, J. P., & LeCompte, M. D. (1984). *Ethnography and qualitative design in educational research.* Orlando, FL: Academic Press.

Gould, S. J. (1981). *The mismeasure of man.* New York: W. W. Norton.

Guba, E. (1981). Criteria for assessing the trustworthiness of naturalistic inquiries. *Education Communication and Technology Journal, 29*(2), 75-91.

Kaplan, A. (1964). *The conduct of inquiry.* San Francisco: Chandler.

Kirk, J., & Miller, M. L. (1986). *Reliability and validity in qualitative research* (Sage University Paper Series on Qualitative Research methods, Vol. 1). Beverly Hills, CA: Sage.

LaTour, B., & Woolgar, S. (1986). *Laboratory life: The construction of scientific facts.* Princeton, NJ: Princeton University Press.

McEwen, W. J. (1963). Forms and problems of validation in social anthropology. *Current Anthropology, 4,* 155-183.

Miles, M. B., & Huberman, A. M. (1984). Drawing valid meaning from qualitative data: Toward a shared craft. *Educational Researcher, 13*(5), 20-30.

Peacock, J. L. (1986). *The anthropological lens: Harsh light, soft focus.* New York: Cambridge University Press.

Pelto, P. J., & Pelto, G. H. (1978). *Anthropological research: The structure of inquiry* (2nd ed.). New York: Cambridge University Press.

Phillips, D. C. (1987). Validity in qualitative research. *Education and Urban Society, 20*(1), 9-24.

Spindler, G. (Ed.). (1982). *Doing the ethnography of schooling.* New York: Holt, Rinehart and Winston. (Revised edition, Prospect Heights, IL: Waveland Press, 1987)

Tyler, S. A. (1986). Post-modern ethnography: From document of the occult to occult document. In J. Clifford & G. E. Marcus (Eds.), *Writing culture: The poetics and politics of ethnography* (pp. 122-140). Berkeley: University of California Press.

Van Maanen, J. (1988). *Tales of the field: On writing ethnography.* Chicago: University of Chicago Press.

Vendler, Z. (1984). Understanding people. In R. A. Shweder & R. A. LeVine (Eds.), *Culture theory: Essays on mind, self, and emotion* (pp. 200-213). New York: Cambridge University Press.

Vidich, A. J., & Bensman, J. (1954). The validity of field data. *Human Organization, 13*(1), 20-27.

Weber, R. P. (1985). *Basic content analysis* (Sage University Paper Series on Quantitative Applications in the Social Sciences). Beverly Hills, CA: Sage.

Wolcott, H. F. (1967). *A Kwakiutl village and school.* New York: Holt, Rinehart and Winston. (Reissued, Prospect Heights, IL: Waveland Press, 1984, 1989)

Wolcott, H. F. (1973). *The man in the principal's office: An ethnography.* New York: Holt, Rinehart and Winston. (Reissued, Prospect Heights, IL: Waveland Press, 1984)

Wolcott, H. F. (1974). *The African beer gardens of Bulawayo: Integrated drinking in a segregated society.* New Brunswick, NJ: Rutgers Center of Alcohol Studies.

Wolcott, H. F. (1977). *Teachers versus technocrats: An educational innovation in anthropological perspective.* Eugene, OR: Center for Educational Policy and Management, University of Oregon.

Wolcott, H. F. (1982a). The anthropology of learning. *Anthropology and Education Quarterly, 13*(2), 83-108.

Wolcott, H. F. (1982b). *Adequate schools and inadequate education: An anthropological perspective.* (Commissioned paper prepared for the School Finance Project, Contract NIE-P-81-0271). Washington, DC: U.S. Department of Education.

Wolcott, H. F. (1983a). Adequate schools and inadequate education: The life history of a sneaky kid. *Anthropology and Education Quarterly, 14*(1), 3-32.

Wolcott, H. F. (1983b). A Malay village that progress chose: Sungai Lui and the Institute of Cultural Affairs. *Human Organization, 42*(1), 72-81.

Wolcott, H. F. (1984). Ethnographers sans ethnography: The evaluation compromise. In D. Fetterman (Ed.), *Ethnography in educational evaluation* (pp. 177-210). Beverly Hills, CA: Sage.

Wolcott, H. F. (1987). Life's not working: Cultural alternatives to career alternatives. In G. W. Noblit & W. T. Pink (Eds.), *Schooling in social context: Qualitative studies* (pp. 303-325). Norwood, NJ: Ablex Publishing.

Wolcott, H. F. (1988). Ethnographic research in education. In R. M. Jaeger (Ed.), *Complementary methods for research in education* (pp. 187-249). Washington, DC: American Educational Research Association.

Wolcott, H. F. (1989). A Kwakiutl village and school—25 years later. Afterword to the second printing of *A Kwakiutl village and school*. Prospect Heights, IL: Waveland Press.

Wolcott, H. F. (1990). *Writing up qualitative research* (Sage University Paper Series on Qualitative Research). Beverly Hills, CA: Sage.

# Teaching and Learning Qualitative Inquiry

*Much of what is published on fieldwork today is not "how-to" material so much as reflections on why it is so difficult to tell people how to do it.*
—Jean E. Jackson, "I Am a Fieldnote," p. 8

*Advisors can tell you only what they did and what you should do, but one person's method does not work for most others, and many advisors and graduate schools refuse to cover these topics.*
—Jean E. Jackson, "I Am a Fieldnote," p. 28

This last part takes a different tack to transforming data, in Chapter 12 by examining what can be done through formal instruction to help students learn these procedures, in Chapter 13 by reviewing what beginning researchers need to know (regardless of whether or not formal instruction is how they acquire it), and in a brief final chapter of personal reflection.

One great way to learn about almost any subject is to teach it. That has certainly proved true in qualitative research. As a newcomer to the professional fields, many of those who teach it have had to learn it just that way, literally by having a teaching assignment thrust upon them.

Chapter 12, "Teaching Qualitative Inquiry," addresses the formal teaching of qualitative research as a graduate level (and perhaps occasionally an upper-division) college course. The topic invites a retrospective look at some of the ideas discussed throughout this volume examined in terms of what I have learned from teaching such courses for more than 20 years.

However, as should be apparent from the discussion of Chapter 10, "The Acquisition of Culture," I am not one to confuse teaching with learning. Although I spent some part of each of 25 years as a student in classrooms, and have spent an overlapping three and a half decades instructing in them, I hold no brief that classrooms are particularly effective places to learn or that the only, or best, way to learn a subject is to take a class in it. Chapter 13, "Learning Qualitative Inquiry," discusses how to learn—and do—qualitative inquiry on one's own. I trust that my enthusiasm for learning by doing will emerge clearly in both chapters.

Most students who take courses in qualitative research find them useful, at least in an instrumental way. For one thing, such courses may now meet program requirements for "methods" courses; statistics and experimental design are no longer the only games in town. For another, students increasingly are using (and being allowed to use) qualitative approaches to provide evidence of their research acumen. I doubt, however, that many students feel well prepared to conduct a qualitative study start to finish after taking a course or two. I know that some feel more rather than less overwhelmed on the basis of brief coursework. Without being quite sure what it was they expected from enrolling in such a class, they are quite sure afterward that they didn't get, or get enough of, what they needed.

From the instructional side, the task of offering an all-purpose course in qualitative approaches is beyond comprehension. In meeting my own responsibility to "teach" qualitative research, my eventual resolution was to offer a choice between two courses. I recommended that students take either one of the alternatives, not both. (Basically, students "take" instructors, not courses. I could never escape a feeling that, because they were offered by the same instructor, my two courses were more alike than I intended them to be.) In one class, I offered a broad introduction and survey of qualitative research (see Wolcott, 1992, for an overview). In the other, I focused exclusively on one specific approach: ethnography. Students were admitted to that class only if they had prior coursework in cultural anthropology or could provide evidence of familiarity with the ethnographic literature.

I urge students to find their way into qualitative work through focused courses whenever possible, such as a course in ethnographic research in anthropology, a course in phenomenology or conversation analysis in sociology. That advice follows my preference for doing fewer things in depth rather than many things in breadth, "doing less more thoroughly."

The institutionalization of qualitative research as a field of inquiry is itself a recent phenomenon, something that began in the 1970s under the very eyes of those of us now becoming seniors. Other than the 25 pages that Malinowski devoted to the topic in his 1922 chapter titled, "The Subject, Method and Scope of This Inquiry," anthropological scholars did not customarily burden readers with the trials of their fieldwork experience. Early fieldworkers were apt to disappear altogether from the settings they were describing, and the practice of writing in the ethnographic present left "the natives" preserved forever in their precontact circumstances, as though the ethnographer had not been there at all. (Note, for example, Sanjek's comment about how Boas reported on "a past from which one hundred years of Western contact was filtered out"; 1990, p. 196.) It was so unusual to reveal fieldwork as personal experience that, when Laura Bohannan wrote *Return to Laughter* in 1954, her account was presented as a novel and published under a pseudonym, Elenore Smith Bowen. By the time Hortense Powdermaker's firsthand account of her career and fieldwork appeared in 1966 as *Stranger and Friend: The Way of an Anthropologist,* I had become a seasoned fieldworker myself, with one study (Kwakiutl Village) completed, a second one (the school principal) under way.

The ensuing years have seen an outpouring of texts and personal accounts on aspects of qualitative inquiry: discipline centered (ethnography, qualitative sociology), topic centered (ethnography of speaking, qualitative approaches in the study of mental retardation), and method centered (issues of reliability and validity, qualitative *versus* quantitative approaches).

If the materials now available have one thing in common, it is that they have far more to say about difficulties to be encountered in initiating a study than about what to do to complete it. Technical skills and the mechanics of recording data are put in broad contexts under favorite headings such as "Gaining Entrée and Maintaining Rapport," "Conducting an Interview," and "Ethical Considerations." Any of these topics is, of course, big enough to fill a book, a lecture, or an entire course. Often that seems to be their main function.

What *do* you do with the data you get? How are data transformed into something else that becomes the completed account? And how does one learn that aspect of qualitative work, or teach it to another? Questions like the first two have received the attention to this point. The focus shifts now to how these aspects *may* be taught and *must* be learned.

Be warned, once again, that these procedures remain "mysterious." What each of us does with the data in any particular study is the "little black box" of qualitative research. Regardless of how many studies have been conducted by others, or whether you have conducted this kind of research yourself, there is a unique and creative process specific to each new data set and its related circumstances. How you variously emphasize or blend description, analysis, and interpretation is ultimately up to you in an inquiry approach that does not rest on pat formulas or universal applications. Doing something *with* data is the hard part.

There are inconveniences and frustrations aplenty in fieldwork, today matched with regulations ad nauseam for gaining entrée or satisfying bureaucratic procedures ostensibly designed to protect human subjects. Nevertheless, the genius of qualitative inquiry ultimately lies within yourself. The success of your efforts will be measured not in the field but at your desk. No one can simulate that experience for you or anticipate all the problems you may encounter. But some classroom activities and orientations may be more helpful than others by way of formal preparation. I start by discussing what I believe can be accomplished in a one-term course.

If you are a student, you may feel that in the first of these chapters I am addressing your instructor rather than talking to you. I did write with an instructor's orientation in mind, particularly instructors with limited firsthand experience in qualitative work. But we are all students of these processes, and a chapter such as this brings still another perspective to the understanding of qualitative inquiry. Furthermore, if you have just enrolled in your first course in qualitative research, you may be surprised to find yourself teaching a similar course in the near future. Thus the issues raised, coupled with reflections on your experience as a student and the reflections of others (e.g., Ely, 1991), may prove helpful sooner than expected.

# References

Bowen, Elenore Smith [Laura Bohannan]. (1954). *Return to laughter.* New York: Harper and Brothers.

Ely, Margot. (1991). *Doing qualitative research: Circles within circles.* Bristol, PA: Falmer.

Jackson, Jean E. (1990). "I am a fieldnote": Footnotes as a symbol of professional identity. In Roger Sanjek (Ed.), *Fieldnotes: The makings of anthropology* (pp. 3-33). Ithaca, NY: Cornell University Press.

Malinowski, Bronislaw. (1922). *Argonauts of the Western Pacific.* London: George Routledge.

Powdermaker, Hortense. (1966). *Stranger and friend: The way of an anthropologist.* New York: Norton.

Sanjek, Roger. (1990). The secret life of fieldnotes. In Roger Sanjek (Ed.), *Fieldnotes: The makings of anthropology* (pp. 187-270). Ithaca, NY: Cornell University Press.

Wolcott, Harry F. (1992). Posturing in qualitative inquiry. In Margaret D. LeCompte, Wendy L. Millroy, & Judith Preissle (Eds.), *Handbook of qualitative research in education* (pp. 3-52). San Diego, CA: Academic Press.

# Teaching Qualitative Inquiry

Several years ago, social studies educators introduced the term *post-holing* as a way to visualize (and perhaps dramatize) the enormity of their assignments (e.g., to "teach" U.S. history, the South, Latin America). The term drew an analogy to *encompassing*—literally "taking in"—a huge territory by stringing fence lines loosely marking the boundaries of an area but secured by well-anchored posts set along the way.

Although the phrase *postholing* did not catch on in educator circles, I rather liked the analogy. I have often thought about it when planning my own teaching strategies, faced as we are with the inevitable challenges of too much to take in and too little in the way of available resources or time.

Nowhere is the problem more serious than in designing and offering a graduate level course in qualitative research. One is never certain just how much territory can be covered or exactly where to "dig in." A philosophically oriented instructor may identify philosophy of science as the territory to be explored most carefully, followed by excursions into problem setting, objectivity and subjectivity, and ethics. The usually unambiguous teach-from-the-text approach prompts a forced choice between alternatives of a focus on method (process) and a focus on results (product). If the objective of such a course is to produce *active researchers* rather than *critical users* of research, further choices must be made among inductive approaches in which students alternatively experience the techniques firsthand and generate their own guidelines for using them, are led through a set of guided field projects (e.g., Crane &

Angrosino, 1992), or study what others who have gone before have passed on by way of "warnings and advice" (Wax, 1971; see also Anderson, 1990; Spindler, 1970). If the emphasis is to be on practical applications, should attention be directed primarily to how one goes about getting started with fieldwork, or should already-limited time be divided further to allow consideration of what to do with data once collected? Finally, can attention also be given to questions related to writing (perhaps including publishing as well), further stretching the boundaries of the territory to be covered? Where do those postholes most need to be placed?

## Learning by Doing

When I first began teaching ethnographic research as a formal "methods" course in education (rather than as a facet of a content-oriented seminar in anthropology and education), I was so determined to impress upon students that ethnography is not quick work that I did not even entertain the possibility that they might pursue modest research projects of their own. Instead, they pored over then newly emerging books on anthropological research (Naroll & Cohen, 1970; Pelto, 1970; Wax, 1971) while I regaled them with accounts of my own ongoing or recently completed fieldwork. The focus was on ways to adapt traditional anthropological fieldwork conducted in unfamiliar settings to research in the all-too-familiar setting of the schools. For my students, fieldwork was a totally vicarious experience.

In any course or workshop I offer these days on qualitative or ethnographic research, firsthand experience with at least one and preferably both of the basic fieldwork strategies—participant observation and interviewing—has become the core activity in which everyone must engage. When possible, a modest field project becomes the focus of each individual's activity for the class; one cannot grasp the essence of qualitative research without coming to grips firsthand with the basic problem of what is to be considered as data.

When time and resources allow for no more, at the very least we engage in a period of collective observation at some nearby public place. Alternatively, following a suggestion made years ago by my colleague John Singleton about using the powerful documentary *Titicut Follies*

(Wiseman, 1967) as a teaching device, I schedule the showing of that or another ethnographic or documentary film (perhaps without its accompanying narration) and ask students to take notes *as though they were on the scene in person as observers.* The idea is to engage them immediately in recognizing some of the dilemmas confronting field observers: what to "get" when you realize you can't get it all; how to observe while you are still in the process of setting the purposes of the observation; how to deal with personal reactions.

Afterward, we review what students did observe, what they managed to record of what they observed, and how they might use their recorded data (or next time watch for and record something else instead) were they to continue the observations. A one-time session and follow-up discussion are hardly enough to resolve all the issues related to fieldwork observations (many of which were identified in Chapter 5), but it is always surprising to realize how quickly the important questions begin to surface, and it can be comforting to realize that problems you thought were yours alone are endemic to field research.

Optimally, students then set to work immediately on a field project of their own. We have come to label these projects as "beginning" ethnographies or "beginning" case studies, even when the fieldwork and rudimentary analysis extend through an entire semester. Initially I referred to the projects as "mini" studies, but students helped me realize that a study carried only through its early stages is not the same as a full-blown study in miniature. Whatever might eventuate as the final product will be influenced by further fieldwork, by a more sharply honed problem, and by an evolving analytical or interpretive framework perhaps not even recognizable in the early stages.

Where I once regarded a full semester as too short for engaging in fieldwork practice, I have more recently set participants in as short as a 5 (consecutive) day workshop to making not just one but two forays into "the field" (e.g., an outdoor market, a shopping mall, a transportation center). I want them to "try on" the role of fieldworker and, especially, to reflect on distinctions between being an *observer* and being a *participant observer.* After the experience, we discuss whether and how they made notes, what they chose to observe and record, and the extent to which they activated a participant observer role or, more often, participated only as unobtrusive observers. The phrase *participant observer,* which James Clifford calls "the misleading formula"

(1990, p. 53), proves curiously complex as we discover our own reticence about being genuine participants in settings where we are endeavoring to be detached observers as well.

When a course extends over several weeks, thus making time available for sustained fieldwork, interviewing not only becomes a possibility but takes precedence as a preferred starting place for students new to this work. Interviewing offers a sense of direction for students unsure about how to get started or what might constitute a reasonable focus for a class project. In the absence of an alternative proposal of their own, I suggest that students locate an informant willing to relate a brief "life story." I ask them to make sure any prospective informant understands that this is a class exercise designed primarily to give students practice at interviewing, transcribing, and putting together a life history account. I am aware of cautions that we should not unleash hordes of students on unsuspecting informants, but with the intrusions that house-to-house and, especially, telephone pollsters and solicitors make into our daily lives, I think that students thoughtfully fulfilling an assignment do not ordinarily put voluntary informants at much risk or inconvenience. We do discuss at length, and "for real," such complex issues as anonymity, reciprocity, and the handling of sensitive information.

For classes in ethnographic research, in which cultural interpretation plays a major role in analysis (discussed more fully in Wolcott, 1988), I add an additional requirement: The informant's cultural background must differ dramatically from that of the researcher. I have added "dramatically" in recent years as students have appeared to become better aware that culture is not restricted to ethnic boundaries. In this case, however, ethnic differences are the ones I hope they will seek out so that they experience the kind of cross-cultural, comparative perspective that gave anthropology its start.

An advantage for neophyte researchers who opt for fieldwork conducted primarily through interviewing is the absence of ambiguity about what constitutes "data." The words spoken during an interview—words that can be recorded and transcribed—are not the only data that result from an interview, but they *are* data. They can be written longhand or keyed into a word processor, they can be sorted and labeled, and they lend themselves superbly to a search for repetitions, regularities, schemata, themes, aberrations, paradoxes, problems, turnings—

whatever mental constructs a researcher intends to employ in the effort to impose some order and to identify leads for pursuing the research. *That* is the stage of the research process that I want students to reach, as quickly as possible. I want them engaged in the critical process of "funneling," making decisions about which data to get more of, which data to get rid of, and how to use data already at hand. Collection, reduction, transformation—another nice trio there!

As with trying to teach students to be better observers, I am once again "saved by the bell"; with the exception of the rare student who has data previously collected and sorted, there is never sufficient time in a one-term course to achieve a "mini" study rather than a "beginning" one. But the scope of class topics has expanded beyond simply collecting data to include considerations of what to do with data. Toward the end of the term, we can address, in terms of their individual projects, questions about a projected ratio among description, analysis, and interpretation. In the final class sessions, when students summarize their progress and describe what they would do were they to continue the research, attention is drawn particularly to using data, rather than the far-less-instructive (though admittedly often more entertaining) accounts we used to hear about tape recorders that failed to record or informants who never returned for a second interview.

In most cases, the project ends when the class ends. If a grade must be assigned, it is based on whatever I have in hand on the final due date. I have found over the years that students unable to write up what they have at that point are not likely to get their projects written at all, and there is no point in prolonging their agony. Occasionally the project serves as a pilot study or inspires, sharpens, or totally revamps a dissertation proposal. At least one "beginning" study was carried through to published account (Hill, 1991).

## Reporting and Feedback

There is an uneasy line between respecting the autonomy of one's students and accepting responsibility as instructor to coach or provide feedback. My resolution of that dilemma is to ask students to submit weekly or semiweekly field reports from the outset of fieldwork. Each report is to include descriptive data, discussion or evidence of rudimentary sorting, categorizing, or other preliminary analysis, and reflection on the fieldwork process itself.

Although I encourage students to conduct most of their work through interviewing, I require only one field report that includes a formally taped and transcribed interview. (My colleague Phil Young tells me that when he teaches a comparable class he is equally insistent that one interview be conducted and recorded *without* the use of a tape recorder.) Similarly, one report is to be based on observation, another on participant observation, with explicit attention to how the two do, or might, differ. As assignments go, that has proved workable, but allowances have to be made. Sometimes informants do not want to be recorded on tape, or private interviews cannot be arranged. In some settings, it is easy to observe but the researcher finds no way to be a true *participant* observer. Occasionally students get swept away in participation and later insist they found "no opportunity to observe." (Participant observation proves a misleading formula indeed!)

A suggested two-column format, using only one column to record original fieldnotes, leaves space for researcher comments, indexing, reflection, and questions for future probing. That second column, although often blank in early field reports, serves as reminder that there is more to be done than simply "collecting" data, more to interviewing than the interview protocol itself.

For their required field reports, students may either submit their original notes or extract a formal report from personal and private diarylike entries. The option is intended to allow them to make note-taking highly personal if they so choose. From private notes, they can always distill any reports that must be shared by others, such as might be required of them on a funded project. We probe constantly for ways to make note-taking as efficient as possible, pending the day we will all have notebook computers at our disposal. Any system that entails mere rewriting quickly shows itself to be time consuming and inefficient.

If confidentiality is a concern (in practice, seldom the case), students can use code names in original notes or, as mentioned above, rewrite selected notes to be submitted formally as class assignments. Most informants seem satisfied with the assurance that the instructor and the student researcher will be the only ones to see the "raw" notes. Neither field reports nor final reports are circulated other than at the discretion of the researcher. Few of the reports contain delicate information, but each researcher has the responsibility for deciding whether his or her work should remain confidential. The level of detail divulged in class discussions is guided by the same conditions.

I take my "hands-on" commitment to teaching qualitative research seriously; the emphasis is on immediate experience. I do select texts for class reading, however, and I identify chapters or sections that I want students to discuss together. I present the texts as resources, ready when needed. We discuss the readings to emphasize universal questions raised and answers proposed. The reading is not "required" in the sense that students worry about being examined on it, although I am attentive to students who demonstrate connections between the problems they encounter in their fieldwork and the discussions in class and in the texts.

## Thinking "Backward"

As with qualitative research itself, teaching a class on the subject proceeds most purposefully if the problem is set properly. Taking as the major expectation of the course the submission of a "beginning" ethnography, life history, or case study, and designing all class readings and discussion to aid in the development of that project, is intended to create a clear sense of purpose. Early class sessions focus on identifying appropriate problems, settings, or informants; getting started; and finding efficient ways to keep up with note-taking, reporting, and reading.

In class, we address student problems first: where to borrow or rent a tape recorder, where to meet informants, what kind of permission is needed, whether to keep fieldnotes in longhand or enter them into the computer, what happens if you are interviewing one spouse but the other insists on answering the questions, and so on.

Eventually I direct attention away from such immediate concerns to discuss end results. I want to get students to "think backward," their intended end point serving to guide their thinking about the kind of data they will need. Cast suddenly, as they have been, into the role of researcher, with course expectations as their immediate problem, questions about how they intend to use data—data they have not even begun to collect—strike them as premature, if not totally irrelevant. Still, I nudge in that direction, perhaps by having them list some categories of data that they are sure they will *not* need. We examine how data have been presented and used in exemplary studies. We pit categories of more-likely-to-be-valuable data against less-likely-to-be-valuable data. After a while, questions about the kinds of data one needs no longer seem so preposterous.

## Keeping Track of Everything

I have mentioned my preference for qualitative research courses that focus on one or a few closely related approaches (e.g., ethnography alone, or ethnography in the company of field study and other participant observation strategies). When the course must be taught in broad survey fashion, I ask students to assist with the "postholing" by taking responsibility for particular issues (ethics, objectivity, validity) and/or approaches (biography, critical theory, ethnomethodology, feminism, history, phenomenology, philosophy, symbolic interactionist). Panel discussions prove livelier than show-and-tell reports, especially when students organize lively discussions around key issues rather than make stiff formal presentations, with class time simply divided among presenters. Loosely structured debate-like formats allow for spirited sessions arguing, for example, whether participant observation or interviewing is the mainstay of descriptive research, whether what people say they do or what you observe them doing provides more reliable data, whether bias is the qualitative researcher's friend or foe, whether theory should precede or follow fieldwork, and so forth. On any student-presented topic, a one-page (maximum) handout outlining history and development of the concept, its major tenets, and a short bibliography helps class members keep track of main points (all this comes at them so fast) and provides the beginning of a resource file for future reference.

For years I maintained and constantly updated a topical working bibliography on method. I developed it from material generously shared by Ray Rist, who in 1988 was already on the seventh edition of a bibliographic effort initiated years earlier. I also initiated a parallel bibliography of completed studies, with a particular emphasis on qualitative studies in the field of education (Wolcott, 1982). Through the years, I have continued to explore ways to categorize these studies (Wolcott, 1990, p. 65; 1992, pp. 29-39).

Qualitative studies now are proliferating so fast that anyone intending to keep abreast of them needs to pinpoint highly specific subareas rather than attempt to keep track of everything. Maintaining a "working bibliography," especially of exemplary studies in one's field of specialization, is a useful activity for any instructor who offers coursework or guides student projects in qualitative work. It is the kind of ongoing project to which each new wave of students can contribute, both by identifying new sources and by recommending deletions of outdated and uninformative ones. Every proposed addition or deletion provides further opportunity to review what qualifies as representative or exemplary qualitative work.

Those of us teaching qualitative research, and thus responsible for bringing the relevant literature to the attention of our students, have a concomitant responsibility to bring our students' studies to the attention of the literature. It is up to us to ensure that good studies are recognized (through awards, citations in our own work), read (by our colleagues' students as well as our own), published—either en toto as (de-dissertationized) monographs or reported more briefly in journal articles—and presented at seminars and professional meetings.

I could have no better personal model than my own mentor, George Spindler, whose two major monograph series, the Case Studies in Cultural Anthropology and the Case Studies in Education and Culture, made it possible not only for senior scholars but for wave upon wave of recently completed doctoral students to have their studies published and widely circulated. As noted in the chapter prefaces, Spindler was directly responsible for my writing two of the chapters in this collection. He has been such a positive influence and help throughout my career that it would not be stretching the point to say that he has been a motivating force in everything I have written.

I am proud to report that two of my students' doctoral dissertations were subsequently published as monographs (Chang, 1992; Cline, 1975) and that most of my former advisees published journal or chapter-length articles from their studies. Still, I do not feel that I have been able to help my students as much as Spindler helped me. Only recently have I realized how important this could prove for qualitative study in general as well as for individual careers. One small but easy step in this regard is for instructors to list their own doctoral advisees by name *and dissertation title* on their curriculum vitae and/or in detachable form that can be distributed among interested colleagues. By way of illustration and example, I have included a roster of my doctoral students and their dissertation titles in the Appendix.

## "We Are All Self-Styled Ethnographers"

Qualitative researcher-author-editor John Van Maanen offered another provocative comment during that luncheon conversation of several years ago when he observed, "We are all self-styled ethnographers." Although I do not cast so wide a net as he does, equating everyone who conducts qualitative research with being an ethnographer, I was taken with his notion that each of us doing qualitative/descriptive research is indeed "self-styled." At first I was tempted to argue that "real" ethnographers—anthropologically trained ones, that is—are the exception to his generalization. Yet as I raced through a mental roster of all the ethnographers I know or have read, I could not think of any *two* whose approach or completed works are so strikingly similar as to demonstrate their "training," except in theoretical predispositions that link them (especially in the eyes of others) with schools, Schools, movements, or eras.

If we are all self-styled researchers, then the teaching/training issue has more to do with how to provide a basic orientation and overall sense of what is involved than with trying to devise a list of minimum essential techniques with which every fieldworker ought to be acquainted. Students need to know how to get technical help and what the available resources are, but they cannot be trained in anticipation of every possible technique they might ever need, every field dilemma they might encounter. Our responsibility, as I see it, is to have them experience directly the two basic fieldwork strategies—participant observation and interviewing—and to confront them with the basic problems of figuring out what data to get and what to do with the data they do get.

The alternative, of course, is to present qualitative research as a collection of procedures and techniques, attempting to cover every important facet from finding an informant to preparing a book prospectus. The guiding philosophy here is that students should be exposed systematically to a preselected set of topics, rather than simply presented an "opportunity" to discover something about conducting research of their own and on their own.

Not too long ago a group of anthropologists did organize collectively to pursue this "techniques" approach, attempting to reach consensus about what "a professional ethnographer, of any theoretical persuasion . . . ought to master" (Plattner, 1989, p. 30). They identified six major topics in their Basic List of Ethnographic Methods: research design, qualitative methods (language skills, direct observation, interview skills), data recording and retrieval, quantitative research (e.g., hypothesis testing, basic statistics, computer analysis), research ethics, and fieldwork logistics. Under "interview skills," from cognitive anthropology alone the examples they identified include free listing, triad tests, free pile sort, paired comparison, belief frames and componential analysis, cultural model research, consensus analysis, and analysis of decision making.

Given a partial list like this and the time constraints of a one-term course, it seems to me that postholing is an instructor's only hope. That does not detract from the usefulness of such a list in guiding one's lifelong journey on the way to becoming a "professional" ethnographer; there are always workshops and materials available on specialized topics. (See, for example, a useful overview by Trotter, 1991, or the *Cultural Anthropology Methods* [CAM] *Newsletter* published by the Department of Anthropology, University of Florida.) Furthermore, Plattner and colleagues were quick to note that, as the skills they identified reach greater and greater specificity (e.g., remote sensing, satellite photography, soil analysis, biomass transects), the nature of the project and "appropriate circumstances" must increasingly be taken into account. On the other hand, they reached general agreement that basic camera and map skills are essential for any fieldworker who can reasonably expect to observe and record physical environments and the people in them, just as there are several interview "types" with which every fieldworker ought to be familiar (e.g., structured interview, semistructured interview on both broad and narrow topics, and the open-ended life history/life cycle interview).

From a quick perusal of a course outline or table of contents, the instructional emphasis one can expect to encounter between a techniques-specific focus and a broad "discovery" approach like my own is easy to detect. Students are not likely to have a choice, but at least they know what they should be able to take away from a class and what they may someday have to learn on their own.

I recall an essay by Jerome Bruner in which he proposed a contrast between education and training. We "train" people, he suggested, when we know what we are doing; we "educate" them when we do not. His remarks were consistent with then-current interest in discovery learning. Like the concept of postholing, Bruner's contrast between training and educating has proved useful for setting my own objectives in teaching.

In offering a course on qualitative research, I do not approach the task with the idea that I will be training students, in the sense of providing pat procedures and set recipes. I find my purpose instead in trying to educate them, exploring possibilities and examining broad categories of problems designed to help them cope *in general* with situations neither they nor I can fully anticipate. Without knowing for sure how it was intended, I take as a compliment the statement a graduate student made to a visitor in one of my qualitative research classes: "Harry never seems actually to *teach* anything. But we learn a lot in his classes anyway." I will be quite satisfied if this book draws a similar reaction— that although it doesn't actually *teach* anyone how to transform qualitative data, one can "learn a lot anyway" from the discussion and examples.

For some students, qualitative research is more than just another course, another set of definitions to learn, another set of names to drop. Those are the students who both recognize and seize an opportunity to immerse themselves in it. They are the ones I want to guide and encourage, through a course that unfolds more like a studio course in the arts or a practicum in the professional schools. I can think of no aspect of doing fieldwork, analyzing it, or writing it up about which I can declare, "No matter who you are, where you are, or what your research is about, this I can tell you for sure . . ." Ah, perhaps there *is* one thing I can tell you for sure: There is no such thing as "unreported" research.

There is a certain amount of conventional wisdom one can pass along, but none of it is free from qualifying footnotes, whether it is the absolute necessity for triangulating and cross-checking data (a great topic in seminar and a terrible dilemma in the field when your key informant learns that you are going around checking up on everything he or she tells you) to rigorous and detailed note-taking (which precludes any hope of your becoming the genuine participant you wanted to be).

I once heard an offhand suggestion that probably the best preparation for fieldwork was to go backpacking! After a lifetime of fieldwork, I must agree that knowing how to take care of oneself and how to meet one's basic needs ranks high on the list. It also makes sense to have a clear idea of what others, conducting research on similar problems or holding similar disciplinary orientations, have done. Not every fieldworker will have need of the heavy skillet recommended by Boas, a big stick for the dogs recommended by Kroeber, or "plenty of marmalade and cheap tennis shoes" as suggested to Jean Jackson (1990, p. 29). There still is no substitute for everyday common sense, especially for conducting such everyday business.

If there is no way to anticipate all the possible problems of fieldwork and to prepare students accordingly, it is even more baffling to figure out how to help them sort and analyze the data that should materialize from that experience if they have no data actually at hand. That is why I want students to engage immediately, from the first week of class if possible, in *a study of their own* to gather *data of their own* that they will try to *analyze or interpret on their own*. I offer whatever guidance I can, relying on their sharing of problems with their classmates to broaden our scope from their site-specific and sometimes picayune concerns to the broader issues facing qualitative researchers in general.

In the absence of data supplied by students themselves, the best way I have yet found to provoke discussion about what one does with data is to bring a box of 35-mm transparencies to class, dump them out on a table, and ask students to describe some possible ways to organize any comparable collection of discrete bits of data for presentation. Previewing, culling, sorting, figuring out what kind of narration to follow, deciding what to do about "gaps," determining what to present, to what audience, for how long a "show"—these are not totally unlike the problems facing the returning fieldworker.

If any single factor seems to weigh in favor of studying with an instructor who has actually done fieldwork, it is that an *experienced* researcher may be more realistic about fieldwork as realized versus fieldwork as idealized, a bit more willing to acknowledge the role of serendipity (in data analysis as well as data gathering), a bit more willing to concede that there are multiple ways to proceed with a study even after the data are in.

As with any generation gap—academic generations included—it can be frustrating for empathic old-timers to watch neophytes make all the same mistakes, with students having to learn on their own lessons the old-timers themselves learned long ago. I am not so sure, however, that our students can benefit from our experiences as much as they need to experience those experiences for themselves. Our task, no different from that of all teachers, is not to remove hurdles but to prepare students to overcome them on their own. I think we can best accomplish that by meeting students where they *are* and we *were*—that is, at those same early stages in our own "self-styling"—rather than fast-forwarding them to where we are today after years of accumulated experience.

While helping students to begin their own research, an instructor can also model the evolution of a career by sharing what he or she is doing in current work. That calls for finding ways to involve, or at least to inform, students about one's ongoing projects, perhaps by soliciting their help as a critical audience. One way to accomplish this is illustrated in Chapter 10 through the vehicle of a working paper about a working paper. Students seldom get such a behind-the-scenes view of academic publishing. Sharing one's own rough drafts of articles or participating in seminars and panel presentations describing one's ongoing work—*including one's problems in analyzing and interpreting it*—are others.

In terms of expectations and advice, however, I believe that instruction should be oriented to where the instructor was at a similar career stage, not to where his or her thinking is at present. That is why I do not begin my classes in qualitative inquiry with philosophical issues, perhaps having students read Norwood Russell Hanson's chapter, "The Act of Scientific Seeing" (1969, pp. 59-198) or Wittgenstein's *Philosophical Investigations* (1953) for starters. Eventually those concerns may come to occupy a major place in a professional career, but they are not the burning issues for a neophyte. I watch for teachable moments to introduce such issues, but I focus class attention to issues as students see them. Logic and tradition may dictate that the philosophical issues come first, but that is the logic that often allows formal education to become such dead and deadly business, the student role so passive.

The same creative effort that goes into figuring out how to tell a qualitative story in writing up research ought to go into designing courses that teach it. Whether broad based or highly focused, such a course offers an opportunity to give students an active role in which they discover for themselves what they know and what they need to know. Ultimately, everything about fieldwork must be translated in terms of individual style, the kinds of problems one intends to address, and the disciplinary or professional recognition one hopes to achieve.

I think we find evidence that we are making headway when we hear our students asking better questions than we ourselves asked. To that end, I try to celebrate rather than to answer the best questions posed by students. They need to know how frequently the questions they assume to be hopelessly naive are the very questions the most experienced qualitative researchers ponder. In those deliberations I now have become especially attentive to questions about analysis and interpretation and what useful purpose may be achieved through distinguishing between them.

I never give, or pretend to give, the Definitive Answer to the good questions students raise as they enter (or peek into) the realm of qualitative inquiry. I want them to join me in trying to ascertain just what constitutes "data" or an "ethnographic question," in pondering how theory can guide inquiry without getting in the way, or in deciding where sorting stops and analysis begins. I suppose I would have to provide pat answers if I believed I was *training* them. But I'm not.

## References

Anderson, Barbara. (1990). *First fieldwork*. Prospect Heights, IL: Waveland Press.

Chang, Heewon. (1992). *Adolescent life and ethos: An ethnography of a U.S. high school*. Bristol, PA: Falmer.

Clifford, James. (1990). Notes on (field)notes. In Roger Sanjek (Ed.), *Fieldnotes: The makings of anthropology* (pp. 47-70). Ithaca, NY: Cornell University Press.

Cline, Michael S. (1975). *Tannik School: The impact of formal education on the Eskimos of Anaktuvuk Pass*. Anchorage: Alaska Methodist University Press.

Crane, Julia G., & Angrosino, Michael V. (1992). *Field projects in anthropology* (3rd ed.). Prospect Heights, IL: Waveland.

Hanson, Norwood Russell. (1969). *Perception and discovery: An introduction to scientific inquiry.* San Francisco: Freeman, Cooper.

Hill, Benjamin. (1991). Solomon Fry, survivor. *Anthropology and Humanism Quarterly, 16*(4), 120-128.

Jackson, Jean E. (1990). "I am a fieldnote": Footnotes as a symbol of professional identity. In Roger Sanjek (Ed.), *Fieldnotes: The makings of anthropology* (pp. 3-33). Ithaca, NY: Cornell University Press.

Naroll, Raoul, & Cohen, Ronald. (Eds.). (1970). *A handbook of method in cultural anthropology.* New York: Columbia University Press.

Pelto, Pertti. (1970). *Anthropological research: The structure of inquiry.* New York: Harper & Row.

Plattner, Stuart. (1989, January). Ethnographic method. *Anthropology Newsletter, 32,* 30, 21.

Spindler, George D. (Ed.). (1970). *Being an anthropologist: Fieldwork in eleven cultures.* New York: Holt, Rinehart & Winston. (Reissued in 1987 by Waveland Press, Prospect Heights, IL)

Trotter, Robert T., II. (1991). Ethnographic research methods for applied medical anthropology. In Carole E. Hill (Ed.), *Training manual in applied anthropology* (pp. 180-212). Washington, DC: American Anthropological Association.

Wax, Rosalie. (1971). *Doing fieldwork: Warnings and advice.* Chicago: University of Chicago Press.

Wiseman, Frederick (Producer). (1967). *Titicut follies* [Documentary film]. Cambridge, MA: Zipporah Films (Bridgewater Film Company).

Wittgenstein, Ludwig. (1953). *Philosophical investigations* (G. E. M. Anscombe, Trans.). New York: Macmillan.

Wolcott, Harry F. (1982). Differing styles of on-site research, or, If it isn't ethnography, what is it? *Review Journal of Philosophy and Social Science, 7*(1, 2), 154-169.

Wolcott, Harry F. (1988). On ethnographic intent. In George & Louise Spindler (Eds.), *Interpretive ethnography of education: At home and abroad* (pp. 35-57). Hillsdale, NJ: Lawrence Erlbaum.

Wolcott, Harry F. (1990). *Writing up qualitative research.* Newbury Park, CA: Sage.

Wolcott, Harry F. (1992). Posturing in qualitative inquiry. In Margaret D. LeCompte, Wendy L. Millroy, & Judith Preissle (Eds.), *The handbook of qualitative research in education* (pp. 3-52). San Diego, CA: Academic Press.

# 13

# Learning Qualitative Inquiry

What do you need to know to conduct qualitative research on your own? This chapter summarizes and reviews what is involved in preparing for, conducting, and completing a descriptively oriented qualitative study. Had I been writing a how-to-do-it text, this chapter might have appeared first, but I placed it here instead as a means for putting in context the issues addressed and illustrated in the previous chapters. I write as though you have asked how best to get started on your own, thus assuming either that formal coursework is not available or has left you with more questions than answers. Your reading has provided inspiration, but you do not feel sufficiently well prepared to initiate a study. Where or how does one begin?

Keep in mind the central idea that prompted this volume: that "using data" rather than "getting data" is the more critical and more difficult task in qualitative research. My effort here to summarize and advise will reflect that theme. Admittedly, however, although the research process ends there (one way or the other), it does not begin there. So, to start at the beginning . . .

## In Anticipation

*Reading.* There are two major avenues to be explored in reviewing the qualitative literature. One leads to the how-to-do-it books that focus on method. The other leads to the results reported in completed studies.

The "methods" literature continues to expand by the minute. (While first writing *that very sentence* on an afternoon in October 1992, I received a telephone call from a publisher asking me to review a prospectus for a monograph addressing the problems of writing qualitative dissertations!) The methods literature includes broad overviews in authored (e.g., Bernard, 1988; Glesne & Peshkin, 1992; Hammersley & Atkinson, 1983; Taylor & Bogdan, 1984) and, more often, in edited collections (Denzin & Lincoln, 1994; LeCompte, Millroy, & Preissle, 1992), and with discipline-specific monographs (e.g., Agar, 1980, on ethnography; Lomask, 1986, on biography) and technique-specific ones (e.g., the Sage Qualitative Research Methods Series under the general editorship of John Van Maanen).

Until you are confronted with the methodological issues that such books and monographs address, I recommend against trying to read everything. When you need help, it will be there (for gaining entrée and doing participant observation, see, for example, Jorgensen, 1989; for recording fieldnotes, Sanjek, 1990; for interviewing, McCracken, 1988; Spradley, 1979; for using computers, Fielding & Lee, 1992; Tesch, 1990; for analyzing, Lofland & Lofland, 1984; Miles & Huberman, 1994a, 1994b; Strauss, 1987; for writing, Becker, 1986; Wolcott, 1990; for publishing, Powell, 1985, Smedley & Allen, 1993; even for preparing a talk from your study, Strauss & Corbin, 1990, chap. 13).

Rather than devote too much attention to reading about method, I suggest that you spend your time perusing completed studies. Focus on results. Study what other researchers have actually done rather than what they say you should do.

If you have not paid close attention to range and variation among qualitative studies, begin by examining a wide range of topics, authors, formats, and disciplinary perspectives. I need not cajole about getting started, for that is what you are doing at this very moment. As you read, here and elsewhere, look especially for studies that might serve as models for your own work. A facet of this work now draws attention to the *reading* of qualitative studies (ethnographic texts in particular, see Atkinson, 1992; Jacobson, 1991), inviting new possibilities for encouraging an active critical readership.

Do not be too persnickety as to what qualifies as a suitable model; I use *model* more in the sense of "pioneering effort" than exemplary case. *Every qualitative study is some author's answer to the question of how to transform data into a final account.* Every study you read ought to help you clarify how to proceed with your own work as you elect to emulate, improve upon, or avoid doing what your predecessors have done. Poorly executed and poorly presented studies often serve as excellent models, especially if they leave you determined to do better. Be critical in your assessment of the work of others. Trust your intuition, but subject it to thoughtful examination: What is it about a study that turns you on? Or off? What various sequences and proportions among description, analysis, and interpretation seem appropriate for handling particular kinds of data or addressing particular kinds of problems?

Avoid any temptation to let your reading of the work of others become a new excuse for not beginning a study of your own. The discussion and illustrative chapters in this volume alone might be sufficient to spur you to action. If so, go to it. If your idea of adequate background reading must assume the proportions of a major undertaking, then make that effort count in its own right by writing up a synthesis and critique of the studies you read. With so many people going off in so many directions on so many small-scale (one researcher, limited time and resources) projects, anyone who prepares a synthesis of a subset of studies selected for relevance to a particular topic renders significant service toward making already available resources more accessible. I trust you recognize that, in preparing such a synthesis, just as with preparing a book review, you will make the same basic strategy decisions as those discussed here. Will you focus essentially on presenting a description of the material under review? A penetrating (and presumably comparative/evaluative) analysis? Your own interpretation? All three? Equally?

The intent of this chapter is to help you get started as an *active* researcher. If that is your objective, you need to get on with your own work. Be prepared to learn as you go, the way you do everything else. Because this is "naturalistic inquiry," why not be natural about it? Resolve real problems as they arise rather than anticipating every possible imaginary one you can dream up. Keep your purpose(s) in mind: What are you trying to find out? Does the topic warrant a major commitment? And what is a reasonable way to go about researching it? If you are already committed to an approach (as I am to ethnography, for example), recognize that you need to frame your research question differently: What can be learned about the topic through the qualitative approach you intend to take?

*"Practicing" qualitative research.* Reading completed studies may seem too passive and too slow for you as a way to step into qualitative study, yet starting "cold turkey" may seem too fast. I have heard cautious (and already overcommitted) midcareer academics new to qualitative approaches wonder about conducting modest "practice studies" instead of jumping in to do the real thing.

Practice studies seem superbly suited as class exercises, but I am not enthusiastic about practice studies conducted as unguided solo efforts. Instead of "practicing" qualitative research, I suggest that the way to begin research is to begin research. Pare down what you attempt, to keep the scope manageable, and proceed with a genuine study, not a pretend one or a warmup exercise. Class exercises are not pretend ones, and they need not be contrived. What at first may seem their unfortunate drawbacks—limited time and resources, someone looking over your shoulder, deadlines to be met—often prove blessings in disguise. You may have to "invent" similar conditions to assure that a self-imposed project gets completed. Even if it is only an instructor looking over your shoulder, a class guarantees you at least one reader; if there is no reader, there isn't much point in going to all this effort. There must always be someone who is or will be looking over your shoulder; write with a sense of your audience in mind. (When term paper formats seem to get in the way of some students, I suggest that they write their papers or reports in the form of a letter or memorandum addressed either to me or to an interested professional colleague. Writing to a specific individual can be a big help in framing what needs to be told, and in what order.)

One possible and often fascinating project is to do a (brief) life history of an older informant, perhaps a member of one's own family. True, the audience for such efforts may be small, but it is there. Family members, both now and in the future, are likely to welcome a taped and *edited* typescript compiled from a set of life history interviews. Completing such a project offers a neophyte researcher opportunity to develop skills in interviewing and taping, opportunity for obtaining concrete data (the interview protocols), and opportunity for textual arrangement, perhaps including the identification of key themes or major "turnings" in the life of another (see Mandelbaum, 1973, for a discussion of "turnings" as a way to organize life history data; see also Langness & Frank, 1981). Everyone has a story to tell if the right person comes along to hear it. Such stories provide good entrée to qualitative research.

For anyone unclear about how to get a research project started or unsure as to what qualitative data look like, student or colleague alike, I am a firm believer in projects that make interviewing the primary field technique. Protocol data from taped interviews have a comforting concreteness about them. They are somebody else's words (in contrast to fieldnotes, which consist primarily of our own), captured on tape and then on paper, and amenable to highlighting, cutting and pasting, sorting—yes, perhaps even analyzing or interpreting.

## Getting Started

*Set a problem.* I began my professional career in an educational era when "problem solving" was the marching order of the day. As a result, I always regarded problems as something to conquer—to be uncovered, routed out, eliminated. Problems were the enemy.

The idea that research can be viewed as problem "setting" rather than problem solving did not set too well when I first encountered it. It seemed to imply that we ourselves are the source of our problems, that we take problems into the field, or construct them there, rather than discover them in the manner of the reconnaissance scout. It was hard to grasp a new perspective that saw problems as an ally, a critical component that gives focus to our work.

I have come to realize that we are the genesis of the problems we address. Regardless of what we choose to label it—problem setting, problem finding (e.g., Wolcott, 1988), problem posing (e.g., Brown & Walter, 1990)—the problems don't come with the territory, they come with us. Problem setting is critical to the conduct of research. All research.

One of the distinguishing (and distinguished) features of qualitatively oriented approaches is that problem setting itself is a transactional process. A general idea may be enough at first, with problem and fieldworker alike maturing as fieldwork continues. The realities of the setting exert their influence; researcher proclivities and ideologies exert theirs. One reason for recounting the story for each chapter in the preceding parts was to show the interrelatedness of circumstances that found me pursuing particular topics in particular ways at different moments in my career.

A researcher lacking a clear sense of purpose—the ability to set a problem—cannot narrow the research focus sufficiently to achieve any purpose at all. This is the role that theory plays for all research and that Theory plays for some researchers, although I think the rhetoric surrounding theory is greatly overblown. As Roger Sanjek (1990) observes, "Theory informs; it need not be worn on one's sleeve" (p. 252).

If theory (or Theory) works for you as a starting place, use it. Better still, Johan Galtung argues in a delightful and straightforward plea for theoretical pluralism, let *theories*—a *family* of perspectives (Galtung, 1990, p. 101)—guide you without allowing yourself to become wedded to any one. Galtung (and many others) would issue a stern caution against the overreliance on storytelling that I may seem to have championed. He acknowledges the empirical richness of thick description but insists that it be joined by "sharp, pointed theories; in plural" to achieve its intellectual potential, both for yielding unexpected insights and for weaving together already known ones (p. 100).

But theory, too, is a matter of balance. My purpose here is to help neophyte researchers. If the turn to theory (theories) does not help, then storytelling is a good place to start, and good storytelling is a great way to start. Galtung calls storytelling the "index-card-intensive" approach: one card, one finding or quote, the cards eventually to be "used as stepping stones for telling a reasonably coherent story" (p. 96). My reaction is this: If telling a reasonably coherent story helps you get your fieldwork written up, do it. Keep things simple and honest. Do not shy away from a (seemingly) simple and direct statement of what you wanted to find out and how you proceeded from there. The longer it takes you to complete that one critical sentence when setting out on a new research venture, the more you need to wrestle with yourself until your ideas begin to take shape: "The purpose of this study is . . ."

*Institutional ethics.* Ethics is among the inviting fieldwork topics that can steal time in texts, classes, and national meetings. A theoretically endless list of potential ethical dilemmas is matched only by the theoretically endless opportunities the topic provides for others to preach about protecting human subjects. But what I would regard as the new "institutional ethics" have become little more than a bureaucratic hurdle. Regulations once intended as minimal guidelines have become checklists for compliance. "Genuine ethics," a topic I take up in the closing chapter, are at risk of giving way completely to meeting the letter of the countless regulations promulgated by institutional review boards. How else can a contemporary fieldworker explain to people at a research site the need to obtain their signed consent to verify that they understand their guaranteed anonymity! How appropriate that the title of the person who looks after such things at my university has been changed to "Research Compliance Officer."

With compliance as the objective, institutional ethics can be dealt with today like any other routine bureaucratic procedure, and there are helpful sources to guide the process (e.g., Murphy & Johannsen, 1990; Sieber, 1992). I suggest you neither tempt your local review board with all the possible risks you might engender among your "subjects" nor get carried away with your sense of humor in response to the seemingly ridiculous questions posed. Tell them what they need to hear. Make your ethical concern a professional and personal responsibility rather than an institutional one. Such review procedures grew out of well-meaning intent, but today the tables have turned; now it is researchers themselves who need to be protected from the bureaucracy.

I do want to note one ethical dimension often overlooked: the responsibility to carry through to completion any research requiring the commitment, time, or goodwill of others. This holds especially for research with life history material that informants believe will be made available to them. If there is not sufficient time to complete a study— including some form of write-up—there is no purpose in beginning it. That is another reason that I do not encourage "practice" studies; there is too little incentive to carry them to completion. With even the briefest of class projects, I want each student to convey clearly to participants whether to expect a product to which participants themselves will be privy. Students are caught by surprise when projects begun rather casually ("It's just for a class") begin to take on increasing significance to researcher and researched alike. When someone "gives" a life story, what should be offered in return?

*Work "start-to-finish" but think "finish-to-start."*  With a problem sufficiently well formed to guide you to *begin* fieldwork, and any required
clearances in hand, the most helpful advice I can offer next is to think
through your project "finish-to-start" rather than "start-to-finish." Think
about the form in which you intend to present your completed account: Monograph? Journal article? Project report? What is the relative
emphasis you intend to give to description, to analysis, to interpretation? That emphasis might reveal itself in a tentative outline or proposed table of contents. Go one step further and assign an estimated
number of pages to be devoted to each subtopic. You may be amazed
at how little space you have for any of them, including even the
descriptive dimension to which you may originally have planned to
devote most of the effort. So much information to convey, so few pages!

Note how thinking "finish-to-start" puts the emphasis on the way
you plan to *use* data, not on data themselves or the techniques employed to gather them. If you can think through the kind of analysis
or interpretation you expect to make, then you ought to have a pretty
good idea about the data to collect. There will be little need for "dark
and stormy night" entries, even in your fieldnotes, if you focus on data
use rather than on data collection. On the other hand, if you plan to go
heavy on description (a good way to hedge your bet, if you entertain
doubts about your sophistication at analysis or interpretation), recognize from the outset that rich detail may be critical and you had better
not rely solely on "headnotes" for it. Be thinking about possibilities for
presenting detailed vignettes and make sure you are recording such
events at an adequate level of detail—"fat" data, to use Peshkin's term
(Glesne & Peshkin, 1992, p. 3)—probably including an abundance of
direct quotations.

*Monitor continuously.*  Your problem statement, like your whole modus
operandi, should remain under continual review, using the end point
(rather than method or the number of interviews conducted) as your
measure of progress. Are you getting the data you need? Do your observations support the tentative analyses or interpretations you plan to
make, or are you turning your observations into a self-confirming
hypothesis? Most observers carry on a dialogue with themselves—
recorded in their notes—raising questions, posing alternative interpre-

tations, listing other sources to consult. Do you have a habit of tracking your thoughts?

## Start Writing

The social nature of fieldwork fosters involvement. One of the great concerns about fieldwork, at least among those who have never done any, is that one might become so involved that all hope of objectivity disappears, along with the possibility of ever completing the account. I have never known anyone actually to become that involved, so this sounds like one more excuse for not getting the writing done (or started?). Granted, fieldworkers typically learn more than they ever want or need to know, especially about aspects in which they have less professional interest. As a consequence, they may feel tempted to report more than is necessary. Our peers, after all, are our primary reference group; we want to be sure they appreciate how much we really found out and, by implication, how well accepted we were!

In the abstract, such problems can be broad, philosophical, and worrisome. Writing helps narrow problems to those actually at hand. Don't fret about the level of detail at which you are going to report; do some writing to see how much detail seems warranted. Writing gives form to otherwise vague thoughts. I have said elsewhere, and I firmly believe, that you cannot begin writing early enough. I have gone so far as to suggest writing a rough draft of a study *before* actually engaging in fieldwork (Wolcott, 1990, p. 20, and again here in Chapter 11). The purpose of such early (and private) writing is to discover, or "uncover," what you already know, and what more you need to know, about a topic on which you already must have a great deal of information to have selected it in the first place. Because early writing is strictly for your own use, there is no reason not to lay bare your preliminary thoughts on analysis and interpretation as well.

Do not, however, be too eager to *share* your ideas—especially your written ones—too early. Newly hatched ideas are fragile, easily crushed or smothered. Give written ideas time to develop. Share your initial ideas orally, where they can be cushioned with rhetoric. Protect them from the rigor of colleagues anxious to help but likely to be too critical with feedback offered prematurely.

Do not think of writing as a stage that follows fieldwork; see if you can make it a necessary and parallel accompaniment to it. If you can't, do not worry unduly about that, either; some fieldworkers (Ottenberg, 1990, pp. 146-148, for example) insist that you need to be away from the field to put things into perspective. My recommendation is to try to capture both perspectives, the close-in one while you are still engaged with the fieldwork, the distanced one of later reflection. Similarly, do not think of time devoted to editing, revising, and soliciting feedback as postresearch activity; it is part of the research process. Anthropologist David Plath (1990) admits to "seven parts filework to one part fieldwork," which he feels is "probably close to the guild average" (p. 374). Deskwork begins in the field, in the same way that fieldwork is completed at one's desk.

## Summing Up

I have discussed two ways to become engaged with qualitative inquiry. The first is to become a consummate consumer, enthusiastic about its contribution and informed about its limits and possibilities for a particular field or discipline. A major purpose in preparing this volume has been achieved if I have succeeded in introducing and inducing you to qualitative inquiry, renewed your enthusiasm and support for it, or provided a useful sourcebook.

This does not presume that the illustrative selections necessarily satisfy you as being well executed, or that the range of topics and approaches explored has sufficient overlap with the problems and approaches that interest you. But the examples are here, and although data cannot speak for themselves, the illustrative chapters must. If you have added "culture acquisition" or "variety-reducing behavior" to your collection of concepts worth knowing, have joined me in my preoccupation with rethinking the "helper" role both formally (education, community development) and interpersonally, rediscovered useful perspectives in contrasting behaviors real and ideal, observed and inferred, or have been reminded again of what Clifford Geertz (1973) has described as "the power of the scientific imagination to bring us into touch with the lives of strangers" (p. 16), my efforts are amply rewarded.

As reader, you have been cast in that consumer role, even in this final section, intended to make an active researcher out of you. The consumer role and active role are not antithetical, however. I find that I consult the work of other researchers more, and in more purposeful ways, when I am actively engaged in writing of my own. (I should add that I try to be engaged in some sort of writing project—including editing and revising—most of the time.)

Throughout these pages, and once again in this chapter, I have called attention to knowing what to do with data as the point on which the qualitative enterprise rests. As fieldwork proceeds, recognizing the kind of data you *do* need allows you to disregard the potential mass of data you *do not* need. Until you recognize that some data are more valuable for your intended purposes than others, there is simply no basis for observing and recording. Anyone who claims that an unbiased observer ought to record "everything" has never thought seriously about the difference between formal and casual observation, let alone attempted a few moments of actually doing it.

The advice to think through a study finish-to-start may not seem helpful to someone whose answer might be, "I guess this could be a journal article, but I haven't a clue about the analysis I'm going to do. What if I can't find a way to analyze it? All I know at this point is that I want to go have a look around."

My response would be to ask: Can you imagine some reasonably  focused set of closely related, perhaps obvious questions about which you could say, "If I want to shed light on this topic, I will need such-and-such data?" A broadly defined problem might comprise the outer parameters for beginning data collection. That could serve as your starting point, at the same time allowing you to keep your options open until your set of guiding questions becomes better honed.

Inexperienced researchers often propose research on topics that cannot be addressed directly. Classroom-focused doctoral students in education, for example, may propose to study what pupils in a classroom "really learn" from a new course of study, or what "really" influences the classroom approach of their teaching colleagues. Addressing the question, "What kinds of data would I have to get?" becomes a reality check on qualitative research's ways of knowing. Taken too literally as the complement to quantitative approaches, qualitative research is sometimes regarded as an all-purpose alternative able to accomplish anything that quantitative work cannot. We would certainly be sitting in the catbird seat if that were true. But on such critical issues as what is "really going on" in people's minds, we, too, remain outsiders, except for trying through introspection to understand something of what is going on in our own.

As a final bit of advice to help you get started, let me put in a word on behalf of the much maligned term *bias*. How a researcher might spend a year teaching a classroom of Kwakiutl Indian children, or make repeated round-trips of a 50-mile drive from Kuala Lumpur to observe a village project, and yet stand ready to deny any hint of bias, strikes me as patently absurd. The biases of our careers, our personalities, and our situations constitute essential starting places for our research attention. Inventory your "good" biases and use the inventory to guide your broad initial problem statement. (The bad biases are called prejudices—pre-judgments; let them help steer you away from topics on which even *attempting* to be thorough and objective is not appropriate for you.)

It is counterproductive to worry about how you will analyze or interpret data if you have no data and no problem before you. Focus on the descriptive possibilities as you look for the story (or "a" story) to be told, and continue to probe for the significance of the story in some broader context. Extend any analysis or interpretation as far as you can, then try your ideas on colleagues or students. If you can't seem to get far, turn your analytic effort on the problem you are having with the analysis. Being analytical—or interpretive—is, after all, a frame of mind. Adopt it.

# References

Agar, Michael M. (1980). *The professional stranger: An informal introduction to ethnography.* New York: Academic Press.

Atkinson, Paul. (1992). *Understanding ethnographic texts.* Newbury Park, CA: Sage.

Becker, Howard S. (1986). *Writing for social scientists: How to start and finish your thesis, book, or article.* Chicago: University of Chicago Press.

Bernard, H. Russell. (1988). *Research methods in cultural anthropology.* Beverly Hills, CA: Sage.

Brown, Stephen I., & Walter, Marion I. (1990). *The art of problem posing* (2nd ed.). Hillsdale, NJ: Lawrence Erlbaum.

Denzin, Norman K., & Lincoln, Yvonna (Eds.). (1994). *Handbook of qualitative research.* Thousand Oaks, CA: Sage.

Fielding, N. G., & Lee, R. M. (Eds.). (1992). *Using computers in qualitative research.* Newbury Park, CA: Sage.

Galtung, Johan (1990). Theory formation in social research: A plea for pluralism. In Else Øyen (Ed.), *Comparative methodology* (pp. 96-112). Newbury Park, CA: Sage.

Geertz, Clifford. (1973). *The interpretation of cultures.* New York: Basic Books.

Glesne, Corrine, & Peshkin, Alan. (1992). *Becoming qualitative researchers: An introduction.* White Plains, NY: Longman.

Hammersley, Martyn, & Atkinson, Paul. (1983). *Ethnography: Principles in practice.* London: Tavistock.

Jacobson, David. (1991). *Reading ethnography.* Albany: State University of New York Press.

Jorgensen, Danny L. (1989). *Participant observation: A methodology for human studies.* Newbury Park, CA: Sage.

Langness, L. L., & Frank, Gelya. (1981). *Lives: An anthropological approach to biography.* Novato, CA: Chandler and Sharp.

LeCompte, Margaret D., Millroy, Wendy L., & Preissle, Judith. (Eds.). (1992). *The handbook of qualitative research in education.* San Diego, CA: Academic Press.

Lofland, John, & Lofland, Lyn H. (1984). *Analyzing social settings.* Belmont, CA: Wadsworth.

Lomask, Milton. (1986). *The biographer's craft.* New York: Harper & Row.

Mandelbaum, David. (1973). The study of life history: Gandhi. *Current Anthropology, 14,* 177-206.

McCracken, Grant. (1988). *The long interview.* Newbury Park, CA: Sage.

Miles, Matthew B., & Huberman, A. Michael. (1994a). Data management and analysis methods. In N. K. Denzin & Yvonna Lincoln (Eds.), *Handbook of qualitative research.* Newbury Park, CA: Sage.

Miles, Matthew B., & Huberman, A. Michael. (1994b). *Qualitative data analysis: An expanded sourcebook* (2nd ed.). Newbury Park, CA: Sage.

Murphy, Michael D., & Johannsen, Agneta. (1990). Ethical obligations and federal regulations in ethnographic research and anthropological education. *Human Organization, 49*(2), 127-134.

Ottenberg, Simon. (1990). Thirty years of fieldnotes: Changing relationships to the text. In Roger Sanjek (Ed.), *Fieldnotes: The makings of anthropology* (pp. 139-160). Ithaca, NY: Cornell University Press.

Plath, David W. (1990). Fieldnotes, filed notes, and the conferring of note. In Roger Sanjek (Ed.), *Fieldnotes: The makings of anthropology* (pp. 371-384). Ithaca, NY: Cornell University Press.

Powell, Walter W. (1985). *Getting into print: The decision-making process in scholarly publishing.* Chicago: University of Chicago Press.

Sanjek, Roger. (1990). The secret life of fieldnotes. In Roger Sanjek (Ed.), *Fieldnotes: The makings of anthropology* (pp. 187-270). Ithaca, NY: Cornell University Press.

Sieber, Joan E. (1992). *Planning ethically responsible research: A guide for students and internal review boards.* Newbury Park, CA: Sage.

Smedley, C., & Allen, M. (1993). *Getting your book published.* Newbury Park, CA: Sage.

Spradley, James P. (1979). *The ethnographic interview.* New York: Holt, Rinehart & Winston.

Strauss, Anselm. (1987). *Qualitative analysis for social scientists.* New York: Cambridge University Press.

Strauss, Anselm, & Corbin, Juliet. (1990). *Basics of qualitative research.* Newbury Park, CA: Sage.

Taylor, Steven J., & Bogdan, Robert. (1984). *Introduction to qualitative research methods: The search for meanings* (2nd ed.). New York: John Wiley.

Tesch, Renata. (1990). *Qualitative research: Analysis types and software tools.* New York: Falmer.

Wolcott, Harry F. (1988). "Problem finding" in qualitative research. In Henry Trueba & Concha Delgado-Gaitan (Eds.), *School and society: Learning content through culture* (pp. 11-35). New York: Praeger.

Wolcott, Harry F. (1990). *Writing up qualitative research.* Newbury Park, CA: Sage.

# 14

# Some Power of
# Reasoning, Much Aided

*Some of my critics have said, "Oh, he is a good observer, but has no power of reasoning." I do not think this can be true, for the Origin of Species is one long argument from beginning to end. . . . No one could have written it without some power of reasoning.*

—Charles Darwin, *Autobiography*, p. 140

*My love of natural science has been steady and ardent. This pure love has been much aided by the ambition to be esteemed by my fellow naturalists.*

—Charles Darwin, *Autobiography*, p. 141

"Be sure to say something about what *you* learned," George Spindler advised as he looked over my proposed table of contents for this volume. And editor Mitch Allen, the first critical reviewer of the complete manuscript (minus this chapter) wondered, at the conclusion of that reading, "What does your 30 years of experience, now plastered over 400 pages of text, tell you about this? . . . Does there need to be a coda?"

It seems to me these pages have been filled with lessons derived from all those years of experience; all those "shoulds," "oughts," and "musts" I want others to purge from their descriptive accounts have reappeared here in my own. But perhaps the call is for something else, something more personal. Let me begin by reviewing my intent in preparing this collection of essays and examples.

I have tried to keep the discussion jargon free, borrowing three everyday terms—*description, analysis,* and *interpretation*—to examine the different emphases we can take in transforming qualitative data. I hope I have made the contrasts sufficiently clear conceptually, in spite of the overlapping that occurs in practice. When you emphasize description, you want your reader to see what you saw. When you emphasize analysis, you want your reader to know what you know. When you emphasize interpretation, you want your reader to understand what you think you yourself have understood. In different ratios, for different purposes, and with differing degrees of success, we try to accomplish all three.

Charles Darwin (1887/1969), the consummate natural observer, might have subsumed the three modes as different facets of the "power of reasoning" as summed up in the conclusion to his autobiography (p. 145): reasoning by "industry in observing and collecting facts" (description); reasoning by "a fair share of invention as well as of common sense" (analysis); and reasoning by "unbound patience in long reflecting over any subject" (interpretation). *Reasoning* seems an old-fashioned term today but maybe it is time to bring it back into our research dialogue. Description, analysis, and interpretation are different ways to "reason" with data.

Description, analysis, and interpretation say something about *what* one does in transforming data, and a purpose of this book has been to suggest *how.* I have not yet addressed the question of *why* do qualitative research.

Assuming inquisitiveness to be a natural human inclination, why do some humans insist on calling special attention to their behavior as "research," and some few of those engage in research in a more particular way variously called naturalistic research, descriptive research, or qualitative research? Why does anyone "research," and why do those who engage in it sometimes seem to act so superior, sometimes seem to get so defensive, and not infrequently seem to be doing both at once?

Like so much of our social behavior, decisions about doing research, and what kind of research to be doing, appear to be overdetermined. That is, once we know how the story ends ("So, after that, I was pretty well hooked on qualitative inquiry!"), we can identify any number of professional and personal factors likely to have influenced the decision. Professionally, two different routes lead to a research orientation in one's career. The direct one leads to research-based disciplines (biology, physics, psychology, sociology) where research is integral to the field itself. The indirect one detours via some practice-oriented field (business, journalism, law, medicine, music, teaching), with research added later, to become another option for, or obstacle to, professional advancement. While professional schools argue interminably over the function and meaning of their own specialized doctorates (Doctor of Education, Doctor of Jurisprudence, Doctor of Medicine, Doctor of Music, Doctor of Public Administration, Doctor of Social Work), *The* Doctorate (i.e., the Ph.D., Doctor of Philosophy) continues to be touted as a *research* degree awarded on the basis of demonstrated ability to make an original and scholarly contribution in one's field. That same preoccupation with research provides the core of most programs leading to an advanced degree; it hangs as specter over them all.

In much the same way that a long-standing tradition requiring foreign language competence as a prerequisite for all Ph.D. degrees has given way to pressure to substitute more pragmatic skills (statistics, computer savvy, even qualitative approaches themselves), so too have long-standing traditions of what constitutes an adequate demonstration of research acumen been subjected to critical review. This is especially true in professional schools where research itself is introduced late in the academic program. The newfound enthusiasm for qualitative inquiry has come largely from these applied areas rather than from the disciplines. I assume that most readers of this book will be faculty or students associated with graduate programs in professional schools or are themselves conducting research under the banner of one of the professions where qualitative approaches appear to be both attractive and "new."

The majority of my career has been spent in the field of education, first as a classroom teacher, then as a researcher and graduate professor. Research entered my professional life relatively late, as a thirty-year-old doctoral student, and as an add-on. Only by the greatest good fortune did my studies take an anthropological turn when a far less appealing (to me) educational psychology might have been my only option. Serendipity again: I happened to attend Stanford University when and where one could pursue studies in the emerging interdisciplinary field of "anthropology and education" because that was one of the places where it was emerging. But I have never dared to regale colleagues in cultural anthropology with this amazing "new" approach called qualitative inquiry. Not only have they been doing it all along, as noted in Chapter 12, many anthropologists today work on behalf of a more rigorous methodology at the very time that recent converts to qualitative inquiry are working to break down overly narrow conceptions of research prevailing in their own fields.

A major appeal of qualitative approaches is a newly perceived freedom to be more exploratory, less regimented. The approaches seem to offer an escape from the tyranny of statistics, control groups, tight treatment design, contrived variables (alienation, burnout, dependency, leadership, morale, organizational climate, power, satisfaction, stress), compulsive measurement, meaningless surveys. Instead, they invite opportunity for creative problem setting; responsive, even collaborative, fieldwork; and small-scale, manageable projects within the grasp of a lone investigator.

We have been less attentive to whatever costs and conditions accompany these advantages, particularly qualitative inquiry's seeming lack of structure. Not all researchers are able to negotiate their way successfully through the vaguely defined and somewhat opportunistic procedures on which qualitative research thrives. Neophyte researchers often want clearly defined sequences that not only can be designed but are virtually guaranteed in advance. To the extent they buy into qualitative approaches at all, cautious beginners often infuse them so heavily with analytical procedures that it is only the research setting that is different, not what one looks for in it.

For those able to resist the temptations of haphazard descriptiveness on the one hand and a preoccupation with measurement—if you can't measure it, measure it anyway!—on the other, the relative lack of structure of qualitative inquiry leaves neophyte researchers more or less on their own, start to finish. There is no research umbrella or safety net, no foolproof Scientific Method recipe to follow, no established principal investigator standing nearby to set the problem, identify relevant theory, provide access to the field, underwrite the funding, direct the analysis, or expedite publication of a final report. Individuals who successfully complete an independent qualitatively oriented study so soon after their initial encounter with the whole research tradition make a remarkable achievement. Modest as their results may be—and I cannot escape a suspicion that qualitative research has led to some decline in the rigor associated with formal studies, dissertations in the professional schools in particular—they have revisited the entire inquiry process on their own. My guess is that today's students have far less technical knowledge about research than did their forebears. The good news is that they understand far more about all that research actually entails.

By "successfully complete," I mean not only producing a study of quality but also achieving a personal sense of accomplishment and a positive mind-set toward conducting further research. Along with the obvious fact that not all students do brilliant research, we need to acknowledge that some who produce satisfactory results have an unsatisfactory experience, finding the whole process (doctoral programs in particular) so demeaning that they learn to eschew the research role in the very process of mastering it.

And if you do happen to "take" to qualitative research, you need also to be alerted to what probably lies ahead as the trajectory of a research career. The more you find a sense of fulfillment in research, a sense of the potential contribution you might make, the greater may be your frustration at the uphill battle to keep research a focal point in your work.

Qualitative research is labor intensive, and, for the most part, the intense labor has to be your own. Time is your precious resource, and there is precious little of it. Your career will evolve and develop around all the other things you do, even if you do them expressly to buy time for research and writing. You are expected to conduct research, but the logistics of when and how will be left up to you. The urgencies of everything else somehow take priority: teaching and advising and endlessly meeting, if you pursue an academic career; facilitating other people's projects and priorities, if you seek professional employment; taking time that must be devoted to worrying about your *next* grant or contract or program evaluation, if you decide to go it independently.

I do not mean to suggest that qualitative research ever leads to a life of regret. Except for students who discover that they have enrolled in the wrong course (i.e., these approaches are not for them), no one has to do qualitative research. On the other hand, those who become competent at it seem to find it intrinsically satisfying and usually have wish lists of topics they would investigate if they could find time to do more.

What I have always found unfortunate among academics in university settings is the way they feel so uniformly hounded by the need to publish, which is invariably assumed to be publication based on original research and that today has spawned a great hope that qualitative research offers a way out of their dilemma. I doubt that it does. If only on the basis of the time required to conduct it, qualitative research is not a good default mode. Furthermore, research is research; those unable to make sense out of one mode of inquiry are not that likely to make sense out of another. They are more likely to have convinced themselves that they are incapable of doing research at all, hardly a strong basis on which to stage a last-ditch effort.

A related misconception among university academics is that all universities are research universities and therefore one's colleagues are all researchers. In my experience, most academics make their contribution through teaching and activities related to it. Some have no conception of research, including even how to read it. I see a greater contribution to be made by scholars who help to make use of studies already existing, particularly through synthesis and critique of action-oriented studies relevant in applied fields. If I feel any frustration at all with the qualitative endeavor, it is that the completed studies are not well, or well enough, used. Nor are we paying sufficient attention to deciding, for scholarly reasons rather than only political and economic ones, what studies most need to be undertaken.

If you intend to engage in qualitative work, you will need to give research a priority of your own—to place it so high among your list of essentials that you *actually* do the research and writing that you tell yourself you would *like* to do. Two things can help. First, recognize that in your entire professional life your total number of significant independent projects will necessarily be limited—perhaps half a dozen in all—including dissertation research. Select your topics with utmost care: nothing hokey, nothing that does not have some relevance for issues that deeply concern you, nothing too ambitious for you to complete in whatever time you can make available in the immediately foreseeable future. And never become involved with a new project full swing when you have no idea when or how you will complete the one you have been working on.

Second, make every effort to maintain independence for and control of your own projects or of your part in larger projects. Try to maintain independent control over publication of your work as well. Don't become involved in other people's projects unless you are hopelessly addicted to, and find satisfaction in, team research. The qualitative or ethnographic dimension sometimes tacked on to larger projects is easily lost in the final reporting. You may find that instead of conducting an independent audit or summative evaluation, you were nothing more than a troubleshooting field liaison. One way to maintain a sort of distanced involvement is to serve in the role of consultant or adviser on larger projects, but only that, with or without remuneration. That way you keep your hand in, and offer help, without tying up your own resources except on an as-available basis.

How about fame and fortune from your publications? Forget it. Descriptive studies have a "thin" market. The chances that Hollywood will want you to adapt your dissertation for a major production aren't too good, either. (My hopes for selling film rights for my Kwakiutl village study were dashed in 1974 when I saw Jon Voight in the title role of "Conrack," an adaptation of Pat Conroy's island schoolroom in *The Water Is Wide*.) Books addressed to *method* fare better, but if you write for that audience, recognize that you are buying time from conducting your own research rather than moving forward with it.

How about rewards in terms of academic promotion and tenure? Your only problem there may be the disappointing realization that qualitative research continues to have problems of "status" vis-à-vis quantitative approaches. Although the most powerful administrators, those who manage to make academic administration a full-time business, tend not to be researchers themselves, they are attentive to the politics of research. Lingering positivist notions (exquisitely captured in the phrase "physics envy" that describes the allocation of resources within today's universities) still hold sway. Your research is not likely to be denigrated, but long-term and painstaking efforts at rich description, careful analysis, and/or insightful interpretation are likely to be judged against quick-and-dirty results that will show up, rather than show off, your capacity for thoroughness. There are still administrators today advising junior colleagues that multiple quick studies are "worth" far more than one careful monograph: quantity over quality. Not the kind of advice for a prospective qualitative researcher to hear—or heed.

The irony I underscore is that, for those who find satisfaction in qualitative work, the opportunities to conduct it are likely to be limited, won at some personal cost, and more hampered than helped by the very institutions that would seem fully in support. I remember the late Wallace Stegner describing the university setting as a "sympathetic sanctuary," but I remain unconvinced about the sympathetic part. Universities seem more adept at pitting colleagues against each other in fierce competition for skimpy resources rather than at providing support or celebrating accomplishment. As someone observed of my own institution, "At least they leave you alone." Given the time required in field-based study, perhaps being left alone was the best thing the university could have done for me. In any case, don't look to your institution as a source of personal recognition.

Darwin relates that his steady and ardent love of natural science was "much aided" by the ambition to be esteemed by his fellow naturalists. Universities seem to have run out of gold watches anyway, but they cannot diminish either one's own personal sense of accomplishment or the esteem bestowed by colleagues or students for work well done. I find qualitative researchers appreciative and attentive readers, sufficiently critical yet free of the nitpicking associated with some styles of inquiry and far more likely to put up an alternative explanation than to put down someone for proposing an inadequate one. If I was not overjoyed by the reviews I received and reported in Chapter 10's "Notes on a Working Paper," I certainly did not feel crushed by them. I knowingly took a risk by going farther afield, and the final product benefited from critiques that I perceived as well meant. The polished and published formal article that resulted from the review process has had a thoughtful reading from colleagues, and colleagues are the principal audience for whom we write. As Mitch Allen explained to me, "The writers of qualitative research are also the buyers of qualitative research. It is a closed system."

There will always be at least a few others watching over your shoulder; you need them there. It is far more important, however, that you yourself be satisfied with, and find satisfaction in, this work. The extrinsic rewards alone can never repay the time and creative energy you will invest. I cite Darwin (1969/1887) in illustration again, noting that he reserved as the first condition for his success (preceded with the modest disclaimer, "whatever this may have amounted to") a passion for natural science: "From my early youth," he wrote, "I have had the strongest desire to understand or explain whatever I observed" (p. 141).

Those of us fortunate enough to forge careers (rather than spend our lifetimes filling "second-rate jobs") surely are drawn to lines of work that let us "work out" our preoccupations through our occupations. That very issue—how others go about organizing their lives and learn what they need to know to do it—has always been of keen interest to me. How do humans navigate between their real and ideal worlds, or find their satisfactions and tolerate their frustrations? What do humans think they are up to, and why do they put up with all they have to put up with? As anthropologist A. F. C. Wallace posed the question, what sustains "the humble endurance of discomfort, protracted over decades, by inconspicuous people in positions of authority" (Wallace, 1961, p. 32)? I find such questions to be of genuine interest. I continue to pursue them in my teaching and in my research, drawn more to sociocultural than to psychological analyses and interpretations.

The cultural framework has proved a blessing for me, offering a broad schema sufficiently flexible that I could adapt it for whatever research opportunities came along. But I have never been free to conduct research on just any topic of my choice. This seemed especially so during my years as a research associate in a federally funded university research center, yet even during sabbatical leaves I discovered how my career dictates to me. Among whatever options presented themselves, however, I have always been able to find researchable topics of genuine interest, working "backward" with method as well as product to ask, "What understanding might an ethnographically oriented researcher bring to this problem?"

Over that 30-plus-year span, I have conducted seven field-based studies. Four of those are represented in the illustrative chapters: chronologically, Kwakiutl Village and School in Chapters 8 and 9; The Man in the Principal's Office, Chapter 4; A Malay Village, Chapter 6; and the Brad Trilogy, Chapters 3, 7, and 11. My other studies have been mentioned in passing, and references to them are included in the Select Bibliography (*The African Beer Gardens of Bulawayo*, 1974, 1975; *Teachers Versus Technocrats*, 1977; and a study of the implementation of instructional television, *A View of Viewers*, 1982, 1984). Seven studies over a 30-year period figures out to a mean but meaningless average of 4.2857 years per study, a statistic that nicely obscures that fieldwork in Malaysia was limited to brief weekly visits during an 8-month period, or that I am still in touch today with Kwakiutl families I first met in 1962.

I trust it is apparent that, in highly personal as well as in professional ways, my studies are of genuine importance to me. Collectively they constitute the essence and tangible evidence of my academic career, the scholarly legacy I bequeath to others. I take pride in them. I also take responsibility for them, in a personal way that brings me around again to ethics. Let me turn to that topic in closing, this time in terms of personal dimensions that affect all qualitative inquiry.

I sometimes express caution to students or colleagues on ethical issues but I do not "preach" to others about ethics in field research. I have endeavored always to be ethical, using as my guideline a restating of the Golden Rule, to *not* do to others anything you would not want them to do to you. Nevertheless, I have reported on human life in too many settings to be above the charge of ever having acted unethically in my behavior or reporting. Perhaps I have simply been luckier than some fieldworkers in never being called upon for an accounting in which well-meaning efforts would have to be weighed against reputed shortcomings. I live with the haunting recognition, boldly stated by Miles and Huberman (1984), that "fundamentally, field research is an act of betrayal, no matter how well intentioned or well integrated the researcher" (p. 233). I prefer to think Miles and Huberman have overstated the case, confusing what might be with what is, but I am careful to weigh any potential gain in understanding that may ensue from my work against its potential harm. As I noted in the Afterword to *A Kwakiutl Village and School* (Chapter 9 here), "My discretion necessarily goes unremarked, while questions of possible indiscretion may arise for each reader anew."

My caution to others is this: Be as ethical as humanly possible—or "as you can possibly stand to be"—*all the time.* (For a starter list of possible transgressions, see Fine, 1993.) Ethics can neither be feigned as a fieldwork pose nor achieved through compliance with institutional checklists. Ethics entails personal integrity and social responsibility. In working with their own real, live informants, I ask students to begin thinking about ethical issues from the first day. The issue of confidentiality is a good starting place, particularly if students intend, or might later want, to protect the anonymity of any individual. There is little point in promising anonymity in a written report if there was no effort from the beginning to assure it. A realistic guideline is to keep the number of people "in the know" as small as possible.

Given the emphasis I have placed here on what one does *with* data rather than on collecting it, allow me to point out that, except for one's personal conduct during fieldwork, even ethics is essentially a matter of decisions made *at the desk* in the process of transforming data. How are you going to present or represent those about whom you write? How much about their lives is to be revealed?

My relationship with Brad is a case in point. I felt I knew Brad so well, so *intimately*, that I would get a straight story—and get the story straight—in spite of his often devious or evasive style. The nature of our personal relationship seemed incidental to the education focus of the original Brad story (the Sneaky Kid of Chapter 3), so I did not discuss it there. That he accepted street hustling as a source of quick and easy money if and when he needed it was deeply distressing to me, but I reported it (in Life's Not Working, Chapter 7) as matter-of-factly as I reported the other options he identified.

The dilemma posed in writing what was to become the third chapter of the trilogy (Chapter 11) was more personal than ethical: whether to continue the Brad story at all. The ethical issue, in any case, was not about the private behavior of consenting adults—even American psychiatry has been gracious enough in the last 20 years to release us from its stronghold—but about what is to be revealed from our inquiries, and for what purposes. I did not have to bring Brad into that account; my immediate assignment was to describe what I do to address the issue of validity. At the same time, the events that had transpired since writing the Sneaky Kid piece had given not only my life but validity itself a good hard bump. I was reeling then, and continue to do so to this day, from realizing how little we ever know or fully understand, heightened in this instance by my feeling that this time, in my own cultural milieu and my own backyard, I had finally "gotten it right." But after years of seeing so much attention devoted to method, I think I finally realized that only *understanding* matters, not how we arrive at it. Qualitative inquiry neither can nor, I think, needs to stand on methodological claims-making. We can give that one away; insight is our forte.

Brad has not been compromised in the final chapter of the trilogy; his anonymity has been protected. He is, in fact, so well protected by our legal system that I am totally unable to learn his whereabouts. In the writing, I have given away something of myself, but I have retained my integrity as a researcher. There's that "heady candor" again. I hope it's contagious. In the current mood so receptive to researcher reflexivity, I think researchers have an opportunity, and an obligation, to be more revealing about relevant aspects of themselves and of their research contexts. There is always more to our stories than we can ever tell, but there is also more to most research stories than we customarily reveal.

The reaction to my disclosure has, for the most part, been nonjudgmental. Consistent with what one hopes are more enlightened times, I have sensed little loss of personal esteem, even from those whom I have "disappointed." I may have gained in professional esteem from other fieldworkers not quite ready themselves to be as self-revealing about the nexus between their constructed professional lives and their lived personal ones. Whatever negative reaction has been reported to me secondhand has lent further support to my decision at the time, consistent with the canons of good scholarship, to render an adequately contextualized account.

It seems sort of like "a tidy first-world ending" after all, doesn't it! I hope you noticed that the emphasis was on description—at least until I've had more time to try to figure things out.

## References

Darwin, Charles. (1969). *The autobiography of Charles Darwin*. New York: Norton. (Original work published 1887)

Fine, Gary Allen. (1993). Ten lies of ethnography: Moral dilemmas in field research. *Journal of Contemporary Ethnography, 22*(3), 267-294.

Miles, Matthew, & Huberman, A. Michael. (1984). *Qualitative data analysis*. Newbury Park, CA: Sage.

Wallace, A. F. C. (1961). Schools in revolutionary and conservative societies. In Frederick G. Gruber (Ed.), *Anthropology and education: The Martin G. Brumbaugh Lectures* (pp. 25-54). Philadelphia: University of Pennsylvania Press.

# Appendix

## Qualitative Dissertations Completed
## by the Author's Doctoral Advisees

As suggested in Chapter 12, we need not only to bring the qualitative literature to the attention of our students but also to bring our students' work to the attention of the literature. One way to accomplish this is to circulate the titles of their studies among colleagues and others interested in qualitative inquiry. To that end, here is a list of the dissertations completed by my doctoral advisees at the University of Oregon. The list is arranged chronologically.

### 1969:

Sabey, Ralph H., *Staroveri and school: A case study of the education of Russian immigrant children in a rural Oregon community* (Educational Administration).

### 1970:

Barnhardt, Raymond J., *Qualitative dimensions in the teaching of American Indian children: A descriptive analysis of the schooling environment in three North Pacific Coast Indian Communities* (Educational Administration).

Olson, John A., *Ecological-demographic considerations for educational planning: A micro-study of a suburban elementary school attendance area* (Educational Administration).

*1972:*

Cline, Michael S., *The impact of formal education upon the Nunamiut Eskimos of Anaktuvik Pass, Alaska: A case study* (Educational Foundations).

*1974:*

Rider, C. Douglas, *The Alaska Rural Teacher Training Corps, 1971-73: A case study and analysis in anthropological perspective* (Educational Policy).

*1977:*

McGeever, James, *Student activities in traditional and individualized instruction in selected elementary classrooms: A descriptive study* (Educational Policy).

*1978:*

Hart, Sylvia, *Social organization for reading in one elementary school* (Anthropology).

*1979:*

Myers, Loretta Ching, *Socialization of neophyte nurses within a hospital cultural system* (Educational Policy).

*1981:*

Harrison, Barbara, *Informal learning among Yup'ik Eskimos: An ethnographic study of one Alaskan village* (Educational Policy).

Pougiales, Rita, *Cultural interpretation of the development of an educational change group: A case study of a sex equity project* (Educational Policy).

*1983:*

Holm, Neil, *Completing the dreaming: Aboriginal and white Australian teachers' perceptions of education* (Educational Policy).

Madsen, Eric, *The Akiak "Contract School": A case study of revitalization in an Alaskan village* (Educational Policy).

*1984:*

Blakely, Mary M., *Refugees and American schools: A field study of Southeast Asians in one community* (Curriculum and Instruction).

*1987:*

Campbell, Jean B., *Cultural contacts as university international students provide service in American schools and communities* (Curriculum and Instruction).

*1988:*

Mills, Geoffrey E., *Managing and coping with multiple educational change: A case study and analysis* (Curriculum and Instruction).

*1989:*

Chang, Heewon, *American high school adolescent life and ethos: An ethnography* (Curriculum and Instruction).

Lincoln, Letty C., *Reality, meaning, and transcendence: An ethnography of an adult mystery school in the 1980s* (Curriculum and Instruction).

*1990:*

Schram, Thomas H., *Coming to terms with becoming a teacher: An anthropological perspective on the veteran as newcomer* (Curriculum and Instruction).

*1991:*

Bamford, Barry E., *Sara, a beginning teacher in a North Queensland primary school: A descriptive account* (Curriculum and Instruction).

Davis, Lee, *Activists as teachers: A case study of nonformal educators and their roles in a social action organization* (Curriculum and Instruction).

Draper, Randall, *On your own: The freshman experience at an American university* (Educational Policy and Management).

*1993:*

Hill, Lyle Benjamin, *Japanese students at an American university in Japan: An ethnography* (Curriculum and Instruction).

Silver, Allen, *Culture transmission in a Jewish day school: An ethnographic case study* (Curriculum and Instruction).

Wohl, Mark, *The small town band director: A descriptive case study* (Curriculum and Instruction).

# Select Bibliography

Each individual chapter, each section introduction, and each new preface prepared for the illustrative chapters is accompanied by a list of references cited. This Select Bibliography includes sources that researchers may find especially helpful in organizing and presenting qualitative data, references frequently cited throughout the volume, and a select bibliography of the author's published work.

Agar, M. M. (1980). *The professional stranger: An informal introduction to ethnography.* New York: Academic Press.

Atkinson, P. (1992). *Understanding ethnographic texts.* Newbury Park, CA: Sage.

Barnhardt, R., Chilcott, J., & Wolcott, H. (Eds.). (1979). *Anthropology and educational administration.* Tucson, AZ: Impresora Sahuaro.

Becker, H. S. (1986). *Writing for social scientists: How to start and finish your thesis book or article.* Chicago: Chicago University Press.

Bernard, H. R. (1994). *Research methods in anthropology: Qualitative and quantitave approaches* (2nd ed.). Thousand Oaks, CA: Sage.

Denzin, N. K. (1989). *Interpretive interactionism.* Newbury Park, CA: Sage.

Denzin, N. K., & Lincoln, Y. (Eds.). (1994). *Handbook of qualitative research.* Newbury Park, CA: Sage.

Dobbert, M. L. (1982). *Ethnographic research: Theory and application for modern schools and society.* New York: Praeger.

Eisner, E. W., & Peshkin, A. (Eds.). (1990). *Qualitative inquiry in education: The continuing debate.* New York: Teachers College Press.

Erickson, F. (1973). What makes school ethnography "ethnographic"? *Council on Anthropology and Education Newsletter, 4(2),* 10-19. [Revised and reprinted in *Anthropology and Education Quarterly, 15*(1984), 51-56.]

Erlandson, D. A., Harris, E. L., Skipper, B. L., & Allen, S. D. (1993). *Doing naturalistic inquiry: A guide to methods.* Newbury Park, CA: Sage.

Estroff, S. E. (1981). *Making it crazy: An ethnography of psychiatric clients in an American community.* Berkeley: University of California Press.

Fielding, N. G., & Lee, R. M. (Eds.). (1992). *Using computers in qualitative research.* Newbury Park, CA: Sage. (Original work published 1991)

Foster, G. (1969). *Applied anthropology.* Boston: Little, Brown.

Galtung, J. (1990). Theory formation in social research: A plea for pluralism. In E. Øyen (Ed.), *Comparative methodology* (pp. 96-112). Newbury Park, CA: Sage.

Geertz, C. (1973). Thick description. In C. Geertz (Ed.), *The interpretation of cultures* (pp. 3-30). New York: Basic Books.

Geertz, C. (1983). *Local knowledge: Further essays in interpretive anthropology.* New York: Basic Books.

Geertz, C. (1988). *Works and lives: The anthropologist as author.* Stanford, CA: Stanford University Press.

Glesne, C., & Peshkin, A. (1992). *Becoming qualitative researchers: An introduction.* White Plains, NY: Longman.

Goetz, J. P., & LeCompte, M. D. (1984). *Ethnography and qualitative design in educational research.* Orlando, FL: Academic Press.

Hammersley, M., & Atkinson, P. (1983). *Ethnography: Principles in practice.* London: Tavistock.

Jacobson, D. (1991). *Reading ethnography.* Albany: State University of New York Press.

Jaeger, R. M. (Ed.). (1988). *Complementary methods of research in education.* Washington, DC: American Educational Research Association.

Jorgensen, D. L. (1989). *Participant observation: A methodology for human studies.* Newbury Park, CA: Sage.

Kirk, J., & Miller, M. L. (1986). *Reliability and validity in qualitative research* (Sage University Press Series on Qualitative Research Methods, Vol. 1). Beverly Hills, CA: Sage.

Lancy, D. F. (1993). *Qualitative research in education: An introduction to the major traditions.* New York: Longman.

LeCompte, M. D., Millroy, W. L., & Preissle, J. (Eds.). (1992). *Handbook of qualitative research in education.* San Diego, CA: Academic Press.

LeCompte, M. D. & Preissle, J., with Tesch, R. (1993). *Ethnography and qualitative design in educational research* (2nd ed.). Orlando, FL: Academic Press.

Lofland, J., & Lofland, L. H. (1984). *Analyzing social settings* (2nd ed.). Belmont, CA: Wadsworth.

Miles, M. B., & Huberman, A. M. (1984). *Qualitative data analysis.* Beverly Hills, CA: Sage.

Miles, M. B., & Huberman, A. M. (1994). *Qualitative data analysis: An expanded sourcebook* (2nd ed.). Newbury Park, CA: Sage.

Miles, M. B., & Huberman, A. M. (1994). Data management and analysis methods. In N. K. Denzin & Y. Lincoln (Eds.), *Handbook of qualitative research.* Newbury Park, CA: Sage.

Noblit, G. W., & Pink, W. T. (Eds.). (1987). *Schooling in social context: Qualitative studies.* Norwood, NJ: Ablex.

Ottenberg, S. (1990). Thirty years of fieldnotes: Changing relationships to the text. In R. Sanjek (Ed.), *Fieldnotes: The makings of anthropology* (pp. 139-160). Ithaca, NY: Cornell University Press.

Patton, M. Q. (1990). *Qualitative evaluation and research methods* (2nd ed.). Newbury Park, CA: Sage.

Ragin, C. C., & Becker, H. S. (Eds.). (1992). *What is a case? Exploring the foundations of social inquiry.* New York: Cambridge University Press.

Sanjek, R. (Ed.). (1990). *Fieldnotes: The makings of anthropology.* Ithaca, NY: Cornell University Press.

Spindler, G. D. (Ed.). (1955). *Education and anthropology.* Stanford, CA: Stanford University Press.

Spindler, G. D. (1963). *Education and culture: Anthropological approaches.* New York: Holt, Rinehart & Winston.

Spindler, G. D. (1974). *Education and cultural process: Toward an anthropology of education.* New York: Holt, Rinehart & Winston.

Spindler, G. D. (1982). *Doing the ethnography of schooling.* New York: Holt, Rinehart & Winston. [Reissued 1987 by Waveland, Prospect Heights, IL.]

Spindler, G. D. (1987). *Education and cultural process: Anthropological approaches* (2nd ed.). Prospect Heights, IL: Waveland.

Spindler, G., & Spindler, L. (Eds.). (1987). *Interpretive ethnography of education: At home and abroad.* Hillsdale, NJ: Lawrence Erlbaum.

Spradley, J. P. (1979). *The ethnographic interview.* New York: Holt, Rinehart & Winston.

Spradley, J. P. (1980). *Participation observation.* New York: Holt, Rinehart & Winston.

Spradley, J. P., & McCurdy, W. (Eds.). (1972). *The cultural experience: Ethnography in complex society.* Chicago: Science Research Associates. [Reissued 1988 by Waveland Press, Prospect Heights, IL.]

Strauss, A. (1987). *Qualitative analysis for social scientists.* New York: Cambridge University Press.

Taylor, S. J., & Bogdan, R. (1984). *Introduction to qualitative research methods: The search for meanings* (2nd ed.). New York: John Wiley.

Tesch, R. (1990). *Qualitative research: Analysis types and software tools.* New York: Falmer.

Van Maanen, J. (1988). *Tales of the field: On writing ethnography.* Chicago: University of Chicago Press.

Werner, O., & Schoepfle, G. M. (1987). *Systematic fieldwork: Vol. 1. Foundations of ethnography and interviewing.* Newbury Park, CA: Sage.

Werner, O., & Schoepfle, G. M. (1987). *Systematic fieldwork: Vol. 2. Ethnographic analysis and data management.* Newbury Park, CA: Sage.

Wolcott, H. F. (1964). *A Kwakiutl village and its school: Cultural barriers to classroom performance.* Unpublished doctoral dissertation, Stanford University, School of Education.

Wolcott, H. F. (1967). *A Kwakiutl village and school.* New York: Holt, Rinehart & Winston. [Reissued 1984 and, with a new Afterword, in 1989 by Waveland, Prospect Heights, IL.]

Wolcott, H. F. (1973). *The man in the principal's office: An ethnography.* New York: Holt, Rinehart & Winston. [Reissued with a new Preface 1984 by Waveland, Prospect Heights, IL.]

Wolcott, H. F. (1974). *The African beer gardens of Bulawayo: Integrated drinking in a segregated society* (Monograph No. 10). New Brunswick, NJ: Rutgers Center of Alcohol Studies.

Wolcott, H. F. (1974). The elementary school principal: Notes from a field study. In G. D. Spindler (Ed.), *Education and cultural process: Toward an anthropology of education* (pp. 176-204). New York: Holt, Rinehart & Winston. [Reprinted in D. Erickson (Ed.), 1977; R. Barnhardt, et al. (Eds.), 1979; and G. Spindler (Ed.), 1987. See above.]

Wolcott, H. F. (1974). The teacher as an enemy. In G. D. Spindler (Ed.), *Education and cultural process: Toward an anthropology of education* (pp. 411-425). New York: Holt, Rinehart & Winston. [Reprinted in G. Spindler (Ed.), 1987. See above.]

Wolcott, H. F. (1975). Criteria for an ethnographic approach to research in schools. *Human Organization, 34*(2), 111-127.

Wolcott, H. F. (1975). Feedback influences on fieldwork, Or: A funny thing happened on the way to the beer garden. In C. Kileff & W. Pendleton (Eds.), *Urban man in Southern Africa.* Gwelo, Rhodesia: Mambo.

Wolcott, H. F. (1977). *Teachers versus technocrats: An educational innovation in anthropological perspective.* Eugene: University of Oregon, Center for Educational Policy and Management.

Wolcott, H. F. (1980). How to look like an anthropologist without being one. *Practicing Anthropology, 3*(1), 6-7, 56-59.

Wolcott, Harry F. (1981). Confessions of a "trained" observer. In T. S. Popkewitz & B. R. Tabachnick (Eds.), *The study of schooling: Field based methodologies in educational research and evaluation* (pp. 247-263). New York: Praeger.

Wolcott, H. F. (1981). Home and away: Personal contrasts in ethnographic style. In D. A. Messerschmidt (Ed.), *Anthropologists at home in North America: Methods and issues in the study of one's own society* (pp. 255-265). New York: Cambridge University Press.

Wolcott, H. F. (1982). *The anthropology of learning. Anthropology and Education Quarterly, 13*(2), 83-108.

Wolcott, H. F. (1982). Differing styles of on-site research, Or, "If it isn't ethnography, what is it?" *Review Journal of Philosophy and Social Science, 7*(1, 2), 154-169.

Wolcott, H. F. (1982). Mirrors, models, and monitors: Educator adaptations of the ethnographic innovation. In G. D. Spindler (Ed.), *Doing the ethnography of schooling* (pp. 68-95). New York: Holt, Rinehart & Winston. [Reprinted 1988 by Waveland, Prospect Heights, IL. See above.]

Wolcott, H. F. (1982). *A view of viewers: Observations on the response to and classroom use of "Think About."* Bloomington, IN: Agency for Instructional Television, Research on the Think About Instructional Television Series, Vol. 4.

Wolcott, H. F. (1983). Adequate schools and inadequate education: The life history of a sneaky kid. *Anthropology and Education Quarterly, 14*(1), 3-32. [Reprinted in Jaeger, R. M. (Ed.), 1988. See above.]

Wolcott, H. F. (1983). A Malay village that progress chose: Sungai Lui and the Institute of Cultural Affairs. *Human Organization, 42*(1), 72-81.

Wolcott, H. F. (1984). Ethnographers sans ethnography: The evaluation compromise. In D. M. Fetterman (Ed.), *Ethnography in educational evaluation* (pp. 177-210). Beverly Hills, CA: Sage.

Wolcott, H. F. (1987). On ethnographic intent. In G. & L. Spindler (Eds.), *Interpretive ethnography of education: At home and abroad* (pp. 37-57). Hillsdale, NJ: Lawrence Erlbaum.

Wolcott, H. F. (1987). Life's not working: Cultural alternatives to career alternatives. In G. W. Noblit & W. T. Pink (Eds.), *Schooling in social context: Qualitative studies* (pp. 303-325). Norwood, NJ: Ablex.

Wolcott, H. F. (1988). Ethnographic research in education. In R. M. Jaeger (Ed.), *Complementary methods for research in education* (pp. 187-249). Washington, DC: American Educational Research Association.

Wolcott, H. F. (1988). "Problem finding" in qualitative research. In H. T. Trueba & C. Delgado-Gaitan (Eds.), *School and society: Learning content through culture* (pp. 11-35). New York: Praeger.

Wolcott, H. F. (1990). Making a study "more ethnographic." *Journal of Contemporary Ethnography, 19*(1), 44-72.

Wolcott, H. F. (1990). On seeking—and rejecting—validity in qualitative research. In E. W. Eisner & A. Peshkin (Eds.), *Qualitative research in education: The continuing debate* (pp. 121-152). New York: Teachers College Press.

Wolcott, H. F. (1990). *Writing up qualitative research* (Sage University Press Series on Qualitative Research, Vol. 20). Newbury Park, CA: Sage.

Wolcott, H. F. (1991). The acquisition of culture: Notes on a working paper. In M. J. McGee-Brown (Ed.), *Diversity and design: Studying culture and the individual* (Proceedings of the Fourth Annual Conference of the Qualitative Interest Group; pp. 22-46). Athens: University of Georgia, College of Education.

Wolcott, H. F. (1991). Propriospect and the acquisition of culture. *Anthropology and Education Quarterly, 22*(3), 251-273.

Wolcott, H. F. (1992). Posturing in qualitative inquiry. In M. D. LeCompte, W. L. Millroy, & J. Preissle (Eds.), *Handbook of qualitative research in education* (pp. 3-52). San Diego, CA: Academic Press.

Wolcott, H. F. (1994). Education as culture transmission and acquisition. *International Encyclopedia of Education.*(2nd ed.). Oxford: Pergamon.

Wolf, M. (1992). *A thrice-told tale: Feminism, postmodernism, and ethnographic responsibility.* Stanford, CA: Stanford University Press.

Zelditch, M., Jr. (1962). Some methodological problems of field studies. *American Journal of Sociology, 67,* 566-576.

# About the Author

Harry F. Wolcott is Professor Emeritus in the Department of Anthropology, University of Oregon, where he continues his teaching and writing at the leisurely pace of semiretirement. His own academic career largely coincided with the development of the field of "anthropology and education," and the illustrative chapters selected for this volume are the chapters of his professional biography as well. As interest expanded in qualitative approaches during those years, he was able not only to pursue his own research and writing but also to help other researchers in education and related professional fields do what cultural anthropologists and field-oriented sociologists had been doing all along. His most recent monograph is a publication in the Sage series on qualitative methods, Writing Up Qualitative Research. A select bibliography of his writing in included in the volume.

Both the preparation of this book and the direction it took were inspired by editor Mitch Allen of Sage Publications. Along the way there were others who influenced its development, particularly through reading early drafts of new material. Special thanks are due Michael Agar, Lee Davis, C. H. Edson, Dianne and Phil Ferguson, Ben Hill, Mark Horney, David L. Morgan, Roger Sanjek, Tom Schram, George and Louise Spindler, Mark Wohl, and Phil Young. Readers of drafts of previously published material are acknowledged in endnotes accompanying those chapters.